Springer Studies in the History of Economic Thought

Series Editors

Harald Hagemann, University of Hohenheim, Stuttgart, Germany

Muriel Dal Pont Legrand ⓘ, CNRS - GREDEG
Université Côté d'Azur, Sophia Antipolis, France

Robert W. Dimand, Brock University, St. Catharines, Canada

Hans-Michael Trautwein, Carl von Ossietzky University Oldenburg
Oldenburg, Germany

Advisory Editors

Arie Arnon ⓘ, Department of Economics, Ben-Gurion University of the Negev
Beer-Sheva, Israel

Tony Aspromourgos, University of Sydney, Sydney, Australia

Michaël Assous, Lumière University Lyon 2, Lyon, France

Vladimir Avtonomov ⓘ, Higher School of Economics, Moscow, Russia

Katia Caldari, University of Padova, Padova, Italy

José Luís Cardoso, University of Lisbon, Lisboa, Portugal

Annie L. Cot ⓘ, Maison des Sciences Économiques, Panthéon-Sorbonne University
Paris, France

Alexandre Mendes Cunha, Universidade Federal de Minas Gerais
Belo Horizonte, Brazil

Ariane Dupont-Kieffer, Université Paris 1 Panthéon-Sorbonne, Paris, France

Evelyn Forget, University of Manitoba, Winnipeg, Canada

Yukihiro Ikeda, Keio University, Tokyo, Japan

Marianne Johnson, University of Wisconsin Oshkosh, Oshkosh, USA

Heinz Kurz, University of Graz, Graz, Austria

Jean-Sébastien Lenfant, Université de Lille, Lille, France

Qunyi Liu, Peking University, Beijing, China

Maria Cristina Marcuzzo ⓘ, Sapienza Università di Roma, Rome, Italy

Sylvie Rivot, Université de Haute-Alsace, Mulhouse, France

Margaret Schabas, University of British Columbia, Vancouver, Canada

Bertram Schefold, Johann Wolfgang Goethe-Universität, Frankfurt, Germany

Richard van den Berg, Kingston University, Surrey, UK

Isabella Maria Weber, University of Massachusetts Amherst, Amherst, USA

Carlo Zappia, Università di Siena, Siena, Italy

This series offers an outlet for research in the history of economic thought. It features scholarly studies on important theoretical developments and great economic thinkers that have contributed to the evolution of the economic discipline.

Springer Studies in the History of Economic Thought (SSHET) welcomes proposals for research monographs, edited volumes, textbooks and handbooks from a variety of disciplines that seek to study the history of economic thinking and help to arrive at a better understanding of modern economics. Relevant topics include, but are not limited to, various schools of thought, important pioneers and thinkers, ancient and medieval economic thought, mercantilism, cameralism and physiocracy, classical and neoclassical economics, historical, institutional and evolutionary economics, socialism and Marxism, Keynesian, Sraffian and Austrian economics, econometrics and mathematical studies as well as economic methodology and the link between economic history and history of economic thought.

All titles in this series are peer-reviewed.

For further information on the series and to submit a proposal for consideration, please contact Johannes Glaeser (Executive Editor Economics) Johannes.glaeser@springer.com.

Claes Berg

Gunnar Myrdal

A Life of Many Dilemmas

Springer

Claes Berg
Retired from Sveriges Riksbank
Hägersten, Sweden

English translation of the original Swedish edition published by Dialogos Förlag, 2023

ISSN 2662-6098　　　　　　　　ISSN 2662-6101　(electronic)
Springer Studies in the History of Economic Thought
ISBN 978-3-031-75074-8　　　　ISBN 978-3-031-75075-5　(eBook)
https://doi.org/10.1007/978-3-031-75075-5

Translation from the Swedish language edition: "Gunnar Myrdal : Ett liv med många dilemman" by Claes Berg, © Author 2023. Published by Inbunden. All Rights Reserved.

© The Editor(s) (if applicable) and The Author(s), under exclusive license to Springer Nature Switzerland AG 2025

This work is subject to copyright. All rights are solely and exclusively licensed by the Publisher, whether the whole or part of the material is concerned, specifically the rights of reprinting, reuse of illustrations, recitation, broadcasting, reproduction on microfilms or in any other physical way, and transmission or information storage and retrieval, electronic adaptation, computer software, or by similar or dissimilar methodology now known or hereafter developed.
The use of general descriptive names, registered names, trademarks, service marks, etc. in this publication does not imply, even in the absence of a specific statement, that such names are exempt from the relevant protective laws and regulations and therefore free for general use.
The publisher, the authors and the editors are safe to assume that the advice and information in this book are believed to be true and accurate at the date of publication. Neither the publisher nor the authors or the editors give a warranty, expressed or implied, with respect to the material contained herein or for any errors or omissions that may have been made. The publisher remains neutral with regard to jurisdictional claims in published maps and institutional affiliations.

This Springer imprint is published by the registered company Springer Nature Switzerland AG
The registered company address is: Gewerbestrasse 11, 6330 Cham, Switzerland

If disposing of this product, please recycle the paper.

Dedicated to my beloved family: Adrienne, Elias and Maria, Daniel and Tove, Jessica and Jimmie, Julia, Lo, Tilda, Nico, Oscar

Preface

The idea of writing a book about Gunnar Myrdal first came to me while working in Mozambique as a teacher and development aid coordinator with fellow aid workers from around the world. The challenges of underdevelopment, rooted in 500 years of colonialism, were paramount, raising critical questions: How can poverty be overcome? What roles do economic planning, market mechanisms, education, and healthcare play in the development of a country? How did nations like Sweden succeed in building functional welfare states?

My interest in the Stockholm School of Economics and Gunnar Myrdal deepened during my economics studies at Stockholm University, where I was influenced by two eminent experts Claes-Henric Siven and the late Rolf G. H. Henriksson. However, after courses led by, among others, Torsten Persson, a leading researcher in macroeconomics and political economics, the focus of my doctoral dissertation became modern macro theory. I was then employed at Sveriges Riksbank (the Central Bank) to participate in the work of restoring the Swedish economy after the collapse in the early 1990s, which broadened my understanding of the intricate relationship between economics, politics, and society. The need for strong international relations also became apparent when I was drawn into cooperation with other EU countries and made contact with leading economists and organizations outside of Sweden.

As I prepared to write this book, I reviewed the existing literature on Gunnar Myrdal, finding it fragmented across disciplines like history, sociology, economics, and journalism. While many authors have explored specific aspects of Myrdal's work, I noticed a gap: hardly any author is trying to cover the full scope of Myrdal's life and scientific, political, and international contributions. This book aims to fill that gap by examining the society that shaped Gunnar Myrdal, how he influenced it, how his theories were applied, impacting both society and research. I also explore how the central dilemmas Myrdal addressed in Sweden, Europe, the USA, and Asia have evolved since his time.

This book is a significantly revised translation of *Gunnar Myrdal—ett liv med många dilemman*, originally published in Swedish in 2023 by Dialogos Förlag. First and foremost, I want to express my deepest gratitude to Stellan Andersson, the leading authority on Myrdal, who reviewed drafts of all the chapters and offered invaluable advice and reading suggestions. I am also immensely grateful to Per Wästberg, who read all the chapters and provided essential information, support, and encouragement that I deeply appreciate.

Gunnar Broberg offered wise insights on the chapters concerning the Emergence of the Welfare State and An American Dilemma just a month before his passing, for which I am profoundly thankful. Warm thanks also go to Stefan Fölster, who facilitated my connection with the Myrdal family, and to Kaj Fölster, who engaged in discussions about my drafts and provided insights into the lives of the family members. I am equally grateful to Janken Myrdal for sharing his perspectives on the secret letters between Gunnar, Alva, and Jan Myrdal, and to Sissela Bok for providing information via email.

I extend my sincere thanks to Irene Wennemo, who read the entire manuscript and offered insightful feedback; to Nils Gottfries for his overall comments; to Richard Swedberg for fact-checking the chapter on the Value Premise of Social Scientists; to Claes-Henric Siven for his helpful comments on the chapter on the Macroeconomic Revolution in Theory and Practice; to Birgit Karlsson for fact-checking the chapters on Post-War Planner and Trade Minister and the UN Economic Commission for Europe; to Allan Larsson for reviewing the chapter on how the Swedish Welfare Model was formed after the war; to Lars E.O. Svensson for his comments on the chapter on the Pinnacle of the Swedish Model and the Nobel Prize; to Daniel Waldenström, who reviewed the chapter on the development of the Swedish Welfare State after Myrdal's death; to Martin Kragh for providing information about his research on the Stockholm School; and to Heléne Lööw for fact-checking.

I also wish to thank the staff at the Swedish Labor Movement's Archive and Library for their assistance in retrieving materials from the collections in the Alva and Gunnar Myrdal archives, as well as the Olof Palme archive. Many thanks to Torgny Wadensjö, Barbro Andersson, Patrik Sundström, and Marie Åhman for their assistance with the Swedish edition, and to Benny Carlson, Ann-Marie Lindgren, Mats Lundahl, Lars Jonung, and Bo Sandelin for their comments on that edition. The translation was facilitated by some support of AI tools from OpenAI. I am also grateful for the support provided by the staff at Springer Nature, especially Executive Editor Johannes Glaeser, Production Editor Vijay Kumar Selvaraj and Production Supervisor Sridevi Suriya.

Finally, my heartfelt thanks go to my beloved wife, Adrienne, who read drafts, provided valuable feedback, and has been a tremendous support in every way. Any remaining ambiguities or errors are solely my responsibility.

Stockholm Claes Berg
December 2024

Permissions

The Cultural Committee at Stockholm's Cultural Administration has decided to provide the works of Alva and Gunnar Myrdal with a Creative Commons license. When the work of Gunnar and Alva Myrdal is cited, the Stockholm's Cultural Administration is the licensor.

Most of the letters written by Gunnar and Alva Myrdal and other information are publicly available at the Swedish Labor Movement's Archives and Library and their use is gratefully acknowledged.

The unpublished work by Stellan Andersson related to Gunnar Myrdal is cited by kind permission.

Author's Endorsements

"At last, Sweden has received a high-quality biography of one of its most important social scientists, Gunnar Myrdal. For much of the twentieth century, he was intensely active in areas ranging from monetary policy and demography to discrimination and development economics. Much of what he did remains astonishingly relevant. The biography is not just a tribute—it provides a comprehensive picture of a complex but brilliant individual by also addressing his inconsistencies, failures, and personal shortcomings."

Irene Wennemo, Director General at the Mediation Institute and PhD in Sociology

"In Berg's book, Myrdal's entire life and work are placed within the context of economic and political history, which the reader receives as a bonus. Much of Alva Myrdal's career is also included. In other words, the book is a valuable addition to the literature on Gunnar Myrdal."

Bo Sandelin, Professor Emeritus of Economics, Gothenburg University

"For a layperson and non-economist, it is easy to read, well-written, and in many ways a textbook for a broader audience, rekindling interest in Gunnar Myrdal's life and work."

Per Wästberg, author and member of the Swedish Academy

Contents

1	**Why Gunnar Myrdal?**	1
	Introduction	1
	Contributions	2
	Alva Myrdal	3
	Personality	4
	Relevance Today	4
	References	5
2	**Childhood, Study Years, Roots, and the Early Years with Alva**	7
	Childhood	7
	Study Years	9
	Alva Reimer	13
	The Swedish Roots	15
	Gunnar and Alva Myrdal	19
	Law Studies and Then Economics	20
	Gustav Cassel	21
	Alva's Dilemma	22
	Gunnar and Alva in the USA	23
	References	24
3	**The Value Premises of Social Scientists Must Be Clarified**	27
	Introduction	27
	The Institutional Background in Sweden	29
	The Value Premises of Social Scientists Must Be Clarified	30
	The Dilemma of Goal Formulation	31
	Critique of the Theory of Value	31
	The Harmony Principle	32
	Neoclassical Economics: Praise and Criticism	33
	Irving Fisher and His Contributions	33
	Social Housekeeping and the Need for Valuation	34
	The Technology of Economics Is Based on Sociology	34
	Conclusions	36
	References	38

4	**The Macroeconomic Revolution in Theory and Practice**	41
	Introduction	41
	Keynes, Wicksell, and the Stockholm School Economists	43
	Myrdal's Dissertation	44
	Bertil Ohlin	45
	Erik Lindahl	46
	Monetary Equilibrium	46
	Pioneers in Economic Stabilization Policy: Myrdal, Ohlin, and Wigforss	48
	Collaboration, Consensus, and Trust	51
	Modernization of Monetary Policy and Recovery from the Depression	53
	Conclusions	58
	References	59
5	**The Emergence of the Welfare State Through Social Engineering**	63
	Introduction	63
	Alva Myrdal	64
	The Welfare State and Social Policy	65
	The Housing Issue and Modernity	66
	Population Issue	67
	Myrdals' Proposals for Solving the Population Issue	70
	All These Inquiries	74
	Gunnar Myrdal Opposed Race Biology in Sweden	77
	Conclusions	82
	References	84
6	**An American Dilemma**	87
	Introduction	87
	Gunnar to the USA	88
	First Trip to the Southern States	90
	Staff Recruitment	91
	Second Trip to the Southern States	92
	Gunnar and Alva Return to Sweden	94
	The American Creed	95
	Back in the USA: Gunnar in Deep Crisis	96
	Alva Back in the USA: Work Gains Momentum	98
	The Value Premises	99
	Three Potential Strategies Affecting Whites' Prejudices	100
	Value Premises on Economic Inequality	101
	Vicious and Virtuous Circles	101
	The Role of Expectations	104
	The Structure and Statistical Basis of the Book	104
	Policy Proposals	105
	The Reception of an American Dilemma	106
	References	107

7	**Postwar Planner and Trade Minister**	109
	Introduction	109
	The Little International	110
	The Post-War Council of the Labor Movement	111
	Interlude in the USA	114
	Alva Myrdal's Work with Refugee Aid and Preparations for Reconstruction	115
	The Commission for Economic Post-war Planning: The Myrdal Commission	117
	Trade Minister	121
	Tingsten's Campaign Against Myrdal	123
	Export Credit to the Soviet Union	124
	Currency Crisis 1946–1947	126
	Conclusions	129
	References	131
8	**UN Economic Commission for Europe**	135
	Europe in Ruins	135
	Reconstruction and the Cold War	136
	UN Economic Commission for Europe	138
	International Top Official	139
	The Marshall Plan	140
	Amidst Strong Headwinds, Feverish Efforts for Cooperation Between the East and West Continued	143
	Duels Between Dag Hammarskjöld and Gunnar Myrdal	147
	A Fearless Leader Sought Competent Staff with High Integrity	150
	The Export Embargo Against Communist Countries	152
	Hard Work for Dag Hammarskjöld	153
	The Bridge Between East and West in Use After Gunnar Myrdal's Innovative Approach	156
	ECSC, the European Coal and Steel Community	157
	Alva Made Herself Independent and the Family Split	159
	Gunnar in Deep Crisis	161
	Conclusions	164
	References	165
9	**The Swedish Welfare Model: Increased State and Societal Capacity**	167
	Introduction	167
	State and Civil Society Both Contribute to the Strong Transformational Pressure	168
	Economic Policy	170
	Social Reforms	172
	Disruptions and Imbalances	175
	Political Ideology and Hegemony of Social Democracy	176
	Conclusions	177
	References	177

10	**Integration, Development, and Aid to Poor Countries**	179
	Introduction.	179
	Lectures and Books on Development and Underdevelopment	180
	Value Premises	180
	Vicious and Virtuous Circles in Underdeveloped Countries and Regions	181
	Planning for Development	182
	Development Aid and Moral Dilemmas	182
	The Bandung Conference	183
	Swedish Development Assistance.	184
	The Central Committee for Technical Assistance to Less Developed Areas (CK).	185
	Committee for International Aid.	186
	Preparation for International Aid Issues	187
	U-Group and Bill 1962:100	187
	Conclusions.	189
	References.	190
11	**Asian Drama**	191
	Introduction.	191
	Value Premises	194
	Modernization Ideals	195
	The Gender Issue	196
	Useful Concepts	197
	Cumulative Processes or Stage Theories?.	198
	The System's Main Variables	199
	Family Planning	200
	Planning for Development	202
	The Ideal Plan Demands Much.	202
	Economic Planning Does Not Work Well in Practice.	203
	Industrialization and Rural Development.	204
	Reception	204
	The Challange of World Poverty: A World Anti-Poverty Program in Outline.	206
	Conclusions.	207
	References.	207
12	**Stances in the 1960s**	209
	Back in Stockholm: Alva Myrdal's Career Takes off	209
	Gunnar Works on Many International Issues	210
	The Civil Rights Movement and Civil Rights Laws.	211
	Revisiting the American Dilemma	211
	More Books and Debates with Kenneth Clark and James Baldwin	213
	Sweden and Western Europe, the First Attempt	217
	Criticism of US Foreign Policy.	218
	The Vietnam War.	219

	Conflict with Jan Myrdal	220
	Gunnar Myrdal Chairman of the Swedish Committee for Vietnam	222
	Olof Palme Secured the Social Democrats' Position on the Vietnam Issue	222
	Interactions with Leading Opinion-Makers	223
	References	223
13	**The Pinnacle of the Swedish Model and the Nobel Prize**	225
	Introduction	225
	Stagflation, Stimulus Policy, and Persistent Inflation	226
	Sweden and Western Europe, the Second Attempt	228
	The Environmental Issue	229
	The Economics Prize in Memory of Alfred Nobel	230
	Reflections	233
	Institute for International Economic Studies	234
	References	237
14	**Revisiting the American Dilemma and the Final Years**	239
	Introduction	239
	Alva Myrdal and the Arms Reduction Game	240
	The Second Revisit to the American Dilemma	241
	Criticism Against the Idea of Assimilation	243
	Myrdal Needs Assistance	245
	How Is the Country Governed?	246
	The Final Years	248
	References	250
15	**The Legacy of Myrdal: Is the Swedish Welfare State Dead?**	253
	Introduction	253
	Did the Swedish Model Also Die?	254
	The Swedish Welfare Model Has Transformed But Is Staying Alive	256
	Some New Dilemmas	258
	Myrdal's Approach to Bridging East and West Expires	260
	Conclusions	262
	References	262
16	**The Legacy of Myrdal: The Role of Institutions in Social Theory**	265
	Analysis of Colonialism and Underdevelopment	265
	Development in Asia After Myrdal's Books	266
	Myrdal's Influence on Modern Theory	267
	New Institutional Economics	268
	State and Civil Society Capacity	269
	Conclusions	272
	References	273

Index 275

About the Author

Claes Berg Claes Berg, Photo: Tove Freiij. (Photo of Claes Berg in profile)

Claes Berg holds a Ph.D. in Economics from the University of Stockholm. He has served as the Chief Economist of the Swedish Central Bank, as the Publisher of its Economic Review, and as a member of the Monetary Policy Committee of the European System of Central Banks and a member of the High Level Monetary Policy Experts of the Organisation of Economic Co-operation and Development (OECD). He has also advised central banks in Asia, and worked as a development coordinator in Southern Africa. He has previously written about economic policy, the Stockholm School of Economics, and authored the textbook *Global ekonomi* (Global Economics).

List of Figures

Fig. 2.1	Gunnar in 1915. (Courtesy of the Swedish Labor Movement's Archives and Library)	10
Fig. 2.2	Alva with her siblings Folke and Rut in 1907. (Courtesy of the Swedish Labor Movement's Archives and Library)	14
Fig. 5.1	Alva and Gunnar Myrdal work together in Villa Myrdal. (Courtesy of the Swedish Labor Movement's Archives and Library)	71
Fig. 5.2	Gunnar and Alva caricatured as housing spies in Nya Dagligt Allehanda 1936	72
Fig. 6.1	Gunnar and Alva with their children Jan, Sissela, and Kaj on their way to the USA in 1938. (Courtesy of Tidningarnas Telegrambyrå (The Newspaper's Telegram Bureau))	90
Fig. 6.2	Ralph Bunche and Gunnar Myrdal on a dangerous journey in the Southern States while working on *An American Dilemma*. (Courtesy of the Swedish Labor Movement's Archives and Library)	93
Fig. 8.1	Gunnar Myrdal and Karin Kock, who were professionally close allies. Karin Kock became Sweden's first female cabinet minister, and the first woman to receive the title of professor in economics. She was the chair of the ECE from 1950 to 1952. (Courtesy of UN Photo)	145
Fig. 8.2	In the drawing, Uncle Sam is seen with Western Europeans around the Marshall cake and Stalin surrounded by Eastern Europeans. The drawing was on the wall in Myrdal's office in Geneva. (Source: The UN brochure published in 2007 on the occasion of the 60th anniversary of the ECE)	148

Fig. 8.3 On April 12, 1957, Gunnar Myrdal's resignation from the ECE was accepted by the UN Secretary-General, Dag Hammarskjöld. (Courtesy of UN Photo) 164

Fig. 9.1 Alva Myrdal and Olof Palme were both known for combining a strong interest in welfare issues with a passionate international commitment. Here they are together at the Social Democratic Party Congress in 1973. (Courtesy of the Swedish Labor Movement's Archives and Library) 174

Fig. 12.1 Martin Luther King, Coretta Scott King, and Ralph Bunche at the UN headquarters on December 4, 1964. Bunche was the first African American to win the Nobel Peace Prize in 1950 and he is here congratulating Martin Luther King for being awarded the same prize in 1964. Ralph Bunche participated in Gunnar Myrdal's *An American Dilemma*, a book Martin Luther King referred to in a speech in 1967, the year before he was murdered. (Courtesy of UN Photo, UN7767857) 212

Chapter 1
Why Gunnar Myrdal?

An introductory overview of Gunnar Myrdal's significant contributions to social science, the Swedish welfare state, international development, and their relevance today.

Introduction

This is the tale of a man born in 1898 in a small chamber of a cottage in a poor and remote part of Sweden, where people emigrated. He was initially named Karl Gunnar Pettersson, like anyone else in the region. During his early years, he was individualistic, headstrong, and rebellious, with poor school grades. However, after a few years, he buckled down, studied his lessons, and improved his grades. He developed an interest in history and social issues and eventually embraced social science without blinders, freeing it from ingrained prejudices. He used insights from economics, political science, sociology, and psychology to identify and solve major societal problems. He was at the forefront of several ideological and moral battles of the twentieth century and was one of the shapers of the modern view that embodies equal rights and opportunities for all, regardless of family, class, or ethnic background. He also laid behind much of what has long been taken for granted in the welfare state: equalization of living conditions, childcare centers, free school meals, and economic policy for full utilization of both labor and capital. By then, he had changed his name and become known as Gunnar Myrdal, a name he was alone in carrying, fitting for someone aspiring to fame and honor.

The dilemma between ideals and reality was central to his work. He first formulated a dilemma or problem in a way that would be accessible to most people. Then he presented a compelling and convincing solution to the dilemma, one that would gain approval and be considered the best.

Contributions

A dilemma he grappled with throughout his life was the gap between a scientific analysis of actual reality and the values of desirable changes. He concluded that those proposing solutions to societal problems should openly declare the values and selection principles underlying their proposals. According to Myrdal, this would stimulate the pursuit of truth and open discussion about the crucial issues of the time.

Gunnar Myrdal believed that a freely functioning market economy does not automatically lead to economic balance and full employment. The state can and should stabilize the economy with demand-side policies. Moreover, the state should support the business sector's capital formation and the mobility of the workforce with supply-side policies. Myrdal aspired to a dynamic society where a strong state and robust companies and organizations spurred each other. He also introduced households' and businesses' future expectations into social analysis. In all these areas, Myrdal's contributions were pioneering and of lasting value, influencing economic policy to this day.

A noticeable dilemma in the 1930s, Sweden was the insufficient efforts to reduce poverty and the reluctance to have children. Social malpractices needed to be addressed with preventive social reform policies, according to Gunnar Myrdal and his wife and colleague Alva Myrdal, who quickly gained support for several of their ideas. Particularly Gunnar had an exceptional influence on government investigative work, but not all proposals became reality. The powerful social minister Gustav Möller sometimes opposed them, especially after Gunnar Myrdal left Sweden in 1938 to undertake a study of the race issue in the USA.

Gunnar Myrdal's extensive analysis of racial oppression in the USA, *An American Dilemma*, published in 1944, led to his international breakthrough. The Supreme Court cited Gunnar Myrdal's book when it decided in 1954, in the case "Brown vs. the Board of Education of Topeka," that all segregation of races in schools and other places is against the American Constitution.[1] The decision became a central impulse in the fight for equal rights in the USA and a template for many similar legal cases. Myrdal's in-depth analysis represents the pinnacle of his authorship.

Gunnar Myrdal became a leading politician in Sweden during some of the war years, played a central role in post-war planning, and joined the government after the war, but his time as Minister of Trade was short. In several cases, he was personally criticized and forced to leave the government. In one instance, a veritable hate campaign against Myrdal was led by his old friend Herbert Tingsten, editor-in-chief of the daily newspaper *Dagens Nyheter*; in another, Dag Hammarskjöld, Chairman of the Riksbank's general council and future Secretary-General of the United Nations, was a central figure.

---

[1] Linda Brown, daughter of Oliver Brown, a black welder and church pastor, was denied a place at a nearby white school in Topeka, Kansas, and was forced by the school board to take a bus to a segregated school for black students. Her father pursued the case all the way to the Supreme Court.

The dilemma of the Cold War between the USA and the Soviet Union was central when Gunnar Myrdal in 1947 assumed the position of head of the UN's new Economic Commission for Europe (ECE) in Geneva. Myrdal worked for 10 years with the challenge of coordinating efforts to rebuild all of Europe, which World War II had devastated. After several years of headwind, Myrdal broke the deadlock between East and West with innovative initiatives regarding economic cooperation in Europe. However, Myrdal and Hammarskjöld found themselves in different roles and clashed in several duels. Myrdal primarily wanted to use the ECE in Geneva to build a bridge between East and West. In contrast, Hammarskjöld focused on supporting the reconstruction in Western Europe in the organization set up to handle the American Marshall Plan, the OEEC in Paris. This contributed to his appointment as UN Secretary-General in 1953 instead of the more experienced Myrdal.

Myrdal then spent many years of his life understanding world poverty and proposing measures to eliminate it. He also participated in shaping the Swedish state's development aid policy, with Olof Palme in a central role. A crucial dilemma in poor countries is the contrast between hopes for an increased standard of living and brakes on development: attitudes toward work, weak institutions, authoritarian, and corrupt regimes. His most comprehensive work was *Asian Drama*.

Gunnar Myrdal was awarded the Sveriges Riksbank Prize in Economic Sciences in Memory of Alfred Nobel in 1974. His work was then carried forward by other researchers in various fields—economics, sociology, and political science—but it happened with a delay; the methods needed to be developed and adapted to his broad perspective.

Alva Myrdal

Alva Myrdal consistently played a central role in her husband's intellectual development, collaborated with him on several books, and participated in the work on both major works, *An American Dilemma* and *Asian Drama*. Conflicts between ideals and reality in their lives and work together developed into crucial dilemmas at several points: once at the beginning of their acquaintance and a second time during the work on the American dilemma. When Gunnar was completely absorbed in his work with Europe's reconstruction at the ECE, Alva's situation became increasingly critical. She then chose to make herself free and accepted a high position at the UN in New York. She left the rest of the family in Geneva but received much collegial support from Gunnar for her new work. Alva Myrdal's upbringing and life are briefly described here, but her contributions are explored in more depth in some areas: work with welfare reforms, refugee work during the war, preparations for Europe's reconstruction, and her role as Swedish ambassador to India.

Personality

Gunnar Myrdal's own personality encompasses several facets. At times, he harbored boundless ambitions; at other times, he fell into a deep depression. He took on many challenging tasks and became wholly absorbed for a while. His work pace was enormous, but his interest in anything other than work was negligible. He liked to delegate tasks to others, but he had difficulty collaborating; he needed to be in control to be content. He had a patented approach to handling setbacks: fleeing to a new, absorbing, and large-scale task. He loved debates on society and politics, especially when he could speak and others listened. Author Sigrid Kahle was present in Cambridge, USA, when Gunnar Myrdal had finished *Asian Drama* and was at his daughter Sissela Bok's home.[2] Kahle noted that when Myrdal was holding the first copy of *Asian Drama* in his hand, he was flipping through it happily. She thought that it must be a happy moment to hold a book in one's hand that one has worked on for 10 years. Just like that, Myrdal must have stood at Princeton's station with the completed manuscript of *An American Dilemma* in his hand, exclaiming, "Done! Everything I have lived for!" Kahle also noted that she had never met a Swede who had such high thoughts about himself. Yet, she liked him and did not doubt his greatness.

Relevance Today

Several of Gunnar Myrdal's dilemmas are highly relevant today. His plea for openness about one's values and selection principles is a memento in today's polarized social climate. The pursuit of truth and rational discourse would benefit if researchers and debaters declare the value premises underlying their analysis of important social issues. Among the most intensely discussed topics are the cracks in many Western welfare states. In Sweden, there is a sharp contrast between the equality ideals and the segregated reality. In recent decades, new social movements have deepened the fight against racial oppression in the USA and shown that the American dilemma remains significant. The idea of equal rights plays a central role in safeguarding Afro-American culture against White dominance—a theme that recurs in debates about Myrdal's dilemma.

In the last decade, the world has also been hit by a wave of autocratization. Many countries with weak institutions have been taken over by authoritarian regimes. This raises the question of the relationship between different forms of state capacity, underdevelopment, and oppression—a dilemma that Myrdal highlighted earlier. Russia's invasion of Ukraine has sparked a need to study the experiences of World War II and the work on rebuilding Europe during the coldest period of the Cold War. Gunnar Myrdal's contributions from that time are little known but, as we shall see,

---

[2] Kahle (2003, p. 723).

worth noting, especially in light of the devastation in Ukraine and the burgeoning Cold War 2.0. Myrdal's work on conflict resolution when an American export embargo was imposed on Eastern countries provides insight into the mechanisms that influence such a conflict and how difficult they can be to manage.

Gunnar Myrdal described his career in economics as spanning three distinct phases. Initially, he was an economic theorist within the neoclassical tradition, aiming to develop theories that surpassed those of his predecessors. Subsequently, the depression of the 1930s led him to evolve into a political and social economist. In the final phase of his career, he emerged as an institutional economist.[3] Thus he recognized that even the focus of attention is on specific economic problems, the study must take account of the entire social system, including everything else of importance for what comes to happen in the economic field.[4]

References

Kahle S (2003) Jag valde mitt liv (I chose my life). Bonnier, Stockholm

Myrdal, G (1968), Objektivitetsproblemet i samhällsforskningen, Rabén & Sjögren, Stockholm. English edition: Myrdal G (1969) Objectivity in Social Research, Pantheon Books, New York

Myrdal G (1978a) Institutional economics. J Econ Issues 12(4):771–783

Myrdal G (1978b) The political and institutional economics, eleventh Geary lecture. The Economic and Social Research Institute, Dublin

Swedberg R (1990) Introduction. In: Myrdal G (ed) The political element in the development of economic theory. Transaction Publishers 2017 edition, Routledge, New York

---

[3] Myrdal (1968, p. 17). Exactly when Myrdal became an institutionalist is not clear, as noted by Richard Swedberg (Swedberg 1990, p. xii). But it is clear that he became one during the 1930s. Myrdal noted later that his political work in Sweden on social equality problems could not be handled scientifically except by broadening the approach to all human relations, Myrdal (1978a, p. 772).

[4] Myrdal (1978b, p. 13).

Chapter 2
Childhood, Study Years, Roots, and the Early Years with Alva

Gunnar and Alva Myrdal's childhood and adolescent years in Sweden are placed in a social and historical context. Their upbringing in the first decades of the twentieth century is described against the backdrop of the transformation from an agricultural society to an industrial society, marked by the emergence of democracy and incipient social welfare. Gunnar's early education suffered due to his lack of diligence and frequent relocations, but he eventually excelled after moving to Stockholm and developed an interest in Enlightenment philosophy and political science. Gunnar and Alva's relationship blossomed into a partnership that would later influence Sweden's social reforms. Most influential in Gunnar Myrdal's early career was Gustav Cassel, considered one of the world's leading economists. In a short time, Gunnar established himself as a scientific star and soon he became one of the leading Stockholm economists, alongside Erik Lindahl and Bertil Ohlin. When studying in the USA he met many renowned economists and sociologists, broadening Gunnar Myrdal's focus to encompass a wider range of social sciences.

Childhood

Skattungbyn is located 10 miles northeast of Orsa, nestled on the slopes of the Siljan Ring within the picturesque Swedish region of Dalarna. It boasts views of the expansive forests in the Finnmark to the west and the serene Lake Skattungen to the east. When Linnaeus passed through the village on his journey through Dalarna in 1734, there were 65 farms, but all the people were out on distant meadows harvesting, so he continued his journey toward Orsa church.[1] Most of the day, he had to travel over moors or heaths. In the morning, the north wind blew. After noon, rain

---

[1] Linnaeus (1984, p. 24).

came after strong heat, though thunder was not heard, but it soon passed, according to Linnaeus.

Karl Gunnar Pettersson was born in the chamber of Nissapers Juggas' cottage in Skattungbyn on December 6th 1898. His father, 22-year-old Carl Adolf Pettersson, and mother, 20-year-old Anna Sofia Pettersson, both from Solvarbo, were temporarily residing in Skattungbyn, as the father was constructing the railway station for the Orsa–Bollnäs railway. "Kalle" was his first nickname, but later it became Gunnar, inspired by a poem by Viktor Rydberg.

Carl Adolf Pettersson hailed from simple circumstances at Myresgården in Solvarbo and had completed 6 years of elementary school. After a brief training at a craft seminar in Hedemora, he broke free from farm work by becoming an entrepreneur and building railway stations in the countryside. Pettersson advanced as a building master in his hometown and then moved with his family to Falun, the largest city in Dalarna and the site of Sweden's largest copper mine, in 1902 and then to Stockholm, the capital, in 1905. However, he maintained his interest in the countryside and bought a farm in Västmanland in 1909, later a couple of farms in Uppland, and finally Gesta farm in Södermanland in 1922, where he lived until his death. He was a forceful and noisy man who rose in Swedish society during the great industrialization process by building houses on contract and through speculative deals. Politically, he was conservative and patriarchal in the family. However, his youth's temperance gave way to alcoholism, and he was unfaithful to his wife.

Anna Sofia Pettersson, née Karlsson, was the daughter of a miller. After marrying Carl Adolf, she devoted herself to their eldest son Gunnar and the three children who followed him: Elsa born in 1900, Mela in 1902, and Robert in 1905.[2] She strived for cleanliness and obedience from the children, and it was she who disciplined them, especially Gunnar, who was considered rebellious.[3] She was religious and family-loving. She was uncomfortable with her husband's ambitious nature, his drinking, and his affairs with other women. She disliked the many relocations caused by her husband's business activities. She lamented her unhappy marriage, but divorce was never an option, for religious reasons. However, she took her role in raising her children to be good citizens very seriously. Gunnar, in particular, was considered talented. The mother instilled in her eldest son the importance of high ideals, a strong work ethic, and community spirit.

In the latter part of the nineteenth century, Dalarna was a poor and relatively remote region from which people emigrated to America. However, it was vividly remembered that Dalarna had never been occupied by foreign power and that King Gustav Vasa, with the help of the Dalecarlians, had chased the Danes out of the country. Gunnar Myrdal strongly identified with his Dalecarlian lineage and origins. He stated in a newspaper interview in Aftontidningen in 1943, quoted in Andersson (1989, p. 7):

> I have always imagined that my most honest identification is with this stubborn, individualistic, tradition-stable, ultra-democratic Dalecarlian region.

---

[2] Bok (1987, pp. 62–64).
[3] Jackson (2021, p. 94).

Gunnar spent his early years in Solvarbo, but when he was 3–4 years old, the family moved to Falun. In the 1943 interview, he recalled how his great curiosity was awakened, quoted in Andersson (1989, p. 10):

> One of my childhood memories is that I walk and see a large, large city – I guess it's Falun – and feel frighteningly curious when I think of all the thousand windows and all the people behind them: men, women, and children, working, eating, and sleeping, arguing and laughing, talking on the phone, and reading newspapers. Where does everyone get their money from? How does everyone get food? Why do people become what they become? Why do they marry each other and have the children they have? Why do they behave the way they do? Why not differently? How would it go then? How does everything fit together?

Study Years

When Gunnar was about 7 years old, the family moved to Stockholm, where they frequently changed residences. The family's many moves contributed to Gunnar's initial schooling suffering. After starting at Maria Elementary School in 1905, he attended two different preparatory elementary schools (Maria and Östermalm) before enrolling in Södermalm Higher General School (Södra Latin) in 1908. His grades were weak or very weak. He received remarks for carelessness, lack of diligence, and disruptive behavior. His mother's admonitions were of little help. He disliked studying for homework. However, he did not need to repeat any class because a teacher said, quoted in Andersson (1989, p. 15): "He does have a little head; it's a pity to stop him."

The family moved out of Stockholm to Västmanland in 1911, and Gunnar had to change schools again, now to the State Co-educational School in Köping. His schooling was soon interrupted when he fell from a downspout and injured his hip. He failed and did not receive satisfactory grades in conduct and diligence. His father considered taking him out of school. He missed the autumn term of 1911 and the spring term of 1912. Once he had recovered, he signed a commitment to, quoted in Andersson (1989, p. 14): "be absolutely nice and obedient and willingly and promptly complete all tasks father assigns me." If he broke the obedience requirement, a severe punishment awaited him with five strokes of a birch rod or stick.

At this time, Gunnar was confirmed, and in his confirmation Bible, his mother had written the priest's parting words: "Be vigilant, stand firm in faith." Gunnar remembered much later in that his father, unusually, studied the Bible and found a sentence more to his liking, quoted in Myrdal (1985): "Through idleness, the house's beams decay, and through neglect, it drips through the roof" (Fig. 2.1).

The father's stern threats and admonitions had the intended effect. Gunnar began to study seriously in high school. He spent the first year at Västerås High School for Boys, living as a boarder in the city.[4] After the family moved back to Stockholm, a

---

[4] He spent the fall of 1914 at the high school in Västerås, but there are no grades from there (Andersson, 1989, p. 16). See also Jackson (2021, p. 99).

Fig. 2.1 Gunnar in 1915. (Courtesy of the Swedish Labor Movement's Archives and Library)

successful study period at the High School on Norrmalm (Norra Real) began in 1915. It was at this time that the father changed the surname of his children from Pettersson to Myrdal. The name came from the family farm in Solvarbo called Myres, meaning the farm at Myrdalen that goes down to the river, situated at the very end.

Gunnar's studies at Norra Real were significant for his social and intellectual development. He met good friends and was taught by knowledgeable teachers, often lecturers with doctorates. He took the time to read a lot on his own. His grades improved significantly, and he was considered very talented.

His teacher in Swedish and history, John Lindqvist, played a particularly important role for the young Gunnar, who talked about him in an interview with Stellan Andersson in 1983, quoted in Andersson (1989, p. 18):

> He used to take time to walk in front of the class and talk about the Enlightenment. It was there I got this attitude towards Enlightenment philosophy, which I increasingly came to regard as a view, that people and their society could be reformed and improved.

Lecturer Lindqvist contributed to insights about the interplay between economic interests, domestic politics, strategic military thinking, and diplomacy. It was probably also Lindqvist who first made Myrdal aware of the objectivity problem in historical research.[5]

Gunnar wrote several essays for Lindqvist, often about Swedish history. Some of the essays showed influences from Rudolf Kjellén, a professor in political science and a member of parliament for a right-wing party. Kjellén was internationally recognized. His work *Stormakterna* (the Great Powers), published in 1905, provided a broad institutional analysis of the drivers of development and conflict, where the struggle for resources and territories was placed within a broad analytical framework that included both subjective political values and objective geographical facts, summarized in the concept of *geopolitics*. Gunnar Myrdal retained his appreciation for Kjellén as a political scientist throughout his life.[6]

Gunnar Myrdal and his fellow students also met in a discussion club, Fraternitas Studiosorum Holmiae, where they discussed various current issues. In the spring of 1919, 20-year-old Myrdal spoke about "The Mass and Intelligence," advocating for an intelligence party to solve problems arising in democratic society.[7] In his speech, Myrdal argued that democratic politics are dumb, dirty, and irresponsible. What was required to gain power was the ability to mesmerize and capture the masses, which were considered almost impervious to rational arguments. As a bulwark against mass suggestion, the intelligence party would defend the general interest against selfishness.

The speech was delivered in a conservative context and contained values that Myrdal would not retain. However, it foreshadowed a departure from classical liberalism and an argument for an enlightened elite to manage the lives of citizens in a democratic society. It has been claimed that Gunnar Myrdal, as a young man, was a member of Sveriges Nationella Ungdomsförbund (Sweden's National Youth Federation), which he has refuted as untrue, but Eric Wärenstam's book about the organization suggests he was a member in 1919.[8]

It has also been pointed out that the ideas about the role of the elite were present outside the conservative sphere where young Myrdal felt at home.[9] References are made to "the avant-garde of the labor movement," to Lenin and the role of

---

[5] Andersson (1989, p. 22).

[6] Kjellén's work played an important role in Myrdal's Asian Drama. He requisitioned his books to New Delhi in 1957 before starting the work, see Andersson (1989, p. 26). In a note from 1985 about Jan Myrdal's autobiography *Childhood*, Gunnar Myrdal mentioned that he still appreciated Kjellén, see Myrdal (1985).

[7] The speech is published in its entirety in Andersson (1989, pp. 26–32).

[8] Jan Myrdal (1982b) claims this, while Gunnar Myrdal asserts it is untrue in Gunnar Myrdal (1985, Sect. 11). Wärenstam (1965, p. 13), however, notes that law student Gunnar Myrdal, like Eli Heckscher, was a member of the Stockholm branch of Sweden's National Youth Association in 1919, which was close to the conservatives (General Voters' Union) but evolved in a far-right and anti-Semitic direction in the 1930s when Gunnar Myrdal was a social democrat and active anti-Nazi.

[9] Appelqvist and Andersson (1998, p. 368).

communist parties, and to elitist thoughts even within the reformist part of the labor movement.

There are also reports that Gunnar tried to give a version of the speech again for the students gathered in Djurgården on Walpurgis Night, April 30th, 1920.[10] However, he was met with boos, everything fell apart, and Gunnar and his friends got drunk. Gunnar Myrdal himself recalls in a letter from Gunnar to Alva on May 1st 1920:[11]

> I was to speak, until I had their minds completely in my power – in old-fashioned academic monotonous rhythms and with the most daring concreteness in the images – I had eaten lozenges for a whole week to have my voice in my power and made a draft of the rhetorical highlights…It was the same usual bunch of nitwits, one the same as the other except for a hair's breadth, eerily empty noisy after the first glass. Everything collapsed – it was unthinkable that I should speak to these – one should have some respect for one's own ideas even if they are misguided.

Gunnar Myrdal graduated from Norra Real in May 1918 with high grades in several subjects: the highest grade, A, in the mother tongue, Swedish essay, and history. He received the second-highest grade, a, in the written test in German, physics, the physical work, geography, philosophical propaedeutics. Then followed the third highest grade, AB, in mathematics, mathematical work, German, biology, and chemistry. He was weaker in English and French, where the grade was BA. In the written English exam, he achieved only a B grade. In the autumn of the same year, he began studying law at Stockholm University. He explained his choice of law in a letter to Alva on October 6th 1919:

> Ever since I started contemplating the matter, I have intended to become a statesman. My ambitious fantasies directed my desire to study, leading me to sacrifice so much of my youth on history – the power plays, intrigues – as well as on political science, politics, and rhetoric. It was for these same reasons that I chose to become a lawyer.

In June 1919, Gunnar, then 20 years old, cycled through Sörmland with two friends. They lived a vagabond life, receiving shelter, food, and lodging from various farmers. One morning, they woke up in a barn in Slagsta, near Eskilstuna. An employee informed the owner, Albert Reimer, saying, "Three vagabonds have spent the night in the hayloft." The vagabonds turned out to be students: a lawyer, a medic, and an engineer. Instead of being turned away, they were invited for coffee by Albert's daughters, Alva and Rut Reimer. A few days later, Gunnar invited 17-year-old Alva to cycle with him and a friend in Dalarna. She accepted, marking the beginning of a lifelong relationship between Gunnar and Alva, one of the most documented and discussed in history.

---

[10] Jackson (2021, p. 193).

[11] The letter collection is available at The Swedish Labor Movement's Archives and Library. The first year's letters are published in Hirdman (2003).

Alva Reimer

Alva Reimer's mother, Lowa, born as Lovisa Larsson in 1877, grew up on a prosperous farm in Slagsta, owned by her family for five generations. She was astute, trained as a seamstress, and showed artistic talent in sewing, weaving, and embroidery. Alva's father, Albert Jansson, was born in 1876 into a poor farming family. Albert's parents had an unhappy marriage. His father was an alcoholic and served a month in prison for domestic abuse.[12] Albert's mother made all her children vow never to touch alcohol. At 12, Albert left school to work in agriculture. His father died when he was 16, and he was humiliated watching his family's possessions being auctioned off. He managed to save enough money for a short course at a practical commercial school in Köping and later worked as a clerk in Eskilstuna. Albert became a teetotaler, co-operator, and social democrat, driven by a strong desire to serve the greater good.

Albert adopted the surname Reimer, influenced by his brother who had changed to this surname. He progressed to an insurance agent in Uppsala, a builder in Älvsjö, constructed multi-family homes for Kooperativa förbundet (the Cooperative Union) in Eskilstuna, and became a Social Democratic city councilor. Albert and Lowa married in 1900, but their marriage was not happy. Albert loathed the church, state capitalism, and read Rousseau, Strindberg, and Zola, while Lowa was religious, politically liberal, and drawn to bourgeois culture. They had five children together. Alva, born in 1902, was the eldest, followed by Rut in 1904, Folke in 1906, Maj in 1909, and Stig in 1912. Her mother was both a dominant controller in the children's lives and a frail woman who occasionally stayed at rest homes. Lowa's brother and sister had both died of tuberculosis, making her fearful of contracting it herself, to the point where she never dared to kiss her children or grandchildren.[13] Her extreme obsession with cleanliness and control made Alva uncomfortable at home. The marital disputes between her parents were also stressful. Alva often described her childhood as "hellish." However, she also said that as a child she received much praise and loved her father. At 16, she wrote in a letter to a former teacher Per Sundberg on April 29th 1918 (Fig. 2.2):

> I am pained to say – but I do not like mother at all. And no one who knows her does. But father, I like him too much. In him, I first love my father, no, the father comes second, first a great soul, a poet's soul. If father were not married to mother, I know his spiritual strength would be immense. But he is married and is held down by unbreakable bonds. To put it bluntly: I certainly do not consider it my duty to love a mother who is not a mother at all.

Alva spent her early childhood in downtown Stockholm, later moving with her family to Älvsjö and eventually to the farm in Slagsta, Lowa's childhood home, which Albert bought to fulfill his dream of owning land and producing food for people. Passionate about reading and studying, Alva had to leave school at 14. Continuing

---

[12] Jackson (2021, p. 22).

[13] Following the birth of their youngest son Stig in 1912, his mother withdrew and lay in bed for over 30 years more than half the day.

Fig. 2.2 Alva with her siblings Folke and Rut in 1907. (Courtesy of the Swedish Labor Movement's Archives and Library)

at a secondary school was out of the question, but she studied typewriting, shorthand, and bookkeeping at a commercial school in Eskilstuna. At 15, she got a job at the city's audit office. She maintained her dream of further studies and saved money for them. Her mother opposed the idea of secondary education. Alva wrote an application for a scholarship to attend a private gymnasium, but her mother tore it up. Initially neutral, her father eventually succumbed to Alva's passion for reading. He fought for the Eskilstuna gymnasium to allow teachers to privately tutor a group of girls. To save time and money, Alva studied the courses at a record pace, and in 1922, she graduated as a private student with oral exams in all subjects at Norra Latin School in Stockholm.

Driven by strong ambitions and aspirations, as a child, Alva wanted to learn everything and become a hero—a police officer, general, actress, missionary. Now, she was keen to study medicine, but her parents deemed it unaffordable. Instead, she chose to study literature, religious history, and Nordic languages at Stockholm University, graduating with a Bachelor of Arts in 1924.

The Swedish Roots

Gunnar and Alva were shaped as social beings during a very dynamic period in Sweden's social history. Their personal development must be understood in a broad social, economic, and historical context. Both had their roots in the Swedish countryside, where most people earned their living from agriculture. In Dalarna, from where Gunnar's family originated, large estates were rare and land distribution was relatively even. In contrast, Södermanland, where Alva spent part of her upbringing, had more large estates with tenant farmers and workers living on "stat," that is, year-round work in exchange for living provisions.

Sweden, since its era as a great power, had a strong central government, developed through war and war preparations, with high administrative capacity at the central level, known as the civil servant state.[14] Unlike many other European countries, Swedish peasants succeeded in preventing serfdom from taking root. The relative independence of the peasant class also contributed to their right to political participation and a fair degree of social mobility compared to other countries.

However, the conditions for agricultural and other workers could be dire. Early on, the mining industry experienced capitalist-organized mass production of industrial products, especially in copper production at Stora Kopparberg in Falun, where Gunnar Myrdal spent his childhood.[15] This mine had long played a significant role in Sweden's economy. When Linnaeus visited the Falun mine on August 17th, 1734, he noted the dreadful conditions.[16] A steady smoke rose from this mine and he understood that the entire description of hell was taken from this or similar mines. Outside a stinging sulfur smoke rose, poisoning the air around, making it difficult to approach. At a depth of 270 meters, 1,200 miners toiled, resembling black devils, surrounded by smoke and dust. With no escape routes, all these doomed souls feared being snatched away from life.

---

[14] Premfors (1999).
[15] Schön (2014, p. 87).
[16] Linnaeus (1984, pp. 148–149).

The Swedish state's economic policy for a long time had a restrictive and conservative influence. Foreign trade was limited through stringent restrictions.[17] The state's role was to secure a proper yield for businesses and contributed to limited new establishments in various professions. This system meant that all workers without employment were obligated to take year-long service with a master in the countryside or city, under conditions prescribed in the servant statutes.[18]

However, the organization of agriculture improved during the first half of the nineteenth century with the enclosure movement, which helped consolidate the scattered lands of farmers and facilitate operations. The agriculture sector gained more freedom, and both production and population grew. But the population increase was so substantial that agriculture could not employ all the new workers, creating pressure for increased employment in other sectors. Simultaneously, industrialization in other countries increased demand for Swedish wood and iron, leading to a liberalization of trade policies to facilitate the transformation into an industrial society.

The more liberal stance of the agricultural sector and the population growth contributed to the liberalization of state policies in other areas as well. The economic policy led to the creation of labor and capital markets. The 1848 joint-stock company law allowed for the accumulation of greater capital in companies, enabling large industrial projects based on new technology. Complete freedom of trade was introduced in 1864, deregulating commerce and crafts in both rural and urban areas.

The state played a significant role in tax collection, law and order, and infrastructure development. It took responsibility for expanding the railway, telegraph, and restructuring the postal service. The construction of railways and urbanization were two major development blocks, driving each other forward, with the state and municipalities in central roles.

Gunnar's father participated in the construction of railway stations, as seen earlier. But looking back a generation, one can understand the social development that took place in Sweden at that time. Gunnar Myrdal's great-grandfather, Myr Erik Ersson, was illiterate.[19] Gunnar's grandfather, Pers Peter Ersson, was 9 years old when the Swedish public school system became universal and compulsory in 1842. When the priest conducted household examinations for church records between 1868 and 1877, it was revealed that even his grandfather was unable to read or understand the Bible.[20] However, Gunnar Myrdal's grandmother, Sara Greta Jansdotter, was literate. She was a woman who gave birth to nine children, six of whom survived to adulthood, and worked in agriculture, often following the plow in all kinds of weather.

When Alva's father, Albert Reimer, started elementary school in the mid-1880s, children of the working class were often looked down upon. Many teachers

---

[17] Montgomery (1947, p. 28).
[18] Montgomery (1947, p. 29).
[19] Jackson (2021, p. 86).
[20] Jackson (2021, p. 86).

considered themselves above teaching students from the "lower class." However, Albert's immense passion for reading led him to excel in his class.[21] Despite receiving special education beyond the curriculum with three classmates until he equaled the teacher's knowledge, his parents' poverty halted further education after elementary school. Albert's class consciousness was solidified while doing hard manual labor at a parsonage, where he was treated as a mere servant. However, he never gave up and saved his own money for additional education. He became involved in the temperance movement, educational work, and the labor movement.

Albert Reimer was not alone in being shaped by the radicalism of the Swedish popular movements. The commercialization of agriculture created a large class of landless workers who took jobs in the burgeoning industry. The concentration of workers in industries and growing cities laid the groundwork for political and union organization. Poverty and unemployment started to be seen as political rather than individual issues. The Social Democratic Workers' Party was formed in 1889, and demands for democratization and the state's active role in social issues grew. Local self-government was strengthened, and an efficient, incorruptible state administration emerged—not as an entity separated from and ruling over society, but as a well-integrated part of it.[22]

Around the time Gunnar and Alva were born, trade and labor unions became central players. Landsorganisationen i Sverige, LO, (The Swedish Trade Union Confederation), was established as the umbrella organization for trade unions in 1898, and in reaction, business leaders formed Svenska arbetsgivareföreningen, SAF, (the Swedish Employers Association) in 1902. Gunnar Myrdal, as a child in Stockholm's Södermalm district, witnessed the great strike organized by LO in 1909.[23] The strike, a result of an economic crisis leading to wage cuts and lockouts by SAF, was a stark example of class struggle. Myrdal remembered how some reliable foremen were equipped with police armbands and pistols, and how the upper-class students were driving garbage in Stockholm. The workers lost the strike. The Swedish trade union leaders then tried to rebuild the trade union movement. They had the wisdom to follow the industrial principle and to start building in enough central, albeit democratically controlled, governance to make it strong and effective, according to Myrdal.

The democratization of governance was a central political issue in Sweden at this time. Alva's father, Albert, voted for the first time in 1911 and became involved in local politics. However, Alva's mother, Lowa, like other women, still lacked the right to vote.[24] It was not until 1918 that the parliament decided to introduce universal and equal suffrage for men, with women's suffrage following in 1921.

The period also saw a leap in industrialization in Sweden. New inventions, such as the sun valve, steam turbines, the milk-cream-separator, electrical generators and

---

[21] Jackson (2021, p. 23).
[22] Rothstein (1992, p. 84).
[23] Myrdal (1977, p. 246).
[24] Jackson (2021, p. 46).

power transmission, air compressors, and the radial ball bearing, contributed to the emergence of globally renowned Swedish engineering companies, AGA, Alfa Laval, ASEA, Atlas Copco, and SKF. Innovations and urbanization led to rapid transformation, rising productivity, and increasing wages. Classic industrial capitalism evolved into organized finance capitalism. The breakthrough of financial capital meant that commercial banks became central in various industrial spheres. Sveriges Riksbank, the world's oldest central bank founded in 1668, was granted the exclusive right to issue banknotes in a law enacted in 1897, the year before Gunnar was born.

The rapid growth of the industrial society increased demands for social reforms. In the 1910s, Sweden's social insurance systems were more extensive than many other European countries. It included state committees for labor disputes, state subsidies to municipal employment agencies, expanded subsidies to health insurance funds, enhanced worker protection, and a general pension insurance law.[25] Representatives from SAF and LO began meeting regularly to discuss common issues such as worker protection, employment, wage formation, and housing policy, fostering trust and dialogue even in areas of significant disagreement.[26] This trust between different parties became a cornerstone of the Swedish model. The dual legacy of a strong state on one hand and the democratic ideals of the parish hall on the other were embraced by the Swedish Social Democracy, which claimed to be both a grassroots movement and a party bearing state responsibilities, as noted by historians Henrik Berggren and Lars Trägårdh in their classic depiction of the Swedish model.[27]

In 1917, during World War I, Sweden faced food shortages, hunger riots, and potato uprisings. Albert Reimer, a member of Eskilstuna's food committee, was tasked with ensuring fair distribution of grain and potatoes. However, Lowa, Alva's mother, secretly ground grain with a hand mill to feed her five children, more than the ration allowed. When Albert discovered the secret stash, it led to a major family crisis. Lowa questioned how he could let his own children go hungry, while he countered with the importance of teaching them about justice in society. Albert's actions deeply influenced his daughter Alva.[28]

By the time Gunnar and Alva met, the foundations of a welfare state were already in place in Sweden, but it would take about a decade and a half before they themselves would engage in its development and reform.

---

[25] Schön (2014, p. 236).
[26] Rothstein (1998).
[27] Berggren and Trägårdh (2015, 2022).
[28] Bok (1987, p. 36).

Gunnar and Alva Myrdal

During the autumn of 1919, it was difficult for Gunnar and Alva to meet. Alva had to lie to her parents when visiting Gunnar in Stockholm for the first time in October 1919. Their correspondence provides a candid insight into their views of themselves, each other, life, and the world. Gunnar was self-absorbed with a strong desire to dominate his surroundings, aware of his masculine traits. Gunnar writes about the difference between them in a letter to Alva on October 27th 1919:

> As is only natural, reflection plays a completely different role for me than for you. My masculine will to act currently has no other field of activity… Systemizing thoughts is a need for me for two reasons. Firstly, my desire for power demands that I master and oversee the material of thought. Moreover, the construction is pleasurable, as I find aesthetic enjoyment in harmonically and purposefully built structures of thought.

He also praises the gods that Alva does not think systematically, but at the same time asserts that feminine thought is superior because it does not get stuck in bloodless fictions and finds all shortcuts. He celebrates female intuition. Alva's response to the letter shows that she is more open to change than he is. She claims that she herself knows nothing, but is content with any enlightenment that might lead to greater self-awareness. In a letter from Alva to Gunnar on November 1st 1919 she also asserts:

> I can assemble some known material into a new structure of thought for me, but then this material is always something easily captured.

In the fall, there is a shift in Gunnar's self-perception and his desire for Alva becomes evident. On December 5th 1919, he writes to her that he used to see himself at the center of the world but now places Alva at the center of his world. He also says that the time feels distant when he was ambitious and wanted to change the world. Now he is no longer eager for glory and a life's work, but for Alva.

Seven months after their first meeting, in early 1920, they "cross the line" in Gunnar's room on Birger Jarlsgatan. These meetings require much planning and secrecy. Alva has to invent reasons and lies to her parents to visit Gunnar in Stockholm. The strains are great for young people trying to have a relationship before marriage. Additionally, Gunnar occasionally falls into depression, calling it his mental illness. At the end of February, he is depressed and chooses to be with a woman he met on the streets of Stockholm. In a letter after the incident, he writes to Alva on April 12th 1920:

> I was desperate. You, my dearest, had disappeared and transformed. I no longer loved you, nor anyone else. The little remaining love for you was barely enough to provoke me to protest… Moreover, it undeniably flattered my vanity and self-esteem to be able to subdue a little creature's will to absolute destruction, to take her from the street, and without ceremonies, talk and hypocrisy command her… When I am unhappy and restless in thought, I always write a lot on account of mental illness, but as soon as I become myself again, I find it cowardly done…

The mental illness mentioned in this letter will continue to play a role in Gunnar's life, as he oscillates between claims of genius and deep depressions. Alva responds to Gunnar's confession in his letter and realizes that she does not know him well and that there are cold and calculating traits in his personality. She concludes a letter to Gunnar on April 14th 1920:

> I am so tired that I cannot soften the coldness of the highly psychological with a single word of love.

Three months later, they have the opportunity to meet in person and discuss Gunnar's behavior and Alva's reaction. Initially, she suppresses her own feelings, not wanting to be a martyr, like her mother. She understands that behind Gunnar's masculine hero mask is a depressive and scared boy and now realizes that she must consider her own needs while also helping Gunnar. This means that Alva chooses to assist Gunnar in his project to create a strong and masculine role in the larger world, while demanding that he considers her needs and her own life projects. Later, in the fall of 1920, Gunnar expresses his great gratitude for Alva's role as an anchor in his life. Without her, he would be lost in dreams, fears, shadows, pain.[29]

Law Studies and Then Economics

Gunnar continued his law studies at Stockholm University, completing them in 1923. He later claimed that he thought legal studies would provide an orientation on how society was organized, but was disappointed.[30] After his law degree, Gunnar served as a deputy notary at the Stockholm City Court and acting mayor in Mariefred, the idyllic city at lake Mälaren, only 40 km from Eskilstuna where Alva's hometown was.

In October 1924, Alva and Gunnar Myrdal married. Both wanted to free themselves from their parents, who were not invited to the wedding.[31] Only their closest friends Märta Fredriksson and Alf Johansson attended the ceremony. After the wedding, Alva and Gunnar settled in a two-room apartment on Atlasgatan in Stockholm. During this time, Gunnar Myrdal helped his father write political articles in local newspapers, mainly about local road and agricultural issues.[32] The articles are written from the perspective of the right-wing party. An article by C.A. Pettersson, published in Strängnäs Tidning on September 10th 1926, was addressed to farmers:

> If right-minded farmers prefer the right-wing program, it is because they realize that they are not served by a class party and a class program. Our well-being is best promoted not in conflict with other social classes. The well-being of all is the well-being of each. Justice for all is our motto.

---

[29] Jackson (2021, pp. 184, 207).
[30] Gunnar Myrdal (1985).
[31] Etzemüller (2014, p. 39).
[32] Andersson (1989).

It would be a few more years before Gunnar—influenced by Alva, his scientific studies, and the economic depression—became an active social democrat. In the 1920s, he lectured occasionally at ABF and Brunnsvik Folk High School, but he did not engage in the party until the early 1930s.[33] Alva Myrdal, on the other hand, had already been in contact with the social democratic youth movement in her youth.[34]

While Gunnar found his legal studies unsatisfactory, they taught him to be precise with words and to identify the core of a problem. But he was dissatisfied with the day-to-day work in law after graduation and became depressed. It was then that Alva stepped in and saved him.[35] She suggested he shift his focus to economics, which suited him better than law because of its similarity to mathematics and science, subjects he had enjoyed at Norra Real. Alva bought Gustav Cassel's textbook "Theoretical Social Economics" and he began reading it and other economic literature while continuing to support himself as a lawyer. He read everything in "Ekonomisk Tidskrift" ("Economic Journal") from its first issue in 1899. He and Alva discussed economics and social problems with economists Alf Johansson and Erik Lindahl, school friend Fritz Thorén, and teacher Märta Fredrikson, among others.

Alf Johansson recalled in 1976 that they regularly gathered, one evening a week in Alva and Gunnar's first shared apartment to discuss.[36] It was Alva who initiated these meetings. They dealt with various issues: primarily economics, where many current controversies in economic theory existed. However, most discussions were about social policy problems.

Johansson also remembered Alva Myrdal's contributions as particularly clear, original, and significant.[37]

Gustav Cassel

Most influential in Gunnar Myrdal's career, however, was Gustav Cassel. Born in 1866, Cassel was a professor at Stockholm University, renowned and frequently sought after as a lecturer and advisor in national and international financial matters. For a period after World War I, he was considered the world's leading economist until John Maynard Keynes took over that position.[38] Cassel made significant contributions in general equilibrium analysis, monetary theory, growth theory, and developed the theory of purchasing power parity between countries' exchange rates.

---

[33] Myrdal (1982a, p. 275).

[34] According to an official biography, both Gunnar and Alva Myrdal joined the Social Democrats in 1932, see Lindskog (1981, p. 21). Before that, she was active in the Social Democratic Youth Association, according to Jackson (1990, p. 55).

[35] Myrdal (1982, p. 274).

[36] Lindskog (1981, p. 17).

[37] Carlson (1990, p. 37).

[38] See Schumpeter (1954, p. 1104) and Myrdal's (1953a, p. 341) obituary of Cassel.

Influenced by the political struggles of the late nineteenth century, he advocated for universal suffrage and workers' rights to collective bargaining. In 1902, he published a book on social policy with a social liberal program in opposition to both extreme liberalism and socialism. However, it was not about solving a distribution problem.[39] Primarily, citizens should rely on their own efforts. But when necessary, social policy could come into play, organized by authorities or private organizations. It was about ensuring that individuals could achieve the best possible development of their own capabilities. It might even become necessary to use coercive measures to create greater real freedom for individuals, according to Cassel.

As an economist, Cassel advocated empirical analysis over untestable theories. Myrdal's (1953a) obituary of Cassel noted his remarkable ability to discern the major trends amidst the myriad of real-world data. He also celebrated academic freedom and valued open debate in his seminars. Cassel formed a study group that included four individuals who later held leading positions in various political parties: Gösta Bagge (Right-Wing Party), Nils Wohlin (Farmers' Union), Bertil Ohlin (Liberal Party), and Gunnar Myrdal (Social Democratic Party). Once Cassel recognized Myrdal's talent, he ensured that Myrdal received a travel scholarship from the Academy of Sciences for studies in England in 1925. Gunnar, along with Alva, spent half a year in London, mostly at the British Museum, and returned with a thesis that was approved. He then wrote his doctoral thesis, *Prisbildningsproblemet och föränderligheten* (The Problem of Price Formation Problem under Economic Change), which was approved with the highest grade in 1927. In a short time, he established himself as a scientific star and Cassel's favorite student, and soon he became one of the leading Stockholm economists, alongside Erik Lindahl and Bertil Ohlin.

Alva's Dilemma

Alva Myrdal, after her rapid Bachelor of Arts degree, found it much harder to establish herself. She faced a dilemma between her desire to have children, continue her studies, and Gunnar's need for total support. After several miscarriages, she gave birth to a son, Jan, in the same year Gunnar received his doctorate. She could not attend the doctoral dinner. Jan soon became a problem and "sadly much a duty" for Alva, who could not count on any assistance from Gunnar. He had obtained a lecturer position at Stockholm University and was constantly away.[40]

Alva began teaching English for her livelihood at ABF (the Workers' Educational Association). A woman was hired as a housemaid and lived in the kitchen alcove of their apartment on Atlasgatan. Alva studied educational psychology and social psychology at Uppsala University, thus gaining an academic background to apply for

---

[39] Hasselberg (2021, p. 143, 150).
[40] Hirdman (2006, p. 138).

foreign scholarships. Gunnar and Alva each sought a Rockefeller scholarship for studies in the USA, which were granted in April 1929.[41] They left their son Jan with Gunnar's parents in Gesta, near the maternal grandparents in Kvicksta, where Albert had bought his own farm and where Jan was as welcome as with his paternal grandparents. Gunnar and Alva spent a few months at the British Museum in London before traveling to the USA, arriving in mid-October 1929, about 10 days before the great stock market crash.[42]

Gunnar and Alva in the USA

In the USA, Alva attended courses in psychology and social psychology and a course on children's mental health and development and nursery schools. She was influenced by the German child psychologist Charlotte Bühler, known for her methods of meticulous observation of children's daily activities, and had the opportunity to interview her when she was a visiting professor in the USA. Gunnar feverishly worked on completing his book *Vetenskap och Politik i Nationalekonomin* (The Political Element in the Development of Economic Theory, Myrdal (1953b)), which critiqued his predecessors in the field. Alva's interest in psychology influenced his approach to asking new questions in the analysis of doctrinal history. She was critical of traditional analysis and called for contributions from multiple scientific disciplines beyond economics. Gunnar met many renowned economists, including Frank Knight, a pioneer in analyzing the entrepreneur's role in the economy, who introduced the distinction between risk and uncertainty. Knight's work was a great inspiration for Gunnar Myrdal, as discussed in Chap. 3. He also met Wesley Mitchell, who founded the empirical analysis of the business cycle based on large datasets, bypassing unnecessary theory.

Gunnar and Alva also encountered sociologists like P. T. Sorokin and William Ogburn, who analyzed the interplay between technological innovation and social change, as well as Robert and Helen Lynd, pioneers in exploring local communities.[43] The Myrdals spent considerable time with sociologists W. I. Thomas, a groundbreaking researcher on social organizations, and Dorothy Thomas, a population expert, who later contributed to the work on *An American Dilemma*. Interacting with these scholars broadened Gunnar Myrdal's focus from being primarily centered on core economic theory to encompassing a wider range of social sciences. The stock market crash and the onset of the economic depression spurred a heightened interest in social reforms.

---

[41] Gunnar's application was conditional upon Alva also being accepted as a fellow.

[42] Gunnar Myrdal himself spread the myth that they arrived in New York the day before the great stock market crash, which is not accurate; the correct arrival date is likely October 14th, 1929, according to Stellan Andersson (email).

[43] Jackson (1990, p. 60) and Etzemüller (2014, p. 54).

However, Gustav Cassel, in a letter in december 1929, asserted that Gunnar Myrdal should see himself as Cassel's successor and continue to develop dynamic analysis in economic theory.[44] Cassel said that he had sought to expand the static perspective and maximize its potential. He told Myrdal that it was his task to establish the foundations of dynamic economy and urged him to provide the world with an elementary and perfectly comprehensible guide to the dynamics of economics. This was Myrdals categorical imperative, as life has presented it to him, according to Cassel.

After his stay in the USA, on Cassel's recommendation, Myrdal became a visiting professor in Geneva from 1930 to 1931. During this time, the Myrdals began to take an interest in the Swedish population issue. They drafted two articles on the subject and sent them to the journal *Tiden* in May 1931. However, the articles were rejected for being too lengthy, according to the editor, Ernst Wigforss.[45] Consequently, they set aside the population issue for 3 years. Gunnar Myrdal instead devoted himself to laying the groundwork for dynamic theory and its application in curbing the depression. He also completed a study on the development of Swedish living standards over a hundred years, titled *The Cost of Living in Sweden 1830–1930*.[46] In the autumn of 1933, Gunnar Myrdal succeeded his mentor Gustav Cassel as professor of economics and financial science at Stockholm University. At the inauguration, Cassel embraced his former student, remarking that Myrdal was the most dangerous man in Sweden, but Cassel was proud to have him as his successor.[47]

References

Andersson S (1989) Gunnar Myrdal. Barn- och ungdomsår. Några minnesbilder och dokument' (Gunnar Myrdal. Childhood and Youth Years. Some Memories and Documents), compiled by Stellan Andersson. The Swedish Labor Movement's Archive and Library, Stockholm

Appelqvist Ö, Andersson S (1998) Vägvisare – Texter av Gunnar Myrdal. Norstedts, Stockholm. English edition: Appelqvist Ö, Andersson S (1998) The essential Gunnar Myrdal. The New Press, New York

Berggren H, Trägårdh L (2015) Är svensken människa?, Gemenskap och oberoende i det moderna Sverige (Is the Swede human?, Community and independence in modern Sweden). Norstedts, Stockholm. English edition: Berggren H, Trägårdh (2022) The Swedish theory of love, individualism and social trust in modern Sweden. University of Washington Press, Seattle

Bok S (1987) Alva, ett kvinnoliv. Bonniers, Avesta. English edition: Bok S (1991). Alva Myrdal. A daughter's memoir. Radcliffe biography series. Perseus Publishing, Cambridge

Carlson A (1990) The Swedish experiment in family politics. The Myrdals and the interwar population crisis. Routledge, London/New York

---

[44] Niskanen (2007, p. 4).

[45] Carlson (1990, p. 46). Gunnar Myrdal's critique of economists' conflation of science and politics was published in 1930 and received praise from Ernst Wigforss, as shown in the next chapter.

[46] Part of a large project led by Gösta Bagge on wages, living costs, and national income in Sweden, funded by the Rockefeller Foundation.

[47] Jackson (1990, p. 75).

References

Etzemüller T (2014) Alva and Gunnar Myrdal. Social engineering in the modern world. Lexington Books, Lanham

Hasselberg Y (2021) Vetenskapens karaktär. Eli Heckscher, del 1. Oberoende liv 1879–1924 (The Nature of Science. Eli Heckscher, Part 1. Independent Life 1879–1924). Gidlunds, Halmstad

Hirdman Y (2003) Alva & Gunnar Myrdal. De blå kuverten. Kärleksbreven juli 1919–augusti 1920 utgivna av Yvonne Hirdman, (Alva & Gunnar Myrdal. The Blue Envelopes. Love Letters July 1919–August 1920 published by Yvonne Hirdman) Gidlunds i samarbete med Arbetarrörelsens arkiv och bibliotek, Falun

Hirdman Y (2006) Det tänkande hjärtat. Boken om Alva Myrdal. Ordfront, Stockholm. English edition: Hirdman, Y (2008), Alva Myrdal: the passionate mind. Indiana University Press, Bloomington

Jackson W (1990) Gunnar Myrdal and America's conscience. Social engineering and racial liberalism 1938–1987. The University of North Carolina Press, Chapel Hill/London

Jackson W (2021) Alva and Gunnar Myrdal in Sweden and America 1898–1945. Unsparing honesty. Routledge, New York/London

Lindskog L (1981) Alva Myrdal. 'Förnuftet måste segra (Alva Myrdal. Reason Must Prevail). Sveriges Radios Förlag, Kristianstad

Linnaeus (1984) Carl von Linnés DALARESA (Carl von Linné's journey through Dalarna). Natur och Kultur, Arlöv

Montgomery A (1947) Industrialismens genombrott i Sverige (The breakthrough of industrialism in Sweden). Almqvist & Wiksell, Stockholm

Myrdal G (1927) Prisbildningsproblemet och föränderligheten (The problem of price formation under economic change). Almqvist & Wicksell, Stockholm

Myrdal G (1930) Vetenskap och Politik i Nationalekonomin (The political element in the development of economic theory). Norstedts, Stockholm

Myrdal G (1953a) Gustav Cassel. In: Schumpeter J, Heckscher E, Lindahl E, Myrdal G (eds) Stora nationalekonomer (Great economists). Natur och Kultur, Stockholm

Myrdal G (1953b) The political element in the development of economic theory. 1990 edition, Transaction Publishers; 2017 edition. Routledge, New York

Myrdal G (1977) "Ett bra land som borde kunnat vara mycket bättre" (A good country that could have been much better). In: Herin J, Werin L (eds) Ekonomisk debatt och ekonomisk politik, Nationalekonomiska föreningen 100 år. Norstedts, Stockholm

Myrdal G (1982a) Hur styrs landet? (How is the country run?). Rabén & Sjögren, Stockholm

Myrdal J (1982b) Barndom (Childhood). Norstedts, Stockholm

Myrdal G (1985) PM (Memorandum) 20.03.1985. The Swedish labour movement's archives and library

Niskanen K (2007) Karriär i männens värld. Nationalekonomen och feministen Karin Kock (Career in a man's world: the economist and feminist Karin Kock). SNS Publishing, Stockholm

Premfors R (1999) Sveriges demokratisering. Ett historiskt institutionalistiskt perspektiv (Democratizing Sweden: a historical institutionalist perspective). SCORE. Report 1999:3. SCORE, Stockholm University

Rothstein B (1992) Den korporativa staten (The corporatist state). Norstedts Law, Stockholm

Rothstein B (1998) Den svenska modellens uppgång och fall. En essä (The rise and fall of the Swedish model: an essay). Statsvetenskaplig Tidskrift 1:41–49

Schön L (2014) En modern svensk ekonomisk historia (A modern Swedish economic history). Studentlitteratur, Lund

Schumpeter J (1954) History of economic analysis. Oxford University Press, New York

Wärenstam E (1965) Sveriges nationella ungdomsförbund och högern 1928–1934, Studia Historica Upsaliensa. Norstedts, Stockholm

Chapter 3
The Value Premises of Social Scientists Must Be Clarified

Between 1870 and 1914 Europe experienced prosperity and stability, facilitated by the classical gold standard. This era prioritized balance of payments over other economic concerns. During this time, an economic theory reached its peak, assuming that perfect markets and minimal government intervention would lead to full employment. However, World War I disrupted the stability, leading to a loss of credibility in governments' fiscal and monetary policies. The war's aftermath saw fiscal disasters and rising unemployment. The expansion of suffrage made unemployment a political issue, challenging the laissez-faire doctrine and leading to calls for government intervention to achieve full employment. Alongside John Maynard Keynes, The Stockholm School economists, including Gunnar Myrdal, emerged, advocating for state intervention to stimulate demand and address unemployment. Gunnar Myrdal's book *The Political Element in the Development of Economic Theory* is a doctrinal critique of three central notions: the idea of value, the theory of free competition, and the theory of public finance. Influenced by Max Weber, Myrdal argued for clear value premises in economic analysis, emphasizing that economics cannot be value-free.

Introduction

From 1870 to 1914, known as *La Belle Époque*, Europe experienced a time of hope, peace, wealth, new technologies, and colonial expansion. The period was characterized by the classical gold standard when the Bank of England directed the global financial system, with the pound sterling still serving as the world's central currency. Exchange rates were tied to the price of gold. This gold standard meant that the focus of monetary policy was on countries' balance of payments. Other national considerations, such as unemployment and economic stabilization, were not on the agenda at all. When monetary policy was tightened in England, it also tightened in other countries. Yet, the classical gold standard, during the period 1870–1914, was characterized by stability. This stability rested on a credible defense of the exchange rate and effective international cooperation. Governments prioritized balance of payments equilibrium. In Britain, France, and Germany, there was no doubt that central banks would defend the gold reserves and the gold standard if necessary. The Scandinavian countries Denmark, Sweden, and Norway established in 1873–1874 a currency union based on the gold standard that also lasted till 1914.

During this time, a significant economic theory reached its peak. This economic theory was seen as complete and able to answer all questions within its scope. It aimed to show how people's desires or needs, with perfect knowledge and limited resources, lead to certain outcomes. The theory assumed that markets worked perfectly, with many companies producing goods and buyers not favoring one over another. This theory was about an ideal economic state where everything is balanced. The general equilibrium model, elaborated by Léon Walras and further developed by Gustav Cassel, is defined as a set of prices such that the relevant quantities demanded and supplied in each market are equal to each other. Competition ensures that price equals cost of production for every production process in operation and all markets clear. In particular, the theory supported the laissez-faire belief that the economy will naturally tend toward full employment without government intervention.

World War I marked the end of stability from the classical gold era, as shown by Barry Eichengreen in his classic book *Golden Fetters: The Gold Standard and the Great Depression, 1919–1939* (1992). The credibility of governments' fiscal policies, central banks' monetary policies, and international cooperation eroded. Meanwhile, the expansion of suffrage in several countries meant that unemployment became a political issue. When the balance of payments and employment were at odds, it was unclear which objective should be allowed to dominate.

Where the independence of monetary policy was most questioned, explosive inflations occurred. The printing press financed budget deficits when state finances were depleted. Especially, in countries with proportional electoral systems such as Belgium, Germany, and France, there were financial wars of attrition for several years after the war, where different social groups fought to avoid bearing the burden of national debt. All groups that could lose from the introduction of new taxes were represented in the parliaments and blocked proposals for budget consolidation. However, in the Netherlands and Scandinavia, proportional electoral systems did not lead to inflationary fires, mainly because these countries were neutral in the war and did not suffer from deteriorated state finances like the belligerent countries.

The dispute between Germany and, in particular, France over the payment of the German war reparations, which amounted to 125% of German national income in 1921, was a significant cause of the German hyperinflation in the early 1920s.

World War I and the fall of the gold standard not only contributed to societal collapses. The dominant economic doctrine of laissez-faire also faced powerful attacks from a new generation of economists who highlighted the need for government intervention to achieve full employment.

The Institutional Background in Sweden

In the generation preceding Gunnar Myrdal and other Stockholm Scool economists, several internationally renowned Swedish professors emerged. Knut Wicksell, born in 1851 and originally a mathematician, was drawn to economics by his keen interest in social issues, eventually becoming one of the world's leading economists and a major inspiration for the Stockholm School. Wicksell strongly opposed the injustices in Swedish society, became a significant reform advocate, and was friends with novelist and playwright August Strindberg and leader of the Social Democratic Party Hjalmar Branting.[1] He despised the bourgeois society's irrational and entangling rituals. According to Gunnar Myrdal, Wicksell had the integrity of a saint and few others had lived a life so untouched by moral compromises as he had.[2] Wicksell refused to marry, opting instead for a free union with Norwegian diplomat Anna Bugge, as arranged by the future Prime Minister Karl Staaff.[3] Anna Bugge Wicksell became a prominent lawyer and advocate for women's suffrage, active in the peace movement, and a Swedish delegate to the League of Nations.

Eli Heckscher, born in 1879, gained fame as both an economist and economic historian. He contributed significantly to theories of international trade, monetary theory, and Swedish economic history. At the Stockholm School of Economics, he was a revered lecturer but a feared examiner. Scoring a high A in Heckscher's economics exam was considered more prestigious than becoming a professor or director-general. Among his students, only six, including Stockholm School economists Bertil Ohlin and Alf Johansson, achieved this feat.[4] Heckscher was active in newspapers, periodicals, and as a radio speaker. He was a fierce debater with strong liberal beliefs and scientific credibility. In Gunnar Myrdal, Heckscher met his match in debate strength and theoretical brilliance.[5]

After overcoming substantial resistance, Knut Wicksell became a professor in Lund in 1901. Gustav Cassel, introduced in the previous chapter, was active at Stockholm University from 1904, and Eli Heckscher at the Stockholm School of Economics from 1909. These three professors were foundational in establishing the field of economics in Sweden.[6] They were all liberals of various shades, engaged in public debate, but not interested in political office. They did, however, participate in governmental inquiries and advise the Riksbank.

The new generation of Stockholm economists included Gunnar Myrdal, Erik Lindahl, Bertil Ohlin, Dag Hammarskjöld, Alf Johansson, Karin Kock, Erik

---

[1] Gårdlund (1956, p. 12).
[2] Myrdal (1972, appendix, p. 271).
[3] Wicksell Nordqvist (1985, p. 95).
[4] Henriksson (1979, p. 512).
[5] Henriksson (1979, p. 515).
[6] The founders also included David Davidson, who became a professor at Uppsala University in 1889 and founded "Ekonomisk tidskrift," the first scientific journal on economics in Sweden, see Jonung (1991, p. 2).

Lundberg, and Ingvar Svennilson. They shared the older generation's desire to engage in socio-political debate and reach a wider audience through their writings. However, they also challenged the older generation's analyses and methods, particularly in the context of Sweden's high unemployment in the 1920s, which required solutions beyond wage reductions. The Stockholm School advocated for state intervention to stimulate demand for goods, services, and labor. Many became influential in politics (Kock, Ohlin, Myrdal), public administration (Hammarskjöld, Johansson, Kock, Lundberg), and international organizations (Hammarskjöld, Kock, Myrdal, Svennilson).

Both generations met in the Economic Club, founded in Stockholm in 1917 by Heckscher to provide Wicksell a platform after his retirement.[7] In 1928, 2 years after Wicksell's death, Myrdal first presented his strong critique of the older generation's faith in the theory of free competition to create maximum wealth, which became the famous book discussed in this chapter. The younger economists, primarily Myrdal, clashed with the older ones, particularly Heckscher, like "sticks and straws in the air."[8]

The Value Premises of Social Scientists Must Be Clarified

Gunnar Myrdal wrote *Vetenskap och politik i nationalekonomin* (The Political Element in the Development of Economic Theory*)* at the behest of his friend Alf Johansson.[9] The book was a sharp critique of mainstream economics and its tendency to confuse empirical truth with valuable ideals, mixing scientific facts with political ideologies. It represented a revolt against the older, distinguished generation of Swedish economists, particularly Eli Heckscher and Gustav Cassel, who took offense at the criticism.

Myrdal's book is a doctrinal critique of three central notions: the idea of value, the theory of free competition, and the notion of Social Houeskeeping. The theory of value, according to Myrdal, employed non-scientific concepts and obscured potential conflicts between political ideals and scientific analysis. The idea of competetive markets, asserting that competition in free markets is the most beneficial system, rested on hidden assumptions not met in reality. Myrdal argued that the Social Housekeeping idea—public finance, as we say today—presupposes a political valuation of the desired society, a realization most economists had not reached.

Regarding the theory of value, Myrdal acknowledged the influence of German sociologist Max Weber, who argued that economics should be a theoretical and value-free science. However, Myrdal believed Weber did not sufficiently critique

---

[7] The most famous meeting in the club took place in 1936, when J.M. Keynes discussed his employment theory with, among others, Ohlin, Myrdal, Hammarskjöld, Finance Minister Wigforss, and Riksbank Governor Rooth, see Henriksson (1987, p. 305).

[8] Henriksson (1987, p. 310).

[9] The inspiration may have come from Keynes (1926), according to Henriksson (1991).

the political speculation inherent in economic theory, being more of a sociologist and historian than an economic theorist.[10] Myrdal was also influenced by Swedish philosopher Axel Hägerström, a prominent value nihilist who argued that moral judgments lack truth value. Myrdal maintained that social science analysis should be value-free to be objective, but he went further in his book.[11]

The Dilemma of Goal Formulation

In the first chapter, Myrdal criticized Knut Wicksell's formulation of societal development goals. In his inaugural lecture as a professor of economics, Wicksell stated that the goal was to spread the greatest possible happiness to all, regardless of social class, race, gender, language, and creed.[12] Myrdal objected that such a broadly formulated goal is impractical in social science. Happiness, as defined, cannot be scientifically measured and weighed. However, Wicksell was both a great scientist and a radical social reformer. Thus, Myrdal began to realize that the perceived conflict between Wicksell's political ideals and economic theory presented a central dilemma. Myrdal (1930, p. 41) said that:

> This problem is not solved merely by asserting that economics should be assumption-free, merely striving for knowledge and not general political norms.

Critique of the Theory of Value

Myrdal devoted a significant portion of his book to a thorough historical examination of the theory of value. He studied the classics, seeking the origins of economic thought. Economics was permeated with values inherited from natural law and utilitarianism, leading economists to use concepts and evaluations that were seemingly objective but actually shaped by scientific tradition and their environment. Concepts like value, utility, and equilibrium were not scientific but fundamentally moral-philosophical. The idea of human equality stemmed from both natural law and utilitarianism. However, there was a value conflict within economics between the principles of harmony and equality. The harmony principle suggested that the state should minimally interfere in economic development, while the equality principle supported creating an egalitarian society.

---

[10] Myrdal (1930, p. 27). Weber became world-famous as a sociologist, but he was trained as a lawyer specializing in commercial law, close to economics, and considered himself an economist. Like Myrdal, he was passionately interested in politics.
[11] Myrdal (1930, p. 31).
[12] Myrdal (1930, p. 39).

The Harmony Principle

Myrdal derived the fundamental idea that the economy develops best if people act unhindered, in accordance with natural laws, laissez-faire, from the French Physiocrats in the late eighteenth century.

The French Physiocrats, more interested in improving the world than in explaining it, introduced the principle of laissez-faire, the idea of letting economic processes run unhindered. According to Myrdal, their system did not reflect the actual societal state at the time but represented a compilation of economic and political norms derived from reality, seen as immutable and universally applicable. Thus, the doctrine of free trade emerged as an unchallenged scientific truth. The ideal state was envisioned as one protecting only individual and property rights, allowing the "natural laws" to manifest themselves.[13]

Despite his critique, Myrdal acknowledged the Physiocrats' significant contribution to the progress of science. They identified a *lawful* relationship between economic phenomena. The idea of basing central price formation on a general analysis of the entire economy is a vital legacy of the Physiocrats.

A key notion in economics is that free price formation in competetive markets leads to a state of *general equilibrium*, mathematically first formulated by Walras. Myrdal traced this idea throughout doctrinal history, noting that the equilibrium principle is among the perilous concepts allowing a slip from theory into normative speculation.[14]

Myrdal challenged the theory of free competition propagated by Adam Smith and his successors. The theory posited that individuals, when left to their own devices, will buy from the cheapest and sell to the highest paying markets. This, following Smith's principle of division of labor, leads to maximal national income or total product under complete freedom.[15]

Myrdal distanced himself from the notion that free competition maximizes national income. He pointed out that the theory assumes several hidden premises, such as rational behavior by individuals, and highlighted the difficulty in measuring national income acceptably.

Myrdal also criticized the common tendency among economists to separate the analysis of the *magnitude of national income* from its *distribution*. If this is done, then the value premise must apply to the benefits of various combinations of these two factors. Fundamentally, this means that proposals for changes should be evaluated in relation to their impact on national income, regardless of the specific value premises they are based on. Myrdal believed that the theory of free competition became a kind of straitjacket for the choice of political value premises.

---

[13] Myrdal (1930, p. 58).
[14] Adam Smith, Léon Walras, and Alfred Marshall are among the economists Myrdal discussed.
[15] Myrdal (1930, p. 194).

Neoclassical Economics: Praise and Criticism

Myrdal was more favorable towards the economists' use of the equilibrium concept when discussing neoclassical economic theories.[16] He believed that the analysis of marginal utility played a crucial role in the development of economics. The theory of marginal utility, based on the impact of consuming or producing an additional unit of a good, has been one of the most fruitful ideas, paving the way for a unified explanation of the entire price formation system in modern equilibrium theory. By introducing marginal utility analysis of both demand and supply, a unified explanation of the entire extensive price formation system in modern equilibrium theory was made possible.[17]

However, Myrdal continued his critical analysis of applying neoclassical economics in practice. He highlighted several difficulties in determining whether a particular action increases or decreases the happiness of all people. He is critical of the theory that starts from the utility maximization of individual persons. The utilitarian value premise that the individual should consider others falls away. Fundamentally, the utilities of all individuals are summed up despite being presumed unaware of each other's utilities. Myrdal argued that neoclassical economists implicitly assume that all people want the same thing, that there is a harmony of interests. Conflicts between individuals and groups do not exist in this theory, which is an unacceptable way to resolve the inherent value conflict between the principle of harmony and the principle of equality.

Irving Fisher and His Contributions

In contrast to his critique of classical and neoclassical economists, Myrdal acknowledged Irving Fisher for developing a practically useful theory. Fisher, born in 1867 and considered a rival to Wicksell, began as a mathematician before becoming a professor in economics at Yale University. He advanced general equilibrium theory, monetary theory, and showed that interest rates reflect the valuation of deferring consumption to the future. Fisher was also a pioneer in combining economics and statistics, known as *econometrics*, and the development of index numbers.

Myrdal appreciated Fisher's detachment from utilitarianism while retaining the aim to statistically measure and compare individual utilities.[18] Fisher proposed that measurements could relate to the psychological valuation of a certain quantity of goods or alternative desirable goods, essentially the preferences present in society. Despite academic skepticism about the feasibility of measuring such preferences,

---

[16] According to him, economists who contributed to the development included William Stanley Jevons, Carl Menger, Léon Walras, and Knut Wicksell.

[17] Myrdal (1930, p. 63).

[18] Myrdal (1930, pp. 154–156).

Fisher argued that in practical human life, such assessments are common. Economists should not refrain from measurements simply because they touch upon a philosophically insoluble problem. In practice, it involved issuing a moral judgment about value, based on as accurate a knowledge of reality as possible. Myrdal, influenced by Fisher, believed in replacing moral judgment with scientifically determined alternatives, using public statistics and new survey methods as a basis for such valuation, which he also demonstrated in later works.[19]

Social Housekeeping and the Need for Valuation

Myrdal also analyzed the concept of social housekeeping (public finance) and its relation to value premises. The doctrine of housekeeping, a direct translation of the term economics, harks back to the absolute monarchy, where a monarch not only cared for the state's finances but also for the welfare of the people. From Adam Smith onwards, the concept referred to an analogy between an individual managing personal affairs and society's overall management.

Myrdal pointed out that for the concept of social housekeeping to be meaningful, a social valuation criterion is required.[20] Myrdals wiew was that it presupposes an ideal form of housekeeping to be intentionally pursued. Further, he thought that a subject for the entire economic process implies a social valuation, and only a social valuation can define the concept of social housekeeping. If this concept is to be scientifically valid—and it is even assumed to be the very definition of the subject of economics—it must be objectively determined, i.e., universally valid, according to Myrdal.

Myrdal also emphasized the significance of institutions and the need to analyze various societal groups' power resources and how political programs benefit or disadvantage them. According to Myrdal, such an approach to economic science could claim objectivity because it only recommends from a specific and established perspective of interest. He called for definite and concretized *value premises*, chosen so broadly that they align with the somewhat divergent interests of powerful social groups.[21]

The Technology of Economics Is Based on Sociology

Myrdal recognized additional complexities. Human motives are not solely driven by economic interests; they intertwine with moral fervor, which can either support or contradict self-interest. Therefore, the technology of economics should be based on

---

[19] See, for example, Myrdal (1944).

[20] Myrdal (1930, p. 218)

[21] Myrdal (1930, p. 285).

both interests and opinions and it is not just a field of interest that we need to build our economic technology upon, but also a field of opinion.[22]

In the English edition of the book, this was sharpened to a technology of economics should not be built upon economic interests, but upon social attitudes.[23] According to Myrdal 'attitude' means the emotive disposition to respond in certain ways to situations. Pride, self-respect and dignity may for example be more important than higher wages for workers on strike. However, when this sentence was retranslated to Swedish in the new edition 1972, Myrdal pointed out that it is not only a field of interest but also a field of opinion.[24] In this final version, Myrdal thus seemed to focus on both economic interests and opinions (or social attitudes), as in the original 1930 edition.

Myrdal discussed how social scientists could determine people's actual attitudes on current political issues, a complex social-psychological problem. However, as he noted in 1930, it was not the same field of opinion needed for the technology of economics research.[25] Simply discovering people's actual opinions was not enough as these opinions are largely based on incorrect notions about social reality and the connections within it. A technology of economics cannot advantageously be built on these opinions, which presuppose not only a certain personal emotional stance towards the problems but also incorrect reality conceptions, according to Myrdal.

Myrdal concluded that economic technology should be built on the opinions people would hold if they observed reality more accurately, meaning if they knew everything that economists already know. First, the relevant field of opinion must be defined, actual opinions ascertained, and then the hypothetical opinions different social groups would hold if their economic insights were more complete and accurate. Myrdal apparently provided a rationale here for how a social engineer could develop proposals for a welfare policy for citizens, which became a central part of his and Alva's message when they began transforming the Swedish welfare state in the 1930s.

Yet, the task was not complete. Myrdal believed it could not be accomplished using purely logical methods. It was impossible to logically derive the values of social groups with more accurate and comprehensive understandings of reality. This led to the realization that what the social scientist does is to choose a new valuation. Political valuations consist either of different social groups' actual stance or their probable stance under certain hypothetical conditions. The connection between opinions, attitudes, and economic interests is social-psychological. According to Myrdal, economic technology is rooted in modern, social-psychologically oriented sociology.

Myrdal continued to work on the role of valuations in social science throughout his career. In his inaugural lecture as a professor, Myrdal (1935), he pointed out that one must ask a question to get an answer and that the question itself constitutes a

---

[22] Myrdal (1930, p. 287).
[23] Myrdal (1953, p. 200).
[24] Myrdal (1972, p. 257).
[25] Myrdal (1930, p. 289)

choice, which to some extent determines the answer. In his view, the answer is not and cannot be without preconditions. In practical research, value premises should be relevant in the sense that they actually correspond to existing social power groups' real attitudes and preparedness to act, according to Myrdal.

Conclusions

My conclusion is that Myrdal was already in the first edition of *Vetenskap och politik i nationalekonomin* acutely aware of the difficulty of conducting objective social science without clear value premises. However, he himself claimed in 1953 that he still believed, while writing the first edition, that by cutting away all metaphysical valuations, there would remain a positive economic theory construction completely independent of valuations.[26] He returned to the issue in 1972, claiming that his view of the value problem had shifted since 1930 when he still believed that there was a value-free economics.[27]

But I argue that a careful reading of the first edition of the book shows that Myrdal's description of his own changes of opinion regarding this book does not quite hold. However, it is true that he continued to work on the issue throughout his life, and the framework of thought in subsequent works both influenced and was influenced by the problems he worked with.

To what extent was he a pioneer in this area of intellectual history? It is clear that German sociologist Max Weber played a significant role for Gunnar Myrdal. Weber is mentioned in several places in the book. Weber believed that strict concept formation is required in science, which requires studying the ultimate axioms underlying what one aims to achieve.[28] Sven Eliaeson has noted that Myrdal was reluctant to emphasize his dependence on Weber, creating an interpretative problem.[29] There is support that Myrdal's work with value premises still represents an improvement and further development of Weber's theory. Like Hägerström and Myrdal, Weber opposed the influence of natural law on social science. According to Weber, the value aspects became important to clarify when social science became secularized.

Weber distinguished between *value neutrality* and *value relevance*. By value neutrality, he meant that a researcher should strive to keep her own valuations and opinions away from the analysis. A problem should be viewed from various perspectives before the researcher can draw neutral conclusions. The concept of value relevance, according to Weber, means that social science cannot be conducted without valuations. The researcher's subject matter can only be understood in a cultural

---

[26] Myrdal (1953, preface, p. xli).
[27] Myrdal (1972, preface to the new Swedish edition, p. 13).
[28] Nilsson (1994, p. 148).
[29] Eliaeson (2009, p. 216).

context and is always related to valuations. Weber thus pointed out a classic dilemma that needs to be resolved.

The issue is about rational and human-constructed valuations. Weber emphasized that value judgments cannot be tested by scientific means.[30] Weber's dilemma is that objective values are needed for a scientific means-ends analysis, but such values are not available. He tried to resolve this dilemma by introducing explicit value aspects to avoid uncontrolled value bias, but he did not go all the way because he did not clarify the foundation of goal valuation. Weber is difficult to interpret. He argued that it is not possible from a scientific viewpoint to indicate which values are best. Yet, he believed that it is possible to scientifically state which means could or could not realize these values.[31]

According to Richard Swedberg, Gunnar Myrdal was aware of the concept of value neutrality in Weber's sense when he wrote the book.[32] However, Myrdal was not aware of the concept of value relevance, according to Swedberg. But a central aspect of value relevance is that Weber believed a researcher should strive to consider competing and antagonistic value systems. This is precisely what Myrdal did as early as 1930 in the Swedish edition of the book. He called for definite value premises chosen so broadly that they align with different social groups' actual or probable stance, based on certain assumptions, as we have seen.

Hedwig Ekerwald and Per Wisselgren argue that in terms of the boundary between science and politics, Weber focused primarily on the scientific nature of social science, while Myrdal was keen to also promote its political relevance and practical societal benefit.[33] We will later see how Myrdal in his works demonstrated how value premises can be used in science and policy analysis. He emphasized that the relationship between science and politics should be one-directional, with social science supporting political decision-making, but politicians should not control research.[34]

There is a critique that Myrdal placed too much emphasis on the social researcher's responsibility to control their own values. The risk then arises that the analyst might tend to seek out societal values that align with their own.[35] However, this critique overlooks the most crucial point of clearly stating one's value premises. By openly disclosing their own values and selection principles, analysts invite a rational discussion about their work, leading to new questions and further evaluations by other reviewers. For Myrdal, it was not the truth, but the pursuit of truth, the rational conversation, that was the primary commandment of scientific work, according to

---

[30] Eliaeson (2009, p. 220).

[31] Richard Swedberg, email 8.2.2023.

[32] Swedberg (1990, p. xxvii).

[33] Ekerwald and Wisselgren (2022).

[34] Gunnar Myrdal published a pamphlet in 1945, *University Reform*, in which he stated that it was necessary to firmly reject any intrusion on our academic self-governance and above all keep political and other interest influences out of the administration of academic management (Myrdal 1945, pp. 69–70).

[35] Ljungar (1999, p. 59).

Appelqvist and Andersson (1998, p. 9). Therefore, it is important that one's own value premises are disclosed as clearly as possible.

Myrdal's book was first published in Swedish, sold a few hundred copies, was discussed relatively little, and received some reviews by economists.[36] A significant review titled *Ungdomens uppror* (Youth's Rebellion) was published in the social democratic magazine *Tiden*, written by Ernst Wigforss.[37] Born in 1881, Wigforss was one of the great intellectual ideologists and pragmatists of social democracy, a friend of both Knut Wicksell and Anna Bugge Wicksell. After becoming a lecturer in Nordic languages in 1913 with a thesis on the dialects of southern Halland (a Swedish landscape), his interest in societal issues and politics grew. Following the outbreak of war in 1914, he systematized documentation on the war's origins, which was published in two volumes in 1915. He was a leading critic of German activism and also directed sharp criticism at imperialism, racism, and racial theories. He collaborated with Anna Bugge Wicksell on peace issues.[38]

Wigforss was elected to the parliament in 1919 and served as Finance Minister for the first time from May 1925 to June 1926. Knowledgeable and well-read in economics, he embraced Keynes' theories earlier than many Swedish economists. He gave Myrdal's book glowing praise in his review. Wigforss appreciated Myrdal's critique of the older, conservative economists. The review led to a close contact and friendship between Wigforss and Myrdal. They interacted significantly in the following years. Only when the book was translated into German in 1932 did it become known on the continent. An English translation was delayed until 1953. *The Political Element in the Development of Economic Theory* first attracted mixed reviews but today it is considered a classic in the doctrinal history of economics. When Myrdal was awarded the Economics Prize in Memory of Alfred Nobel in 1974, it was mentioned as a pioneering critique of how political values in many areas of research are inserted into economic analysis.

References

Appelqvist Ö, Andersson S (1998) Vägvisare – Texter av Gunnar Myrdal. Norstedts, Stockholm. English edition: Appelqvist Ö, Andersson S (1998) The essential Gunnar Myrdal. The New Press, New York

Eichengreen B (1992) Golden Fetters. The gold standard and the great depression, 1919–1939. Oxford University Press, New York

Ekerwald H, Wisselgren P (2022) Alva och Gunnar Myrdal. Policyorienterade samhällsforskare (Alva and Gunnar Myrdal. Policy-oriented social researchers). In: Eklund L, Isenberg B (eds) Sociologins klassiker. Upptäckter och återupptäckter. Studentlitteratur, Lund

---

[36] Reviews were written by, among others, Johan Åkerman and Sven Brisman, see Strang (2007).
[37] Wigforss (1930).
[38] Wicksell Nordqvist (1985, p. 177).

References

Eliaeson S (2009) Gunnar Myrdal som en Weberiansk offentlig intellektuell. Arvet efter Max Weber (Gunnar Myrdal as a Weberian public intellectual. The legacy of Max Weber). Statsvetenskaplig tidskrift 3:215–237

Gårdlund T (1956) Knut Wicksell. Rebell i det nya riket (The life of Knut Wicksell). New edition: 1990. SNS Publishing, Stockholm

Henriksson R (1979) Eli F. Heckscher och svensk nationalekonomi (Eli F. Heckscher and Swedish economics). Ekonomisk Debatt 8:510–520

Henriksson R (1987) Nationalekonomiska klubben 1917–1951 (The Political Economy Club 1917–1951). Ekonomisk Debatt 4:305–317

Henriksson R (1991) The political economy Club and the Stockholm School, 1917–1951. In: Lars J (ed) The Stockholm School of Economics revisited. Cambridge University Press, Cambridge

Jonung L (ed) (1991) The Stockholm School of Economics revisited. Cambridge University Press, Cambridge

Keynes JM (1926) The end of Laissez-Faire. Hogarth Press, London

Ljungar E (1999) Gunnar Myrdals relevans för dagens sociologi. Värdepremisser och kumulativ kausalitet (Gunnar Myrdal's relevance for today's sociology. Value premises and cumulative causality). Sociologisk forskning 3:37–67

Myrdal G (1930) Vetenskap och Politik i Nationalekonomin (The political element in the development of economic theory). Norstedts, Stockholm

Myrdal G (1935) Den förändrade världsbilden inom nationalekonomin (The changed world view in economics) Installationsföreläsning den 31 mars 1934, i Samhällskrisen och socialvetenskaperna Två installationsföreläsningar. Kooperativa förbundet, Stockholm

Myrdal G (1944) An American Dilemma The Negro problem and modern democracy, first edition: Harper & Row Publishers, New York; cited edition: Transaction Fiftieth Anniversary Edition 1996. Transaction Publishers, New Jersey

Myrdal G (1945) Universitetsreform. Tiden, Stockholm

Myrdal G (1953) The political element in the development of economic theory, 1990 edition, Transaction Publishers. 2017 edn. Routledge, New York

Myrdal G (1972) Vetenskap och politik i nationalekonomin, revised edition, retranslated from the English edition. Rabén & Sjögren, Stockholm

Nilsson JO (1994) Alva Myrdal En virvel i den moderna strömmen (Alva Myrdal: a whirlwind in the modern stream). B Östling's Publishing House Symposion, Stockholm

Strang J (2007) Overcoming the rift between 'is' and 'ought'. Gunnar Myrdal and the philosophy of social engineering. Ideas Hist II(1):143–177

Swedberg R (1990) Introduction. In: Myrdal G (ed) The political element in the development of economic theory. Transaction Publishers; 2017 edn. Routledge, New York

Wicksell Nordqvist L (1985) Anna Bugge Wicksell En kvinna före sin tid (Anna Bugge Wicksell A Woman Before Her Time). Liber förlag, Malmö

Wigforss E (1930) Ungdomens Uppror (The Youth's revolt). Tiden 22:525–538

Chapter 4
The Macroeconomic Revolution in Theory and Practice

The Wall Street crash of 1929 and the ensuing economic crisis, the Great Depression, was exacerbated by the return to the gold standard in many countries after the war and led to global economic downturns. Sweden abandoned the gold standard in 1931 and emerged from the depression faster than many other Western countries. The Swedish Social Democracy evolved into a radical reform party and began its long-standing period in government in 1932. Gunnar Myrdal developed a dynamic theory where the future expectations of households and businesses played a central role. Stockholm economists, finance minister Ernst Wigforss and his closest ally Myrdal developed the theoretical reasons for expansive fiscal policy in a depression, which became practical policy in Sweden. Sweden's recovery also involved currency depreciation and a pioneering price level target for monetary policy. The consensus between the employers' organization and the workers' organization culminated in the establishment of negotiation rules to prevent costly conflicts. In line with Myrdals theory, improved and credible future expectations played an important role when economies began to recover during the depression, first in Sweden and then in the USA.

Introduction

During the 1920s, Swedish politics were characterized by parliamentary crises, minority governments, and frequent changes in government. Three Social Democratic governments were formed, which could not implement much of their socialist party program due to lacking a parliamentary majority. The liberal politician C.G. Ekman became influential with his kingmaker policy: alternating cooperation between the left and right.

This decade's economy faced high unemployment and numerous strikes, but was also marked by continued industrial progress and a rising standard of living. More people gained access to new advancements—electricity, radio, film—and many countries referred to the mid-decade as the "roaring twenties." However, the decade abruptly ended with the Wall Street crash on October 24, 1929. The following economic crisis provided Social Democracy a golden opportunity to transform into a radical reform party on the basis of the existing society.

Towards the end of the 1920s, the first signs of a serious downturn in the American economy were noted. It was the Federal Reserve's tightening of monetary policy at the end of the 1920s and the stock market crash that triggered the Great Depression of the 1930s. The Great Depression has remained somewhat of a mystery to historians and economists. Barry Eichengreen argued in his book *Golden Fetters* (1992) that the main reason for the global depression was the reintroduction of the gold standard after World War I, in a situation where eroded state finances and international disputes destroyed the possibilities for a credible defense of fixed exchange rates. Prominent researchers in the field include former Federal Reserve Chair Ben Bernanke, co-winner of the Nobel Memorial Prize in Economic Sciences in 2022, who showed in his *Essays on the Great Depression* (2000) how widespread bank collapses in the early 1930s exacerbated the downturn in the USA, following the Federal Reserve's monetary policy tightening. The gold standard linked countries' exchange rates through a fixed price against gold and contributed to the depression becoming worldwide. When the Federal Reserve raised interest rates, all other central banks had to do the same; otherwise, they faced gold outflows. By the end of the 1920s, the money supply fell more in Europe and Latin America than in the USA. Protectionism and tariff wars hastened the collapse of world trade, which fell by 25% between 1929 and 1932. In the spring and summer of 1931, Germany, Hungary, and Austria were forced to suspend the gold standard. Against the background of reparations obligations since World War I and the economic downturn, Germany faced continuing shortfalls in government financing. The disaster in Germany not only ravaged the domestic economy and led to high unemployment, which paved the way for Adolf Hitler's ascent, but also sent shockwaves through the international financial system. Britain had substantial sums invested in Germany that it could not repatriate after the German financial crisis in the summer of 1931.[1] The Swedish financier Ivar Kreuger had given a loan to the German government in 1929, in exchange for the match monopoly, thereby tying both his own and Sweden's finances to Germany's solvency.[2] International investors ceased to consider Sweden a safe haven after the German financial crisis. In September 1931, the currency crisis spread to Britain, Sweden, Denmark, Canada, Norway, and other countries and they left the gold standard. The international economy now split into, among others, a sterling block, which included Sweden and traded primarily with Britain, and a gold block—consisting of Belgium, France, the Netherlands, Poland, Switzerland, and the USA—which continued to adhere to the gold standard.

---

[1] Straumann (2019).
[2] Straumann et al. (2016).

After Ivar Kreuger's suicide in March 1932, the Stockholm Stock Exchange collapsed. The Kreuger Crasch hit investors and companies worldwide. Kreuger's conglomerate, involved in match production and other industries, was heavily reliant on loans and complex financial structures. Following the Kreuger Crash several thousand Swedes and small banks lost their savings and investments as a result. Swedish Match recovered after the crash as did most of the industrial companies within the Kreuger empire. The banks related to other industrial spheres (Wallenberg, Stenbeck, Handelsbanken) took over most of the companies in the Kreuger group. The Swedish government intervened to stabilize the situation and implemented stricter financial regulations, which resulted in commercial banks establishing holding companies for their ownership of industrial shares. The intervention also contributed to the significant shift in economic policy, with the state playing a more active role in the economy.

After several countries had left the gold standard and devalued their exchange rates, Sweden emerged as one of the winners. Eventually, the gold block also disintegrated. The depression was deep and prolonged. Unemployment lines were long, in the USA, Germany, and many other countries. The democratic welfare state had not yet been introduced—but the depression contributed to its emergence in several countries. The depression contributed to revolutionize economic theory, and in Sweden, the new ideas quickly became practical, reformist politics.

Keynes, Wicksell, and the Stockholm School Economists

Economic and political problems have always significantly influenced the development of economics. The Great Depression of the 1930s contributed to the formulation of employment theory by John Maynard Keynes in *The General Theory of Employment, Interest and Money* in 1936.

Stockholm economists Gunnar Myrdal, Bertil Ohlin, and Erik Lindahl anticipated aspects of Keynes' theory. However, some researchers regard their central message as different from Keynes. Don Patinkin argued that the Stockholm School did not anticipate the novel central message of *General Theory*: the equalibrating role of changes in output.[3] Demand for goods and services may prove inadequate, resulting in the economy becoming entrenched in a state of suboptimal capacity utilization equilibrium. Keynes central message was that overall economic demand determines employment and conducted a static analysis of escaping a depression caused by insufficient demand.

Based on Knut Wicksell's works, the Stockholm School developed a dynamic analysis, where the formation of expectations played a crucial role in a strikingly modern way. Myrdal's and the Stockholm School's analysis, according to this

---

[3] Patinkin (1982, p. 53).

viewpoint, had a different primary message, one actually missing in Keynes' famous book.

Wicksell realized that the quantity theory of money was inadequate for explaining the development of prices when the money supply largely consisted of bank deposits. He thus developed a new theory where the relationship between the loan rate of interest and the *natural* rate (the rate of return on newly created real capital) plays a crucial role in price level changes.[4] Wicksell showed how credit expansion in the banking system lowered the loan rate of interest below the natural rate, stimulating companies to borrow money, invest, and expand production. Demand for goods and labor increased across the economy, leading to widespread price increases, inflation. This inflation continues as long as normal interest rate is lower than the natural return on business investments. A Wicksellian cumulative process can be visualized as a succession of equilibria whose equilibrating variable is price, as pointed out by Claes-Henric Siven (1997). Wicksell laid the foundation for policy decisions in monetary policy, still a focus for many of the world's central banks: the monetary policy steering rate should be aligned with the rate that creates stable price development.

Wicksell also laid the groundwork for analyzing cumulative processes in the economy, or the potential for virtuous/vicious cycles. Some economists have interpreted the cumulative process as a disequilibrium phenomenon, Gunnar Myrdal was one among them. In his version of dynamic theory, disequilibrium was the nonfulfilment of expectations. Later in life, he would apply and extend the cumulative causation theory in several ways, as will be discussed in following chapters.

Myrdal's Dissertation

The economists of the Stockholm School, drawing inspiration from Wicksell, made significant strides towards dynamic analysis.[5] In his dissertation titled *Prisbildningsproblemet och föränderligheten* (The Problem of Price Formation under Economic Change), Gunnar Myrdal argued that the traditional assumptions of static analysis and perfect knowledge in economic theory were no longer applicable. He was influenced by Frank Knight, a distinguished and eclectic

---

[4] In Wicksell (1898), the natural rate is defined as a certain rate of interest which is neutral with respect to commodity prices, and tends to neither raise nor lower them. This is necessarily the same as the rate of interest which would be determined by supply and demand if no use were made of money and all lending would be effected in the form of real capital goods. It comes to much the same thing as the current value of the natural interest on capital. Wicksell (1906) changed the definition of the natural interest to the rate of interest at which the demand for loan capital and savings exactly agree and, which more or less corresponds to the expected yield on the newly created capital – the normal rate of interest.

[5] Hansson (1982), Hansson (1991), Lundberg (1996), Siven (1991), Siven (1997), Siven (2003), and Siven (2006) contain insightful analysis of the dynamic theory of Knut Wicksell, The Stockholm School and Gunnar Myrdal's contributions.

economist from the University of Chicago who authored *Risk, Uncertainty, and Profit* in 1921. Introducing the distinction between risk and uncertainty in the book, Knight delineated *economic risk* as scenarios with unknown outcomes that nonetheless have a calculable probability distribution, in contrast to *economic uncertainty* where neither outcomes nor probabilities can be estimated in advance. Gunnar Myrdal's thesis distinguished itself as groundbreaking work, drawing influence from Cassel's analysis of general equilibrium, Knight's examination of uncertainty, and the contributions of several other economists, such as Marshall, Fisher, and Keynes.

According to Myrdal, the element of time introduces uncertainty as well as inertia within capital and production structures.[6] He explored the importance of uncertainty for profit generation and the role of intertemporal planning in such contexts. He examined how entrepreneurs predicted future economic shifts and how these predictions influenced the formation of prices in the current period. For each entrepreneur, there exists a certain level of objective risk associated with their expectations of future outcomes, which varies based on their experience and expertise. Additionally, there are personal risks taken by credit suppliers with respect to the entrepreneur. Myrdal emphasized that the non-neutral evaluation of risk is a critical issue, as either underestimation or overestimation of risks can have significant impacts on the cost of bearing risk.

Myrdal differentiated changes as either planned developments over time or adaptations to unexpected shifts in the company's environment, stressing that only unexpected changes had significant implications. Anticipated changes, he argued, were already considered by firms and thus did not lead to new gains. It was the discrepancy between *expectation* and *outcome* that drove changes in company profits and potential equilibrium prices, or "normal prices." In his analysis, anticipations were treated as explicit variables alongside resources and technology within a formal economic theory.

Bertil Ohlin

Bertil Ohlin, a contemporary and notable young economist, made his mark in the 1920s and early 1930s. Studying under Cassel at Stockholm University and Eli Heckscher at the Stockholm School of Economics, Ohlin's major contributions were in international trade theory, where he merged Cassel's general equilibrium theory with Heckscher's trade theory into the Heckscher-Ohlin model. When Myrdal earned his doctorate in 1927, Ohlin was already a professor in Copenhagen, but his return to Stockholm marked the beginning of a fruitful intellectual dialogue with Myrdal. In 1937, Ohlin brought the Stockholm School to international attention through an article in the *Economic Journal*, highlighting its focus on aggregate

---

[6] Lundberg (1996, p. 29).

analysis and the distinction between looking forward and looking backward perspectives, applying casuistic reasoning for precision.[7] Ohlin made significant contributions to the development of the Stockholm School and the analysis of Swedish policy issues related to stabilization. He also rose to prominence as an influential politician, serving as the leader of the Liberal Party for several decades.

Erik Lindahl

Erik Lindahl, a colleague of Gunnar Myrdal and Bertil Ohlin, distinguished himself with a more deliberate pace of work and a modest demeanor. Nonetheless, his contributions to public economics and monetary theory have garnered significant international recognition.

In 1929 and 1930, Lindahl published seminal works on monetary theory and policy, drawing inspiration from Wicksell. Contrary to the quantity theory of money, Lindahl, following Wicksell, emphasized that price level fluctuations should be understood through the lens of demand and supply dynamics for goods. Their perspectives diverged, however, on the optimal objective for monetary policy. While Wicksell advocated for a stable price level as the central bank's target, Lindahl proposed a more flexible goal: a price level that adjusts inversely to productivity changes similar to David Davidson's norm. When discussing his monetary rule, Lindahl proposed that the central bank must be allowed a certain margin of error, a tolerance band, but committed to take action against any price developments beyond this margin.

Lindahl also challenged Wicksell's concept of a discrepancy between the normal loan interest rate and the natural rate of interest, arguing that the price system inherently adjusts to equate the two rates. This assertion rested on the premise of temporary equilibrium, where all markets reach equilibrium simultaneously. According to Lindahl's equilibrium model, anticipated prices result in a demand-supply balance in each period, fulfilling all expectations. Lindahl conceptualized the dynamic process as a sequence of temporary equilibria, albeit without establishing connections between successive periods. The reliance on the temporary equilibrium methodology was later deemed a conceptual impasse by Myrdal.

Monetary Equilibrium

Gunnar Myrdal critically assessed the concept of temporary equilibrium, instead advocating for a dynamic theory that emphasized the discrepancy between expectations and actual outcomes in monetary theory.

---

[7] Ohlin (1937).

The dichotomy of *ex ante* (looking forward)–*ex post* (looking backward), implicitly present in the thesis, was launched by Myrdal in a lengthy essay on monetary equilibrium, published in Swedish in 1932, in German in 1933 and in English in 1939.[8] In *Monetary Equilibrium*, Myrdal wanted to project his own ideas within Wicksell's framework. According to Lindahl, Wicksell had asserted that (1) a normal loan interest rate brings equilibrium by matching the natural interest rate, (2) equate the supply of and the demand for savings, and (3) guarantee a stable price level, primarily of consumption goods. Myrdal argued that these criteria are not synonymous and that only the first two conditions could be considered consistent.

In his reformulation of the first equilibrium condition Myrdal stated that the natural rate has to be redefined as the rate of profitability of *planned* investments. The difference between the natural interest rate and the loan rate of interest rate can then be replaced by the relation between the capital value and the cost of production of planned real investment. He noted that capital values express *anticipations* of future price and production conditions. It was necessary to consider not only capital values but also the cost of production of real capital to be sums of anticipations, discounted to a point in time.

Myrdal thus developed a forward-looking definition of the natural interest rate. He redefined the natural interest rate as the relation between net income during a future unit period and the reproduction cost of real capital, both discounted to the present. Myrdal showed what should influence investments was the ratio between the value of investing and the cost of investing, anticipating Tobin's q-theory of investment.[9] Myrdal also pointed out that the value of investments can be estimated by employing indices of stock values of shares and bonds of industrial firms, in a modern and useful way.

Myrdal's central contribution in *Monetary Equilibrium* was to express distinction and emphatic contrast between two temporal viewpoints. Households and businesses form expectations about the future (*ex ante*) at the beginning of a certain period and establish plans for their actions. However, the outcomes of expectation variables may be different at the end of the period (*ex post*) than anticipated. If expectations are not met, it can trigger revisions of both expectations and plans for

---

[8] The original Swedish text is dated 1931 but was actually published in 1932. The German translator Gerhard Mackenroth suggested the terms *ex ante–ex post*, in the German translation of the book, published in 1933. It was then given a more systematic presentation in the book in English, Monetary Equilibrium, published in 1939. See Myrdal (1931b), Myrdal (1933), Myrdal (1939) and Patinkin (1982, p. 47).

[9] See Myrdal (1931b, p. 208). Klaus Schmidt (1995) gives evidence for Myrdal anticipating the q theory in Tobin (1969) by at least 30 years. It is also clear that the tradition of analysis linking investment to the financial structure of the company has its origins in the writings of Knut Wicksell, Thorstein Veblen and Keynes (1930, 1936), as pointed out by Dieudonné (2019). In Keynes's *A Treatise on Money* (1930), the value of the company's capital assets is the result of the capitalization of expected returns at the capital markets rate. In the *General Theory* (1936) Keynes develops the notion of marginal efficiency of capital, the relation between the prospective yield of one more unit of capital and the cost of producing that unit, that refers to the q theory.

the next period. The unexpected gap between expectations and outcomes is thus a central part of Myrdal's and the Stockholm School's message.

G.L.S. Shackle has stated that Myrdal was the first economist to explicitly base economic theory on people's assessment and quantification of future, unknown quantities. By asserting that the future and the past are distinct, and that the perception of a specific time period can change from its start to its end, Myrdal freed economic theory from the limiting assumption that the economy moves predictably like planetary orbits, according to Shackle.[10]

It is also clear that Myrdal discussed the equilibrating role of changes in output and unemployment in *Monetary Equlibrium,* already in the Swedish and German versions, which was the central message in Keynes's *General Theory*. Myrdal elucidated the downward Wicksellian process triggered by a credit contraction and resulting in a new equilibrium. The new equilibrium featured significantly lower capital values due to higher interest rates or tighter credit, slightly lower wages, especially in capital goods industries, considerable unemployment, particularly in those industries, and a generally reduced production volume.[11] This implied a shorter production time structure, reduced savings, and new investments that were less extensive and more direct.

Thus, there are in Myrdal's book obvious parallells to Keynes theory of unemployment. But Myrdal did not consider the equilibrating role of changes in production to be his *central* message in this book, as pointed out by Don Patinkin. It is also clear that Myrdal did not provide an explicit model for analyzing the conditions for monetary equilibrium as an analytical instrument in situations outside equilibrium, as noted by Siven (2006). However, during the depression, Gunnar Myrdal became one of the most important policymakers when a new economic policy was introduced in Sweden, in order to combat both unemployment and deflation.

Pioneers in Economic Stabilization Policy: Myrdal, Ohlin, and Wigforss

The younger generation, the Stockholm School economists, became pioneers in reducing unemployment and stabilizing business cycles through economic policies, primarily fiscal policy, but also proposals for modernization of monetary policy. Two of them, Gunnar Myrdal and Bertil Ohlin, also became highly politically active. Bertil Ohlin proposed as early as 1931 that the state budget should not be balanced annually but over an entire business cycle.

Gunnar and Alva Myrdal returned to Sweden in the fall of 1931, at a time when the depression had deepened, the liberal government was weakened, and Social

---

[10] Shackle (1967, p. 116).
[11] Myrdal (1939, pp. 164–169).

Democracy was led by a generation of reform-minded politicians: Per Albin Hansson (party chairman), Gustav Möller, Ernst Wigforss, and Östen Undén.

It was also around this time that the Myrdals began to become publicly known. Gunnar traveled around Sweden giving lectures on fiscal policy, planned economy, and social housing policy. Newspapers reported on the ambitious and hurried man who was never dull.[12] The first public photograph of Gunnar and Alva, featured in their functionalist apartment on Kungsholms strand, appeared in the weekly magazine *Idun* in November 1931, showing Gunnar reading a (significant) text while Alva looks into the camera.

A new expansive economic policy was launched in the spring of 1930, in a motion drafted by Wigforss. Wigforss ensured that Gunnar Myrdal participated in drafting a major crisis motion in the spring of 1932, which became the basis for the election campaign and the government declaration in the fall of 1932.[13] Myrdal contributed to the 1933 state budget proposal under the leadership of the new finance minister, Wigforss. In the annex *Konjunktur och offentlig hushållning* (Business cycle and public finance) Myrdal provided a theoretical legitimization of active, counter-cyclical fiscal policy.[14] He noted that it was quite natural that the depression, extraordinary in both depth and duration, forced this viewpoint into relevance. Fiscal policy could assist the distressed business sector and thereby also reduce the number of unemployed due to the stagnation in business life, according to Myrdal. This means that the young generation of economists, who formed the core of the Stockholm School, and Wigforss backed Keynesian stimulus policies in practical politics before the publication of Keynes (1936).

There were additional institutional conditions for establishing the Stockholm School economists.[15] Among them was *Arbetslöshetsutredningen* (*The Unemployment Investigation*), which started working in 1927, that produced around 140 memorandums and appendices, and a final report in 1935. Eli Heckscher was instrumental in setting up the investigation, which included members such as Gösta Bagge, professor of economics and future Member of Parliament and party leader for the Right-Wing Party, and Ernst Wigforss, then a Social Democratic Member of Parliament. Several Stockholm economists participated as experts.[16] Dag Hammarskjöld was the secretary in drafting the final report and wrote an appendix, which he used as the basis for his doctoral thesis.[17] Bertil Ohlin wrote five memorandums and an appendix. In Ohlin (1934), he studied various means of fighting unemployment. The model he used might be described as a simple version of the Keynesian macroeconomics of the 1950s, as noted by Siven (2003). Ohlin used

---

[12] Etzemüller (2014, p. 56).

[13] Hirdman (2006, p. 186).

[14] Appelqvist and Andersson (1998, p. 85).

[15] See Jonung's preface (1991, p. 7), and references to articles by Craver and Wadensjö in the book.

[16] Bagge became a Member of Parliament in 1932 and was the leader of the Conservative Party from 1935 to 1944. Wigforss left the commission when he became Finance Minister in 1932. He was Finance Minister from 1932 to 1949 (with a brief break for a few months in 1936).

[17] Hammarskjöld (1933).

multiplier analysis to determine national income and the accelerator to determine investments. Ohlin also asserted that in a depression, the central bank's monetary policy could play a role in stimulating the economy and improving future expectations. He rejected a general wage reduction to decrease costs, as it would reduce purchasing power and hence the overall demand in the economy. Ohlin said that the cost for one person is income and a source of demand for another person, a formulation he had borrowed from Keynes.[18] Ohlin called for societal measures, including public works, to increase production and employment.

Gunnar Myrdal contributed to *The Unemployment Investigation* with a memorandum and an appendix. In the memorandum, Myrdal (1934), there are chapters with macroeconomic analysis anticipating the income analysis in *General Theory* by Keynes.[19] Myrdal became, alongside Ernst Wigforss, the foremost advocate for active fiscal policy. It was explicitly noted that policy should not be influenced by the natural price equilibrium but by a specific valuation of the desired equilibrium. Budget policy should primarily mitigate the country's economic depression.[20] Myrdal (1934) pointed out that if a government expenditure significantly increased the nation's production and real capital formation, by employing unused production resources for this purpose, this expense represented a strengthening of the state's finances from a deeper financial perspective, regardless of how it was covered.

Myrdal also advocated for public works, arguing that since they lead to increased employment and higher incomes, the tax base would also grow. Therefore, the state's deficit would be lower than the original expenditure. Myrdal had a clear insight into the multiplier effect of government spending in a recession: state expenditures lead to income for others, initiating a virtuous cycle in the economy. According to Bent Hansen both Ohlin and Myrdal demonstrated clear understanding of the dynamics of the multiplier process, but only Myrdal had a full understanding of the *convergence* of the process.[21] It is also important to stress that Myrdal was cautious in his advocacy for counter-cyclical fiscal policy. He was a proponent of fixed norms in fiscal policy and believed that the state's budget should be balanced over the business cycle.

In the final *Report II* of the *Unemployment Investigation* (1935), a complete Keynesian model was sketched by the draftsman, most probably Dag Hammarskjöld. However, the draftsman failed to analyze the model correctly, according to Bent Hansen.[22]

Ernst Wigforss himself wrote some memorandums for the *Unemployment Investigation*, clearly showing his early insights into Keynesian thinking. He described how the automatic price mechanism could be rendered ineffective in a

---

[18] Larsson (1998, p. 95).

[19] Myrdal (1934) part 4, Chaps. 3 and 4, contains analysis anticipating Keynes (1936), see Siven (2006, p. 682).

[20] Appelqvist and Andersson (1998, p. 87).

[21] Hansen (1981, p. 275). Hansen also notes that Myrdal may have been inspired by Erik Lindahl who visualized the possibility of underemployment equilibria in Lindahl (1929).

[22] Hansen (1981, p. 276).

crisis situation. Falling prices might not lead to increased demand but could instead create expectations of more price drops, further stifling demand. A cumulative process would ensue, with decreasing production and rising unemployment as consequences. He also noted that wage reductions would not be an effective means against unemployment in such a crisis, contrary to what classical economists usually claim.[23]

In the fall of 1931, Wigforss published *The Economic Crisis*, which provided an accurate analysis of the mechanisms of the depression and a theoretical justification for expansive fiscal policy as a means to stimulate employment and growth. The publication fueled the extensive debate about the relationship between Keynes, the Stockholm economists, and Wigforss, with recent claims even suggesting that it, in some respects, predated Keynes *General Theory*.[24] In the election year of 1932, it was followed up with an election pamphlet *Can We Afford to Work?* where Wigforss summarized the Social Democrats' election program, calling for a more expansionary economic policy.

Wigforss was thus unusually mentally prepared for the new theoretical winds beginning to blow in economics in the 1930s and contributed significantly to this shift.

Collaboration, Consensus, and Trust

Collaboration with other parties and establishing a trust-based consensus with the business sector were crucial as Swedish Social Democracy solidified its position as a ruling party in the 1930s. When the Social Democrats came to power in 1932, Per Albin Hansson assumed the role of Prime Minister, Ernst Wigforss became Finance Minister, and Gustav Möller took on the position of Social Minister. In the parliamentary election of 1932, the Social Democrats did not secure a majority and sought the support of another party, the Farmers' Union. This collaboration resulted in the so-called "cow trade" of 1933, aimed at addressing the significant pressure on

---

[23] Wadensjö (1987, p. 300).

[24] Landgren (1960) argued that Wigforss was the driving force for an expansionary fiscal policy, influenced by Keynes. Keynes' ideas about large public investments to counter unemployment are found in Keynes and Henderson (1929), which Wigforss had read. Steiger (1971) contested Landgren's analysis and highlighted the domestic roots of the Swedish theoretical development. Wigforss himself noted influences from British liberals and Keynes but emphasized the social democratic and socialist roots of the new policy, see Wigforss (1951, p. 287). Sten O. Karlsson (2001) argued that Wigforss was strongly influenced by the English idea debate, especially the guild socialists in the Fabian Society, who aimed for local worker control, contrasting with Gunnar Myrdal's top-down perspective. Wigforss adopted early ideas on combating unemployment from the Minority Report by Beatrice and Sidney Webb 1909. Karlsson also claimed that Myrdal became a bridge between Wigforss' experimental Fabianism and Per Albin's People's Home, contributing to the victory of the social democratic welfare policy, see Karlsson (2001, p. 389, 412, 648). Kragh (2014) argued that Wigforss (1931) developed the motives for expansionary fiscal policy independent of the Stockholm School economists and in some respects anticipated Keynes (1936).

agriculture from the disproportionate drop in prices of agricultural products compared to other goods during the depression.[25] The agreement between the Social Democrats and the Farmers' Union on regulating the trade in agricultural products—through tariffs, quotas, and income-policy motivated pricing—enabled the Social Democrats to gain parliamentary support for their expansive economic policy aimed at combating unemployment, as championed by Wigforss and Myrdal. At the party congress in March 1932, Wigforss advocated for a planned economy to achieve full employment, drawing inspiration from Keynes and the Stockholm School economists, without resorting to the nationalization of the business sector.[26]

The government assumed social responsibility for tackling unemployment, allowing trade unions to concentrate on improving conditions for workers. The Swedish Trade Union Confederation (LO) emerged as the leading organization for workers. The mutual interest of the working class in industrial development and growth, along with the role of rationalizations in increasing wage space, strengthened the trust between parties—a trust that had begun to develop in the 1910s through state-facilitated dialogue to address common interests.[27] The consensus between the Employers' Organization, Svenska Arbetsgivareföreningen SAF, and Landsorganisationen LO, culminated in the establishment of negotiation rules and methods to prevent the costly conflicts of the 1920s. The Saltsjöbaden Agreement, signed in 1938, became a foundational element of the Swedish model, which gained strength after World War II.

A second pivotal event in 1938 was the reform of corporate taxes to introduce free depreciation allowances for machinery and equipment, benefiting large, profitable, and capital-intensive firms, as highlighted by Peter Högfeldt.[28] These rules, generous by international standards, enhanced the acceptance of the Social Democratic economic policy among large firms.

A third significant move allowed major banks to transfer their substantial corporate assets, acquired during the depression of the early 1930s, to holding companies. Consequently, the leading banks became the principal owners of the largest listed firms, further integrating the financial sector with industrial development.

These modifications were pivotal in fostering collaboration between labor and capital within the Swedish model. The economic policy did not necessitate the nationalization of private enterprises, provided that capitalists continued to invest. The strategy for economic growth emphasized large-scale production and the expansion of firm sizes, arguing that resources are more efficiently allocated within a structured hierarchy than in market environments, especially for significant investments and research and development (R&D) activities. It was believed that larger firms would highlight the social nature of production and encourage the incorporation of societal interests into corporate decision-making processes. The envisioned

---

[25] Schön (2014, p. 303).
[26] Wigforss (1951, pp. 363–366).
[27] Rothstein (1998).
[28] Högfeldt (2005, pp. 538–547).

model was a corporatist society featuring capitalist enterprises but devoid of individual capitalists. Capital would be retained within companies, as investments were to be funded through tax-subsidized retained earnings. The objective was to establish a stakeholder economy enriched with elements of strategic planning, deemed more effective than the myopic and erratic market economy, which was often characterized by high unemployment rates and resource wastage.

Modernization of Monetary Policy and Recovery from the Depression

The Swedish economy emerged from the 1930s depression, characterized by falling prices and rising unemployment, far better than many other Western countries, especially those that adhered longer to the gold standard. This was largely due to Sweden abandoning the gold standard in September 1931, the depreciation of the krona and the Swedish central bank's goal to stabilize the Swedish krona's purchasing power. The Social Democratic government that took office in 1932 pursued an expansive fiscal policy, including increased loan financing of public works. However, the immediate impact of fiscal policy on the economic upswing during the Great Depression was not as significant as that of monetary policy. Fiscal policy acted as a slight positive impulse for economic recovery, but taxes also increased in order to finance government actions. Although fiscal policy was slightly counter-cyclical, monetary policy was mainly responsible for the recovery.[29] However, the recovery of the Swedish economy was aided by the political commitment to combat unemployment and stabilize household incomes. Additionally, demographics and improved confidence in the future contributed to increased household formation. Finally, new development blocks around electrification and automobile usage became central factors behind Sweden's relative success in the 1930s.[30]

In October 1931, a month after Sweden left the gold standard, leading Swedish economists gathered to discuss a proposal for monetary policy.[31] Gunnar Myrdal had drafted an analysis for discussion. However, it proved impossible to reach agreement between the younger generation of economists, led by Myrdal, and the older generation led by Heckscher. Myrdal and the younger economists advocated for monetary policy to focus on stabilizing consumer prices. Heckscher, on the other hand, wanted stabilization of producer prices to be the target of monetary policy. Additionally, Myrdal proposed a number of regulatory interventions in the economy that Heckscher considered deviations from liberal theory. The differences

---

[29] Lundberg (1953, p. 106) and Kavonius (2010).
[30] Schön (2014, s 307–313).
[31] Henriksson (1991, pp. 54–56).

were so significant that Heckscher chose to write his own book on monetary policy, to which Myrdal quickly responded by publishing his own book.[32]

Myrdal's book, *Sveriges väg genom penningkrisen* (Sweden's Path Through the Monetary Crisis) is today considered remarkably modern for focusing on domestic price stabilization of consumer prices as a means to achieve general stability. Myrdal dismissed a return to the gold standard, unlike older economists like Cassel and Heckscher, who supported the goal of price stabilization but advocated a return to the gold standard as soon as the international monetary system stabilized. Gunnar Myrdal did not want to introduce a fixed exchange rate for the Swedish krona. He considered it better to pursue a "free currency policy," arguing that it is the currency's internal stability that should be defended. This was also what the government had stated when announcing a month earlier that Sweden was leaving the gold standard: "Monetary policy should be aimed at using all available means to preserve the domestic purchasing power of the Swedish krona," a formulation likely from Cassel.[33]

Myrdal also linked the need to state value premises for his proposals. He argued that a monetary policy program can only be stated based on the interests and views of certain specific social groups. However, Myrdal believed that in the current crisis situation, the interests of many different social groups coincided, suggesting that consensus on the proposals could be achievable.[34] There was a common interest in raising prices on industrial goods, which became the *value premise* for the monetary policy program.[35] However, higher prices on industrial goods would raise the cost of living for the working class, and this price increase had to be limited, which became the *objective* of monetary policy.

Myrdal presented an astute analysis of what the central bank could and should do. He advocated a monetary policy program that openly declares the level of price stability promised. He could envision a tolerance range around this level. The central message was that a monetary policy declaration can lead to the fulfillment of the indicated price development as long as the public trusted the central bank's ability to implement its intentions.[36] Myrdal was thus early in incorporating the importance of psychology into practical monetary policy. He argued that the price level tended to move in the direction people believed it will, anticipations were the cause of their own fulfillment.[37] Myrdal was also aware that expectation formation in a critical situation could have a destabilizing function, such as in an international crisis that lead to a significant change in the exchange rate. Such a crisis could cause the public

---

[32] Heckscher (1931) and Myrdal (1931a).

[33] Finance Minister Felix Hamrin's statement from September 27, 1931, was apparently formulated by Gustav Cassel, who was assigned the task by Hamrin the day before, see Berg and Jonung (1999, p. 528).

[34] Myrdal (1931a, p. 5).

[35] Postscript to Myrdal's *Value in Social Theory* (1958) cited in Appelqvist and Andersson (1998, p. 58).

[36] Myrdal (1931a, p. 78).

[37] Myrdal (1931a, p. 60).

to mistrust the central bank's ability to meet the crisis. The psychology could then turn against the central bank's monetary policy and inflation or deflation that started in this way, could prove quite difficult to control with the central bank's normal methods.[38]

Myrdal analyzed which price indices to consider when monetary policy is aimed at achieving price stability. He rejected the use of producer prices in industry and concluded that monetary policy should focus on stabilizing a *cost-of-living* index.[39] According to Myrdal, the central bank's monetary policy declaration should entail the following: the central bank should use all its power to prevent an increase in a cost-of-living index, at most five%, likely less, and, without shying away from a certain price increase in the industry's finished products, keep the industry profitable and production going. He also emphasized that higher employment should be achieved through improved returns in the industry, not through reduced wages, as many economists advocated. He called for a coordination of several forms of government policy: fiscal policy, industrial policy, and policy to make the workforce more mobile. Erik Lundberg later noted that Myrdal was early with ideas that became relevant 25–30 years later.[40] Regarding the proposal that monetary policy should be based on a credible inflation target with a tolerance band, Myrdal was, in my opinion, 50–60 years ahead of his time. Erik Lindahl's norm, the inverse productivity rule, is more akin to present day suggestions of nominal income targeting, as pointed out by Fregert (1993).

In the work on the book about monetary policy, Gunnar Myrdal enlisted the help of Karin Kock, the only woman among the Stockholm economists. Karin Kock, who earned her doctorate in 1929 with a dissertation on the empirical analysis of interest rate formation, was a skilled statistician, economist, and administrator who became a friend and colleague of Gunnar Myrdal early on. Kock handled much of the logistics for the Stockholm School economists, organizing meetings and conferences, reviewing manuscripts and statistics.[41] However, she did not receive the same support from older professors Bagge, Cassel, and Heckscher as her male classmates Myrdal, Ohlin, and Lindahl. The young men quickly became informal and close with the older men (Brother Myrdal) and secured their livelihood in academic life, while she remained Miss Kock and supported herself with bank work after her doctorate.[42]

Karin Kock was a hardworking professional woman and became the first Swedish woman to make an academic career in economics, became an associate professor in economics, received a professorial title, and became Sweden's first female minister.

---

[38] Myrdal (1931a, p. 60).

[39] Increased import prices on input goods and raw materials can worsen the return in domestic industry. Monetary policy should then not add further burden by pushing down the average prices of finished goods. He preferred to stabilize living costs. One reason was to achieve a calm labor market. He, therefore, wanted a measure to assess the working class's standard of living.

[40] Lundberg (1984, p. 23).

[41] Jonung and Jonung (2013).

[42] Niskanen (2007, p. 48).

It was Karin Kock who wrote the appendix, *Hur Sverige tvingades överge guldmyntfoten* (How Sweden Was Forced to Abandon the Gold Standard) to Myrdal's book on monetary policy. She also put extensive work into Myrdal's own text and became a very important collaborator for him. He supported her academic career.

Karin Kock participated in several important investigations under his leadership, substituted for his professorship, and participated as the Swedish representative in the United Nation's (UN's) Economic Commission for Europe during Myrdal's time as executive secretary, as narrated in later chapters. One interpretation of the alliance between Myrdal and Kock in the 1930s is that it was based on an unspoken agreement that Kock got work corresponding to her education and competence, while Myrdal got a competent substitute who did not undermine his position at Stockholm University.[43]

The Swedish central bank, the Riksbank, became a pioneer in the world of central banking in the 1930s by introducing a monetary policy program to stabilize falling prices (deflation), establish a consumer price index, and announce how the goal of stable monetary value would be achieved. The Riksbank's management, led by Ivar Rooth, requested assistance from both older and younger economists in the autumn of 1931. Three economists from the older generation (Cassel, Davidson, and Heckscher) were asked to answer a survey on suitable goals and means for monetary policy. Erik Lindahl, the prominent Stockholm economist who produced significant work on monetary policy, took an active part in setting up the Riksbank's consumer price index, which began to be compiled weekly.[44] A younger Stockholm economist, 26-year-old Dag Hammarskjöld, was employed to participate in the practical work. However, the consumer price index was not the only target variable for monetary policy; the development of other price indices was also analyzed. The Riksbank was evaluated by the parliament, which was the bank's principal, and set its goals. The program was adopted by parliament in May 1932.[45]

The goal was in line with Wicksell's norm of stable prices and played an important role in breaking the downward price spiral and anchoring future expectations. The evaluation of the monetary policy program took place annually in the Parliament's Banking Committee. On two occasions, there was also a public evaluation of monetary policy by the Finance Minister Wigforss.

At the first evaluation in May 1933, Wigforss was critical. The goal of price stabilization had not yet been achieved, despite the interest rate cuts the Riksbank had made after abandoning the gold standard.

The price decline, which had been ongoing since September 1931, slowed down significantly in Sweden after the announcement of the price stability target. Although the decline was much milder thereafter, Ernst Wigforss called for a more active monetary policy and coordination with fiscal policy. He was inspired by Keynes,

---

[43] Niskanen (2007, p. 67).

[44] Erik Lindahl was for many years one of the most consulted academic economists by the Ministry of Finance and the Riksbank, see Landberg (2012 p. 160).

[45] Berg and Jonung (1999).

Myrdal, and Ohlin.[46] As a result, Sweden's monetary policy became even more expansionary in 1933, with continued interest rate cuts. Additionally, from May the Riksbank ensured that the krona was undervalued against the pound, facilitating recovery in the export industry.[47] The Riksbank's purchase of pounds provided liquidity to the money market and commercial banks, leading to a gradual reduction in bond interest rates. The expansionary monetary policy created monetary space for a significant increase in production and employment in Sweden, while consumer prices recovered in a stable manner.

Gunnar Myrdal was the faculty opponent when Dag Hammarskjöld defended his doctoral thesis in economics in November 1933.[48] Myrdal focused only on the theoretical sections, leaving the empirical part to the second opponent, Karin Kock. Hammarskjöld's thesis, although difficult to read and not one of the Stockholm School's most significant contributions to doctrinal history, resulted in one of the longest defenses ever. At the doctoral dinner, Myrdal was seated next to Dag's brother Bo Hammarskjöld, who, after a few drinks, expressed his opinion about Myrdal's opposition. Bo objected to Myrdal's use of the word "sloppy" to describe the thesis, which was not tolerated in the Hammarskjöld family, a traditional civil servant lineage. Myrdal, reportedly alarmed, responded, "You must remember that I spoke on behalf of the office."[49]

The grading of the thesis was also prolonged. However, Hammarskjöld eventually became a docent, although it was not as a scientist that he was called, as Myrdal had already pointed out during the defense.[50] Hammarskjöld continued his work with the Unemployment Commission and at the Ministry of Finance and the Riksbank, where there was a tug-of-war over the talented civil servant. This competition was temporarily resolved when Dag Hammarskjöld was appointed as state secretary to Ernst Wigforss at the Ministry of Finance in 1936. However, a significant future role awaited him at the Riksbank and more clashes with Gunnar Myrdal, as discussed in later chapters.

In May 1937, during the second evaluation of the Riksbank's monetary policy program, Ernst Wigforss was more satisfied than at the first evaluation in 1933. The depression in Sweden had given way to economic upswing. The price decline was replaced by a price increase, with prices now close to pre-depression levels. Price stability continued to be the goal for monetary policy, but it was supplemented with goals for a stable economy and full employment. The Riksbank's monetary policy

---

[46] Landgren (1960, p. 13).

[47] The krona weakened against the pound from 18.40 in January 1933 to 19.50 in May 1933. The Riksbank then bought all pound currencies on the market to prevent the krona from strengthening. In July 1933, the Riksbank introduced a fixed exchange rate between the krona and the pound at 19.40, which remained until the outbreak of war, see Lundberg (1953, p. 250). Some researchers also argue that it is hard to reconcile the Riksbank's striving for a fixed exchange rate with the claim that it adopted price level targeting, see Straumann and Woitek (2009).

[48] Hammarskjöld (1933).

[49] Andersson (1998).

[50] Appelqvist (2008).

was to be coordinated with fiscal policy. This can be interpreted as the price stabilization program being replaced by a broader economic program, where price stability was subordinated to other goals, especially full employment, which became evident in the post-war period.[51]

Sweden emerged from the 1930s depression faster than the USA, which held onto the gold standard longer and suffered severely from bank collapses. When Franklin D. Roosevelt assumed the presidency in the USA in 1933, he broke with traditional economic dogmas. The USA left the gold standard, and a large number of federal programs, The New Deal was launched to repair the banking system and pull the economy out of its deep slump. The central explanation for the American economy's upturn after Roosevelt's inauguration was changed future expectations. When the USA left the gold standard, a commitment was also made to keep current and future interest rates low, which, according to modern research—along with a better functioning banking system and expansive fiscal policy—played a significant role in the economy's upturn.[52] The federal expenditures and budget deficits in The New Deal were relatively small compared to the size of the American economy, but they represented an important break from the dogma of a balanced budget and created credible expectations of higher future production and incomes. It is psychology that can explain why policy measures, not sufficient in themselves, created a more optimistic outlook for the future that became self-fulfilling. This development was in line with Myrdal's vision of "anticipations causing their own fulfillment."

Conclusions

We have seen that Myrdal significantly contributed to the young generation of Swedish economists, the Stockholm economists, in renewing economic theory and practice in the 1930s. They developed a dynamic theory where the future expectations of households and businesses played a central role. Myrdal introduced the crucial distinction between looking forward, *ex ante*, and looking backward, *ex post*. This laid the foundation for analyzing the gap between expectations and outcomes, which is central in the social sciences today. Ernst Wigforss developed the theoretical reasons for expansive fiscal policy in a depression and, as finance minister, ensured that they became practical policy. Gunnar Myrdal was Wigforss' most important economic ally in the early 1930s.

It is also clear that the theories of Myrdal, the Stockholm economists, and Wigforss have significant similarities with Keynes' theory. A freely functioning market economy does not lead to economic balance and full employment on its own. Keynes' model shows how the economy can get stuck in an equilibrium with

---

[51] Berg and Jonung (1999, p. 545).
[52] Eggertsson (2008, p. 1476–1516).

low employment. Myrdal demonstrated a full understanding of the dynamics of the multiplier process and its convergence.

Myrdal's formulation of a monetary policy program was also very modern. He highlighted that the central bank—if crediblecan actively influence future expectations and advocated that monetary policy should focus on stabilizing household living costs. Price stability was important but needed to be complemented with measures in other areas, such as fiscal policy and industrial policy. Stabilization of the price level also became a fixed norm in Sweden from the fall of 1931 until 1939 and was accepted by both economists and politicians. Deflation and unemployment were countered with an expansionary policy, but it should not lead to high inflation.

The second confidence factor concerned fiscal policy. Alongside Wigforss, Myrdal was the foremost advocate in Sweden for using active fiscal policy to stimulate the economy during the depression, but confidence was a factor he took seriously.[53] Large and growing government budget deficits could lead to negative market reactions, potentially slowing the recovery. Myrdal believed in the soundness of state finances, which implied a requirement to balance the state's budget over the economic cycle.[54]

The development of macroeconomic theory in the decades after the 1930s was dominated by Keynes—not the Stockholm economists—thinking. This was largely because Keynes' equilibrium theory was more pedagogical and easier to grasp. The Stockholm economists often used process analysis, arguing that reality is complicated. However, if the economy was subject to many different disturbances that needed consideration, the result quickly became difficult to oversee. Myrdal's introduction of expectations into the mainstream of economics was a pioneering contribution of lasting value. Changed and credible expectations indeed played a decisive role when monetary policy programs, Keynesian stimulus policies, and the repair of the American banking system helped counter the depression and economies began to recover, first in Sweden and later in the USA.

References

Andersson S (1998) Skiss till en fallstudie Gunnar Myrdals beslut att skriva Asian Drama (Sketch for a case study Gunnar Myrdal's decision to write Asian Drama). Manuscript. The Labor Movement's Archive and Library, Stockholm

Appelqvist Ö, Andersson S (1998) Vägvisare – Texter av Gunnar Myrdal. Norstedts, Stockholm. English edition: Appelqvist Ö, Andersson S (1998) The essential Gunnar Myrdal. The New Press, New York

Appelqvist, Örjan (2008), A Hidden Duel. Gunnar Myrdal and Dag Hammarskjöld in Economics and International Politics 1935–1955. Stockholm Papers in Economic History 2

Berg C, Jonung L (1999) Pioneering price level targeting – the Swedish experience. J Monet Econ 43(3):525–551

---

[53] Lundberg (1987, p. 283).

[54] Lundberg (1953, p. 269).

Bernanke BS (2000) Essays on the great depression. Princeton University Press, Princeton

Dieudonné M (2019) Thorstein Veblen's contributions to Q and insider/outsider analysis. The European Journal of the History of Economic Thought 26(2):294–326

Eggertsson G (2008) Great expectations and the end of the great depression. Am Econ Rev 98(4):1476–1516

Eichengreen B (1992) Golden fetters. The gold standard and the great depression, 1919–1939. Oxford University Press, New York

Etzemüller T (2014) Alva and Gunnar Myrdal social engineering in the modern world. Lexington Books, Lanham

Fregert K (1993) Erik Lindahl's norm for monetary policy. In: Jonung L (ed) Swedish economic thought. Routledge, London

Hammarskjöld D (1933) Konjunkturspridningen En teoretisk och historisk undersökning (The spread of economic fluctuations a theoretical and historical study) Bilaga 4 till Arbetslöshetsutredningens betänkanden SOU 1933:29

Hansen B (1981) Unemployment, Keynes, and the Stockholm school. Hist Political Econ 13(2):256–277

Hansson B (1982) The Stockholm school and the development of dynamic method. Croom Helm, London

Hansson B (1991) After the Stockholm school. In: Jonung L (ed) The Stockholm School of Economics revisited. Cambridge University Press, Cambridge

Heckscher, Eli (1931), Sveriges penningpolitik. Orientering och förslag (Swedish Monetary Policy, An Orientation and Proposals). Norstedts, Stockholm

Henriksson R (1991) The political economy club and the Stockholm school, 1917–1951. In: Jonung L (ed) The Stockholm School of Economics revisited. Cambridge University Press, Cambridge

Hirdman Y (2006) Det tänkande hjärtat. Boken om Alva Myrdal. Ordfront, Stockholm. English edition: Hirdman, Y (2008), Alva Myrdal: the passionate mind. Indiana University Press, Bloomington

Högfeldt P (2005) The history and politics of corporate ownership in Sweden. In: Morck R (ed) A history of corporate governance around the world. Family Business Groups to Professional Managers University of Chicago Press, Chicago

Jonung C, Jonung L (2013) Ekonomporträtt Karin Kock 1891–1976 (Economist Portrait Karin Kock 1891–1976). Ekonomisk Debatt 7(13):66–78

Jonung L (ed) (1991) The Stockholm School of Economics revisited. Cambridge University Press, Cambridge

Karlsson S (2001) Det intelligenta samhället (The intelligent society). Carlsson, Stockholm

Kavonius I (2010) Fiscal policies in Europe and the United States during the great depression. Government Institute for Economic Research, Working Papers 13, Helsinki

Keynes JM (1930) A treatise on money: the applied theory of money: volume 1: the pure theory of money. Macmillan & Co, London

Keynes JM (1936) The general theory of employment, interest and money. Macmillan & Co, London

Keynes JM, Henderson H (1929) Can Lloyd George do it? an examination of the Liberal pledge. Collected Writings IX:86–125

Kragh M (2014) The 'Wigforss connection' the Stockholm school vs Keynes debate revisited. Eur J Hist Econ Thought 21(4):635–663

Landberg H (2012) På väg ... Dag Hammarskjöld som svensk ämbetsman (On the way Dag Hammarskjöld as a Swedish Civil Servant). Atlantis, Stockholm

Landgren KG (1960) Den nya ekonomien i Sverige J M Keynes, E Wigforss och B Ohlin och utvecklingen 1927–39 (The new economics in Sweden JM Keynes, E Wigforss, and B Ohlin and the development 1927–39). Almqvist & Wiksell, Stockholm

Larsson SE (1998) Bertil Ohlin Ekonom och politiker (Bertil Ohlin economist and politician). Atlantis, Stockholm

References

Lindahl E (1929) Penningpolitikens mål (The ends of monetary policy). Förlagsaktiebolaget, Malmö

Lindahl E (1930) Penningpolitikens medel (Means of Monetary Policy), Förlagsaktiebolaget, Malmö

Lundberg E (1953) Konjunkturer och ekonomisk politik (Business cycles and economic policy). Konjunkturinstitutet, Stockholm

Lundberg E (1984) Kriserna & ekonomerna (Crises & economists). Liber, Stockholm

Lundberg E (1987) Minnen kring Stockholmsskolan (Memories around the Stockholm School). Ekonomisk Debatt 4:280–286

Lundberg E (1996) The development of Swedish and Keynesian macroeconomic theory and its impact on economic policy. Cambridge University Press, Cambridge

Myrdal G (1927) Prisbildningsproblemet och föränderligheten (The problem of price formation under economic change). Almqvist & Wicksell, Uppsala

Myrdal G (1931a) Sveriges väg genom penningkrisen (Sweden's path through the monetary crisis). Natur och Kultur, Stockholm

Myrdal G (1931b) Om penningteoretisk jämvikt: en studie över den 'normala räntan' i Wicksells penninglära. Ekonomisk tidskrift 33:5–6. (German translation in Myrdal (1933), English translation in Myrdal (1939))

Myrdal G (1933) Der Gleichgewichtsbegriff als Instrument der Geldtheoretischen Analyse. In: Hayek FA (ed) Beiträge zur Geldtheorie. Springer Verlag, Vienna, pp 361–488

Myrdal G (1934) Finanspolitikens ekonomiska verkningar (Economic effects of fiscal policy), SOU 1934:1. Norstedts, Stockholm

Myrdal G (1939) Monetary equilibrium. W Hodge, London

Niskanen K (2007) Karriär i männens värld Nationalekonomen och feministen Karin Kock (Career in a man's world: the economist and feminist Karin Kock). SNS Publishing, Stockholm

Ohlin B (1934) Penningpolitik, offentliga arbeten, subventioner och tullar som medel mot arbetslöshet (Monetary policy, public works, subsidies, and tariffs as remedies against unemployment). Bilaga 7 till Arbetslöshetsutredningens betänkande, SOU 1934:12

Ohlin B (1937) Some notes on the Stockholm school theory of saving and investment I–II. Econ J 47:53–69. (I), 221–240 (II)

Patinkin D (1982) Anticipations of the general theory. The University of Chicago Press, Chicago

Report II of the Unemployment Investigation (1935) Åtgärder mot arbetslöshet (Measures against unemployment), SOU 1935:6

Rothstein B (1998) Den svenska modellens uppgång och fall. En essä (The rise and fall of the Swedish model: an essay). Statsvetenskaplig Tidskrift 1:41–49

Shackle G (1967) The years of high theory: invention & tradition in economic thought 1926–1939. Cambridge University Press, Cambridge

Schmidt K (1995) Tobins q? – Myrdals Q! Credit & Capital Markets – Kredit und Kapital 28(2):175–200

Schön L (2014) En modern svensk ekonomisk historia (A modern Swedish economic history). Studentlitteratur, Lund

Siven CH (1991) Expectation and plan the microeconomics of the Stockholm school. In: Jonung L (ed) The Stockholm School of Economics revisited. Cambridge University Press, Cambridge

Siven CH (1997) Capital theory and equilibrium method in Wicksell's cumulative process. History of Political Economy 29(2):201–217

Siven CH (2003) Heertje, Heemeijer, and Samuelson on the origin of Samuelson's multiplier-accelerator model. History of Political Economy 35(2):323–327

Siven CH (2006) Monetary equilibrium. History of Political Economy 38(4):665–709

Straumann T (2019) 1931: debt, crisis, and the rise of Hitler. Oxford University Press, Oxford

Straumann T, Woitek U (2009) A pioneer of a new monetary policy? Sweden's price-level targeting of the 1930s revisited. Eur Rev Econ Hist 03:251–282

Straumann T, Kugler P, Weber F (2016) How the German crisis of 1931 swept across Europe: a comparative view from Stockholm. Econ Hist Rev 70(1):224–247

Steiger, Otto (1971), Studien zur Entstehung der Neuen Wirtschaftslehre in Schweden, Duncker & Humblot, Berlin

Tobin, James (1969), A General Equilibrium Approach to Monetary Theory, Journal of Money, Credit and Banking, 1, February, pp 15–29

Wadensjö, Eskil (1987), Före Stockholmsskolan. Arbetslöshetsutredningen, Ernst Wigforss och Gösta Bagge (Before the Stockholm School. The Unemployment Investigation, Ernst Wigforss and Gösta Bagge), Ekonomisk Debatt, 4/87, pp 298–304

Wicksell K (1898) Geldzins und Güter Preise: Eine Studie über den Tauschwert des Geldes bestimmenden Ursachen. Verlag von Gustav Fisher, Jena. English edition: Wicksell K (1936) Interest and prices: a study of the causes regulting the value of money. Macmillan and Co, London

Wicksell K (1906) Föreläsningar i nationalekonomi II: Om penningar och kredit. Fritzes, Stockholm. English edition: Wicksell K (1935) Lectures on political economy volume II: money. George Routledge and Sons, London

Wigforss E (1931) Den ekonomiska krisen (The economic crisis). Tiden, Stockholm

Wigforss, E (1950, 1951, 1954) Minnen I, II och III (Memoirs I, II, and III). Tiden, Stockholm

Chapter 5
The Emergence of the Welfare State Through Social Engineering

Gunnar and Alva Myrdal played a crucial role in shaping the Swedish welfare state in the 1930s. Their book *Crises in the Population Question* addressed the societal issue of declining birth rates and proposed concrete social reforms. Gunnar Myrdal led government investigations to support and implement these reforms and was elected to parliament. The Myrdals' ideas influenced various welfare reforms, emphasizing general benefits over poor relief. Their proposals included improved housing, maternal care, child health services, general child allowances, and nursery schools to support families. However, their proposals faced modifications and rejections, notably by Social Minister Gustav Möller, who preferred cash benefits over the Myrdals' in-kind support. The Myrdals' work highlighted tensions between state intervention and individual autonomy and laid the groundwork for the Swedish welfare state's expansion and its recognition as a model of balancing capitalism and socialism.

Introduction

In the early 1930s, Sweden increasingly embodied the modern breakthrough in society and culture. The radical cultural magazine *Spektrum* was founded in 1931, with editors like poets Karin Boye and Gunnar Ekelöf, aiming to provide space for modernist literature, philosophy, psychoanalysis, architecture, and social policy. It was in *Spektrum* that T.S. Eliot's poem *The Waste Land* was published in translation by Karin Boye and Erik Mesterton. Contributors included author Artur Lundkvist, who played a significant role in the breakthrough of modernism in Sweden and was part of the Myrdals' circle. Gunnar Myrdal joined the *Spektrum* writers, publishing popular science articles on social policy, a hot topic in the 1920s.

Several social reforms were implemented under the liberal politician C.G. Ekman as prime minister. His minority government, in the 1920s, carried out a school reform with support from the Social Democrats, introducing a common basic education for all. Along with the center-right parties, Ekman's government also introduced a law on collective agreements and a joint employer–employee labor court, which eventually became an important part of the Swedish welfare model. In Ekman's tenure as prime minister, decisions on health insurance and maternity insurance were also made in 1931, with support from the Social Democrats. Health insurance was still voluntary, but state support and regulation of health funds increased.

In the 1930s, Gunnar Myrdal vigorously and creatively participated in further developing the Swedish welfare state. Along with Alva Myrdal, he became one of the most influential idea generators for new social policy. However, the most significant role in the welfare state's development phase was played by Gustav Möller, the Social Democratic social minister from 1924–1926 and for most of the period 1932–1951.[1] Along with Wigforss, Möller, and others, the Myrdals helped modernize the vision of the welfare state into the noble goal and collective project that a good state should formulate. According to this view, the state's task is not to make one class happy but to look after the common good of the entire society, as stated by Sten O. Karlsson in his thesis *Det intelligenta samhället* (The Intelligent Society).[2]

Alva Myrdal

In Geneva in 1930–1931, Alva Myrdal expanded her knowledge by studying under Jean Piaget, a psychologist, educator, and pioneering theorist of knowledge. Back in Sweden, she studied theoretical philosophy and pedagogy in Uppsala and gained practical experience as an assistant at the forensic psychiatric clinic on Långholmen in Stockholm. She also organized the country's first study circle in parental education under the auspices of Workers' Educational Association (ABF). Alva Myrdal increasingly became a public spokesperson for the rational upbringing of both children and parents. While Gunnar was portrayed as a new type of professor—charming, eloquent, and open—Alva was seen as a committed, straightforward, and elegantly dressed speaker. Both were associated with the image of their modern, functional living room, furnished with beautiful pieces from Svenskt Tenn.[3]

In fact, Alva Myrdal was a pioneer in developing a view of women's role in society.[4] In 1934, she wrote an article for the magazine *Idun*: "Uppfostran till äka quinnlighet" ("Education to True Femininity"). In the article, she questioned the prevailing gender power order and the traditional female role, arguing that there is no scientific evidence for natural differences between women and men. Environmental factors

---

[1] Möller was Minister of Social Affairs in 1924–1926, 1932–1936, 1936–1938, and 1939–1951.
[2] Karlsson (2001, p. 652).
[3] Etzemüller (2014, p. 57).
[4] Jackson (2021, p. 219).

are crucial in how individuals develop their personalities. Girls are told early on that they are less valuable than boys, and their play is focused by their environment on household chores. Women are socialized into subordination. Marriage is not a financial guarantee for women and cannot be their ultimate goal. A year after Hitler's rise to power in Germany, she distanced herself from the Nazis' view of women, which meant that a woman's role is to take care of children, the kitchen, and the church. More than a decade before Simone de Beauvoir, she anticipated the idea that one is not born a woman but becomes one.[5]

By writing the books *Riktiga leksaker* (The Right Toys) and *Stadsbarn: en bok om deras fostran i storbarnkammare* (City Children: A Book on Their Upbringing in Large Nurseries) Alva Myrdal also became an established child expert.

The Welfare State and Social Policy

Alva Myrdal's insights were a significant driving force in the book she wrote with her husband Gunnar, *Kris i Befolkningsfrågan* (Crisis in the Population Question), which became a major breakthrough for the Myrdal couple. Gunnar's part began with two articles in *Spektrum* titled Socialpolitikens dilemma (The Dilemma of Social Policy).[6] In Myrdal (1932, p. 24) he noted:

> We provide the poor with poor relief, the unemployed with unemployment benefits, put the sick in hospitals, intern alcoholics in homes for alcoholics, the insane in asylums, etc., but do very little to prevent these conditions from arising. Maladies in society should be addressed with preventive measures; the evil should be eradicated at its roots; social policy should be prophylactic and ensure that wounds do not occur.

Years earlier on January 18, 1928, Per Albin Hansson delivered his famous speech on *Folkhemmet* (the People's Home) in the Second Chamber of the Riksdag:

> The foundation of the home is community and empathy. The good home knows no privileged or disadvantaged, no favorites or stepchildren. There, no one looks down on another; no one tries to gain advantage at another's expense, the strong do not oppress and plunder the weak. In the good home, there is equality, consideration, cooperation, helpfulness. Applied to the great people's and citizen's home, this would mean the dismantling of all social and economic barriers that now separate citizens into privileged and disadvantaged, ruling and dependent, rich and poor, propertied and impoverished, plunderers and plundered.

The idea of the People's Home became one of the Social Democrats' central ideas. There has been speculation that Rudolf Kjellén, who the young Gunnar Myrdal was influenced by, is the originator of the concept of the People's Home, but this is not accurate.[7] However, the idea of the People's Home state has a prehistory dating back to the nineteenth century and originates from a conservative ideological tradition.

---

[5] Jackson (2021, p. 220).
[6] Appelqvist and Andersson (1998, p. 146).
[7] Edström (2014, pp. 33–38).

Per Albin Hansson often spoke more about citizens than classes. Even Hjalmar Branting was early in turning to broader groups than the working class for support to reform society. According to Branting, in a country as backward as Sweden, the middle class still played a very important role.[8] The working class needed the help it could get from this quarter, just as the middle class, in turn, needed to have the workers behind them to stand up against common enemies.

The Housing Issue and Modernity

For Gunnar and Alva Myrdal, along with their economist and functionalist architect friends like Sven Markelius and Uno Åhrén, the house, home, and housing embodied the realization of a better and more modern life for citizens. At this time, housing standards in Sweden were worse than other industrialized countries like England and Germany. Particularly, workers' housing was subpar, with one-room apartments being the most common. Their friend Alf Johansson, one of the Stockholm School economists, pointed out that there is nothing fantastical in the thought that a people and a culture could perish due to the inability to solve its housing issue.[9] The housing issue encapsulates several of the most vital conditions for all societal life, according to Johansson.

Gunnar and Alva Myrdal realized the explosive potential of the housing issue and that it could be used to radically reshape society. Gunnar Myrdal and architect Uno Åhrén both wished to analyze the housing issue in a broader context. Åhrén was a leading proponent of functionalism in Sweden, known for the modernist architecture's first manifesto in Sweden, *Brytningar* (Breaks) published in 1925.[10] According to Åhrén, the new architecture meant the entrance of health and wellness into everyday life. The functional was to have aesthetic value, with form expressing the functions of things. The useful is the beautiful, according to a slogan at the Stockholm Exhibition in 1930. Housing became a hygienic modernization project in a comprehensive transformation of society. A new functional architecture could contribute to creating a new and rational lifestyle, even a new, modern human.

One searching for the new human at this time was the author Ivar-Lo Johansson, famous for his realistic and detiled depictions of landless Swedish peasants. In an autobiographical novel, Lo-Johansson (1957, ch. 1) wandered along the main street to the great Stockholm Exhibition of 1930. It was summer and scorching hot. The sun of the new decade shone on his head. A completely new city of steel, glass, and concrete had been erected on the plain where there had been a void. The functionalist era had blown in. The style of the new times was precisely the scraping away of

---

[8] Branting (1886).
[9] Hirdman (1989, p. 100).
[10] Åhrén (1925).

styles. Its naked language was called fact. Lo-Johansson went around looking for the new human.

Gunnar Myrdal and Uno Åhrén lobbied intensely for an investigation into the state of housing in Sweden. Wigforss, the new finance minister, supported an initial investigation, while Möller, the new social minister, later greenlit a major housing social investigation with Gunnar Myrdal and a radical circle of architects and doctors as participants.[11]

Alva Myrdal, together with architect Sven Markelius, engaged in creating a functionalist and utopian collective house. It was assumed that both man and wife would be working; the collective house took over responsibility for children, laundry, meals, and cleaning. In the house, cleanliness, fresh air, nourishing food, and regular medical checks reigned. Children were supervised by trained pedagogues. The dominant perspective was the desire to free women from degrading household work and change the conditions of small-scale life.[12]

Sven Markelius and Alva Myrdal led a group proposing that Sweden's first collective house be built in the form of three parallel ten-story buildings in Alvik, a suburb in western Stockholm.[13] However, the project was not realized as the City Council deemed it too daring. Instead, a collective house with 57 apartments was built on Kungsholmen in Stockholm City, completed in 1935. Alva Myrdal noted in an interview that it was not the working class who could afford to move into the collective house. However, many people from the cultural elite of the time did move in, including the architect Sven Markelius, feminist pioneer Elise Ottesen-Jensen, and radical child psychiatrist Skå-Gustav Jonsson.

Clearly, the explosive potential of the housing issue was not enough to reshape society and affect people as radically as Gunnar and Alva Myrdal had hoped.

Population Issue

They therefore returned to the population issue and the article drafts that were rejected in 1931 by *Tiden*, deciding to write a book on the subject. The population issue had long been driven by conservative politicians but also engaged a radical economist, Knut Wicksell. With the book *Kris i befolkningsfrågan* (Crisis in the Population Question) published in 1934, the Myrdals succeeded in turning the issue away from the dominating themes of the Swedish debate.

Traditionally, the population issue was about the risk of overpopulation. When Thomas Robert Malthus published his famous book *Essay on the Principle of Population* in 1798, the main thesis was that the majority of the world's population

---

[11] Hirdman (2006, p. 188, 403).

[12] Hirdman (1989, p. 111, 116–117).

[13] Nilsson (1994, pp. 246–251).

cannot get better off.[14] As soon as incomes in a society begin to rise, so does its population. Although agricultural production could increase, the "passion between the sexes" causes the population to grow even faster. When the population becomes too large in relation to the production of food, it decreases due to malnutrition and diseases.

In normal times, both population and income per capita tend to be stable. In the preindustrial society, infant mortality was high and life expectancy low. Every woman had to give birth to many children for some of them to survive.

Malthus visited Sweden in 1799, a difficult year for farmers with famine following drought and livestock deaths. The population had nevertheless increased significantly to over 3 million from 2.2 million in the mid-eighteenth century. Malthus observed that the lower classes endured the severe strains surprisingly well. This was due to their reliance on their own strengths and being convinced that they were subject to the laws of necessity and not the whims of their rulers.[15]

In the mid-nineteenth century, industrialization led to improved health conditions and a decrease in infant mortality. However, childbearing did not decrease, as families did not know how many children would survive. Thus, the net reproduction rate (the number of daughters per woman) increased during this period, contributing to rapid population growth.

The risk of overpopulation engaged many, and in Sweden, Knut Wicksell became the leading neo-Malthusian. He traced all of Sweden's social problems to overpopulation. One of his famous pamphlets, published in 1880, was titled "Några ord om den viktigaste orsaken till social misär och dess bot med speciell hänvisning till dryckenskap" (A Few Words on the Most Important Cause of Social Misery and Its Cure, with Special Reference to Drunkenness).[16] In it, Wicksell described a vicious circle of overpopulation, poverty, and alcoholism as Sweden's most important social issue.

Wicksell (1880) provided a harrowing account of the dire conditions within the working class at the time and reported from a visit to a cobbler:

> As I opened the door to his residence, a thick white smoke immediately poured out, and the air that hit me was so suffocatingly unhealthy that I gasped for breath for a good while. Once I finally mustered the courage to step in, I had before me a room not much larger than my own small student room, but which was literally packed full of people. In the middle of the floor sat the master himself with an apprentice, working, surrounded by as many of his numerous children as were not in school. At the stove, finally, his wife and a couple of other women were busy processing a larger sugar dough, from which Danish caramels were to be made for sale; and I assure my audience that the strong smell of burnt sugar combined with an equally strong smell of wet leather, especially when added to the necessary evaporation from so many people, formed a whole for which at least my nose was not sufficiently hardened… the memory I carry with me, I will not easily forget. And yet what I had seen was by no means an extraordinary or rare hardship, only average, ordinary poverty.

---

[14] Berg (2012, p. 456, 459).
[15] Malthus (1798, second ed. 1803).
[16] Lundberg (1984, p. 55) and Kock (1944).

The demographic and social background to Wicksell's lecture was an increasing number of surviving children per family, migration of young people from the countryside to the cities and abroad (emigration), a large increase in the number of children born out of wedlock, low living standards, and poor housing conditions.[17]

Malthusianism was often the topic Knut Wicksell recommended to those wishing to write academically in economics. Those who did not accept Malthus were not fully accepted by Wicksell. Wicksell wrote a threatening message to a younger, untenured colleague, whom he hoped would revise his views on population; otherwise, he would take him under special treatment. An economist who was not thoroughly permeated with Malthus was like a sailor without a rudder, compass, and ballast, according to Wicksell.[18]

Wicksell did not advocate for sexual abstinence or delayed marriages. From 1880 onwards, he instead proposed marital cohabitation at a young age, education and access to contraceptives, and the right to abortion, a highly radical program for its time.[19]

Eventually, birth rates began to decline in the 1880s and thereafter. Initially, birth rates decreased in older age groups, i.e., families that already had children. In the next step, birth rates also decreased for younger women, who chose to have their first child later in life and also increased the time interval to the next child.[20] But only at the beginning of the twentieth century was the net reproduction rate in Sweden down to the same levels as at the end of the eighteenth century. Urbanization meant that the proportion of the population employed in agriculture decreased from three-quarters in the 1870s to one-third in the mid-1930s. This meant that the need for children, who in agriculture were seen as a resource, decreased due to rapid urbanization. Instead, the costs of having children increased in industrial society. Longer education required more resources per child. More children also limited women's opportunities for wage work. Neo-Malthusianism gained a strong hold on the working class; child limitation was seen as a sign of responsibility in broad layers, which also gained support within social democracy.[21]

For conservative politicians, the population issue was a matter of national interest. They believed that falling birth rates should be countered with laws against the use of contraceptives and opposed women working outside the home.

Better health conditions, a larger urban population, and neo-Malthusian ideas contributed to Sweden's net reproduction rate being too low by the mid-1920s. Between 1880 and 1930, the average number of children per family dropped from six to two.[22] The country's population was no longer increasing. The problem of overpopulation was replaced by the risk of underpopulation. In the mid-1930s,

---

[17] Kock (1944, p. 81).
[18] Gårdlund (1956, p. 242).
[19] Jonung (2001, p. 34).
[20] Schön (2014, p. 212).
[21] Hatje (1974, p. 16).
[22] Schön (2014, p. 212).

when the Myrdals' book was published, the net reproduction rate was lower than required to prevent a decrease in population size.

The population issue thus became a matter of the risk of depopulation of Sweden if measures were not taken to increase birth rates. There is also a hypothesis that the Myrdals pursued the population issue as a pretext for the reforms they wanted to implement anyway.[23] Additionally, Gunnar Myrdal was driven by his own ambition—to become his era's Malthus —by forming a conception of reality so irresistible that the political program it implied had to be followed by all, regardless of political affiliation.[24]

Myrdals' Proposals for Solving the Population Issue

The Myrdals successfully wrested the population issue from the political right with radical proposals that influenced both production and reproduction. They believed that low birth rates in Sweden were due to the conflict between having more children and a reasonable standard of living. Solutions included policies for increased production, higher incomes, and lower unemployment. Emphasis was placed on creating a new economic basis for the family as a social institution. Housing loans and housing allowances facilitated family formation, free maternal care, child health centers, and school doctors were responsible for children's health, general child allowances and school meals supported the family's economy, and free nursery schools (day care centers) freed women from the home. Additionally, targeted benefits in kind were proposed for those most in need, i.e., clothes and food directly to poor children and mothers (Fig. 5.1).[25]

The Myrdals saw a contradiction between individuals' actions at the microlevel and the results of their actions for society as a whole. Therefore, the state's intrusion into private life can be given scientific legitimacy. People's trust in their rationality is not taken for granted. Households' own preferences, as expressed in their choices, cannot be accepted by a responsible state authority. Thus, it is about clarifying and implementing rational actions that people would wish for, if they had improved knowledge. Irene Wennemo has shown that the Myrdals here had a different view than Knut Wicksell, who believed that what was rational at the individual level was also the best for society as a whole.[26]

Alva Myrdal also called for an effective public housing inspection that relied on laws and police power and ensured that homes did not deteriorate and that

---

[23] Hirdman (1989, p. 119) and Carlson (1990, p. 194).
[24] Hirdman (1989, p. 119).
[25] Hirdman (1989, p. 122).
[26] Wennemo (1991).

Fig. 5.1 Alva and Gunnar Myrdal work together in Villa Myrdal. (Courtesy of the Swedish Labor Movement's Archives and Library)

intervened against a family allowing its children to live below the approved, housing-hygienic norms through their own fault (Fig. 5.2).[27]

With gifts from the state also came demands. People's consumption and lifestyle needed to be regulated. Gunnar Myrdal advocated for publicly built housing, He claimed that it was important to gradually accustom people to live practically and educate them to a rightly adjusted housing demand from their own perspective. Consumption actually needed to be directed in the consumers' own interest. In Myrdal's view, people had to be accustomed to brushing their teeth and eating tomatoes before they came to appreciate that kind of consumption, and the same was true with sensibly arranged housing.[28]

Kris i befolkningsfrågan (Crisis in the Population Question) became immensely talked about and read by many people in 1934 and 1935. The book was launched with the help of extensive opinion-building.[29] Lecture tours followed one after another. Gunnar addressed church people, for instance, meeting a professor of theology, who was critical of Myrdal's view of collective child-rearing and sex life but still recognized the need for social reforms. Alva gave lectures to businesswomen, women's clubs, and social democratic women's associations. Gunnar appeared for

---

[27] Myrdal (1944, p. 302).

[28] Hirdman (1989, p. 123) referring to Myrdal (1932), Do social reforms cost money?, Architecture and Society, p. 43

[29] Carlson (1990, pp. 112–114).

Fig. 5.2 Gunnar and Alva caricatured as housing spies in Nya Dagligt Allehanda 1936

the first time on the radio with a lecture on the population issue. Sveriges Radio also organized a study circle on the subject between October 1935 and April 1936. For the study circle, Gunnar produced a study guide, "Acta och facta i befolkningsfrågan" (Acts and Facts in the Population Issue).

The book's success was also due to its skillful articulation of a problem that many people recognized. It also spoke plainly about reproduction, sexuality, and pleasure. The problem of too low childbirth rates appeared inevitable and common, a problem that everyone had an interest in solving. Finally, a clear plan was laid out for how the problem should be solved; there was no doubt about what had to be done.[30]

The book and the debate about it led to the word "Myrdal" being used frequently in various contexts. "Myrdalshus" (Myrdal houses) became the name of the new houses built with the ambition to create bright and practical homes for families with children. "Myrdal" even became slang for having intercourse, and condoms were called "myrdalare."

Herbert Tingsten, a political scientist who became a professor at Stockholm University and a friend of the Myrdals at the time, praised the book in *Stockholms-Tidningen*.[31] According to Tingsten it was a remarkable synthesis of thorough knowledge, sharp intellect, and social passion.[32] Many of the sociological sketches and idea analyses were considered masterpieces of controlled irony by Tingsten.

---

[30] Hirdman (2006, p. 190).

[31] The relationship between Gunnar Myrdal and Herbert Tingsten leading to a breakup is described in more detail in Chap. 7.

[32] Lindskog (1981, p. 37).

However, the book also faced criticism from both the left and right. Some in trade unions and among communists were strongly opposed to poor people having more children for the bourgeois state.[33] Conversely, conservative and liberal economists attacked the book for advocating materialism and collectivism.[34] Gustav Cassel wrote five critical articles in the newspaper *Svenska Dagbladet*, recognizing the need for a prophylactic social policy but arguing that the Myrdals presented the population problem in a way that required socialism or even communism. Eli Heckscher wrote four articles in the newspaper *Dagens Nyheter* and, along with his wife Ebba, wrote several personal letters to the Myrdals. Heckscher argued that the Myrdals failed to understand the psychological background to decreased birth rates and resorted to a simplistic materialistic explanation. He accused the Myrdals of wanting to replace the traditional nuclear family with collective upbringing. The correspondence led to very strained relations between the Heckscher and Myrdal couples.

Within social democracy, the book had significant impact. Prime Minister Tage Erlander remembered how it was a shocking experience that the labor party would engage in the population issue, which had been a rallying banner for conservative forces. According to Erlander, it did not take long before he understood that Alva and Gunnar Myrdal were right.[35] At least the government should try to create a social system that allowed citizens to decide for themselves how many children they wanted. Erlander did not want economic coercion or the desire for a reasonable standard to stand in the way.

Following the publication of their book, Gunnar Myrdal participated in several government inquiries to find support for and implement the proposals in their joint book. Alva Myrdal was assigned a more subordinate role, but continued to work in many contexts.[36] She played a central role as the director of studies and later as the principal of the Social Pedagogical Seminar, which she helped start in 1936. The Social Pedagogical Seminar took on the new task of educating staff who would work in what we now call preschool, but at that time was referred to as kindergartens or large nurseries.[37] Alva structured the teaching on how to help children grow, dividing the education into full semesters of theory and practice. The practical training was designed to immerse students in the full day-to-day life of a child, while the theoretical training included all the new social–psychological findings from pioneers abroad, as well as courses in social studies. Gunnar and Alva Myrdal shared a strong belief in reason. However, according to Sissela Bok, their eldest daughter, the

---

[33] Lindskog (1981, p. 36).

[34] Lundahl (2021, ch 3).

[35] Lindskog (1981, p. 38).

[36] She became vice-chairman of the Women's Club in Stockholm in 1932, chairman of the National Association of Professional Women in 1936, secretary of a committee on women's employment appointed by Wigforss in 1935, active member of the Social Democratic Women's Association, lecturer for ABF, Young Eagles, and Marx Society. See Hirdman (2006, p. 221) and Lindskog (1981, p. 51).

[37] Bok (1987, pp. 117–120).

collective thoughts were more influenced by Alva than Gunnar. When Sissela commented on the book *Kris i befolkningsfrågan* she noted that Alva and Gunnar's faith in reason and its ultimate victory knew no bounds.[38] When they talked about the need for collectivist thinking within schools, families, and even marriages themselves she heard Alva's voice. Gunnar never had Alva's reverence for collectivism and was not concerned about the selfishness and egocentricity condemned in the book.

All These Inquiries

The population issue became so important in the public debate that in the spring of 1935, the Social Minister Gustav Möller appointed a population commission, led by Nils Wohlin, a professor of statistics, general director of customs, and a member of parliament for the Farmers' Union.[39] The commission produced a large number of reports and opinions across the entire social field: the status of working women, preventive maternal and child care, midwifery training, nutrition issues, family taxation, maternity benefits and maternal aid, housing loans, clothing allowances for children, nurseries, subsidies for children of widows, public dental care, and other components of a state-developed care policy. Gunnar Myrdal was the most driving force in the commission until the spring of 1938, when he took a break to visit the USA.[40] Alva Myrdal became an expert in the commission and participated by producing a report on nurseries and summer colonies, meaning that much of the Population Commission's work during its first years was shaped by the Myrdals' values and analyses.

Gunnar Myrdal's influence over the commission was exceptional. It lasted from mid-1935 to mid-1938 and was due to his intense activity in the commission's work and his leading of more inquiries than any other member. He was also the most active member of the steering group, consisting of three people. Myrdal was adept at intellectually dominating and convincing other commission members. He formed a close bond with the chairman, Nils Wohlin, who he courted as if he were an older relative.[41]

Myrdal was also adept at pushing his views by raising them in the inquiries, outmaneuvering, or winning over opponents to his side. For instance, he managed to get a majority for his idea that Swedish children should receive free school lunches paid by the state, regardless of family income.[42] He also exercised control

---

[38] Bok (1987, pp. 104–105).

[39] Statistician Richard Sterner participated in the work, and economist Torsten Gårdlund was secretary.

[40] He gave lectures at Harvard and also discussed with the president of the Carnegie Corporation, which led to him accepting the assignment to lead the major study on the American race issue.

[41] Carlson (1990, p. 132).

[42] Carlson (1990, p. 133).

over the staff employed by the commission. Richard Sterner, a statistician who became one of Myrdal's most central collaborators, noted that he formally answered to Wohlin, but in practice took orders from Myrdal.[43]

Gunnar Myrdal was the author of several reports and played a central role in the 1936 Sexual Inquiry, which was appointed because a new sexual morality was needed in society to increase childbearing. Alva Myrdal also participated in the Sexual Inquiry and wrote two appendices.[44] The Inquiry, opposed to old, musty sexual morals, saw sexuality as something healthy and proper. Both the Sexual Inquiry and the Population Commission believed that marriage should be the norm for sexual relations.[45]

Gunnar Myrdal was innovative in writing appendices that established the theoretical analytical framework. Some researchers even believe that Myrdal set assumptions and conditions that guided the analysis and conclusions in his desired direction.[46] One of the appendices referred to Myrdal's book, *Vetenskap och politik i nationalekonomin* (The Political Element in the Development of Economic Theory) and attempted to base the population issue on an analysis of value premises.[47]

Myrdal discussed how population development is normally related to several social factors. Different assumptions painted a picture of several possible future courses. Myrdal argued that one must also envision how a certain population development in itself affects other social factors. The connections were of a sociopsychological and sociological nature. Normally, one would rationally evaluate the effects according to certain social norms. But these social norms did not correspond to all individuals' norms. This meant that the assessment of birth control, for example, the use of contraceptives, was a valuation that individuals would have if they made "more accurate representations of reality" and based them on the assumed social norms. The goal for future population development was ultimately a subjective valuation of different alternatives, their effects, and the means required for their realization. The valuations should be conscious and be expressed premises for the conclusions.

---

[43] Carlson (1990, p. 133).

[44] Alva Myrdal wrote "Barnantalets familjepsykologiska betydelse" (The Family-Psychological Importance of Child Numbers) and "Föräldrafostrans socialpedagogiska uppgifter och organisation" (Social-Pedagogical Tasks and Organization of Parental Education), Appendices to SOU 1936:59, Report on the Sexual Question.

[45] At this time, the contraceptive law was still valid. It was in force from 1911 to 1938 and criminalized the distribution of knowledge and use of contraceptives to the public. The investigation considered that childless marriages and marriages with only one child and in most cases even marriages with two children did not constitute a truly happy form of cohabitation. The most important result of the Sexual Investigation was to see sexuality as an instrument for the state to increase birth rates. Sexuality was liberated from stale morality, contraceptive techniques were taught, marriage was promoted as the norm, but extramarital relationships were accepted. Hirdman (1989, p. 135, 143).

[46] Carlson (1990, p. 144).

[47] Myrdal, G. (1936).

In an appendix that Myrdal wrote together with the professor of statistics, Sven Wicksell—son of Knut Wicksell—it was noted that there is a lack of exhaustive empirical research on the connections between social and population development.[48] But after analyzing the historical statistics for Sweden, population forecasts were made under various assumptions. The conclusion was that it was almost certain that Sweden's population would soon start to decrease.

The Population Commission also conducted an extensive census in 1936.[49] It consisted of a normal census and a new population-political survey that involved visiting 1.3 million people—one-fifth of the population—to answer a questionnaire with 30 questions. It included time, place, and other details about childbirths. Questions about children in different family constellations, parents' education, employment, incomes, and the extent to which women cease gainful employment after marriage were asked. Questions about the size of dwellings, number of rooms, and bathrooms were also included.

Before the survey, Gunnar Myrdal based much of his analysis on a statistical analysis by Karl Arvid Edin, who showed that increased incomes tended to be related to higher birth rates.[50] Edin had used advanced statistical methods for his time but only studied data from Stockholm. The 1936 survey covered a larger sample and was used to analyze the issue. It supported Edin's hypothesis. Higher incomes were related to larger families across the country. Thus, Myrdal got the ammunition he needed to push his line in the commission in favor of creating an economic basis for the family as a social institution.[51]

The general conclusion for Gunnar Myrdal and the Population Commission was that society should be arranged in such a way that people do not need to be ignorant or moral to act in the interest of society, which meant having an average of three children per family.[52] The housing issue also continued to play an important role as society's responsibility for welfare increased. The Housing Social Inquiry, which had been approved by Social Minister Möller, became a subcommittee to the Population Commission. Alf Johansson, a Stockholm economist and one of Gunnar Myrdal's closest friends, became the chief secretary in this work and had a significant influence on the development of a new housing policy, which will be revisited in Chap. 8.[53]

The situation of women in the labor market also became the subject of a government inquiry, investigated by the Women's Work Committee, led by Kerstin Hesselgren and with Alva Myrdal as secretary and Karin Kock as an economic expert. Kock contributed with an appendix, "Kvinnoarbetet i Sverige" (Women's Work in Sweden) a pioneering work that described and analyzed the strong

---

[48] Myrdal G, Wicksell S. (1936).
[49] Carlson (1990, p. 134).
[50] Carlson (1990, p. 90).
[51] Carlson (1990, p. 134).
[52] Hatje (1974, p. 230).
[53] Myrdal (1982, p. 192).

segregation between men and women in the labor market. Women systematically had lower wages than men for the same work.

Karin Kock worked with empirical data in the broad institutional perspective and emphasized the role of values in line with Gunnar Myrdal. She argued that the wage difference between men and women was influenced by prejudices. The wage difference, in turn, affected how companies were organized, and the segregation ensured that the perception that women were not worth the same wage as men was maintained. The lower wages for women were due to the demand side of the traditionally bound notion of a "normal" wage difference between male and female workers. In the context of the supply side, a key finding was how the married woman's bond to family and home impacted the scenario.[54] A conclusion drawn was that increasing women's wages would break down the preconceived notions about the level of women's wages, which were so significant for wage formation.[55] Karin Kock's innovative work was rediscovered at various times by feminists and gender researchers from the 1960s onwards.[56]

Gunnar Myrdal Opposed Race Biology in Sweden

An important issue in the 1930s was the prevailing views on race biology and racial hygiene. In the 1920s, discussions on population issues were influenced by beliefs in the superiority of the Nordic race and the dangers of racial mixing. In 1921, a racial biology institute was established in Sweden to give such views scientific status. Its head, Herman Lundborg, held explicit racist beliefs.[57] In conservative circles, declining birth rates among the "educated classes" caused fears of deteriorating "Swedish stock."

Myrdals refuted race- and class-based biological theories in *Kris i befolkningsfrågan* (Crisis in the Population Question), citing modern research. Intellectuals like political science professor Herbert Tingsten and Gunnar Dahlberg, a docent in medical heredity research and medical statistics, played significant roles in discrediting race biology in Sweden. Gunnar Myrdal was instrumental in changing both the leadership and direction of the racial biology institute. The racial biologist Herman Lundborg was expected to retire in 1933 but stayed to pave the way for a likeminded successor. After a complex and prolonged expertise procedure, the institute's board majority favored Torsten Sjögren, a candidate aligned with Lundborg's racial biology ideology. Opposing him was Gunnar Dahlberg, an active anti-Nazi

---

[54] Kock (1938, p. 470).
[55] Kock (1938, p. 467).
[56] Niskanen (2007, p. 93).
[57] See Appelqvist and Andersson (1998, pp. 172–175) for a description of Myrdal's relation to racial biology.

who did not accept racial concepts.[58] In a 1933 article in the cultural magazine *Ord & Bild* Dahlberg demolished Lundborg's racial concepts, emphasizing the lack of correlation between appearance and intelligence.[59] There was no scientific basis to infer intellectual ability from hair color, eye shape, or head form.

Gunnar Myrdal emerged as a decisive figure, influencing the responsible minister, Östen Undén, leading to Herman Lundborg's replacement by Gunnar Dahlberg. Myrdal's intervention marked a turning point, with racial hygiene losing its foothold and legitimacy in Swedish societal debate.[60]

However, the Myrdals' book included a chapter titled "Socialpolitiken och folkets kvalitet" (Social Policy and the Quality of the People) discussing how the quality of the population could be improved in line with modern life's demands. Despite the problematic wording for modern readers, their conclusions advocated social reforms. They argued that the most crucial method to enhance the "quality of human material" was the elimination of unemployment, particularly youth unemployment.[61]

The Myrdals and other Swedish population researchers also inadvertently provided support for repressive state measures, particularly regarding the *sterilization* issue.[62] In 1934, the Swedish Parliament decided that mentally ill individuals under guardianship could be sterilized, considering hereditary risks. The Myrdals supported these thoughts in their book, suggesting extending the hereditary perspective of sterilizations to include social–pedagogical aspects, considering the unsuitability of the upbringing environment for children.

However, there was no scientific basis to determine which social groups possessed different traits. The Sexual Investigation rejected the hereditary biological arguments on scientific grounds, but its method—sterilization—was accepted from a social perspective.[63]

It's evident that the Myrdals lost their scientific rigor and critical perspective when supporting the expansion of the sterilization law, as noted by Yvonne Hirdman.[64] It's also difficult to understand, in a contemporary context, why this view wasn't controversial at that time. The Population Commission's sterilization

---

[58] Gunnar Dahlberg was a member of the anti-Nazi association Kulturfront and the Committee for Exiled Intellectuals, which worked to grant work permits in Sweden to Jewish doctors in exile.

[59] Hagerman (2015, part 5, The Great Sami Investigation).

[60] Broberg and Tydén (2005, pp. 47–48).

[61] Myrdal (1934, ch. 7).

[62] The policy of sterilization was adopted in several Western countries in the early decades of the twentieth century and was given scientific legitimacy. The German Nazis' racial extremism led to mass murder of the mentally ill and handicapped and systematic extermination of Jews, Gypsies, and homosexuals.

[63] Hirdman (1989, p. 147).

[64] Hirdman (2006, p. 199).

proposal wasn't addressed in Parliament until the war, in 1941, when a new sterilization law was enacted.[65]

It's important to stress that the Myrdals didn't accept theories of racial or class-based collective differences in intelligence.[66] They focused on environmental factors, emphasizing society's role in care and education and creating jobs for all, even those marginalized due to increasing intelligence demands in tasks.

Alva Myrdal also played a significant role in enabling physically and mentally handicapped individuals to leave institutions and enter the workforce. She was one of the initiators of establishing "protected workshops" under government management.[67]

Gunnar Myrdal joined the first chamber of the Swedish Parliament in 1936. His strong will to pursue his views began to draw attention. On some occasions, his proposals conflicted with those of Finance Minister Wigforss, especially regarding a 1937 proposal by Wigforss to provide teachers and other civil servants with cash child benefits. Myrdal opposed this, advocating for child benefits in kind, such as clothing and food items, directly to families. His stance was motivated by a radical and rational "consumption socialism." Myrdal swayed other Social Democrats, and Wigforss's proposal was dropped in the internal process.[68] However, the internal debate on the nature of child benefits within the Social Democratic Party continued. The key figure in this political process was Social Minister Gustav Möller.

Gustav Möller, born in Malmö in 1884 and raised in poverty, was deeply influenced by his upbringing.[69] His political actions were marked by his mother's difficult life. According to Möller, a significant part of social policy aimed to prevent such fates as his mother's. There were no pensions for grandmothers to ease his mother's burden, no support for widows with children and poor incomes, and society did nothing to eradicate living conditions that contributed to early deaths. There were no regulated working hours, paid holidays, or opportunities for housewives' breaks.[70]

During Möller's tenure as Social Minister, much of Sweden's social safety net was established. This included introducing or improving a social insurance system to protect citizens against sickness, unemployment, and old age. The political

---

[65] The 1941 law was in effect until 1975. It allowed sterilization based on three indications: eugenic indication, a person who by hereditary factors can pass on mental illness or mental retardation, or other severe illness; social indication, a person deemed manifestly unfit to take care of children due to mental illness or mental retardation or asocial behavior; medical indication, if pregnancy poses a risk to the woman's life. A person who cannot give consent to sterilization due to mental disorder can be sterilized involuntarily. Source: Wikipedia, 1934 and 1941 Sterilization Laws. See also Broberg & Tydén (2005, p. 102).

[66] Myrdal completely rejected a memorandum by Nils von Hofsten, which claimed the existence of hereditary biological differences between different social groups, see Hatje (1974, p. 180).

[67] Appelqvist and Andersson (1998, p. 174).

[68] Carlson (1990, p. 175).

[69] Edebalk (2021, p. 10).

[70] Myrdal (1982, p. 282).

scientist Bo Rothstein has pointed out that Möller was keen to ensure that social policy would strengthen the autonomy of citizens and grant them well-defined rights, rather than arbitrarily organizing their lives.[71] Möller, therefore, opposed several proposals from the Myrdals, including the idea of in-kind child benefits. He preferred cash grants for families with children. Fundamentally, he had a different view of the role of experts than Alva and Gunnar Myrdal. The Myrdals strongly believed in the role of social engineers to make the right decisions. However, as Irene Wennemo observed, Möller was critical of the role of experts and traditional bureaucracy. He wanted to break up old bureaucracies and replace them with new ones, and he was keen on transferring power to local and popularly established bodies.[72]

Several of the Population Commission's key proposals were decided by the parliament in 1936 and 1937. Some proposals to create a new economic foundation for the family as a social institution were approved by the parliament with some adjustments. Free maternity care, preventive maternal and child care, and advance payments for single mothers, as well as state housing loans, were decided. Additionally, special child allowances were introduced for orphans, fatherless, and disabled children. However, Möller opposed the Commission's proposal for a general maternity allowance, which would be independent of income. He argued that many would have difficulty understanding why people in a favorable position should receive state support. Instead, maternity allowance was introduced based on a fairly generous income test.[73] An income limit was retained, but it was set so high that 90% were eligible.[74]

The law prohibiting the dissemination of the use or knowledge of contraceptives was abolished. Discrimination against women in the labor market was forbidden, through a new law that made it punishable for employers to dismiss women who became pregnant or got married. The tax system was adjusted to finance the reforms, and the income tax became more progressive. However, other proposals from the Population Commission were postponed in an increasingly uncertain situation ahead of the outbreak of the war, for example, costly proposals for daycare and free school meals, much to Gunnar Myrdal's chagrin. Another setback for Myrdal was that the Commission's main proposal for in-kind child benefits was not tested by the parliament before the war.[75]

Gunnar Myrdal left the Population Commission when he moved to the USA in September 1938. One reason for his departure was likely that Prime Minister Per Albin Hansson spoke of a "reform pause" in the spring of 1938. Ernst Wigforss noted in his memoirs that social policy plans were maturing and there were desires

---

[71] Rothstein (2010, p. 225).
[72] Wennemo (2014, p. 195).
[73] Edebalk (2021, p. 49).
[74] Wennemo (2014, p. 157).
[75] Edebalk (2021, p. 50).

for wage and productivity increases.[76] The balance between rising state expenditures in various areas was also influenced by the demands to strengthen the defense due to the international crisis situation.[77]

Gustav Möller and Nils Wohlin ensured that Myrdal lost his leading role in the commission when the final report was prepared. There were formulations in it that were foreign to Myrdal.[78] The eugenic element was given a different role in the report than he had given it.[79] He was in the USA when the final report was written and, according to a decision by Möller, had not been allowed to submit any particular opinion or reservation to the report.[80] He appealed in letters to the Social Democratic members of the commission not to accept the report.[81] According to Myrdal, there was too much in the report that Social Democrats could not simply sign off on and that would be used by their opponents.

When the final report was formally approved at the Population Commission's last plenary meeting on December 18, 1938, there were three delegates who indicated that they would reserve themselves against it. Two of them, Social Democrats A. L. Persson and Disa Västberg, prepared an opinion in line with Myrdal's objections, but at the last moment, they refrained from issuing any opinion without stating the reason. Gunnar Myrdal's pleas had reached them, but they did not have the intended effect; the writings remained.[82] The question of whether the state's support for child families would be in kind, as Myrdals wished, or with cash grants, as supported by Möller and Wigforss, continued to be investigated during the war, and only a few years after the end of the war were cash child benefits introduced, as Möller had wished.

---

[76] Wigforss (1954, p. 109).

[77] Myrdal stated in a 1970 interview that feared defeats regarding the financing of the commission's proposals contributed to his departure to the USA, see Hatje (1974, p. 45). In later conversations with Stellan Andersson, Myrdal cited several reasons for the move: fatigue with investigative work and its slowness, opposition to family policy reforms, financial problems, and persecution in the press, see Andersson (2022, p. 30).

[78] "It must rather be considered as a biologically necessary assumption that the division within a people into different occupations and professions, however powerful the social position and other environmental factors may influence, at least in some cases to some extent depends on the individual's disposition, which is connected with their hereditary traits." SOU 1938:57, p. 64, see Hirdman (1989, p. 151).

[79] Nils Wohlin himself had demonstrated eugenic sympathies, was one of the initiators of the racial biology institute, and was a friend of Herman Lundborg, see Hagerman (2015, part 3, Racial Biological Lobbying).

[80] Hatje (1974, p. 180).

[81] Broberg and Tydén (2005, p. 82).

[82] Carlson (1990, pp. 182–183).

Conclusions

Gunnar and Alva Myrdal had a significant impact with their ideas when the Swedish welfare state began to expand in the 1930s. Gunnar Myrdal's general ideas about preventive social policy led to the work of writing the influential book *Crises in the Population Question* together with Alva Myrdal. They convincingly described the problem of low birth rates; showed that it was a problem that concerned everyone in society and concluded with a catalog of concrete proposals for action.

After the publication of the book, it was Gunnar Myrdal who took the largest place in government investigations to practically ensure analyzing, finding support for, and finally trying to implement the proposals. He was also elected to the parliament and could thereby participate in the implementation of some of the Population Investigation's proposals. Alva Myrdal was assigned a more subordinate role in the most central political processes of the time, even though she continued to work vigorously in several contexts and participated in the work with both the Population Commission and the Sexual Investigation.

A number of welfare reforms over the next few decades had their origins in the Myrdals' book. A key idea in the reform strategy was that social reforms should be general, benefit everyone regardless of income, and not be characterized by poor relief thinking.

The central idea to gain general support for welfare policy was that state support was required to, in the national interest, slow down the population decline. Thus, it can be said that the Myrdals managed to capture the population issue from the conservative right and create a foundation for social reforms. Gunnar Myrdal himself claimed that many people with conservative convictions in intellectual professions such as teachers, priests, and doctors realized that it would be in their own interest to counter a declining population with social reforms.[83]

It can also be argued that the Myrdals used the population issue as a battering ram for reforms that they wanted to implement anyway. Their program for the Swedish welfare state has been seen by the historian Alan Carlson as victories on several fronts.[84] Feminism triumphed over an older form of socialism, reason triumphed over religion and tradition, and the state triumphed over local society and the family, according to Carlson. But it is also important to emphasize that several of the Myrdals' proposals did not become reality or were modified by the powerful Social Minister Gustav Möller.

The welfare state also committed abuses. The application of sterilization policy was perhaps the most tangible example of state abuse in Sweden during the twentieth century.[85] As part of social policy, sterilization became more than a medical

---

[83] Myrdal (1940, p. 96), see Barber (2008, p. 59).
[84] Carlson (1990, pp. 196–197).
[85] Between 1935 and 1975, 63,000 people were sterilized in Sweden, of which 93% were women, see Broberg and Tydén (2005, p. 97). Women were given a subordinate position, and their lives were regulated from a male top-down perspective, see Hirdman (1989, p. 230). According to

issue. It became a means to intervene against the neglected, the deviant, against all those on the periphery who did not fit into the normal and orderly society, all those considered "undesirable in the welfare state," a concept coined by historians Gunnar Broberg and Mattias Tydén.[86]

However, it can be argued that the general welfare policy has contributed to the abolition of the basis for this repressive side of social policy, as pointed out by the author Sven Lindqvist.[87] But when the state takes over responsibility for many aspects of people's social lives, there is a risk that individuals are subordinated to motives formulated by others, the social engineers who want to set life right for the citizens, according to Yvonne Hirdman's terminology in her influential partial report to the Study of Power and Democracy in Sweden in 1990.[88] However, I would argue that the emergence of the Swedish welfare state after the war was mostly characterized by the dynamics, cooperation, and competition between a strong state and a strong civil society, which contributed to increased capacity in both sectors, which I will return to in later chapters.

A new population investigation was appointed in 1941 and presented its main report in 1946. The investigation was led by Möller's state secretary, Tage Erlander, and was thus clearly linked to the Ministry of Social Affairs and Gustav Möller himself. It was then that family policy had a more tangible breakthrough with, among other things, free school meals, housing allowances for families with children, and state subsidies for daycare centers.[89] It was also then that the old battle between the Myrdals and Möller over the design of child benefits was decided. Möller's line with cash child benefits, money directly in hand, triumphed over Myrdal's proposal for in-kind benefits, clothes, and food items instead of money. The reform with uniform, cash child benefits took effect in 1948. It was Gustav Möller's merit that the cash child benefits went directly to the mothers and that the concept of the household head was never established in Swedish social policy.[90]

After the successes with a faster recovery from the 1930s depression than in many other countries and the talked-about social reforms, interest in Sweden grew significantly in the outside world. There was talk of a country that had found a

---

Gunnar Broberg and Mattias Tydén, it is not possible to determine how many Swedes were sterilized against their will. Even though most signed their application themselves, many were in a coercive situation or did not know what they were signing, see Broberg and Tydén (2005, p. 143). Thomas Etzemüller (2010, p. 88) however states that about 20,000 people were forcibly sterilized in Sweden from 1935–1975. Ola Larsmo estimates that 30,000–33,000 sterilizations were performed under persuasion or coercion, and at least 15,000 of them were in direct violation of the law, see Larsmo (2022, p. 245). In 1999, a law was introduced to compensate those who were sterilized against their will.

[86] Broberg and Tydén (2005, p. 184).
[87] Lindqvist (1997).
[88] Hirdman (1989).
[89] Edebalk (2021, p. 76).
[90] Rothstein (2010, p. 230).

middle way between capitalism in the USA and communism in the Soviet Union.[91] In the USA, attention was paid to both the Swedish economic and social policy and one of its main architects.

By that time, it was evident that Gunnar Myrdal had shifted his methodological approach from high theory to institutionalism.[92] In Sweden he became involved in social equality problems, which he found could not be handled scientifically except by broadening the approach to all human relations. When he accepted the responsibility for the study of race relations in the USA, this took him farther away from conventional economics. From then on more definitely Gunnar Myrdal came to see that there are no economic, sociological, or psychological problems, but just problems, and they are all mixed and composite.

References

Åhrén, Uno (1925), "Brytningar", Svensk slöjdförenings årsbok
Andersson S (2022) Några anteckningar i samband med läsningen av Maribel Moreys bok White Philantropy (Some notes in connection with reading Maribel Morey's book White Philantropy). Manuscript. Labor Movement's Archive and Library, Stockholm
Appelqvist Ö, Andersson S (1998) Vägvisare – Texter av Gunnar Myrdal. Norstedts, Stockholm. English edition: Appelqvist Ö, Andersson S (1998b) The essential Gunnar Myrdal. The New Press, New York
Barber W (2008) Gunnar Myrdal an intellectual biography. Palgrave Macmillan, New York
Berg C (2012) Global ekonomi – en introduktion till samhällsekonomi och politisk ekonomi (Global economy - an introduction to economics and political economy). SNS Publishing, Stockholm
Bok S (1987) Alva, ett kvinnoliv. Bonniers, Avesta. English edition: Bok S (1991) Alva Myrdal. A daughter's memoir. Radcliffe biography series. Perseus Publishing, Cambridge
Branting H (1886) De närmaste framtidsutsikterna (The immediate future prospects), Social-Demokraten 1.11.1886. In: Alsterdal A, Sandell O (eds) (1970) Hjalmar Branting Socialism och demokrati; ett urval (Hjalmar branting socialism and democracy; a selection). Prisma, Stockholm
Broberg G, Tydén M (2005) Oönskade i folkhemmet Rashygien och sterilisering i Sverige (Unwanted in the welfare state Eugenics and sterilization in Sweden), 2nd edn. Dialogos, Stockholm
Carlson A (1990) The Swedish experiment in family politics. The Myrdal's and the interwar population crisis. Routledge, London & New York
Edebalk PG (2021) Gustav Möller En legendarisk socialpolitiker (Gustav Möller a legendary social politician). Arkiv förlag, Lund
Edström B (2014) Inledning. In: Björk EB, Lundén T (eds) Rudolf Kjellén Geopolitiken och konservatismen. Introduction. In: Björk R, Edström B, Lundén T (eds) Rudolf Kjellén geopolitics and conservatism. Hjalmarson & Högberg, Stockholm
Etzemüller T (2014) Alva and Gunnar Myrdal social engineering in the modern world. Lexington Books, Lanham

---

[91] A bestseller at the time was the book Sweden. The Middle Way by Marquis Childs from 1936.
[92] He articulated this change in direction in Myrdal (1978, p. 772).

References

Gårdlund T (1956) Knut Wicksell. Rebell i det nya riket (The life of Knut Wicksell). In: Ny upplaga 1990. SNS förlag, Stockholm. English edition: Gårdlund T (1996) The life of Knut Wicksell. Edward Elgar, Cheltenham

Hagerman M (2015) Käraste Herman Rasbiologen Herman Lundborgs gåta (Dearest Herman The Enigma of the race biologist Herman Lundborg). Norstedts, Stockholm

Hatje, A-K (1974) Befolkningsfrågan och välfärden Debatten om familjepolitik och nativitetsökning under 1930- och 1940-talen (The population issue and welfare the debate on family policy and birth rate increase during the 1930s and 1940s), Dissertation. Allmänna förlaget, Stockholm

Hirdman Y (1989) Att lägga livet till rätta Studier i svensk folkhemspolitik (Arranging life properly, studies in Swedish welfare policy). Carlsson, Stockholm

Hirdman Y (2006) Det tänkande hjärtat. Boken om Alva Myrdal. Ordfront, Stockholm. English edition: Hirdman, Y (2008), Alva Myrdal: the passionate mind. Indiana University Press, Bloomington

Jackson W (2021) Alva and Gunnar Myrdal in Sweden and America 1898–1945. Unsparing honesty. Routledge, New York/London

Jonung L (2001) Inledning. In: Wicksell K (ed) Att uppfostra det svenska folket. Opublicerade manuskript. Introduction. In: Jonung, L, Hedlund-Nyström T, Jonung C, Wicksell, K (eds) Educating the Swedish people, Unpublished Manuscripts. SNS Publishing, Stockholm

Karlsson S (2001) Det intelligenta samhället (The intelligent society). Carlsson, Stockholm

Kock K (1938) Kvinnoarbetet i Sverige (Women's work in Sweden). Appendix 1, SOU 1938:47

Kock K (1944) Nymalthusianismens genombrott i Sverige (The breakthrough of neo-malthusianism in Sweden) Studier i ekonomi och historia Tillägnade Eli F Heckscher den 24 November 1944, pp 73–88

Larsmo O (2022) Lektion 11: En bok om rasbiologi (Lesson 11: A book on racial biology). Kaunitz-Olsson, Falun

Lindqvist S (1997) Välfärd stoppade steriliseringar (Welfare halted sterilizations) Dagens Nyheter, August 30, 1997

Lindskog L (1981) Alva Myrdal. 'Förnuftet måste segra (Alva Myrdal. Reason must prevail). Sveriges Radios Förlag, Kristianstad

Lo-Johansson I (1957) Författaren, Kapitel 1 (The author, Chapter 1). Bonnier, Stockholm

Lundahl M (2021) The dynamics of poverty circular, cumulative causation, value judgements, institutions, and social engineering in the world of Gunnar Myrdal. In: Cohen A, Harcourt G, Kriesler P (eds) Palgrave studies in the history of economic thought. Palgrave Macmillan, Cham

Lundberg E (1984) Kriserna & ekonomerna (Crises & economists). Liber, Stockholm

Malthus T R (1798) An essay on the principle of population, excerpts from the 2nd ed. 1803 published in Swedish in Borgström G (1969) (Ed.) Malthus om befolkningsfrågan, LTs förlag, Stockholm

Myrdal G (1932) Socialpolitikens dilemma II (The dilemma of social policy II). Spektrum 4:24–28

Myrdal G (1934) Finanspolitikens ekonomiska verkningar (The economic effects of fiscal policy) Bilaga 5 till Arbetslöshetsutredningens betänkande. SOU 1934:1

Myrdal G (1940) Population a problem for democracy. Harvard University Press, Cambridge

Myrdal A (1941) Nation and family The Swedish experiment in democratic family and population policy. Harper & Brothers, New York. Swedish edition: Myrdal A (1944) Folk och familj, Kooperativa förbundets bokförlag, Stockholm

Myrdal G (1978) Institutional economics. J Econ Iss 12(4):s771–783

Myrdal G (1982) Hur styrs landet? (How is the country run?). Rabén & Sjögren, Stockholm

Myrdal, G. (1936), Bilaga 1, Några metodiska anmärkningar rörande befolkningsfrågans innebörd och vetenskapliga behandling, SOU 1936: 59, Betänkande I sexualfrågan (Appendix 1, Some methodological remarks regarding the importance and scientific treatment of the population issue. Report on the Sexual Question)

Myrdal G, Wicksell S. (1936), Bilaga 8, Utsikterna i fråga om den framtida befolkningsutvecklingen i Sverige och de ekonomiska verkningarna av olika alternativt möjliga befolkningsutvecklingar. SOU 1936:59, Betänkande I sexualfrågan. (Appendix 8, Prospects for future population development in Sweden and the economic effects of various alternatively possible population developments. Report on the Sexual Question.)

Nilsson JO (1994) Alva Myrdal En virvel i den moderna strömmen (Alva Myrdal: a whirlwind in the modern stream). B Östling's Publishing House Symposion, Stockholm

Niskanen K (2007) Karriär i männens värld Nationalekonomen och feministen Karin Kock (Career in a man's world: the economist and feminist Karin Kock). SNS Publishing, Stockholm

Rothstein B (2010) Vad bör staten göra? (What should the state do?). SNS Publishing, Stockholm

Schön L (2014) En modern svensk ekonomisk historia (A modern Swedish economic history). Studentlitteratur, Lund

Wennemo I (1991) Arbetarrörelsen och befolkningsfrågan Knut Wicksells och makarna Myrdals befolkningsteorier (The labor movement and the population question Knut Wicksell's and the Myrdals' population theories) Forskningsrapport. Department of Sociology, Stockholm University

Wennemo I (2014) Det gemensamma Om den svenska välfärdsmodellen (The common welfare about the Swedish welfare model). Premiss Publishing, Stockholm

Wicksell K (1880) Några ord om den viktigaste orsaken till social misär och dess bot med speciel hänvisning till dryckenskap' (A few words on the most important cause of social misery and its cure, with special reference to drunkenness). Eget förlag

Wigforss E (1950, 1951, 1954) Minnen I, II och III (Memoirs I, II, and III) Tiden, Stockholm

Chapter 6
An American Dilemma

In 1938 Gunnar Myrdal began his study of the American race issue on behalf of the Carnegie Corporation. Myrdal began by assembling a diverse team from leading institutions, including Ralph Bunche and Doxey Wilkerson from Howard University. Myrdal identified the American Creed as central to understanding racial dynamics, rooted in Enlightenment philosophy, Anglo-Saxon legal traditions, and Protestant religion. These ideals of equality starkly contrasted with the reality of racial discrimination in America. Myrdal proposed the theory of vicious and virtuous circles, where discrimination and poor conditions for black Americans reinforced each other, creating a cycle of oppression. Conversely, reducing discrimination could improve living conditions and decrease prejudices, fostering a virtuous circle. Myrdal's book *An American Dilemma* published in 1944 became a seminal work, highlighting the moral conflict in American society. It received widespread acclaim, influenced civil rights legislation, and became a key reference in the fight for racial equality in the USA.

Introduction

During their work on housing and population issues, Alva and Gunnar Myrdal decided to improve their own living standards. The family had grown with the addition of two daughters, Sissela born in 1934, and Kaj in 1936, necessitating larger and better-organized space. They moved from a rented villa on Thaliavägen in Ålsten to a modern functionalist-style villa, constructed in 1937 on Nyängsvägen in Bromma, designed by architect Sven Markelius.

Alva actively participated in the villa's design, which spanned two floors. The ground floor housed rooms for children, a nanny, and a maid, along with a common room. The upper floor contained the parents' joint office and a bedroom, which could be divided by a sliding wall between the beds. According to their son Jan, the house resembled a steamboat, with round vents in the bathroom, a large command bridge, and teak railings.[1] He also claimed that the children's sleeping quarters were intended only for sleep; during the day, the children were expected to play outdoors or collectively in the common room. Sissela recalled the house more fondly and noted that she and Kaj had a bright, spacious nursery with a large doodle board on the wall, which was the exact opposite of the dwellings Alva described where nurseries "house each a languishing and confined human section."[2] The press joked about Villa Myrdal, which had a large outdoor terrace on the upper level, where Gunnar and Alva could sunbathe nude. When Gunnar attempted this, a neighbor from the slope above called the police. Jan claimed that the neighbor must have climbed onto his roof to see Gunnar naked on the terrace, to which Gunnar exclaimed, "pervert!" However, Kaj and Sissela insisted that no neighbors could see onto the veranda, and Sissela also remembered being able to play both outdoors and indoors—on both floors and the terrace.[3]

Jan also claimed he could hear his parents' conversations from the upper floor due to an unplanned acoustic effect. This was because Markelius designed the house with an offset lower floor relative to the upper one. The staircase winding down from the upper floor to the hall of the lower floor, near the large common room, essentially created an old phonograph horn. According to Jan, the acoustics were so peculiar that if he stood right at the wall, where the hall turned into the common room, every whisper from upstairs sounded as if they were standing right behind his ear. However, Kaj and Sissela disagreed, saying that their parents' conversations on the upper floor could not be heard downstairs.[4]

The villa remained the Myrdals' home until 1947, although they did not reside there throughout the entire period. A new assignment awaited Gunnar in the USA in 1938.

Gunnar to the USA

In April 1938, Gunnar Myrdal traveled to the USA to give lectures at Harvard University on the population issue. He was also to meet Frederick Keppel, president of the Carnegie Corporation, a philanthropic organization interested in engaging an independent intellectual to undertake a study on the American race issue.

Andrew Carnegie, the foundation's founder, was born in Scotland in 1835 and moved to Pittsburgh at age 12. He worked his way up in American society and amassed a fortune in the steel industry. At 65, he sold his company for 480 million dollars, equivalent to 15 billion dollars today. Carnegie dedicated himself to

---

[1] Jan Myrdal described the house in Myrdal (1984, pp. 45, 92–93, 95–96).
[2] Bok (1987, pp. 109–110).
[3] Interview with Kaj Fölster on May 17, 2023, and email from Sissela Bok on June 6, 2023.
[4] Interview with Kaj Fölster on May 17, 2023, and email from Sissela Bok on June 6, 2023.

philanthropy and advising the most significant politicians of his time. He also had a special interest in financing vocational training for black people in the USA, primarily practical training in agriculture and industry, interpreted as a means to preserve blacks' subordination in American society.[5]

Frederick Keppel, the son of Irish immigrants, was educated at Columbia University, where he later became the president. He then worked internationally for the Red Cross and the US Chamber of Commerce and became president of the Carnegie Corporation in 1923, where he remained until his retirement in 1941 (Fig. 6.1).

Keppel was considered a very competent and driven bureaucrat, inspiring great respect in Gunnar Myrdal, similar to Gustav Cassel a decade earlier. Keppel, in Carnegie's spirit, had a significant interest in the status of blacks in the Anglo-Saxon part of the world. He ensured that the Carnegie Corporation funded two studies, *The Poor White Problem in South Africa* (1932) and *An African Survey* (1938), to provide a basis for white decision-makers regarding their governance over black people in English-speaking colonies in Africa. Keppel's intentions with the extensive project he entrusted to Gunnar Myrdal were largely to provide the white population in the USA with a basis for handling the racial issue in the country. He aimed to make the issue of African Americans' conditions and status a national matter but hardly sought to fundamentally change the system.[6] He also took significant risks by investing unusually large resources in the study.

Myrdal was asked to undertake the extensive project because he was seen as a neutral Scandinavian who could analyze with unbiased eyes. Gunnar accepted, feeling like a Swedish frigate from the era of great power, firing all cannons at once.[7] Keppel personally took a lot of responsibility for ensuring that the study had good office space, in the Chrysler Building in New York, and plenty of money to hire staff. In total, the Carnegie Corporation contributed 280,000 dollars—equivalent to 5 million dollars today—between 1938 and 1942, making it one of the most expensive social science research projects in US history.[8]

A few weeks later, Gunnar secured an apartment on Riverside Drive in New York for the entire family, whom he fetched from Sweden. They arrived in New York on September 10, along with Swedish statistician Richard Sterner, who would participate in the book's work, his wife Margareta, and two nannies.

---

[5] Morey (2021, Chap. 2).
[6] Morey (2021, Introduction and Chap. 6).
[7] Hirdman (2006, p. 225).
[8] Morey (2021, p. 154).

Fig. 6.1 Gunnar and Alva with their children Jan, Sissela, and Kaj on their way to the USA in 1938. (Courtesy of Tidningarnas Telegrambyrå (The Newspaper's Telegram Bureau))

First Trip to the Southern States

Keppel suggested that Myrdal familiarize himself with the race issue on-site in the Southern States before delving into the literature.[9] Therefore, in October, Gunnar and Sterner embarked on a two-month tour through the American South, guided by Jackson Davis, a reformist school bureaucrat raised in the South who advocated

---

[9] Jackson (1990, p. 90).

reforms in education for blacks within the practical framework of racial segregation. Myrdal and Sterner tired of the school environments Davis showed them and made sure to visit agricultural plantations, tobacco and textile industries, huts as dwellings, and all kinds of environments where the black population lived. They were shocked by the masses of malnourished black people, the poor tenant farmers, the impoverished families, and all the untapped resources.

Back in New York, Davis submitted a secret report to Keppel, complaining about Myrdal, whom he felt made judgments about the South too quickly. However, Keppel disregarded the report, giving Myrdal full confidence to conduct the extensive study on the blacks' situation as he planned. Davis himself continued to assist Myrdal in the writing process and eventually admitted that *An American Dilemma* surpassed his boldest hopes.[10] Gunnar Myrdal now immersed himself in existing research in the USA.[11] This included works by sociologists like Robert Park and William Fielding Ogburn from the University of Chicago, Howard Odum from the University of North Carolina, and W.E.B. Du Bois, born in 1868. Du Bois was a black professor of economics and history at Atlanta University who had conducted pioneering sociological work on the conditions of black Americans in the late nineteenth century and spent several decades outside the academic environment working for civil rights, co-founding NAACP (National Association for the Advancement of Colored People) in 1909.

Du Bois was a prominent and pioneering social researcher whose work became a model for many of today's social scientists.[12] His analysis of race, racism, and the construction of whiteness laid the foundation for current research in the field. Du Bois developed a cultural concept of race that considered shared history, law, and religion. He believed that the collective history of African Americans was shaped by the legacy of slavery, encompassing both subjugation and resistance, creating a distinct African American culture. Gunnar Myrdal highly valued Du Bois. He included many of Du Bois's books in his bibliography. However, as we will see, Myrdal chose a different approach in his analysis of the American dilemma.

Staff Recruitment

By January 1939, Myrdal had prepared an initial memorandum for Keppel on how he intended to structure the study. General ideas and value premises were discussed, but not yet the fundamental concept of the conflict between the American belief system (creed) and the actual living conditions of blacks. He addressed black organizations and economic conditions and emphasized the possibility of using social

---

[10] Morey (2021, p. 189).

[11] The list of all people Myrdal consulted at the beginning of the study is given in the preface to the book and is very long.

[12] Esseveld and Eyerman (2022).

engineering to improve the situation of African Americans. Du Bois was among those who commented on the memorandum. In the spring of 1939, the process of recruiting staff for the study began. Myrdal reached out to all leading academic institutions in the analysis of race issues: the universities of Chicago, North Carolina, and Atlanta, as well as Yale, Howard, and Columbia.

For the leadership team, Myrdal selected knowledgeable academics: Guy Johnson (a white sociologist from the University of North Carolina), Dorothy Thomas (a white sociologist and population expert who had long known Myrdal), Ralph Bunche (a black professor of political science from Howard University), Doxey Wilkerson (a black professor of education at Howard University), Paul Norgren (a white economist from Harvard University), and Richard Sterner (a Swedish statistician and population expert, with experience from the Population Commission). He also regularly consulted Donald Young, head of the Social Science Research Council.

In addition, 31 researchers were hired to write analyses on a wide range of areas. About 70 researchers were involved in the project in total. Several researchers Myrdal recruited were black and radical, some of them Marxists, which he did not find particularly strange since it was difficult to find black intellectuals who were not radical at the time.

In the summer of 1939, the idea of basing the study on American ideals began to take shape. Myrdal wrote a lengthy memorandum about the need for clear value premises. He revisited the analysis in *The Political Element in the Development of Economic Theory*. The risk was that the study would lack relevance without specified value premises.

Second Trip to the Southern States

Myrdal traveled around the country, interviewing people in various settings without always revealing the purpose of his work in the USA. The idea was to gain an understanding of people's opinions without biases. However, Myrdal realized it might be difficult for him to interview black people himself. Therefore, he invited Ralph Bunche, the first African American to earn a Ph.D. in Political Science in the USA, a radical and brilliant individual with a promising future, to accompany him on a trip to the Southern States in the fall of 1939. This journey proved to be an eye-opener for Myrdal.

Bunche and Myrdal had to stay in separate hotels and eat in different restaurants in line with the segregation of the time. Myrdal grew tired of the segregated existence and decided to defy racial separation. He took Bunche to white-only restaurants and other places. He was defiant in several contexts and didn't realize that his behavior could pose risks for Bunche (Fig. 6.2).

Myrdal himself recounted an episode where he and Bunche decided to break the racial rules. Bunche grew up in the Northwestern USA in an area with little racial discrimination. He was the captain of his school's football team and knew the rules

Fig. 6.2 Ralph Bunche and Gunnar Myrdal on a dangerous journey in the Southern States while working on *An American Dilemma*. (Courtesy of the Swedish Labor Movement's Archives and Library)

of the white world. Myrdal and Bunche entered a hotel where Myrdal had booked two rooms. They engaged in lively conversation and behaved generally like normal white people of the educated class. Like Myrdal, Bunche kept his hat on, normally impossible for a black man in the Southern States. None of the whites in the hotel lobby showed any signs of alarm. Myrdal interpreted it as ordinary white Southerners actually did not perceive Ralph's skin color when they saw them enter the hotel, relaxed and confident, and literally did not believe their eyes.[13]

It was also during this trip that Myrdal and Bunche hastily had to leave Georgia after an arrest warrant was issued for Gunnar Myrdal. He had independently visited a fanatical white woman, Mrs. Andrews, who spoke at length about black men's lust and desire for white women, leading Myrdal to ask if she was aware of the psychological theory that people with such sexual phobias actually desire what they claim to despise. When the woman realized what Myrdal meant, she threw him out of her house and called the police, who issued an arrest warrant for him on charges of obscene language.[14]

Myrdal and Bunche became close allies in the fight against racial politics. Bunche was also the person who first presented a radical critique of Myrdal's main thesis about a conflict between white people's values and racial discrimination. Bunche argued that it was not particularly difficult for many white people to rationalize their prejudices against black people. Ralph Bunche later became one of the most celebrated African Americans of the twentieth century. He was awarded the

---

[13] Myrdal (1987, p. 72).
[14] Jackson (1990, p. 124).

Nobel Peace Prize in 1950 for his work in mediating peace between Israel and Egypt as the UN's chief negotiator. In the 1960s, Bunche also became one of the civil rights movement's most important spokespersons and worked closely with Martin Luther King.

While Gunnar was fully immersed in the work on *An American Dilemma*, Alva began writing the book *Nation and Family*, describing the Swedish experiment with democratic family and population policy for an English-speaking audience. The book was based on *Crisis in the Population Question* and the Population Commission's reports. Alva Myrdal's choice of topics meant that she was categorized in the gender field for women's issues. This was also due to the organized women's world requesting her participation on various levels. She built a large network, wrote articles, gave lectures, and in 1938 was appointed vice-chair of the International Federation of Business and Professional Women.[15]

Gunnar and Alva Return to Sweden

In the fall of 1939, the World War II broke out, casting a shadow over the work of both Gunnar and Alva. Following the German invasion of Denmark and Norway on April 9, 1940, they decided to return to Sweden to serve their country. Keppel accepted this and appointed Samuel Stouffer from the University of Chicago as the acting head of the study. Richard Sterner remained in the USA, as his wife Margareta was Jewish, and continued as an important assisting resource in the work. The Myrdal family returned on the cargo ship Mathilda Thordén, a convoy vessel loaded with barrels containing explosives bound for Petsamo in Finland, from where they traveled to Stockholm with a Swedish military delegation that had unloaded war material from the ship's hold.

However, no major assignments awaited the Myrdals in Sweden. The Swedish coalition government, led by the Prime Minister Per Albin Hansson, was preoccupied with handling the ongoing war drama in the nearby world. Gunnar approached the prime minister and suggested that Sweden should prepare an effective refugee government in case of occupation and prepare radio broadcasts from abroad.[16] Per Albin listened not unsympathetically but argued against such actions. You don't think I'm afraid, said Per Albin in conclusion, which Myrdal did not. According to historian Alf W. Johansson, Per Albin Hansson's negative reaction is not hard to understand.[17] Rumors that the party was preparing for illegality could be interpreted as defeatist and create a lack of confidence in the will to defend, particularly sensitive before the upcoming parliamentary election. The intellectual friends, who had

---

[15] Lindskog (1981, p. 55).

[16] Myrdal (1982, p. 286).

[17] Johansson (1985, p. 191).

taken a stance against the Nazis, such as Herbert Tingsten, discussed unlike Gunnar Myrdal how they would need to flee the country if Sweden was invaded.

Alva Myrdal, however, did not let go of the issue and, together with Sonja Branting-Westerståhl (social democratic politician and daughter to Hjalmar Branting), wrote a memorandum to the party's executive committee with a complete program on how the party should prepare for a possible upcoming illegality. They argued that the Social Democrats, alongside military defense plans, must quickly develop cultural and political defense plans. The program contained details about psychological warfare, anti-Nazi writing series, names for replacements in important trust positions, proposals for purchasing radio transmitters and portable printing presses, and much more, but it did not lead to any known actions when it was processed by the executive committee in September 1940.[18]

In the summer of 1940, Alva and Gunnar sent their children to the countryside and began writing a book, *Kontakt med Amerika* (Contact with America), a description of the USA for Swedish readers, published in 1941. They painted an idealized picture of Roosevelt's America as a beacon of democracy in the world, inspiring hope in the fight against Nazism. It was in connection with this narrative that the idea arose that racial discrimination in the USA could be analyzed against the backdrop of its conflict with the American creed. The comparison with Nazi racial ideology led the Myrdals to emphasize that the American ideal is about equal rights for all, thus representing a clear and explicit rejection of racial ideology.

The American Creed

Gunnar and Alva Myrdal contended that America was the Western country with the most unified, clearly articulated, and vividly present system of expressed ideals for human coexistence. These principles were consciously and explicitly present in all strata of society. Every American had these ideals, the American Creed, imprinted in their mind.[19] The American Creed has three roots: the philosophy of the Enlightenment of the eighteenth century, Anglo-Saxon legal thinking, and low-church Protestant religiosity. From the Enlightenment philosophy comes the belief in individual rights. The state should be strong, but it exists for the sake of the people. All individuals have the same rights toward each other and before the state, regardless of race, religion, and external status.

The Anglo-Saxon legal concept originated in the struggle for equality before the law against the monarchy and government bureaucracy in England and was brought to America by the English Puritans during colonial times.

The Christian religion shapes America more than any other Western country, according to the Myrdals. At that time, half of the population voluntarily belonged

---

[18] Johansson (1985, p. 435).
[19] Myrdal and Myrdal (1941, p. 33).

to a church denomination. The other half was less turned away from religion and church than the average Swede. The strongly humanitarian element in the American view of society has a noticeable and conscious connection with religion.

The American political creed emerged from these three roots. It was able to develop freely, protected by two oceans, without the threat of foreign cultural, political, or military oppression.[20]

Back in the USA: Gunnar in Deep Crisis

Richard Sterner penned a letter from the USA, proposing that no task Gunnar Myrdal could undertake in Sweden would eclipse the significance of fulfilling his obligations to the work he had initiated in America.[21] Gunnar Myrdal then realized that his most important task was to complete *An American Dilemma* on-site in the USA. In January 1941, he traveled back via Moscow, the Trans-Siberian Railway to Vladivostok, boat to Japan, then to Honolulu and San Francisco, and after a two-month journey, reached New York.

He spent time in Jackson, Mississippi, gaining further insight into the conditions of segregation.[22] In Mississippi, there was a total prohibition on alcohol to harass the black population. However, liquor flowed freely in the restaurants where blacks were forbidden. Myrdal began reading his colleagues' memoranda but missed Alva; it was hard to work without her by his side.

He continued to Dartmouth College, in the small university town of Hanover, New Hampshire, to tackle the vast material that the researchers had compiled for him. But before he could seriously focus on the American dilemma, he had to deal with the contrast between his own ideals about life with Alva and how their marriage was actually playing out. Gunnar read and wrote incessantly but could not find peace. He missed Alva and wrote letter after letter to her, requesting that she leave the children behind in Sweden and come to him in the USA.[23] He claimed that her destiny was linked with his and the world's—not her "toy tasks" in Sweden. But he was beginning to grasp the American dilemma. On July 6, 1941, he wrote to Alva:

> The Western culture will survive in a few individuals superior to the nervous, short-sighted everyday people. I feel myself like an enormous accumulator of intelligence.

But beneath the surface, he was still desperate and jealous of Alva. He continued his blackmailing tactics against her, who was with the children; Jan was 14 and having problems at school, Sissela was 7, and Kaj was 4. Gunnar continued to assert that the most important relationship was between husband and wife, not between parents

---

[20] Myrdal and Myrdal (1941, p. 49).
[21] Myrdal (1982, p. 287).
[22] Myrdal (1987, p. 29).
[23] The letter collection is available at The Swedish Labour Movement's Archives and Library. Some of the letters related to the work with *An American Dilemma* are cited in Hirdman (2006).

and children. He needed Alva to complete the great book and portrayed himself in various roles in a long letter: the lone and angry man, the little child needing his mother, the patient speaking out to the analyst, the intellectual mentor scolding a student.[24]

In early July, Alva received a letter from Gunnar written on June 29, in which he threatened divorce and to take his secretary on a trip in the mountains. Alva was upset and replied with both a telegram and a letter on July 8. In the letter, she gave him the green light to have an affair with another woman but also admitted that she herself had had an affair with a man in Stockholm.[25] When Gunnar read this letter, he was upset. He now realized that he had to be as open and honest with Alva as he tried to be in his scientific work. Their marriage was at stake; he had to save it through complete honesty. He wrote a long letter and confessed to having had a brief affair with a Swedish woman in New York, an event that meant nothing to him. He also confessed to a brief encounter with a woman in the Southern States in 1938 and a few meetings the previous summer with the wife of a colleague in Stockholm.

Gunnar and Alva's marriage was now in deep crisis, but after exchanging several letters and telegrams about how difficult life could be, they decided to continue together. Alva wrote a long letter in August and announced that she had decided to save them both.[26] She argued that one cannot be in love with more than one person at the same time. She also gave reasons for her own affair. She wanted to make Gunnar realize that his own affairs could have catastrophic consequences for their marriage; he had to stop them. She wrote candidly about her own pain, criticized his behavior, and affirmed that she wished for them to reunite. Gunnar replied that he loved Alva 100% and also claimed that his own dark side threatened the good side in him. By completing the study in the USA, he would contribute to the struggle for black liberation and thereby restore his own moral status.[27]

It was also around this time, July–August 1941, that Gunnar sent a draft to Alva, with the insight that racial discrimination in the USA was the white man's problem—a moral problem between the American ideals and the subjugation that blacks were subjected to. Gunnar began by pointing out that the problem had its roots in himself in a letter on July 26, 1941:

> It must be laughable for you to read my draft of the negro book: from the first to the last page it is only about me and us and about my fatal life problem: it should be written with my blood. It shall deal with the groaning of creatures and the distress of humanity, but do not be afraid: it will still be the book about the negroes with all the facts and data, with fine curves and inspiring discussions for future research; the great pattern is my life problem, but it becomes true anyway, for it does not look coincidental but "natural" in the true sense, sprung from Nature through me: brought up to this level of generality, all the incidental in my life problem is cleaned away, and only the elementary tragedy of humanity remains: that

---

[24] Jackson (2021, p. 235).
[25] Jackson (2021, p. 238).
[26] Jackson (2021, p. 267).
[27] Jackson (2021, p. 271).

good people make life a true hell when they have to live in social relations: in family and society.

In another letter on July 23, 1941, there is a key sentence, noticed by Yvonne Hirdman: "You do not need to cry," he wrote, "it is I who am the problem, the moral problem." It is I—not you—the approach recurs in *An American Dilemma*. Alva called it the genius stroke in a telegram to Gunnar.[28] Racial discrimination is the white, American man's problem—not the blacks'.

Alva Back in the USA: Work Gains Momentum

In August, Alva sent a telegram to Gunnar, informing him of her impending departure. She secretly flew on a British military plane over Norway to Scotland but stayed a month in London. There, she spent her time writing articles about England for the Swedish press and providing British authorities with information about the situation in Finland, which she had recently visited. She then flew to Lisbon, where she had to wait another month before it was possible to fly to the USA. She was reunited with Gunnar in Princeton in October 1941, where he was completing *An American Dilemma*, and could now again devote his full attention to the work.

However, the large staff from the initial phase was no longer there. Gunnar Myrdal was supported by Richard Sterner and a new assistant, Arnold Rose, a young sociologist from the University of Chicago. Both played a central role in drafting the book's many chapters.[29] Rose also became important as an editor for the English text since he was the only one among the three who had English as his native language.

Alva Myrdal also played a central role in the creation of the book. She was particularly important for the text describing the similarities between the situations of women and African Americans. The text dedicated to this issue was a work of Alva, though it was Gunnar who held the pen.[30] The Myrdals argued that the similarity in how African Americans and women are treated in society is not coincidental, as both groups' positions originated in a paternalistic social order. Frederick Keppel, president of the Carnegie Corporation, however, believed that such a description could offend both groups and persuaded Gunnar Myrdal to move the text to an appendix.[31]

By early September 1942, the manuscript was nearly completed. Gunnar Myrdal handed it over to Arnold Rose, who was tasked with the final editing of the book.

---

[28] Hirdman (2006, p. 252).
[29] Jackson (1990, p. 161).
[30] Hirdman (2006, p. 262).
[31] The text constitutes Appendix 5 in the book, see Myrdal (1944, p. 1073) and Jackson (2021, p. 279).

When it was published in early 1944, it consisted of 45 chapters and 10 appendices—nearly 1500 pages in total.

The Value Premises

In *An American Dilemma* it is primarily the introduction and the first three methodological appendices that deepen and concretize how value premises play a crucial role in the analysis. In the introduction to the book, Myrdal claimed that it deals with the moral dilemma between, on one hand, the American creed in thoughts, speech, and actions under the influence of high national and Christian ideals and, on the other hand, how values are expressed in reality, when individuals and groups, with the help of prejudices and self-interest, unite against other individuals or groups. Myrdal pointed out that the dilemma regarding the situation of the African American population involved a century-long delay in public morals adapting to American ideals. The African American population had not yet received the elementary civic and political rights that these ideals prescribe, nor had they been given the opportunity to earn their livelihood on equal terms.[32]

Myrdal specified the difference between "beliefs" and "valuations." He stated that people with "opinions" express both their beliefs and their valuations. It is common for people not to distinguish between what they think they know and what they like or dislike. Alva Myrdal played a central role in assessing how people's own values and inner conflicts can influence the analysis.[33]

In the book's first appendix on methodology, Myrdal (1944, p. 1028), he noted:

> The expressed valuations and beliefs brought forward as motives for specific action, or inaction, are selected in relation to the expediencies of the occasion. They are the "good" reasons rather than the 'true' reasons. In short, they are "rationalizations."

In the same page, he also stated that even repressed values influence actual behavior:

> In this treaty, therefore, behavior is conceived of as being typically the outcome of a moral compromise of heterogeneous valuations, operating on various planes of generality and rising in varying degrees and at different occasions to the level of consciousness.

Myrdal observed in the book's main text that in the USA, many beliefs about the African American population serve a purpose, to rationalize and maintain racial oppression. The African American population's low standard of living and cultural isolation contribute to the belief in negative characteristics of African Americans as a group or caste. These characteristics are perceived as innate by many whites, especially in the American South. The whites' beliefs about African Americans become more important in the analysis of the current situation than various, more objective,

---

[32] Myrdal (1944, p. 24).

[33] Alva Myrdal familiarized herself with the survey research used to find out people's opinions on various issues by companies like Fortune and Gallup. She was also interested in the bias present in measurements of IQ among different groups, see Cherrier (2009, p. 47).

facts about the African Americans' situation. The whites' beliefs are, therefore, opportunistic, according to Myrdal. They have a definite purpose; they keep down the African American population group, or caste.[34]

Thus, Myrdal established that it is the whites' beliefs about African Americans that constitute a fundamental dilemma in the USA. Once this is done, the analysis begins of what strategies exist to address the dilemma. The analysis is then deepened by describing his own value premises in line with the framework he had introduced in *The Political Element in the Development of Economic Theory*.

Three Potential Strategies Affecting Whites' Prejudices

Myrdal argued that if the value premise were to reduce the bias in whites' beliefs about the African American population, there were three strategies. The first would be to improve the status and behavior of African Americans, which is made difficult because the root problem is the whites' prejudices. The second strategy would be to correct the ordinary white person's own observations of the African American population and demonstrate why they are incorrect. Scientific studies are needed of what objectively matters for the African American group's conditions. Scientifically based information can then be disseminated through media and schools to demonstrate the inaccuracies in many observations. A third strategy could be to more directly focus on the moral question and make it clear to white people that their beliefs are in conflict with American ideals. It's crucial to reinforce the significance of these ideals in valuing all groups equally. Any effort to alleviate racial oppression reduces the moral conflict in the heart of an American and the need to defend false racial perceptions. All three strategies have a role to play, according to Myrdal, since each can have a certain effect and collectively contribute to turning the tide towards a better path.[35] Meanwhile, Myrdal emphasized the need for thorough studies to distinguish opportunistic notions from more objectively founded facts with the help of science.

Myrdal took great care to clearly explain the background of the value premises he chose for his analysis in the book. The central hypothesis is the theory of the vicious circle. The attitudes and beliefs of white people keep the black population down in several respects and contribute to living conditions that, in turn, reinforce white prejudices.

[34] Myrdal (1944, p. 111).
[35] Myrdal (1944, pp. 109–110).

Value Premises on Economic Inequality

Regarding economic inequality, Myrdal identified the following three value premises:

Black people should be given equal opportunities. This value premise was the most important, according to Myrdal. To the extent that poverty in the black community is caused by discrimination, this value premise challenges the application of the American creed's principle of equal opportunities, "regardless of race, belief, skin color," in practice. Thus, Myrdal also placed the concept of discrimination at the center of his broad analysis of the American dilemma. The value premise of equal opportunities becomes a central starting point for Myrdal in later works.

No American population group's standard of living should be allowed to fall below a certain minimum level. This value premise acknowledged the importance of the living standards of the black group (and other groups). It justifies that living conditions should be subject to political assessment and supports the idea of welfare policy.

Economic inequality itself is not wrong. This value premise may seem strange to a modern reader of the book. The main reason he chose it was to stay within the framework of the conservative reform agenda in the American economic debate of the time. Class analysis and class divisions have never been a central part of the American creed, which rather focuses on equal opportunities for all individuals.

Vicious and Virtuous Circles

It was in working on *An American Dilemma* that Gunnar Myrdal seriously began to develop the theory of vicious or virtuous circles, originally from Knut Wicksell's monetary policy book.[36] In fact, Myrdal was so inspired by the idea that he made the theory of the cumulative process the most central value premise in the book, later using it in several other works. The idea is that an economic system, a society, or a social group can be affected by an initial change that propagates and intensifies in various ways, leading away from the starting point. This can involve both negative and positive spirals: in the economy, about inflation—or deflation—that continues as long as the central bank's policy rate is too low—or too high—relative to the rate that gives price stability.

In *An American Dilemma*, the value premise is that the discrimination by white Americans contributes to the low standard of living, education, health, and values of black Americans, which in turn reinforces white prejudices and antipathies against blacks.

---

[36] Wicksell (1898).

The following quote taken from Myrdal (1944, p. 208) and originally from Johnson et al. (1935) about the conditions of black sharecroppers in the Southern States provides a background:

> Shiftlessness and laziness are reported as reasons for the dependent state, whereas in fact, in so far as they exist, they are not necessarily inherent, but are caused by the very conditions of the share-cropping system. It is a notorious and shameful fact that the stock arguments employed against any serious efforts to improve the lot of cotton tenant are based upon the social and cultural conditions which tenancy itself creates. The mobility of the tenant, his dependency, his lack of ambition, shiftlessness, his ignorance and poverty, the lethargy of his pellagra-ridden body, provide a ready excuse for keeping him under a stern paternalistic control. There is not a single alleged trait which, where true, does not owe its source and continuance to its imposed status itself.

A problem Myrdal noted is that the separation between blacks and whites tends to contribute to a self-fulfilling vicious cycle.[37] Discrimination and working conditions mean that black Americans are not allowed to work in certain industries; where they are allowed, they cannot do so alongside white workers; they are forced into dirty and poorly paid jobs that whites do not want; white people rarely meet black people and do not understand them. The black people's tasks mean that they are kept far down and far away from the lives of the whites in a way that creates a stereotypical image of them, which in turn confirms the whites' prejudices and reinforces discrimination.

Discrimination manifested itself in several ways. Many white workers generally think that blacks should have equal chances at work, but oppose their participation in the industry or company where they themselves are employed. Many customers object to being served by a black person unless he is in a clearly subordinate position. Many employers believe that black people are inferior workers to whites, except in dirty, heavy, hot, and other unattractive occupations. They also greatly consider white customers' and white workers' prejudices in this matter.

Discrimination was self-preserving in this respect. Myrdal assumes, as an example, what can happen if a single employer stops discriminating against blacks while all other employers continue. This leads to that unique employer attracting a large proportion of black workers, who flock to his company. Rumors spread, and the proportion of blacks exceeds that of whites in the company.

Eventually, a company may find itself in a situation where no white workers are employed any longer. The conclusion from this simple example is that *discrimination breeds discrimination.*[38] Myrdal himself acknowledged a predecessor, Edwin Embree, in applying the theory of vicious circles to the experiences of African Americans in the USA. Myrdal (1944, p. 1069) citing Embree (1931):

> There is a vicious cycle in caste. At the outset, the despised group is usually inferior in certain of the accepted standards of the controlling class. Being inferior, members of the degraded caste are denied the privileges and opportunities of their fellows and so are pushed still further down and then are regarded with that much less respect, and therefore are more

---

[37] Myrdal (1944, p. 391).

[38] Myrdal (1944, p. 381).

rigorously denied advantages, and so around and around in the vicious circle. Even when the movement starts to reverse itself—as it most certainly has in the case of the black people—there is a desperately long unwinding as a slight increase in goodwill gives a little greater chance and this leads to a little higher accomplishment and that to increased respect and so slowly upward toward equality of opportunity, of regard, and of status.

On this quote, Myrdal commented that although there is an element of time delay, the theory of vicious circles is a reason for optimism rather than pessimism, as the cumulative process goes both ways.

Let's now take a more detailed look at how Myrdal himself analyzed vicious and virtuous circles. He started from a system where a primary change affecting any of the core parts of the system—the economy, the living conditions of black Americans, or the prejudices of whites—would contribute to changes in the other parts of the system and lead to an overall transformation.[39] A central idea is that no single cause is solely responsible for where the process leads. The theory of the cumulative process describes how many factors can interact and reinforce or counteract each other.

Myrdal analyzed a system where he assumed that the prejudices of whites and the inferior conditions of African Americans mutually reinforced each other. If no changes occur, the two forces can seemingly balance each other. But if one of the forces changes, a process begins where the other force reacts and contributes to a continuous change in the system as a whole, which is greater than the initial change.[40] Myrdal, for example, posited that if the prejudices of whites decrease and thus discrimination, the living standards of black Americans could increase, which in turn leads to fewer prejudices from the white side and so on.

In a more detailed description of the theory, Myrdal suggested that many more subvariables to the living conditions of black Americans could be considered.[41] The prejudices and discrimination of the white group are assumed, via the cumulative process, to affect all subcomponents of living conditions. These conditions include employment, wages, housing, diet, clothing, health, education, stable family, cleanliness, punctuality, reliability, law-abidingness, social loyalty. The assumption is now that if the level of one of these components moves towards the level of the white group, the whites' prejudices decrease. This, in turn, leads to improvements in all subcomponents of the black population's conditions. The effect of an improvement in a subvariable of the blacks' conditions can thus, through its reducing effect on the whites' discrimination, lead to an improvement in all subcomponents of the blacks' living conditions, a strong assumption. It is an example of how the total strength of a cumulative, positive spiral can become greater than the initial change if the theory's assumptions are met.

---

[39] Myrdal (1944, p. 208).
[40] Myrdal (1944, p. 76).
[41] Myrdal (1944, p. 1066).

The Role of Expectations

The formation of expectations was also given a place in this work. Myrdal notes a possible difference between how the whites' prejudices might be influenced by an actual increase in the living conditions of black Americans and an expected increase in them. He assumed that an actual increase in the conditions of African Americans leads to reduced prejudices among whites against blacks, at least after a certain time. But he did not exclude that an expected improvement in the blacks' living conditions might instead lead to increased prejudices, especially in the short term, and particularly in the Southern States. According to Myrdal, it is entirely possible to work with the hypothesis that poor whites react negatively to expectations of improved conditions for the black population, even in the slightly longer term. This is a question for science to resolve.[42]

Myrdal was thus keen to include the dominant importance of the time factor in the analysis. The effect is influenced by which variable is analyzed. An increase in employment for black people tends to quickly contribute to a higher standard of living, while better education and health standards take longer to achieve, which delays the effect when a virtuous circle is about to be established.

The Structure and Statistical Basis of the Book

An American Dilemma was written from an institutional perspective with a focus on a broad analysis of various legal, social, and economic institutions and conditions. The theoretical framework of the book was derived from several social disciplines. However, the content of the book is not structured according to concepts and theoretical starting points.

Instead, the structure is determined by the institutional framework: the economy (agriculture, labor market, business, public sector); politics (ideologies, party structure, legal and illegal activities, voting participation and absence of suffrage); justice (police, courts, violence and threats); social inequality (segregation, education, housing, social and sexual relations); social stratification (caste and class structure); leadership and coordinated actions (patterns of leadership, protest movements, church, newspapers). Each main section begins with a historical look back at slavery and its consequences for the current theme.

Myrdal used the concept of caste to describe the status of black Americans. The idea is that the caste concept captures the white group's way of treating black people differently because of their skin color, an example being the taboo against marriage across racial boundaries. Protests against segregation are judged to be quite inward-looking and the organizations are led by a petty-bourgeois black elite; the influence of the working class is considered too weak. Myrdal also analyzed the role of the

---

[42] Myrdal (1944, p. 1068).

church for African Americans but underestimated its importance and later realized that he had not foreseen in the book how important the church would become in the struggle for civil rights.[43]

The book utilized a large amount of official quantitative statistics for the labor market, education, health care, and household income and expenses, which in many cases classify residents by "race" and enable a comparison of black and white people from different perspectives. Myrdal also set up his own projects to collect data where such data were missing, for example, for the political system and the judiciary. For the analysis of the central issue of the spread of poverty, data from censuses are combined with data from the labor market to illuminate differences in land ownership, access to financing, wage differentials, occupations, and so on.

The official statistics showed, for example, that black families are discriminated against in terms of access to public services, housing, and other things, despite contributing as much in taxes. Segregation was a way for white politicians at the local level to keep down public expenditures, which spoke for the need for federal legislation to enforce fair behavior at the local level.

The book also used qualitative evidence, based on the commission's own interviews, newspapers, and popular culture, often indicated in footnotes to the main text. An important reason for the interviews was to clarify denials, rationalizations as well as contradictions when people talk about their own values in the race issue.

Policy Proposals

Myrdal's policy proposals for solving the American dilemma were largely about interventions at the federal and local levels.

A central underlying premise in Myrdal's policy message was the concept of assimilation. He assumed that assimilation into American ideals was a kind of core value inherent in these ideals. The assumption was that all ethnic groups in the USA strive to be assimilated. Myrdal chose to ignore research in the area that did not support this assumption.[44] He also saw the American nuclear family as an ideal for black people, whose family relationships were broken by the devastating living conditions of slavery and migrant labor.

At the federal level, Myrdal's policy proposals were about initiatives for full employment, migration, and vocational training policies that would help the poor in rural areas in the Southern States to jobs in the cities in the north, educational efforts to encourage companies to hire black people, and support for family planning. The Supreme Court should ensure that the constitutional amendments on equal rights to

---

[43] Jackson (1990, p. 223).

[44] The research included works by Randolph Bourne, Horace Kellen, Robert Park & W.I. Thomas, see Jackson (1990, p. 225).

higher education and voting rights in the Southern States were complied with. He also called for a national education program aimed at prejudices.

In the Southern States, Myrdal suggested that the poll tax be abolished. African Americans' voting rights should be gradually extended. A federal program was needed to build schools and a better program for police training. There was also a need for support for civil organizations for legal aid and support for organizing trade unions for black rural workers.

Myrdal, however, did not say much about where the political and economic resources for the changes would come from.[45] Obviously, he counted on Roosevelt's New Deal as a first step towards a welfare state and a stronger mobilization of resources for African Americans, especially at the local level, where the welfare deficiencies were so extensive.

The Reception of an American Dilemma

The book was published in January 1944 and met with positive reviews in the major newspapers and several academic journals. Many of the reviewers were white intellectuals who saw Myrdal's book as a sharper and more detailed analysis of racial discrimination than they had previously read. Many black intellectuals were also positive about the book's analysis and the message that the race problem fundamentally stemmed from the whites' conceptions. W.E.B. Du Bois, the most senior black American researcher in the field, praised the book as a monumental study without competition.[46] However, critical voices pointed out weaknesses in the book's description of black culture and the use of the caste concept, which doesn't consider the dynamic developmental possibilities mentioned elsewhere in the book. In the Southern States, the book was met with polite skepticism and some frontal attacks from white intellectuals.

There were also examples of serious researchers who doubted the idea that white people actually experience a moral dilemma in the way assumed.[47] There was no strong sociological support for the belief that Americans truly adhere to the American ideals. However, it has also been argued that this type of criticism missed Myrdal's important point.[48] He continually heard in schools and political assemblies that American ideals were central to people's worldviews. By basing his analysis on the gap between ideals and reality, Myrdal opened a discussion that otherwise would not have occurred, a way to navigate through difficult scientific terrain.

---

[45] Jackson (1990, p. 211).
[46] Jackson (1990, p. 245).
[47] Jackson (1990, p. 253).
[48] Lyon (2004, p. 207).

Another type of criticism came from the left. Myrdal was considered too positive about the reform willingness of the white upper class.[49] By asserting that the problem is about moral values in the white person's heart, he effectively obscured the fact that racial discrimination was caused by the economic system. Myrdal's analysis risked shifting focus away from the fight against the established capitalist system.

Overall, the positive response to An American Dilemma was much stronger than the criticism. Myrdal's book began to be compared with classic works about the USA by Alexis de Tocqueville and James Bryce, and it gained an extraordinary position in the postwar debate.[50] In the first decades after its publication, the book was considered the leading analysis of the race issue in the USA. It became a textbook at universities and a guideline in many policy issues, and it was the reference point that long dominated the debate on race in the USA.

As early as 1946, President Harry S. Truman issued an executive order and established a committee for human rights. In 1947, this committee published a report specifying the federal government's central roles in addressing Myrdal's dilemma.

Myrdal's book was hugely significant for the civil rights movement and the legislation on civil rights. In 1954, the Supreme Court decided that all segregation of races in schools and other places was against the American constitution and referred, among other things, to Myrdal's book. The decision became an important support for the fight for equal rights in the USA and influenced many subsequent legal cases. We will return in Chaps. 12 and 14 to the book's significance and the development of the American dilemma.

References

An African Survey (1938) A study of problems arising in Africa South of the Sahara. Published under the auspices of the Royal Institute of International Affairs and funded by the Carnegie Corporation. Oxford University Press, London
Bok S (1987) Alva, ett kvinnoliv. Bonniers, Avesta. English edition: Bok S (1991) Alva Myrdal. A daughter's memoir. Radcliffe biography series. Perseus Publishing, Cambridge
Cherrier B (2009) Gunnar Myrdal and the scientific way to social democracy, 1914–1968. J Hist Econ Thought 31(1):33–55
Embree E (1931) Brown America. The Viking Press, New York
Esseveld J, Eyerman R (2022) WEB Du Bois Ras, institutionell rasism och social ojämlikhet (WEB Du Bois race, institutional racism, and social inequality). In: Eklund L, Isenberg B (eds) Sociologins klassiker Upptäckter och återupptäckter. Studentlitteratur, Lund
Hirdman Y (2006) Det tänkande hjärtat. Boken om Alva Myrdal. Ordfront, Stockholm. English edition: Hirdman Y (2008) Alva Myrdal: the passionate mind. Indiana University Press, Bloomington

---

[49] Jackson (1990, p. 258).
[50] Alexis de Tocqueville was a French writer whose work, *Democracy in America*, was published in two parts in 1835 and 1840. James Bryce was a British jurist, historian and ambassador to the USA whose book on the institutions of the USA, *The American Commonwealth*, was published in 1888.

Jackson W (1990) Gunnar Myrdal and America's conscience. Social engineering and racial liberalism 1938–1987. The University of North Carolina Press, Chapel Hill/London

Jackson W (2021) Alva and Gunnar Myrdal in Sweden and America 1898–1945. Unsparing honesty. Routledge, New York/London

Johansson A (1985) Per Albin och kriget (Per Albin and the war). Tiden, Stockholm

Johnson C, Embree E, Alexander W (1935) The collapse of the cotton tenancy. New edition 2013. The University of North Carolina Press, Chapel Hill

Lindskog L (1981) Alva Myrdal. 'Förnuftet måste segra' (Alva Myrdal. Reason Must Prevail). Sveriges Radios Förlag, Kristianstad

Lyon S (2004) Researching race relations Myrdal's American dilemma from a methodological perspective. Acta Sociol 47:203–216

Morey M (2021) White philanthropy, Carnegie Corporation's an American dilemma and the making of a white world order. The University of North Carolina Press, Chapel Hill

Myrdal G (1944) An American Dilemma the Negro problem and modern democracy, 1st edn. Harper & Row Publishers, New York; cited edition: Transaction Fiftieth Anniversary Edition 1996, Transaction Publishers, New Jersey

Myrdal G (1982) Hur styrs landet? (how is the country governed?). Rabén & Sjögren, Stockholm

Myrdal J (1984) En annan värld (another world). Norstedts, Stockholm

Myrdal G (1987) Historien om an American dilemma (the tale of an American dilemma revisited). SNS Publishing, Stockholm

Myrdal A, Myrdal G (1941) Kontakt med Amerika (contact with America). Bonniers, Stockholm

The Poor White Problem in South Africa (1932) Report of the Carnegie commission. Pro ecclesiadrukkery, Stellenbosch

Wicksell K (1898) Geldzins und Güter Preise: Eine Studie über den Tauschwert des Geldes bestimmenden Ursachen. Verlag von Gustav Fisher, Jena. English edition: Wicksell K (1936) Interest and prices: a study of the causes regulating the value of money. Macmillan and Co, London

Chapter 7
Postwar Planner and Trade Minister

During World War II, Gunnar Myrdal, Willy Brandt, and Bruno Kreisky led the Little International in Stockholm and published a peace manifesto proposing cooperation among nations on a federal basis, embedded in a new global organization to succeed the League of Nations. Gunnar Myrdal also played a significant role in the Swedish Post-War Council of the Labor Movement which called for full employment, fair distribution, greater efficiency, and more democracy in business. It argued for a planned economy without extensive nationalization of industry. Instead, it focused on supporting private sector production with policies to maintain economic stability and full employment. Gunnar Myrdal served as Trade Minister after WWII but faced challenges, including controversy over trade agreements with the Soviet Union and domestic economic crises. Alva Myrdal worked on refugee aid and postwar reconstruction, advocating for Sweden's moral responsibility in Europe's recovery. The Myrdal Commission, led by Gunnar, developed comprehensive economic policies for Sweden's post-war era but was met with mistrust from business organizations and political opponents. Ultimately, Gunnar Myrdal's tenure as Trade Minister was marked by controversy and opposition, leading to his departure in 1947. Despite challenges, his ideas were highly influential in shaping Sweden's post-war policies and modernization efforts.

Introduction

An *American Dilemma* turned out to be the pinnacle of Gunnar Myrdal's career. This book is considered his most prominent and internationally influential work. After dealing with the American race issue, Myrdal returned to domestic matters for a period shorter than anticipated. Gunnar Myrdal became a leading politician in Sweden during some of the war years, played a central role in postwar planning, and joined the government after the war but failed as a minister. His strong opinions on central issues clashed with a challenging reality. Alva Myrdal engaged in refugee work and preparations for Europe's reconstruction during the war.[1] Their combined efforts in social reforms and postwar planning influenced Sweden's development for a long time.

The Little International

The Swedish coalition government took office in December 1939 with Per Albin Hansson as Prime Minister. Other Social Democrats in the coalition government included Finance Minister Ernst Wigforss and Social Minister Gustav Möller.

After completing his work on *An American Dilemma*, Gunnar Myrdal resumed his professorship at Stockholm University. Neither he nor Alva Myrdal could stay away from Swedish politics. In 1942, they hired a housekeeper, Karin Anger, to take care of home and children, and she stayed as a "substitute mother" for almost 8 years.[2] Jan was 14, Sissela 7, and Kaj 5.

During the war, Gunnar and Alva Myrdal were drawn into discussions about postwar planning among social democratic refugee circles in Stockholm, including Willy Brandt, later Chancellor of West Germany, and Bruno Kreisky, later Chancellor of Austria. Gunnar Myrdal became chairman and Willy Brandt secretary of what became known as the Little International.[3] Unlike other social democratic organizations at the time, the Little International focused on a continental social democracy attempting to serve as a bridge between the West and the East. The organization represented 14 different nationalities, including many Scandinavians and Germans, as well as Czechs, Poles, and Hungarians.[4] The Little International published a peace manifesto authored by Brandt, Myrdal, and Kreisky proposing regional economic and social cooperation among nations on a federal basis, embedded in a new global organization to succeed the League of Nations and act as a bridge between the Anglo-Saxon powers and the Soviet Union.[5] Such an organization was established after the war with Gunnar Myrdal as head of the UN's Economic Commission for Europe. Several other members of the Little International in Stockholm later took up international roles. David Owen, a liaison officer for the British Royal Air Force during the war, became Assistant Secretary-General of the UN and was the one who suggested Myrdal as head of the UN's Economic Commission. Polish economist Wladek Malinowski became head of the UN's regional section, coordinating activities for the UN Economic Commission under Myrdal's leadership.

---

[1] In the 1940s, Alva Myrdal also focused extensively on educational issues and became a member of the 1946 School Commission, see Lindskog (1981, p. 78).
[2] Bok (1987, p. 163).
[3] Lindskog (1981, p. 73).
[4] Stinsky (2018, p. 53).
[5] The manifesto was published on May 1, 1943, see Stinsky (2018, p. 54).

The Post-War Council of the Labor Movement

Alva Myrdal became active in the Social Democratic Women's Association and, along with August Lindberg, Chairman of LO (the Swedish Trade Union Confederation), proposed in December 1942 that the social democrats should undertake postwar planning.[6] The Post-War Council of the Labor Movement was established in April 1943, on the suggestion of LO's leadership, which in turn had received the proposal from the new head of LO's research department, Richard Sterner, a long-time and central collaborator of Gunnar Myrdal. The Council addressed political issues of the postwar period, led by Wigforss, and consisted of representatives from the union, the party, the women's association, and the youth association, with Sterner as the main secretary. Alva Myrdal became a member representing the women's association.[7] Gunnar Myrdal was called in as an expert, quickly gaining significant influence. In a comprehensive memo in July 1943, he criticized the government's policy on various points, including fiscal policy. The Council published its action program at the end of April 1944, demanding full employment, fair distribution, greater efficiency, and more democracy in business, among other things. Wigforss had finalized the text just before the May Day demonstrations and the party congress.

Economic planning played a key role in the postwar program. The debate on economic planning in Sweden had been ongoing since the mid-1920s and at times was very intense.[8] The most well-known academic opponents of economic planning were Gustav Cassel, Eli Heckscher, and Gösta Bagge, who warned that it would lead to a loss of citizens' freedoms, while the main academic proponents were Bertil Ohlin and Gunnar Myrdal, who argued that economic planning did not equate to socialism. The rational and efficient use of production resources was central for both Ohlin and Myrdal. Economic planning was already discussed at the Social Democrats' party congress in 1932. Ernst Wigforss then stated in a speech that economic planning is possible without nationalizing the economy. Political scientist Leif Lewin argues in his thesis *Planhushållningsdebatten* (The Economic Planning Debate) that the socialization theory was thus replaced by the economic planning ideology at the party congress.[9] The goal for the Social Democrats was still freedom from economic misery and the coercion of capital. By increasing the state's economic influence, the freedom of many people could be realized. Sten O. Karlsson in his thesis *Det intelligenta samhället* (The Intelligent Society) argues that the vision of the welfare state was transformed into a laboratory for creating a highly efficient societal machine under the leadership of social engineers like Gunnar Myrdal.[10]

---

[6] Appelqvist (2000, p. 96).

[7] At this time, Alva Myrdal was also a member of the committee for international aid. She remained vice president of the International Federation of Business and Professional Women.

[8] Carlson (2018).

[9] Lewin (1967, p. 75).

[10] Karlsson (2001, p. 549).

Gunnar Myrdal himself claimed that the first time he heard about economic planning was in a presentation by Dag Hammarskjöld sometime toward the end of the 1920s.[11] In his inaugural lecture as professor at Stockholm University in March 1934, he gave an overview of the roots and purpose of economic planning.[12] He argued that the legacy came from both the left, socialism, and the right, conservatism. For the left, it was about replacing the private capitalist market economy with a planned, social needs-based economy. For the conservatives, economic planning was a way for the state to contribute to a lasting and class-appropriate organization of production, primarily benefiting the upper classes. Common to both the left and the right's economic planning ideas, according to Myrdal (1935), was a rejection of the liberal ideology that harmony arises if the market is left undisturbed. Economic planning demands—from both the left and the right—had contributed to a dynamic view of society and social institutions, breaking down and relativizing the liberal static societal abstraction under "the system." Myrdal argued that deep economic crises greatly contributed to increased state intervention in production. The volume of government actions had become so large that coordination was necessary for effectiveness. Myrdal envisioned a systematic regulation of production to ensure certain basic needs of citizens. However, there was a risk that the interests of different social groups would not align. Hence, a robust economic policy was needed, according to Myrdal (1935), to ensure the alignment of citizens' interests, which was feasible especially due to unemployment and the surplus of other unused production resources.

Gunnar Myrdal played a central role in the development of the post-war program of the labor movement in 1943–1944. According to the introduction to the program, the primary task ahead is to coordinate economic activity into a planned economy so that labor and material resources are consistently utilized for efficient production.[13] Such coordination should occur under societal leadership and be oriented such that individual interests are subordinated to the goals collectively pursued. The main thesis of the program was that the private sector is inefficient. Post-war, an economic policy in line with Keynesian and Stockholm School of Economics' central ideas was needed. This meant maintaining the lowest possible interest rates and actively using fiscal policy to stabilize the economy. However, active fiscal policy supporting total demand for goods and services would not be sufficient to maintain employment. Even the excessively high unemployment during economic booms needed to be eliminated.[14] This involved stimulating the total supply in the economy, both corporate investments and labor mobility. With supply-side policies, more resources could be mobilized. The business sector needed a new organization, and society had to be transformed in a socialist direction, but the program did not demand a general nationalization of industry. Myrdal's and the program's focus was

---

[11] Landberg (2012, p. 101).
[12] Myrdal (1935).
[13] Arbetarrörelsens efterkrigsprogram (1944).
[14] Lundberg (1983, p. 136).

not on state measures like public works. Instead, the policy should ensure that the business sector's own production was maintained. It would be supported with general demand support and subsidies for increased production on inventory.

The points in the postwar program concerning the business sector also showed an understanding of the conditions of business, and that everyone loses when enterprise falters during a crisis or depression. It was noted that if private enterprise successfully fulfills the task of providing the masses with as much of life's goods as possible with full resource utilization, it can be allowed to operate roughly as before in the future. The most important task must be to maintain full capacity in the ordinary business sector.

However, there were several controversial points in the program.[15] Regarding planning of investment activity, the expansion of an extensive state business banking operation was proposed. The insurance industry was to be nationalized to achieve rationalization gains and increased control over the capital market. Investment activities would be led by a public cooperation body. Another point demanded nationalizations in areas where private enterprise led to mismanagement or monopoly.

Although Gunnar Myrdal advocated for planned economy concepts, he did not question the private sector and its profit motive. Neither Myrdal nor Wigforss pushed for extensive nationalizations of the business sector as proposed in France and Britain at the same time.[16] In his book on monetary policy, Myrdal (1931, p. 127), noted that elements of a planned economy might be needed to preserve an unbroken development of Sweden's democratic and private capitalist structure. Together with Alva, he also wrote in a later book, Myrdal and Myrdal (1941), that in Sweden, the state had always owned land, forests, and waterfalls, controlled iron mines, operated banks, and built the most important railway lines. They pointed out that a tobacco monopoly was introduced by a right-wing government and a liquor monopoly thanks to the temperance movement. Most public institutions were owned and operated by municipalities and had been built up by conservative local politicians with a sense for good business. They claimed, with some exaggeration, that Sweden stopped socializing only when social democracy came to power.

It is also clear that after the war, social democracy abandoned many ideas in the postwar program: socialization of the credit market, investment planning, socialization of monopolies for efficiency reasons or industries with too little large-scale production. The coordination of production under societal leadership did not materialize.[17] One reason was the liberalization of world trade, which meant that Swedish trade escaped the restrictions expected to persist after the war. The dominant issue in the postwar program became instead the policy for full employment, which later became central in Sweden. The policy for full employment was built up with innovative labor market policy, under wide consensus in parliament, a decade after the

---

[15] Bergström (1977, p. 125).
[16] Appelqvist (2000, p. 104).
[17] Bergström (1977, p. 133).

program was developed.[18] Erik Lundberg spoke of an optimized market economy under general state control.[19] It was a combination of free foreign trade and strict general fiscal policy that yielded competition-driven prices and set tight limits for cost compensation. Emerging unemployment was slowed down through systematic selective subsidy measures, The state thereby gained general power over structural development.

Interlude in the USA

The coalition government decided in 1943 to send Gunnar Myrdal to the USA to investigate trade relations and restore good relations with the superpower after Sweden's policy of adaptation to Germany. He was given diplomatic status as a Councelor at the Swedish Embassy in Washington. Tore Browaldh, a young lawyer and economist and future head of one of the largest banks, Handelsbanken, accompanied him as a personal assistant. The journey across the Atlantic to the USA took place in four stages in the summer of 1943. An ABA plane took them to Scotland, dropped them off, and was then shot down by the Germans on the way back. Gunnar and Tore boarded a troop train to London, then a troop transport plane to Ireland, and finally a Pan American flying boat flew them to New York.[20]

Tore Browaldh learned much from Myrdal's work approach during their stay in the USA. Browaldh had learned shorthand before the trip, which was very useful for recording the personal conversations Gunnar had with important people. Gunnar read copiously and made excerpts from documents that were then systematized by topic.[21] His other method of gathering facts was through personal conversations with various notables. The subjects of these in-depth interviews were a cross-section of the academic and political world, in particular the leadership of the trade unions, the leaders of major corporations and also a number of journalists. He had great respect for the integrity of American journalists and their incorruptibility regarding data publication.

In the USA, Gunnar Myrdal also met several well-known economists such as Alvin Hansen, one of the key Keynesians at the time, but the impression from the meetings was that the experts responsible for the major reforms of the New Deal were losing influence in Washington. This formed a rather dark background for the new book he began working on, about the risks in the world after the war.

---

[18] Bergström (1977, p. 133).
[19] Lundberg (1983, p. 138).
[20] Browaldh (1998).
[21] Appelqvist and Andersson (1998, p. 26).

Alva Myrdal's Work with Refugee Aid and Preparations for Reconstruction

During this time, Alva Myrdal felt that her work was not taken as seriously as her husband's. Yet, she had been the main secretary for the Women's Work Committee's report in 1938, participated in the workers' movement postwar program, and published several of her own books, the latest being *Nation and Family*, published in 1941 and translated into Swedish a few years later. She perceived her activities as being seen as a female and thus subordinate version of Gunnar Myrdal's work. She found it offensive to be compared only to other women and not to be compared with men, who lived in a sphere with higher public status.[22] However, she worked tirelessly as a journalist, author, helping refugees, and preparing for the reconstruction after the war. Uno Willers, future national librarian, used to serve Alva Myrdal as a young official at the Riksdag Library in the summer of 1941, assisting her with publications from the International Labour Office. Willers had never experienced such an intense concentration on plowing through the material—and requesting new. Alva Myrdal did not give a moment's time to the surroundings and irrelevant details.[23]

Swedish policy toward Jewish refugees seeking protection from Nazi Germany was for a long time very restrictive, due to complacency, discrimination, and national selfishness. The author Göran Rosenberg has pointed out that as late as February 1942, when the forced deportations of European Jews "eastward" were already known to the Swedish Foreign Ministry, Jewish "emigrants" were denied residence permits in Sweden.[24] He also noted that for the few who were granted permission at this time, it was usually too late. After the deportation of Norwegian Jews in the fall of 1942, Sweden began to open its doors to Jews fleeing the threat of the Holocaust.[25] When Jews in Denmark were threatened with deportation in the fall of 1943, the Swedish government declared its willingness to accept them all, and nearly all were smuggled across the Øresund.

Alva Myrdal regularly wrote articles and columns on social policy, foreign policy, and the need for reconstruction after the war. She was among those who early on drew attention to the Holocaust, writing in April 1943 Aftontidningen, quoted in Myrdal (2011, Section II, Article 5):

---

[22] Niskanen (2007, pp. 122–124).

[23] Willers (1971).

[24] Rosenberg (2021, ch.: At the End of Words), with references to Levine (1998, pp. 116–119) and Rudberg (2017, p. 186).

[25] In Norway, mass arrests of mostly male Jews occurred on October 25–26th, 1942, leading to actions to help Jews escape across the border into Sweden. A new wave of mass arrests of mostly Jewish women and children took place in November. On November 26th, 1942, 532 Norwegian Jews, men, women, and children, were deported from Norway by the ship Donau to Poland; most of them were murdered in the gas chambers of Auschwitz. About 1100 Jews fled from Norway to Sweden. In connection with rescue operations for Danish Jews in October and November 1943, Sweden received 7800 people. See Åmark (2016, Chap. 15–16).

The material on what the modern, scientifically systematic, and militarily disciplined persecution of Jews really is, is now being gathered in great abundance and reliability. The Polish government's official note to the Allied governments in December 1942 was followed by a report from the Inter-Allied Commission of Inquiry a week later. We do not lack a well-documented overview of what is happening to the Jews country by country. Two million of Europe's Jews have already been "liquidated." The remaining 4–5 million still face the danger of death.

The Cooperative Committee for Democratic Reconstruction (SDU) was established in the spring of 1943 with Professor Einar Tegen as chairman and Alva Myrdal as vice-chair.[26] The SDU engaged in helping refugees who had come to Sweden and in planning for Sweden's contributions to the reconstruction of Europe after the war. Alva Myrdal was active in the executive committee. It involved responsibility for studies of democracy and dictatorship, translation and assistance in restoring destroyed literature, inviting Swedish and German organizations to participate in post-war reconstruction work, establishing contact with refugees and their organizations, and preparing technical assistance with doctors, engineers, and other specialists after the war. Fundamentally, it was about ideologically detoxifying the Germany that was realized to be defeated.[27]

Initially, the financing for the SDU consisted of funds from the Cooperative Union and LO, with state support becoming available later. In June 1944, an SDU conference was held where Alva Myrdal asserted that Sweden could and had a moral responsibility to help in the reconstruction of Europe. Alva Myrdal, cited in Mays (2011, p. 44):

> Not that we should feel guilty for not participating in the war. But rather that we still have a debt of gratitude to those who fought even for our freedom. Those who have already been alone in paying in blood should not also have to be alone in paying in money, goods, and services.

Alva Myrdal also initiated the creation of a book with interviews of survivors from concentration camps in Germany and Poland.[28] The interviews were conducted by a professional witness psychologist, Valdemar Fellinius, and a translator, Dory Engströmer. After intense work in 1945, it was published and translated into German, reaching the ongoing Nuremberg trials. Some of the material was presented in Einar and Gunhild Tegen's book *De dödsdömda vittnar* (The Condemned Bear Witness) (1945).[29]

In September 1945, the SDU began publishing a magazine, Via *Suecia*, with Alva Myrdal as the responsible publisher. The magazine was aimed at refugees in Sweden. On the first page of the first issue was a picture and statement by Prime Minister Per Albin Hansson addressing the refugees. Per Albin's hope was that

---

[26] Mays (2011).

[27] Hirdman (2006, p. 277).

[28] Mays (2011).

[29] Pia-Kristina Garde interviewed some of the individuals several decades later and published a book, De dödsdömda vittnar. 60 år efteråt (2004) (The condemned testify. 60 years later). See Åmark (2016, p. 609).

when the refugees returned to their homelands, they would be convinced that in democratic Sweden they have friends who want to preserve, defend, and improve the democratic order, increase social progress, and create jobs for all. Göran Rosenberg has noted that Via *Suecia* was a fascinating mix of Swedish and Jewish.[30] On the same page, one could read about the fight against the housing shortage in Sweden and what the Talmud had to say about the equal value of all people. There were also articles that could have an appealing effect on camp inhabitants who had no home to return to and were beginning to consider the possibilities of staying.

Alva Myrdal was also active in the Swedish Committee for International Relief Work (SIH), established in January 1944 as a committee with state support. SIH was an umbrella organization for other aid organizations like the Red Cross and Save the Children. Initially, the aid focused mainly on the Nordic countries, and later the relief work gradually expanded to cover all of Central Europe. In several countries, children's homes and hospitals were built with Swedish aid funds. By mid-1947, a daily Swedish feeding program for a quarter of a million children in European schools was underway.[31]

The Commission for Economic Post-war Planning: The Myrdal Commission

Gunnar Myrdal performed so well in the post-war council that he was appointed chairman of the state commission for economic post-war planning, the Myrdal Commission, established in February 1944.[32] The commission included top leaders from the business community and trade unions, and politicians from the Social Democrats and bourgeois parties. Karin Kock was a member and the main secretary of the commission. She organized its statistical surveys and wrote several reports and statements.[33]

The background to Myrdal's work as chairman of this important commission included the action program from the post-war council and the analysis in his book *Varning för fredoptimism* (Warning for Peace Optimism) published at the beginning of 1944. The book contained a famous warning of a post-war depression, which did not materialize, and concern for escalating tensions between the Anglo-Saxon powers and the Soviet Union, which became a reality. The analysis was based on the risk that the American economy, in transitioning from the war boom, might face shortages in some areas and overcapacity in others. Myrdal warned of mass unemployment in large regions. If U.S. imports collapsed, the depression could then spread to

---

[30] Rosenberg (2021, ch.: "Judgment of the Future").
[31] Sevón (1995, p. 75).
[32] Gunnar Myrdal resumed his parliamentary seat in 1944, became a member of the Banking Committee, and took a place on the Board of the Swedish Central Bank in the spring.
[33] Niskanen (2007, p. 103).

the rest of the world. However, Myrdal was not alone in warning of a post-war depression. In fact, it was a common assessment at the time among many prominent Keynesian-oriented economists in the USA, Britain, and Sweden, including the head of *Konjunkturinstitutet* (the National Institute of Economic Research), Erik Lundberg.[34] Myrdal also warned that the USA and Britain might not succeed in building a sustainable international economic system after the war. He expressed great concern that once the war was won, peace would be lost, and he warned of what later became the Cold War. He also believed that for Sweden, an overriding political interest was to achieve intimate and good relations with the Soviet Union.[35]

For Myrdal, fiscal policy was central to achieving full employment.[36] Industrial policy should be aimed at supporting and directing regular employment, rather than providing public works for those not employed by the private sector. Trade policy should be oriented toward supporting exports to new world markets and assisting companies with export credits and insurance. In the area of monetary policy, Myrdal wanted to maintain the regulations introduced because of the war—currency control and price control—aimed at price and wage stability. He also wanted to combine low-interest-rate policy with high taxes, but this idea of high taxes did not gain acceptance with Wigforss.

The Myrdal Commission worked for just over a year and issued 10 reports and 26 statements. Political scientist Leif Lewin argued in his thesis *Planhushållningsdebatten* (The Debate on Planned Economy) (1967) that the commission reached a more advanced macroeconomic holistic view of the industry than had previously occurred in Swedish politics, anchored in empirical studies.[37] He believed that the work was a straightforward application of the macroeconomic efficiency concept that the Social Democrats had made their own in the 1930s.

However, during the work of the commission, Gunnar Myrdal became increasingly controversial. Liberal economists like Gustav Cassel and Eli Heckscher had warned in the 1930s about the risks of a planned economy leading to restrictions on freedom in society. Friedrich von Hayek's book *The Road to Serfdom* warned that a planned economy would lead to the downfall of freedom of thought and expression. Cassel, Heckscher, and Hayek articulated a concern that had long existed within the bourgeoisie and gave it ammunition for its positions. The criticism against planned economy was threefold: socialization, central planning, and dictatorship.[38]

Lewin notes that the bourgeoisie's interpretation of the Social Democrats' postwar plans appears to be a deliberate or inadvertent misunderstanding.[39] They did not understand, or did not want to understand, that the Social Democrats were taking

---

[34] Lundberg (1983, pp. 116, 122).

[35] See Myrdal (1944a, ch. The Economic Outlook after the War and ch. Sweden's Interest).

[36] Örjan Appelqvist has reconstructed Myrdal's initial values for the work in the commission in his dissertation, see Appelqvist (2000, p. 78).

[37] Lewin (1967, p. 252).

[38] Lewin (1967, p. 272).

[39] Lewin (1967, p. 278).

their own path, one that did not lead to nationalizations of the business sector and planned economic dictatorship. For Ernst Wigforss and Gunnar Myrdal, economic planning meant increasing production and employment within the framework of a capitalist society.[40] Their mantra was that the business sector should operate at full capacity. According to Lewin, Hayek's thesis that democracy was under threat was inapplicable to Sweden's political conditions.[41]

Gunnar Myrdal was fearless and easily attracted criticism. He publicly advocated combining high taxes with low interest rates, as a central part of post-war policy.[42] The idea was to resolve a dilemma. A policy of low interest rates risks leading to inflation, but when combined with high taxes, this risk is negated. At the same time, high taxes could dampen investments, but if coupled with low interest rates, this risk is also negated. Thus, with low interest rates and high taxes, the economy could grow with full employment without inflation taking off, a remarkable feat of economic magic.[43]

However, Wigforss considered this thought experiment dangerous, as there were those who had an interest in misunderstanding the proposal.[44] His words of caution proved justified, as there was significant opposition to high taxes in the business community and among the bourgeoisie. In the commission, there was also distrust of the Riksbank's ability and means to implement the monetary policy program from the 1930s aimed at price stabilization.[45] Instead, the Myrdal Commission referred to the Price Control Board's power to directly intervene to press down prices even after the war.

Myrdal continued on his path without much hesitation, becoming the most questioned Social Democrat of the time. He even went beyond the original scope of the Myrdal Commission, setting up working groups on fiscal policy and organizational rationalization and productivity in various industries on his own initiative.

This contributed to the business community beginning a general mobilization against the Myrdal Commission in the fall of 1944. Within the bourgeoisie and business world, distrust of Myrdal increased significantly. He increasingly symbolized the risk that a planned and regulatory economy, along with extensive tax increases, would ruin the country. The campaign against social democracy and Myrdal was dubbed by Prime Minister Per Albin Hansson as the Resistance to Planned Economy.

Myrdal also found it increasingly difficult to gain support for his ideas from Wigforss. Contributing to this was the fact that Dag Hammarskjöld had been the state secretary to the finance minister since 1936. Hammarskjöld played a crucial

---

[40] Lewin (1967, p. 281).
[41] Lewin (1967, p. 283).
[42] The essay was published in a Festschrift for Eli Heckscher, see Myrdal (1944b).
[43] Myrdal (1944b, pp. 165–166).
[44] Appelqvist (2000, p. 95).
[45] Lundberg (1953, p. 285).

role in formulating fiscal policy and had a more restrictive view of its possibilities than Myrdal.[46]

In the summer of 1944, Myrdal presented a new, more expansive norm for fiscal policy at a meeting with the Commission for Post-War Planning, which included, among others, Chairman of the Employers' Organization (SAF) Gustaf Söderlund and Dag Hammarskjöld. Myrdal criticized the norm of stabilizing national debt at its current level and that borrowing should only occur for productive purposes. He argued that increased state borrowing was justified if it financed activities that in turn generated tax revenues to cover the additional interest expenses.[47] However, Dag Hammarskjöld was dismissive of Myrdal's proposal. Hammarskjöld, who had been the architect behind the budget policy in the years just before the war, sought a return to that approach. Myrdal's proposal did not find support.

In the fiscal plan for 1945, Myrdal's influence was not as noticeable as in the government bill of 1932/33. Myrdal himself noted much later in his book *Hur styrs landet?* (How is the country governed?) that Wigforss had insisted on deciding the government's economic policy alone, without Myrdal, before forming the government.[48] Wigforss proposed export credits for Swedish companies, low-interest policy, housing construction plans, and increased spending on social reforms, but was relatively restrained, considering the risk of an inflation-driving surplus of purchasing power or *inflation gap*, as pointed out by Erik Lundberg, head of Konjunkturinstitutet (National Institute of Economic Research).[49] The assessment made by the Economic Institute at the turn of the year 1944/45 highlighted the risks of high demand and inflation.[50] Lundberg began to realize that there would not be a post-war depression, as he and many other Keynesian-oriented economists had previously feared.

In the fall of 1946, Erik Lundberg made calculations of the surplus of purchasing power for 1947, which had a significant impact and posed problems for Gunnar Myrdal. Lundberg's forecast turned out to be accurate in one respect but missed in another.

---

[46] Appelqvist (2005).

[47] Discussion memo from a meeting on June 29, 1944, see Appelqvist (2000, p. 229).

[48] Myrdal (1982, p. 228).

[49] Erik Lundberg was one of the foremost Stockholm economists. In his 1937 dissertation, he gave a more general analysis of the employment issue than Keynes had in 1936, see Berg (1991). Lundberg was also early in formulating a macro model for surplus purchasing power and inflation and how it could be quantified. Here he was a few years ahead of Keynes, who tackled the issue in the autumn of 1939, shortly after the outbreak of the war.

[50] Metelius (1987, p. 23).

Trade Minister

After the end of World War II, the coalition government resigned and was replaced by an entirely Social Democratic government in July 1945. Per Albin Hansson remained as Prime Minister, Ernst Wigforss as Finance Minister, and Gustav Möller as Social Minister. The new Foreign Minister was Östen Undén, an experienced politician who had been the Swedish representative at the League of Nations, Foreign Minister in two previous terms, and a recognized expert in international law. The new Minister of Education was Tage Erlander, who had been a state secretary to Möller since 1938 and a consultative minister since 1944, and who just over a year after the new government's formation would succeed Per Albin Hansson as Prime Minister following his unexpected death, holding the position for 23 years. Gunnar Myrdal was appointed Trade Minister, succeeding Bertil Ohlin, who had been trade minister in the coalition government since 1944. Gunnar Sträng also entered the government as a consultative minister, beginning his career as one of the prime architects of the welfare state, in positions such as Minister of Agriculture, Social Minister, and long-serving Finance Minister.

The Social Democratic government inherited several issues from the coalition government. The German and Baltic extradition in 1945–1946 attracted significant attention.[51] About 2700 German soldiers had fled to Sweden at the end of the war. A number of them, 167 soldiers, were of Baltic origin. In June 1945, the Soviet Union demanded that all soldiers who had fled to Sweden be extradited. The coalition government decided in June 1945 to comply with the Russian request, but the Swedish public was not informed. The matter only became known in November 1945. The Baltic internees began a hunger strike. A storm of public opinion now demanded that the Baltic soldiers not be extradited to the Soviet Union. The government faced a difficult dilemma between the coalition government's promise of extradition and the Swedish opinion that stood up for the desperate Balts. Foreign Minister Undén was among those in the government who began to doubt whether to proceed with the extradition; he seemed to have the support of the Prime Minister. But a majority in the government wanted to stick to the original decision to deport, made by the coalition government. Among the majority were Ernst Wigforss and Gunnar Myrdal, who at the decisive government meeting most strongly argued for the extradition of the Balts. For them, it was both about building bridges between East and West and a desire to increase trade with the Soviet Union.

When Gunnar Myrdal was appointed Trade Minister, he brought the Myrdal Commission to the Ministry of Trade. But work in the commission stalled. Myrdal failed to gather the commission into the national unity he had hoped for. One of the sticking points, which led to the commission reaching its end, was the question of the state's role in the structural rationalization of industry. Proposals to appoint permanent state bodies to scrutinize competition and efficiency conditions industry by industry had crossed an important line. It was about how cooperation between

---

[51] Bjereld et al. (2008, pp. 72–79).

the state and industry should be structured. The Saltsjöbaden Agreement of 1938 and the compromise negotiated between social democracy and industry in 1939 were important cornerstones of the Swedish model.[52]

The business community accepted cooperation with the state as long as all cooperation occurred between the state and the industry's organizations. The state should never choose its own partners within the business community. The state should also not influence the organizations' decisions.[53] Myrdal's proposals in this area were to cross a line that should not be crossed. Myrdal, who had been one of social democracy's brightest intellectuals, now increasingly proved to be a burden as a politician. His period as Trade Minister was short, lasting just under 2 years.

After the war, there was no international currency system. Myrdal advocated for orderly international free trade, but before that, bilateral agreements were required. He spent much time concluding bilateral credit and trade agreements with the Nordic neighbors, and in May 1946, it was noted that trade agreements had been concluded with a total of about 30 countries, including Argentina, Australia, and Czechoslovakia.

However, the most debated was the agreement on the so-called Russian credits, which led to intense debate in the press. A principal decision on the Russian credit was taken by the Swedish coalition government in June 1945.[54] The background was that Swedish export companies believed they had lost their markets in the West and South due to the war. They needed the government's help to enter the Soviet market. Negotiations began on a credit and trade agreement with the Soviet Union. The Swedish coalition government accepted a proposal from the Soviet Union in June 1945, which meant that Sweden would provide a state credit for the purchase of Swedish goods worth 1 billion kronor, as a basis for negotiations.[55] The basic terms of the agreement had thus been formed when Bertil Ohlin, the Leader of the Liberal Party, was the Trade Minister in the coalition government, yet it was still subjected to an intense press campaign led by Herbert Tingsten, editor-in-chief of the daily newspaper *Dagens Nyheter*.[56] Tingsten argued that the Swedish government had unreasonably bowed to the communists in the East.

---

[52] Söderpalm (1976, pp. 48–59) provides a detailed description of the background to the negotiations between the government and the business community in June 1939 and how the outbreak of war interrupted the negotiations, leading the parties to focus on the new supply policy tasks.

[53] Appelqvist (2000, p. 170).

[54] Karlsson (1992, p. 120).

[55] Karlsson (1992, p. 49).

[56] Söderpalm (1976, pp. 129–138) depicts the background of the press campaign.

Tingsten's Campaign Against Myrdal

In the 1930s, Gunnar Myrdal and Herbert Tingsten were both Social Democrats and close friends. They jointly published their inaugural lectures as professors at Stockholm University in 1935, with Tingsten becoming a professor of political science and Myrdal in economics. Tingsten claimed in his memoirs that the Myrdals initiated a friendship that, with some interruptions, lasted until the spring of 1945. Myrdal and Tingsten occasionally organized joint seminars for doctoral students in political science and economics, often leading to arguments between them.[57]

At the beginning of World War II, when Myrdal was in the USA, he received a letter from Tingsten dated December 8, 1939, with dollar checks that Tingsten asked Myrdal to deposit in an account. The money was to be used if Tingsten needed to flee Sweden in case of war. Myrdal reply was dated January 12, 1940.[58] According to Myrdal, Gunnar and Alva were very shaken by the current development and had been on the verge of returning to Sweden for the past 6 months. He welcomed Tingsten to America and offered him their apartment and their children. He also stated that, personally, they didn't like the idea of becoming refugees. He added that peasants and workers can never become refugees, as they must stay in their country come what may. It is only intellectuals who can run away, according to Myrdal.

How Tingsten reacted is unknown, but he likely was furious at being likened to a flight-prone intellectual, in contrast to Myrdal's steadfast stance aligned with peasants and workers. In September 1944, Gunnar Myrdal attended a gentlemen's dinner at his publisher Tor Bonnier's, in the company of, among others, Eli Heckscher, Herbert Tingsten, and Marcus Wallenberg. Myrdal and Tingsten engaged in a significant domestic political quarrel, where Tingsten, moving away from social democracy, sharply criticized the strong state and its control of the economy, while Myrdal argued that economic planning was an excellent thing for capitalists.[59]

In his memoirs, Tingsten claims that the definitive break between him and Myrdal occurred in connection with an article in Tiden in 1945. Myrdal attacked Nazis, German sympathizers, and home Englishmen, isolated intellectuals who experienced neutrality as a psychological trauma, who were ashamed of Swedish politics and desired anti-Russian activism. Tingsten stated in his memoirs that what was unpleasant was that Myrdal said it was directed against "Tingstens type" and, above all, that during the many conversations during the war, Myrdal had gone further than Tingsten in the direction Myrdal now rejected, and even accused Tingsten of not attacking the government more sharply in debates and lectures.[60]

Tingsten left social democracy and became a liberal in 1945. When he was appointed editor-in-chief of the daily newspaper *Dagens Nyheter* (DN) in 1946, he took every opportunity to take revenge on Myrdal. He wrote an editorial that was a

---

[57] Wirtén (2013, p. 115).
[58] Johansson (1995, pp. 66–67).
[59] Hederberg (2004, p. 164).
[60] Tingsten (1962, p. 54).

character assassination of Myrdal, who was described as unreliable, power-hungry, and self-centered.[61] Tingsten was also the one who initiated the fierce press campaign against the government's Russian credit and ensured it became a vendetta against Myrdal. DN claimed that the government, and especially Myrdal, exerted pressure and threats against Swedish business to force it to fulfill the export quotas to Russia, which the government wanted to please. The basis for these claims was provided to DN by a director at ASEA (a major electrical equipment manufacturer).[62]

Professor of History Birgit Karlsson, who assessed the basis for these claims, believes they are far-fetched. ASEA had stated in a letter that the quantities requested by the Soviet Union could only be achieved under certain conditions. Among other things, the government had to guarantee access to labor and raw materials.[63] What Myrdal primarily focused on in the talks with ASEA was the lack of labor.[64] The government could never guarantee the availability of labor. But it could take measures to facilitate companies getting labor, for example, by allowing increased housing construction in Västerås.[65] Myrdal believed it would be beneficial for ASEA to face domestic competition, an opinion not shared by the ASEA chief.[66] When Myrdal spoke to him about invigorating domestic competition, he perceived it as a threat, but it could also be interpreted as a desire to make Swedish capitalism more efficient.

Myrdal noted that the ASEA director had also colorfully depicted his conversations with Myrdal. DN sought to exaggerate and dramatize the information. A hearing was held in the Foreign Affairs Committee of the parliament with the ASEA director on October 21, 1946. In the communiqué following the hearing with the director, there was nothing to suggest that he had been subjected to pressure by Myrdal.[67] However, Tingsten did not give up and continued to accuse Myrdal of lying. The ASEA director then issued his own communiqué distancing himself from the attacks on the government and the Trade Minister in DN.

Export Credit to the Soviet Union

Despite the fact that the leading representatives of the business community had participated in drafting the agreement with the Soviet Union, it was difficult to find anyone in the business world who publicly defended it. The agreement fits well with the government's goal of maintaining employment during an expected recession.

---

[61] Johansson (1995, p. 67).
[62] Johansson (1995, p. 86).
[63] Karlsson (1992, p. 89).
[64] Johansson (1995, p. 87).
[65] Karlsson (1992, p. 89).
[66] Karlsson (1992, p. 89).
[67] Johansson (1995, p. 93).

However, companies had, in the time between the principle decision and the negotiations, made their own planning.[68] They accepted orders from old customers in the West to a greater extent than calculated. National-level planning came into conflict with company-level planning.

ASEA, the company most affected by the Russian agreement, wanted to limit its commitment for economic reasons. ASEA had already been burned by too-large Russian orders in 1940. Moreover, trade with Eastern countries often faced problems with credits and various disruptions. Finally, the post-war economic boom meant that there was an exceptional demand for the company's products from traditional customers in the West, which was easier to handle than the socialist planned economies of the East.

The agreement also received strong criticism from the USA, which in a note to the Swedish government claimed that the agreement meant that Sweden's trade would be tied to the Soviet Union for a long time, contrary to the principles of multilateralism.[69] Yet, Myrdal continued to push the issue forward. The commercial reason remained: to support Swedish industry's exports. There was also another thought from earlier about a bridge-building purpose with the credit to the Soviet Union. It was intended to inspire the USA to give the Soviet Union a giant credit and create a spirit of cooperation between East and West after the war. Finally, Myrdal himself was driven by the idea that post-war world trade should be organized on as broad a basis as possible, including the socialist countries. Increased trade with the Eastern countries would help pave the way for free trade.

It is possible to interpret the negotiations and the escalated debate as a game between three parties with three entirely different starting points. Myrdal approached the macroeconomic whole picture. For him, the nation's interest in expanded markets and increased and stable economic growth was the overarching goal. For the ASEA director, the company's interest was the main objective. He did not concern himself with the nation's growth but with his company and its employees. Herbert Tingsten emerged as a political ideologue, seizing the opportunity to strike against Myrdal and social democracy.

If there were conditions for understanding between Myrdal and Ericson (the ASEA director) based on clarifying what was in the nation's interest and what was in the company's interest, these completely disappeared with Tingsten's entry onto the scene, according to Birgit Karlsson.[70] Tingsten gave theoretical form and a new dimension to the threat perceived by Ericson. Not only was ASEA threatened but the entire democratic societal structure, in his view.

Despite internal and external pressures, Myrdal managed to ensure the negotiations were completed. Parliament made a decision on the agreement in November

---

[68] Karlsson (1992, p. 120).
[69] Appelqvist (2000, pp. 376–384).
[70] Karlsson (1992, p. 92).

1946.[71] But for Myrdal, it was a Pyrrhic victory; he was now both politically and personally a marked man. Prime Minister Tage Erlander wrote in his diary that the Myrdals had begun to tire of political life.[72] Erlander understood them, as the campaign against them was one of the more nerve-wracking ever experienced. Erlander supported Myrdal to go on the offensive but Myrdals proposal to arrange a special interrogation debate about the campaign against him was very firmly rejected by the government.

Currency Crisis 1946–1947

The monetary policy in the first years after the war was expansive, featuring low interest rates and high credit growth. Fiscal policy also stimulated demand. Together, these policies contributed to significant deficits in the balance of payments. The Riksbank sold gold and foreign currency from its reserves but kept the long-term interest rate stable by offsetting currency sales with the purchase of bonds and short-term interest-bearing securities from commercial banks for almost the same amount. The expansive monetary policy led to significant price and wage increases from 1945 to 1948. An attempt to curb price increases occurred when the Riksbank revalued (increased the value of) the krona against the dollar and pound by 17% in July 1946.

Dag Hammarskjöld, chairman of the Riksbank's governing board, was a central figure behind this decision.[73] A few months before the coalition government was succeeded by a Social Democratic government in July 1945, Hammarskjöld chose to resign as state secretary in the Ministry of Finance to serve as a financial consultant for the entire Government Offices. He was thereby somewhat detached from the political loyalty demands associated with the role of state secretary, which was further underscored when he began as a financial expert and envoy in the Ministry for Foreign Affairs in January 1946 ahead of the major post-war international economic negotiations.[74]

Hammarskjöld's influence over economic policy was exceptional. It was based on formal top positions at the Riksbank and the Ministry for Foreign Affairs, as well as a strong informal role through his previous work at the Ministry of Finance. After a visit to the USA in early summer 1946, Hammarskjöld realized the risk of major American price increases, which could spread to the rest of the world. He pushed the issue of a Swedish revaluation in the governing board. The exchange rate issue was raised in the government and the foreign affairs committee before the Riksbank's

---

[71] The Swedish Parliament made the decision on November 13, and the credit amount was 1 billion kronor, see Harrison (2017, p. 197). The agreement was also modified in many respects before it was decided in the Parliament, see Söderpalm (1976, pp. 134–135).
[72] Erlander (2001, p. 149).
[73] Appelqvist (2005).
[74] Landberg (2012, p. 269).

governing board revalued the krona on July 12.[75] However, purchasing power continued to rise, most of the wartime import regulation was dismantled during 1946, and the turnover tax, introduced in 1941, was removed at the end of 1946.[76] The revaluation of the krona contributed to increasing imports, and the government's economic policy did not slow the deterioration of the trade balance. The domestic tightening that the Riksbank had sought did not materialize.[77]

By the end of 1946, Sweden was heading into a financial crisis. At this time, there was no international capital market; international payments were mainly regulated by bilateral agreements. The availability of foreign currency was therefore a serious restriction on economic policy. The Riksbank's foreign currency reserves rapidly diminished as imports increased much more than exports. The Riksbank increasingly supported government bonds to stabilize the long-term interest rate. The Riksbank, with Ivar Rooth as its head and Dag Hammarskjöld as its chairman, alerted the government about the situation.

Erik Lundberg of the National Institute of Economic Research wrote a confidential memo detailing an estimation of an excess demand of 2 billion kronor for 1947, contrary to Finance Minister Wigforss's government bill, which he shared with Trade Minister Myrdal, who immediately latched onto the memo.[78] The memo, titled "PM regarding inflation," dated December 2, 1946, was intended for discussion with Finance Minister Wigforss on December 9.[79] Lundberg himself believed that the excess demand would primarily lead to inflation but also recognized the risk of an import surplus and reduced currency reserves.[80]

On the evening of December 5, 1946, Gunnar Myrdal gave a widely discussed speech before the National Economic Association.[81] According to him, without a significant slowdown in the ongoing increase in incomes and purchasing power within the country, Sweden would be forced to abandon the relative free trade in terms of imports in 1947. It would also be necessary to limit the part of the imports that was judged as non-essential through direct regulations. The speech prompted attendees to rush out and place last-minute import orders by phone. Erik Lundberg's words about the meeting have become classic: "Myrdal's loose talk made the country lose money."[82] However, Örjan Appelqvist, who studied the statistics, did not

---

[75] Wetterberg (2009, p. 330). Myrdal later claimed in a memoir that the measure was never directly discussed with Wigforss and Myrdal, see Myrdal (1982, p. 229).

[76] Wigforss had planned to abolish the turnover tax by January 1, 1948, but opposition leader Bertil Ohlin wanted it done earlier in the Parliament, a move Erik Lundberg thought would exacerbate the inflation gap The Parliament settled for July 1, 1947, but requested Wigforss to consider an earlier termination, leading to his decision for January 1, 1947, see Landberg (2012, p. 308).

[77] Lundberg (1953, p. 297).

[78] Lundberg (1984, p. 25).

[79] Metelius (1987, p. 28).

[80] Metelius (1987, p. 28).

[81] Metelius (1987, p. 29) and Lundberg (1984, p. 25).

[82] Appelqvist (1999, p. 35).

find any significant differences in import development before and after Myrdal's speech.[83]

Myrdal also addressed the export credit to the Soviet Union in his speech. He defended it from a long-term perspective, pointing out that it was about not becoming too one-sidedly dependent on the unstable systems of the USA and Western Europe. He called for an organized system of free trade that included the socialist states in the East. Eli Heckscher responded skeptically to the speech, expressing concern that Russian demand for Swedish goods would not be large or stable, as there was no difference between economy and politics in a dictatorship state. Myrdal then replied that Professor Heckscher may not have listened so carefully to what he said.[84] Myrdal also said that it was quite difficult to keep up since this involves extremely complex matters. Myrdal invoked an unanimously known opinion within the large circle of experts worldwide that agreed with him. He concluded by saying that Professor Heckscher could retreat to his study and say that the problem was insoluble—a defeatist stance.

It soon became clear that it was Myrdal himself who had to retreat. The financial crisis continued, the balance of payments deficits grew, and the currency reserves were reduced. After a few months of political discussion, the Riksbank's governing board met on March 13, 1947. Hammarskjöld argued that the abolition of price regulations, the removed turnover tax, and wage policy were explanations for the imbalances, that is, the government's policy rather than the Riksbank's. However, it cannot be denied that the Riksbank's appreciation of the krona in 1946 contributed to increased imports. The Riksbank's reluctance to raise the discount rate also meant that it pursued a low-interest rate policy, which had not yet been questioned to any significant extent. Gunnar Myrdal even stated that taxes could replace interest as a control mechanism for investments.[85]

The Swedish economy needed to be cooled down. Following the Riksbank's urging, the government decided to impose a general import ban from March 15, 1947. A system of import licenses was introduced, and rationing was imposed on coffee and cocoa. The Trade Minister was accused in the media of being personally responsible for the problems, and his wife, Alva, was accused of hoarding coffee well in advance. Myrdal later claimed that the government's paralysis was due to Wigforss, who had not realized the problems in time and had been prepared to act.[86] There are also historians who have pointed out that the primary responsibility lay with Finance Minister Wigforss, who, together with the Minister of Supply Axel Gjöres, was responsible for import issues in the government and had until the last moment rejected any measures aimed at limiting imports.[87]

---

[83] Appelqvist (2000, p. 458).
[84] Lundberg (1984, pp. 26–27).
[85] Myrdal (1944b, p. 167).
[86] Myrdal (1982, p. 233).
[87] Appelqvist (1999, p. 47).

Even in this matter, sharp criticism came from the USA. The American government submitted a note claiming that the Swedish decision constituted a breach of the trade agreement and that the Swedish government, considering the Riksbank's warning in December 1946, had had plenty of time to discuss the issue with the USA.[88]

All this led to Myrdal having enough. He left the post of Trade Minister and took up the position of Executive Secretary for the UN Economic Commission for Europe in Geneva in April 1947.

Erik Lundberg's forecast of the purchasing power surplus was both right and wrong. The import surplus for 1947 turned out to be precisely 2 billion kronor.[89] But it was mainly the external balance that was affected by the increase in the purchasing power surplus between 1946 and 1947, not inflation.[90]

Conclusions

Gunnar Myrdal's tenure as Trade Minister was indeed short. A common view of him is that he was not suited for the ministerial role.[91] Tage Erlander, who became party chairman and Prime Minister after Per Albin's death in October 1946, quickly realized that Myrdal would cause problems in government work and that Myrdal had to be subdued or removed. He was causing a lot of trouble domestically, but perhaps even more abroad.[92] Erlander also felt that Myrdal was not fit to negotiate with the business sector. He took Myrdal aside and discussed with him for 2 hours without getting clarity on what he had actually said during a meeting with the business community. According to Erlander Myrdal understood nothing of the prime ministers absolute demand for clarity, consistency, and order.[93] Everything was here and there and Myrdal had said peculiar things to his "friends" the entrepreneurs. Myrdal could probably be defended by saying that he has always been in good faith, according to Erlander, who was ready to fight for him as best as he could. Gunnar Myrdal himself later claimed that a significant reason for his constant defeats in the government was that Social Minister Gustav Möller, one of the heaviest ministers, faithfully adhered to the silent agreement not to interfere in Wigforss's matters.[94]

---

[88] Appelqvist (2000, p. 389).

[89] Bengt Metelius at KI had forecasted an import surplus of precisely 2 billion kronor, a figure Erik Lundberg doubted, Metelius (1987, pp. 28, 31).

[90] The Riksbank's consumer price index rose in 1947 by 0.9% while the National Board of Health and Welfare's cost of living index increased by 2.8%. The moderate inflation rate was partly due to the removal of the turnover tax, see Metelius (1987, p. 31).

[91] Harrison (2017, p. 188).

[92] Erlander's diary, October 18, 1946, see Erlander (2001, p. 144).

[93] Erlander (2001, p. 146).

[94] Myrdal (1982, p. 231).

In January 1947, Tage Erlander noted in his diary that Myrdal could eventually be placed in the UN, but so far no position of significant importance had been available to lure Myrdal.[95] Erlander also noted that Myrdal was not a burden among their own voters. Myrdal was a great asset among social democrats, while several ministers in the government considered Myrdal "risky," including Minister of National Economy Axel Gjöres, Finance Minister Ernst Wigforss, and Foreign Minister Östen Undén.[96] Ernst Wigforss remarked in his memoirs that intellectual talents of Gunnar Myrdal's rare kind did not have their place in practical politics.[97] To gain influence and respect requires intellectual gifts that had never been particularly bestowed upon Myrdal, according to Wigforss. He also noted that personalities with a touch of genius, which he at least could not fail to recognize in Myrdal, often also had something of the childishly open and trusting, and were easily hurt by the world's mockery or malice. Myrdal later polemicized against Wigforss's memoirs, claiming that he was impossible to cooperate with, power-hungry, scheming, opportunistic, and did not understand how to handle the currency crisis and was cowardly regarding the credit to the Soviet Union.[98]

There were also Swedish diplomats who worked against Myrdal. The head of the political department at the Ministry for Foreign Affairs, Sven Grafström, advised the leader of the Liberal Party, Bertil Ohlin, that the best way to attack Wigforss and Myrdal would be to attack the government for unclear signals about the communists.[99] Grafström also told Ohlin to put personal freedom at the forefront of his liberal program, go with it, use irony and facts in this battle, which the Liberal party leader promised to do the next day in parliament.

It is also apparent that Herbert Tingsten and the bourgeois opposition loathed the Trade Minister. What Tingsten wrote in the third volume of his memoirs can be interpreted as the truth not mattering in his campaign against the Russia agreement and against Myrdal.[100] In fact, it turned out that he actually regretted some of what he had written. When Tingsten looked back he found quite a bit that he would like to have unwritten and a couple of really unpleasant digressions (especially when Myrdal was accused, based on information in another newspaper, of exploiting the "import stop" for his own gain).[101]

Myrdal also fell victim to his own illusion that all debate is good. Debates were his lifeblood; he had a belief in open discussion and public debate playing an important role in developing a democratic society. But as a politician, open conversation could lead to wading in blood. According to Myrdal, a politician must tolerate lies

---

[95] Erlander's diary, January 22, 1947, see Erlander (2001, p. 160).
[96] Erlander's diary, January 22, 1947, see Erlander (2001, p. 160).
[97] Wigforss (1954, pp. 362–364).
[98] Myrdal (1982, pp. 196–238, 296–302).
[99] Bjereld, Johansson and Molin (2008, p. 82).
[100] Johansson (1995, p. 103).
[101] Tingsten (1963, p. 153).

and scolding just as a surgeon must dare to see blood, admitting that it was not fun to go wading in blood all day.[102]

It is also possible to point out that Gunnar Myrdal's difficulties as a minister were due to the hard-to-master reality after the end of the war.[103] During the war, he had presented the USA under Roosevelt as a beacon embodying an internationalist world order. After the war, he clung to Roosevelt's ideals in foreign policy. However, American foreign policy was reoriented toward clear interest politics, and the Cold War between the USA and the Soviet Union escalated. The Swedish trade agreement with the Soviet Union did not gain the significance anticipated, with barely half of the credits utilized.[104] Myrdal's statements about Sweden achieving more intimate relations with the Soviet Union worked against him. It then became difficult for Myrdal to formulate the small state's self-interest in relation to the superpower USA, which made demands on Sweden regarding both the trade agreement with the Soviet Union and the import restrictions.

When the Swedish model took shape during the record years after the war, Myrdal's thinking still influenced many of the welfare reforms and policies for modernization, rationalization, and full resource utilization of both labor and capital, as we shall see in Chap. 9.

References

Åmark K (2016) Att Bo granne med ondskan Sveriges förhållande till nazismen, Nazityskland och Förintelsen (Living next to evil Sweden's relationship with Nazism, Nazi Germany and the holocaust). Bonnier, Falun

Appelqvist Ö (1999) Gunnar Myrdal i svensk politik 1943–1947 (Gunnar Myrdal in Swedish Politics 1943–1947). NORDEUROPAforum 9(1):33–51

Appelqvist Ö (2000) Bruten brygga Gunnar Myrdal och Sveriges ekonomiska efterkrigspolitik 1943–1947 (Broken bridge Gunnar Myrdal and Sweden's post-war economic policy 1943–1947). Santérus, Stockholm

Appelqvist Ö (2005) Civil servant or politician? Dag Hammarskjöld's role in the Swedish government policy in the forties. Economic Review, Sveriges Riksbank, vol 3, pp 33–49

Appelqvist Ö, Andersson S (1998) Vägvisare – Texter av Gunnar Myrdal, Norstedts, Stockholm. English edition: Appelqvist Ö, Andersson S (1998b) The essential Gunnar Myrdal. The New Press, New York

Arbetarrörelsens efterkrigsprogram (1944) The post-war program of the labor movement. Published online at: Marxistarkiv.se

Berg C (1991) Lundberg, Keynes, and the riddles of a general theory. In: Jonung L (ed) The Stockholm School of Economics revisited. Cambridge University Press, Cambridge

Bergström V (1977) Nationalekonomerna och arbetarrörelsen (Economists and the labor movement). In: Herin J, Werin L (eds) Ekonomisk debatt och ekonomisk politik Nationalekonomiska föreningen 100 år. Norstedts, Stockholm

---

[102] Vinterhed (2003, p. 145).

[103] Appelqvist (2000, p. 467).

[104] Bjereld et al. (2008, p. 81).

Bjereld U, Johansson A, Molin K (eds) (2008) Sveriges säkerhet och världens fred (Sweden's security and world peace). Santérus, Stockholm

Bok S (1987) Alva, ett kvinnoliv. Bonniers, Avesta. English edition: Bok S (1991). Alva Myrdal. A daughter's memoir. Radcliffe biography series. Perseus Publishing, Cambridge

Browaldh T (1998) Inledning (Introduction). In: Appelqvist Ö, Andersson S (1998) Vägvisare – Texter av Gunnar Myrdal, Norstedts, Stockholm. English edition: Appelqvist Ö, Andersson S (1998b) The essential Gunnar Myrdal. The New Press, New York

Carlson B (2018) Swedish economists in the 1930s debate on economic planning. Palgrave pivot, London

Erlander S (ed) (2001) Tage Erlander Dagböcker 1945–1949 (Tage Erlander Diarys 1945–1949). Gidlunds, Hedemora

Harrison D (2017) Jag har ingen vilja till makt, Biografi över Tage Erlander (I have no will to power, biography of Tage Erlander). Ordfront, Stockholm

Hederberg H (2004) Sanningen, inget annat än sanningen sex decennier ur Alva & Gunnar Myrdals liv (The truth, and nothing but the truth six decades from Alva & Gunnar Myrdal's life). Atlantis, Stockholm

Hirdman Y (2006) Det tänkande hjärtat. Boken om Alva Myrdal. Ordfront, Stockholm. English edition: Hirdman, Y (2008), Alva Myrdal: the passionate mind. Indiana University Press, Bloomington

Johansson A (1995) Herbert Tingsten och det kalla kriget Antikommunism och i liberalism i Dagens Nyheter 1946–1952 (Herbert Tingsten and the cold war anti-communism and liberalism in Dagens Nyheter 1946–1952). Tiden, Stockholm

Karlsson B (1992) Handelspolitik eller politisk handling Sveriges handel med öststaterna 1946–1952, (Trade policy or political action Sweden's trade with the Eastern Bloc 1946–1952?, dissertation). Department of Economic History, University of Gothenburg

Karlsson S (2001) Det intelligenta samhället (The intelligent society). Carlsson, Stockholm

Landberg H (2012) På väg … Dag Hammarskjöld som svensk ämbetsman (On the way Dag Hammarskjöld as a Swedish civil servant). Atlantis, Stockholm

Levine P (1998) From Indifference to Activism, Swedish Diplomacy and The Holocaust 1938-44. Uppsala Studia Historica Uppsaliensis

Lewin L (1967) Planhushållningsdebatten (The debate on planned economy). Almqvist & Wiksell, Stockholm

Lindskog L (1981) Alva Myrdal. Förnuftet måste segra (Alva Myrdal. Reason must prevail). Sveriges Radios Förlag, Kristianstad

Lundberg E (1953) Konjunkturer och ekonomisk politik (Business cycles and economic policy). Konjunkturinstitutet, Stockholm

Lundberg E (1983) Ekonomiska kriser förr och nu (Economic crises then and now). Studieförbundet Näringsliv och Samhälle, Stockholm

Lundberg E (1984) Kriserna & ekonomerna (Crises & economists). Liber, Stockholm

Mays C (2011) For the sake of democracy, Master's thesis. Department of History, Uppsala University

Metelius B (1987) De första tio åren (The first ten years). In: Henriksson R (ed) Konjunkturinstitutet under Erik Lundbergs tid. Tillbakablickar vid 50-årsjubileet, Konjunkturinstitutet. Norstedts, Stockholm

Myrdal G (1931) Sveriges väg genom penningkrisen (Sweden's path through the monetary crisis). Natur och Kultur, Stockholm

Myrdal G (1935) Den förändrade världsbilden inom nationalekonomin (The changed world view in economics) Installationsföreläsning den 31 Mars 1934, i Samhällskrisen och socialvetenskaperna Två installationsföreläsningar. Kooperativa förbundet, Stockholm

Myrdal G (1944a) Varning för fredsoptimism (Warning against peace optimism). Bonnier, Stockholm

Myrdal, G (1944b) Höga skatter och låga räntor (High taxes and low interest rates). Studier i ekonomi och historia Tillägnade Eli F Heckscher den 24 November 1944, pp 160–166

References

Myrdal G (1982) Hur styrs landet? (How is the country run?). Rabén & Sjögren, Stockholm

Myrdal A (2011) Kommentarer, e-bok, utgiven av Stockholms stadsbibliotek (Comments, e-book, published by Stockholm City Library), Stockholm

Myrdal A, Myrdal G (1941) Kontakt med Amerika (contact with America). Bonniers, Stockholm

Niskanen K (2007) Karriär i männens värld Nationalekonomen och feministen Karin Kock (Career in a man's world: the economist and feminist Karin Kock). SNS Publishing, Stockholm

Rosenberg G (2021) Rabbi Marcus Ehrenpreis obesvarade kärlek (Rabbi Marcus Ehrenpreis's unrequited love). Albert Bonniers Publishing, Stockholm

Rudberg P (2017) The Swedish Jews and the Holocaust, Routledge, London and New York

Sevón C (1995) Visionen om Europa, svensk neutralitet och europeisk återuppbyggnad 1945–1948 (The vision of Europe, Swedish neutrality, and European reconstruction 1945–1948). Bibliotheca Historica 3, Helsinki

Söderpalm SA (1976) Direktörsklubben Storindustrin i svensk politik under 1930- och 40-talen (The directors' Club big industry in Swedish politics during the 1930s and 40s). Tema Teori 12 Zenit/Rabén & Sjögren, Stockholm

Stinsky D (2018) A bridge between east and west? G Myrdal and the UN economic commission for Europe 1947–1957. In: Christian M, Skott S, Ondrej M (eds) Planning in cold war Europe competition, cooperation, circulations (1950s–1970s). De Gruyter, Oldenburg

Tingsten H (1962) Mitt liv 2 Mellan trettio och femtio (My life 2 between thirty and fifty). Norstedts, Stockholm

Tingsten H (1963) Mitt liv 3 Tidningen 1946–1952 (My life 3 the newspaper 1946–1952). Norstedts, Stockholm

Vinterhed K (2003) Kärlek i tjugonde seklet En biografi över Alva och Gunnar Myrdal (Love in the twentieth century a biography of Alva and Gunnar Myrdal). Atlas, Stockholm

Wetterberg G (2009) Pengarna & makten Riksbankens historia (The money & the power the history of the Riksbank). Sveriges riksbank och Atlantis, Stockholm

Wigforss, E (1950, 1951, 1954) Minnen I, II och III (memoirs I, II, and III). Tiden, Stockholm

Willers U (1971) Fredspristagarna (The peace prize winners). In: Hertz U (ed) Alva och Gunnar Myrdal i fredens tjänst. Rabén & Sjögren, Stockholm

Wirtén P (2013) Herbert Tingstens sista dagar Berättelsen om ett liv (Herbert Tingsten's last days the story of a life). Bonniers, Stockholm

Chapter 8
UN Economic Commission for Europe

The UN established the Economic Commission for Europe (ECE) in Geneva to aid post-war reconstruction. Gunnar Myrdal became its first Executive Secretary in 1947, advocating for East-West collaboration despite Cold War tensions. However, the Marshall Plan in 1947 shifted its focus, leading to the establishment of the Organization for European Economic Co-operation (OEEC) for Western Europe in Paris, sidelining the ECE. Nonetheless, the ECE played a crucial role in managing coal distribution, promoting trade, and developing technical cooperation in Europe. Myrdal's efforts to bridge East and West faced resistance, notably from Dag Hammarskjöld's pro-Western stance. Despite the Cold War's peak, Myrdal facilitated bilateral trade consultations, contributing to eventual trade resumption. His tenure saw significant economic studies and fostering international cooperation, albeit amid personal and professional challenges. Hammarskjöld's appointment as the UN Secretary-General was a harsh blow to Myrdal's self-esteem. Alva Myrdal became a prominent UN official and then Swedish ambassador to India. Gunnar Myrdal's work concluded in 1957 when he transitioned to research in India, for his work on *Asian Drama*.

Europe in Ruins

When World War II ended, many European countries lay in ruins. The European continent had been liberated from Nazism, but the devastation after 5 years of war was unimaginable. Nelly Sachs, the Jewish poet who managed to leave Germany at the last moment and fled to Sweden on May 16, 1940, described in a poem how children died in the gas chambers under the supervision of horrific guards who had taken the place of mothers (Lagercrantz 1966). In total, 35 to 40 million human lives were lost in Europe during World War II.[1] Cities and villages were destroyed. Homes, industrial buildings, and infrastructure lay in ruins. A large part of the agricultural land was littered with war materiel, remnants of shells and unexploded bombs. Social, economic, and international relations that had existed for many hundreds of years had collapsed. One example was Warsaw, visited by John Vachon, part of the UN relief team.[2] After the war, 90% of Warsaw was destroyed. There were large remnants of buildings without roofs or walls, with people living in them. The exception was the Ghetto, which was just a large field of bricks, twisted beds, bathtubs, sofas, framed pictures, bags, and millions of other things sticking out among the rubble. It was incomprehensible, so evil that it was beyond understanding, according to Vachon.

A Swedish author, Stig Dagerman, went to Germany in the fall of 1946 at 23.[3] He noted that in German cities, people often asked the stranger to confirm that their city is the most burned down in all of Germany. It was not about finding consolation in misery; the misery itself had become a consolation. Dagerman also noted that the people got despondent when he told them he had seen worse elsewhere, and maybe the foreigner did not have the right to say it; every German city was the worst when you had to live in it.

Reconstruction and the Cold War

After the war, the USA emerged as the leading superpower in the West. The USA pushed the idea that Europe needed help with reconstruction. The most immediate aid to Europe came from the United Nations Relief and Rehabilitation, UNRRA, established in November 1943 with participation from 44 allied countries, including the USA, the UK, the Soviet Union, and China. The operation was funded 70% by the USA.[4]

Three intergovernmental organizations were established in 1945 to help restart production and trade in Europe: a European Coal Union (ECO), an Economic Emergency Committee (EECE), and a European Transport Organization (ECITO). The Soviet Union only participated in the latter organization, and only to a limited extent; its territory was also not covered by ECITO's work. The USA participated in all three organizations, which played a crucial role as the USA was the only country at this time capable of exporting coal, wheat, and other central goods to distressed countries.

After the chaos of currency, world depression, and world war, stability in the global economy also needed to be restored. In 1944, a conference in Bretton Woods

---

[1] Lowe (2012, p. 13).
[2] Lowe (2012, p. 5).
[3] Dagerman (1947, p. 24).
[4] Kostelecký (1989, p. 12).

laid the foundation for the General Agreement on Tariffs and Trade (GATT), the International Monetary Fund (IMF), and the World Bank (IBRD). The UN Charter was adopted in San Francisco in June 1945, and member states agreed to strive for a world characterized by higher standards of living, full employment, and economic and social progress and development.

By the end of 1945, however, it became clear that the three intergovernmental organizations in Europe—ECO, EECE, and ECITO—were not up to the task of long-term assistance in rebuilding Europe. The international political climate hardened in 1946. Stalin delivered an ideological speech in February. This led to the American diplomat George Kennan sending a more than 5000-word telegram from Moscow to his superiors at the State Department in Washington on February 22, 1946. In the "Long Telegram", Kennan warned that what the world was now witnessing was that the Russian regime, despite being clothed in new attire, international Marxism, and offering fair promises to a desperate and war-weary world, was more dangerous and insidious than ever before.[5] According to Kennan, regardless of what it said, the Soviet Union would always seek to undermine the Western world; it was in the Russian nature. However, the Soviet Union was also weakened by significant destruction during the war and did not desire war but rather sought other opportunities for increased influence. Unlike Hitler's Germany, the Soviet power was not adventurous and would not take unnecessary risks. Therefore, it was important for the USA to show determination as soon as Moscow made noise. If the USA ensured that it extended its help to the democracies in Europe so that they knew who they could rely on, and otherwise took care of its affairs, there was no reason to fear a third world war, according to Kennan's assessment.

Winston Churchill, who had been the British Prime Minister during the war, gave a public speech in Fulton, Missouri, in March 1946, warning of a threatening and expansionist Soviet Union that oppressed its own people.[6] He warned against Stalin and spoke of the importance of securing security, prosperity, freedom, and progress in all countries. Europe was now on the verge of being divided into two halves. From Stettin in the Baltic to Trieste in the Adriatic, an "iron curtain" had descended across the continent. The iron curtain became a powerful metaphor that everyone could understand. Behind that line lied all the capitals of Central and Eastern Europe and belonged to the Soviet sphere. Churchill proposed a special relationship between the USA and the British Commonwealth as a counterforce to Soviet expansion. He also emphasized the importance of European integration and foresaw the supranational organizations that later came into being in Europe.

George Kennan's Long Telegram meant that he was brought back to the State Department to reinforce the analysis of the Soviet Union. President Truman became increasingly skeptical of Stalin's intentions. The Soviet Union delayed withdrawing troops from Iran, as agreed upon, and refused to join the World Bank and the IMF. Russian espionage on atomic secrets was revealed in Canada. In January 1947,

---

[5] Menand (2021, p. 22).
[6] Iron Curtain Speech, Encyclopedia Britannica,

Kennan wrote an essay on the psychological background of Soviet foreign policy.[7] He argued that Soviet pressure against the free institutions of the western world was something that could be contained. He proposed the application of counterforce at a series of constantly shifting geographical and political points. This would correspond to the shifts and maneuvers of Soviet policy. The Soviet Union could not be charmed or talked out of existence. Kennan thus formulated the basis of what was called the doctrine of containment. The USA sharpened its tone against the Soviet Union, and in March 1947, the Truman Doctrine was announced, aimed at keeping the communist countries contained or blocked and supporting governments threatened by the Soviet Union.

UN Economic Commission for Europe

The UN Economic and Social Council, ECOSOC, set up a temporary sub-commission for the reconstruction of areas in Europe destroyed by the war. On the suggestion of Poland, the United Kingdom, and the USA, the sub-commission proposed in September 1946 the establishment of the UN ECE with the aim of initiating and participating in reconstruction efforts.[8] The Soviet Union was critical and emphasized that reconstruction should take place on each country's own terms. There was a fear that the new body would require economic statistics from the Soviet Union and send observers to the country. The USA and the United Kingdom wanted to give ECE extensive powers, but the commission would be subordinate to the UN's bodies in hierarchical order. The Soviet Union, on the other hand, wanted ECE's tasks concerning member states to be limited while ECE should be independent in relation to the UN hierarchy. The USA and the United Kingdom argued that in such a case, ECE risked developing into an independent body outside the UN framework, under Soviet influence. In the vote on ECE's tasks, the Soviet delegate abstained, while all others voted in favor. After long deliberations, the General Assembly in December 1946 unanimously recommended the establishment of ECE.[9]

ECE became the largest of the UN's organizations located in the Palace of Nations in Geneva. The palace was a legacy of the League of Nations, which was formed in 1920 because of the peace conference in Versailles after World War I. During the 1930s, the League of Nations proved incapable of preventing Japan, Italy, and Germany from expanding their territories by force. Its palace was completed only in 1938 and was barely put into use before World War II broke out. Shortly after the outbreak of the war, the organization was forced to leave the

---

[7] Menand (2021, p. 24).

[8] Sevón (1995) and Stinsky (2018, 2021) describe the genesis and development of the ECE.

[9] A formal decision was taken by ECOSOC in March 1947, and a committee with participation of the great powers was tasked to specify the ECE's duties.

palace, effectively ceased to function, and was formally dissolved in 1946. However, ECE took over several of its premises and a very extensive library. ECE also inherited the way of organizing conferences from the League of Nations, as well as the idea of making economic cooperation between countries technical issues.[10] However, open diplomacy, which the League of Nations had tried to practice, became more difficult for ECE to use, given the onset of the Cold War. ECE also drew inspiration from the UN's organization for refugee aid, UNRRA, which was the first civilian UN organization and focused on practical fieldwork rather than bureaucratic diplomacy. ECE needed to work in a similar way and establish a strong independence for its organization. To carry out this task, a strong and independent leader was needed.

International Top Official

Already in 1946, Gunnar Myrdal had begun looking for job opportunities abroad. However, the first to receive a job offer outside Sweden at this time was Alva Myrdal. She was offered the position of Deputy Director at the newly formed UNESCO in Paris, which was to promote the reconstruction of education and culture after the war. Alva declined, out of consideration for the family. Gunnar did not want to move to Paris but asked Alva to add in her reply telegram that he was interested in the leadership of the UN Economic Commission for Europe.[11] This created opportunities for Gunnar's continued career but also meant that Alva's career path was closed for a period. Her subordinate role in the sphere of women became apparent.

In early 1947, Gunnar Myrdal's path out of Sweden was opened when he was offered the position of Executive Secretary of the ECE by the UN's first Secretary-General, Trygve Lie, which the UN was to establish in Geneva. The person who proposed Myrdal for the chief position was David Owen, Deputy Secretary-General for Economic Affairs, an economist from Wales in the United Kingdom who knew Myrdal from his time in Sweden in 1942–1943.[12] Gunnar accepted the position on April fourth, 1947, and resigned from the government on April 11th.

Alva Myrdal had to abandon all activities in Sweden. In Switzerland, she was not allowed to work professionally, other than for the UN; however, the organization's regulations did not allow a husband and wife to work in the same place. But she wrote texts, participated in meetings, and organized conferences.

As usual, it was Alva Myrdal who organized the move, which now went to a large villa, Les Feuillantines, opposite the Palace of Nations, overlooking Lake Geneva. The daughters Sissela and Kaj accompanied her to Geneva, along with the

---

[10] Stinsky (2021, p. 22).
[11] Bok (1987, p. 181).
[12] Sevón (1995, p. 117) and Stinsky (2018, p. 53).

housekeeper Karin Anger. Jan, however, had now moved out and stayed in Sweden but visited Geneva.

The villa had 13 rooms on three floors. The entire ground floor was for guests, except for the library. Sissela and Kaj set up under the roof ridge, enjoyed having their rooms, set up a ping-pong table in the attic, and took possession of all the new things.[13] A lush park with moss-covered stone benches was part of it, as well as a chauffeur's house, which was used by Jan when he visited with his family.

The first meeting with ECE was held from May second to 15th, 1947, with Gunnar Myrdal as the newly appointed chief. Sweden was represented by Karin Kock, who had entered the government after Myrdal's resignation, first as a consultative minister and later as Minister of National Supply.[14] Myrdal had a good cooperation with her and with the Swedish Foreign Minister Östen Undén. But tensions between East and West emerged at ECE's first meeting. There was disagreement over the choice of chairman. It was difficult to agree on rules for voting. However, Myrdal managed to formulate compromises on how the activities of the three E-organizations should be incorporated into ECE. He was tasked with contacting the authorities in the four zones of Germany occupied by the allied countries: the British in the north, the American in the south, the French in the West, and the Soviet zone in the East.

After the initial meeting with the ECE, the reaction in the Anglo-Saxon world was one of disappointment. In the United States, the press believed that the Soviet Union's participation was merely to ensure that the commission achieved nothing. The head of the American delegation, William Clayton, was pessimistic, viewing the ECE as utterly useless for American aid efforts. He feared that smaller countries would be paralyzed by the Soviet Union, which could block all activities.[15]

However, just 3 weeks after ECE's first session, the diplomatic landscape regarding aid to Europe was dramatically altered by a famous speech by George Marshall, the U.S. Secretary of State.

The Marshall Plan

George Marshall, who had served as Chief of Staff of the United States Army during World War II, attended a foreign ministers' meeting in Moscow in April. There, he realized that Stalin had no intention of reaching a settlement regarding the conflict between the West and the East. Upon returning from Moscow, Marshall gave a radio address, describing Europe's situation as: "The patient is dying while the doctors deliberate." He then summoned George Kennan, the head of the State Department's

---

[13] Fölster (1992, p. 78).
[14] Karin Kock was a consultative minister in 1947–1948, Minister of National Economy in 1948–1949, and Director-General of the Central Bureau of Statistics from 1950 to 1957.
[15] Sevón (1995, p. 120).

Policy Planning Staff, and tasked him with devising a plan to save Europe. Marshall's only advice was to "avoid trivialities" leading to extensive work and the swift development of a plan, which was presented in a speech on June fifth, 1947.[16]

The cornerstone of the Marshall Plan originated from William Clayton, the U.S. representative to the ECE. After the first ECE meeting in early May, Clayton wrote a memorandum highlighting that the U.S. had greatly underestimated Europe's devastation.[17] He noted that not only was the infrastructure destroyed, but the war had also caused political, social, and psychological disasters. Clayton estimated that European reconstruction would require aid of at least 2.5 billion dollars per year for at least 3 years. He also argued that the U.S. must manage the aid efforts independently.

The Marshall Aid ended up being larger than Clayton anticipated. It involved U.S. aid to Western Europe between 1948 and 1951, amounting to around 17 billion dollars (equivalent to 205 billion dollars in 2020).[18] The aid played a central role in the post-war reconstruction, with the largest assistance going to the United Kingdom, West Germany, and France.

Before the implementation of the Marshall Plan, intense diplomatic activities unfolded among the great powers and other stakeholders. In his speech, Marshall announced that the U.S.'s extensive aid effort to Europe was open to all, increasing the tension between the East and West.[19] Gunnar Myrdal, a fervent lobbyist, argued that the large aid project planned by the U.S. should be managed by the ECE. However, there was no unanimous support among the Western powers for the ECE and the UN to handle the Marshall Aid. Myrdal, on his initiative and without invitation, traveled to London. He warned the British representatives of the evident risk of a division between the West and East if the ECE was not given responsibility for the Marshall Aid. After meeting with the British, he sent a telegram to Trygve Lie, the UN Secretary-General, suggesting that even if "our plans" were rejected, the Western plan would tend to lean towards the UN.[20]

Myrdal also traveled to Moscow, where he was well received and stayed from June 16th to 23rd, 1947.[21] Moscow radio expressed support for the ECE in relation to the Marshall Plan. However, Pravda condemned the plan as American propaganda with unacceptable conditions. Myrdal met with Foreign Minister Vyacheslav Molotov and insisted that the ECE should not become part of a Western bloc, aligning with Soviet goals. Molotov commented that the Soviet Union would support the

---

[16] Sevón (1995, p. 125).

[17] Stinsky (2021, p. 82).

[18] The Marshall Plan was replaced by the Mutual Security Act at the end of 1951, costing $7.5 billion per year until 1961.

[19] The idea to offer Eastern European countries Marshall Aid came from Kennan, who believed that it would achieve one of two goals. Either they would refuse as expected, which would put the blame for the East-West split on the Soviet Union, or if they accepted, the Marshall Plan could be used to detach Eastern European economies from the Soviet grip, see Gaddis (2005, p. 65).

[20] Sevón (1995, p. 135).

[21] Sevón (1995, pp. 141–146).

ECE, but conditionally. If the commission began to represent any group interests, relations with the ECE would be redefined. Regarding the Marshall Plan, Myrdal emphasized that the initiative concerned ECE's areas and that the UN was best suited to understand Europe's needs.

Myrdal confessed to Molotov that his trip to London was self-initiated. He noted that his arrival was not particularly welcomed by those seeking to divide Europe, but highlighted that other groups in England, especially broad circles within the working class, wished to bring the Marshall Aid to the UN and ECE. He also proposed how ECE member governments should respond to the Marshall Plan. They should, according to Myrdal, include a reconstruction plan on the agenda for ECE's second session in July. Molotov, however, responded evasively, noting that much was still unclear and it was difficult to convey an exact position. On the day Myrdal left Moscow, he learned that Molotov had agreed to a meeting in Paris with the foreign ministers of France, Georges Bidault, and the United Kingdom, Ernest Bevin. Myrdal believed his visit had influenced the Russian decision and sent a telegram to Lie, cautiously assuming that the Soviet government wished for the ECE to handle the Marshall proposals.[22]

In late June and early July 1947, a tripartite meeting was held in Paris between Molotov, Bidault, and Bevin. However, negotiations stalled after Molotov received a telegram from Moscow with information from spy sources in London about the negotiations between U.S. Undersecretary of State Clayton and the British. According to this secret information, the Soviet Union was misled about several aspects of the Marshall Plan.[23]

The Marshall Plan was to be a plan for restructuring the economies of the countries involved. It was not to be implemented under the UN framework, as Germany was not a member of the UN. Germany was considered key to Europe's economy and needed to be considered by the Western powers. The U.S. and the UK also opposed the Soviet Union's desire for continuous war reparations from production in Germany. Realizing this, Molotov understood that the time had come. Germany and war reparations had no place in the directives he had brought to the meeting. Molotov telegraphed Stalin that there was no possibility for a joint decision. He left Paris for Moscow. A few days later, on the eve of ECE's second session, the United Kingdom and France invited all European countries except Spain to a conference in Paris on July 12th, 1947, to discuss Europe's reconstruction based on Marshall's initiative.[24]

---

[22] Sevón (1995, p. 157).

[23] Sevón (1995, p. 174).

[24] The following countries were invited to the meeting by France and the United Kingdom: Albania, Belgium, Bulgaria, Denmark, Finland, Greece, Iceland, Italy, Yugoslavia, the Netherlands, Norway, Poland, Portugal, Switzerland, Sweden, Romania, Czechoslovakia, Turkey, Hungary, and Austria, see Sevón (1995, p. 176).

Sweden was represented by Dag Hammarskjöld at the Paris meeting on Marshall Aid.[25] This participation marked Sweden's first involvement in the post-war deliberations of the Allied states.[26] The work of the commission led to the formation of the OEEC in 1948 in Paris, with Western European members, to coordinate the efforts of the Marshall Plan. This marked the beginning of an integrated Western Europe supported by the U.S., in which Sweden participated, while Eastern Europe was separated, contrary to Myrdal's intentions.[27]

The Soviet Union and its allies were not allowed to participate in efforts controlled by the U.S., as per Stalin's directives.[28] This contributed to the intensification of the nerve war that had begun between the East and West and was now being referred to as the Cold War. The Marshall Aid was focused on rebuilding Western Europe as a defense against communist expansion.[29]

Amidst Strong Headwinds, Feverish Efforts for Cooperation Between the East and West Continued

When ECE's second session began on July fifth, 1947, the atmosphere was tense. The ECE and the UN were not considered as bases for the Marshall Plan. This was clarified when the United Kingdom and the Soviet Union agreed to limit the commission's tasks so that the Marshall Plan fell outside the scope of ECE's work.[30] However, they had different motivations for their actions. The United Kingdom wanted to exclude the Soviet Union from the cooperation. The British were concerned that the ECE alternative would focus on the Soviet Union and Eastern countries when the Marshall Aid was discussed in the U.S. Congress, risking the entire project.[31] The Soviet Union, having already positioned itself outside the group,

---

[25] The European countries met in 1947 in the CEEC (Committee of European Economic Co-operation), which was reformed into the OEEC (Organization for European Economic Cooperation) in 1948. It was transformed in 1961 into the OECD (Organization for Economic Cooperation and Development), an international economic cooperation organization for Western countries. Today, many emerging countries in Eastern Europe and other parts of the world participate in the organization or its cooperative projects.

[26] It took time and much adaptation to the US before Sweden could access dollar loans within the Marshall Aid framework. The loans to Sweden amounted to around 100 million dollars, given in three rounds in 1948/49, 1949/50, and 1950/51, see Karlsson (1992, p. 236) and Sevón (1995, p. 279).

[27] In 1948, the OEEC included the following countries: Belgium, Denmark, Finland, France, Greece, Ireland, Iceland, Italy, Luxembourg, the Netherlands, Norway, Portugal, Switzerland, the United Kingdom, Sweden, Turkey, and Austria. West Germany was initially represented by the British, American, and French occupation zones.

[28] Holmström (2011, p. 48).

[29] Jackson (1990, p. 323).

[30] Sevón (1995, p. 185).

[31] Sevón (1995, p. 285).

sought to ensure that its satellite countries in the East were also excluded from the Marshall Aid.

Western countries constituted a growing market for American exports, which also affected the ECE's role in the Cold War. The ECE largely became a matter for Western Europe and the U.S., which were still among Germany's occupying powers. Western countries significantly influenced the technical organization. Eastern states, particularly Poland and Czechoslovakia, initially participated in the technical committees. However, large plenary meetings were affected by the socialist countries' delegates delivering political speeches against the Marshall Plan and U.S. imperialism.[32]

Following the Paris meeting, Myrdal's approach at the ECE was to defend the territory it had acquired when the three E-organizations were taken over by the commission. In the autumn of 1947, the ECE established an office in Minden to handle contact with the Western powers' occupation authorities in Germany.[33] Analysis of how goods, particularly coal needed for recovery, should be allocated across zone borders, including the Russian zone, was necessary.

At this time, coal was a vital source of energy and heat. During the winter of 1945–1946, the coal shortage in Western Europe was estimated to be three million tons per month.[34] It is noteworthy that historians have underestimated the central role played by the ECE in distributing coal from Germany to other countries and in supporting Europe's reconstruction after World War II.[35] Between 1947 and 1950, it was the ECE that was responsible for the international allocation of coal.[36] A British delegate in the ECE, Lord Derek Ezra, recalls that most of the coal needed for the reconstruction plans came from the Ruhr area and was distributed by the ECE, with both Western and Eastern countries participating.[37] According to Gunnar Myrdal, there was a real coal shortage in Europe after the end of the Second World War. The coal could then be rationed among countries by binding decisions of government representatives in the UN's European Commission. Even the secretariat of the organization had the trust to adjust the decided rationing until the next meeting, based on changes that occurred. The sanction behind the unanimity was that the alternative was chaos in the coal trade, which no one could benefit from (Fig. 8.1).[38]

The tension between East and West meant that the ECE played a crucial role on several occasions. When Yugoslavia under Tito's leadership broke with Stalin's Soviet Union in 1948, it was cut off from coal supplies from Czechoslovakia.[39] Until then, Yugoslavia had participated to a limited extent in the ECE's technical

---

[32] Barber (2008, p100).
[33] Sevón (1995, p. 241).
[34] Stinsky (2021, p. 76).
[35] Stinsky (2021, p. 194).
[36] Stinsky (2018, p. 59).
[37] Stinsky (2018, p. 59; 2021, p. 194).
[38] Ekström et al. (1971, p. 125).
[39] Stinsky (2021, p. 199).

Fig. 8.1 Gunnar Myrdal and Karin Kock, who were professionally close allies. Karin Kock became Sweden's first female cabinet minister, and the first woman to receive the title of professor in economics. She was the chair of the ECE from 1950 to 1952. (Courtesy of UN Photo)

committees. Yugoslavia was not part of the Western bloc and did not participate in the OEEC. But now, they utilized their UN membership, sent a representation to the ECE, and requested access to coal shipments from the Ruhr, which was granted.

Gunnar Myrdal also had ideas about investigating how Eastern European countries could be supported with equipment that produced goods needed by Western Europe for recovery. However, a clear jurisdictional conflict arose with the Paris-based OEEC, which took over more and more tasks entrusted to the ECE and created technical committees and a permanent machinery. Particularly, the United Kingdom pushed this development and opposed the ECE.[40]

But the USA and the State Department wanted to keep the ECE in Geneva, believing it was needed and could work in parallel with the OEEC in Paris. There were four reasons, according to the Americans, for retaining the ECE.[41] A shutdown of the ECE would have negative repercussions on the entire UN, as it was

---

[40] Sevón (1995, pp. 250–251).
[41] Stinsky (2021, p. 89–90).

considered one of the most successful of the UN's commissions. Another reason was that the ECE could ensure that Western Europe had access to raw materials, agricultural crops, coal, and timber from Eastern Europe needed for reconstruction. Additionally, the ECE's continued work could relieve the OEEC from everything except administering the Marshall Aid, which was seen as the USA's most important contribution to Europe at the time. Finally, the USA believed that the ECE could help strengthen the dependence of Eastern states on the West, thereby limiting Stalin's influence.

Thus, the USA tried to consolidate Western Europe through the Marshall Plan and the OEEC, while maintaining some contact with Eastern Europe by allowing the ECE's continued existence.

However, the Marshall Aid and OEEC meant that the ECE risked being marginalized against Myrdal's wishes. He then tried to use the fact that countries from both West and East Europe participated in the ECE, complementing the analysis done by the OEEC and working for economic cooperation between East and West. But Myrdal faced resistance from various quarters and did not have access to as much information as the OEEC. The ECE still managed to produce a report on the state of Europe in 1947, considered better than the corresponding report from the OEEC.[42]

The ECE also developed a system of informal consultations, mainly bilateral but also multilateral, conducted out of the public eye. Such consultations often took place in conjunction with meetings of the Subcommittee on Industry and Materials. In September 1948, a first informal meeting was held, gathering information on bilateral trade agreements between all European countries—both in the West and East—to analyze what could be done, item by item, to increase trade for the mutual benefit of the countries. However, rivalry between the ECE and the OEEC persisted for several years regarding analysis and assessments of countries' production and trade of coal, coke, scrap iron, and iron.

Karin Kock, Sweden's representative in the ECE, was to participate in a commission meeting in Geneva in the fall of 1950. She was disappointed with "the serious consequences" for the work in Geneva, resulting from the OEEC setting up special committees for coke, iron, and scrap iron.[43]

Gunnar Myrdal wanted the ECE to function as a bridge between East and West and tried to counteract the growing divide between the blocs during the Cold War. After the Prague Coup in February 1948, when the Communist Party took power in Czechoslovakia, and the death of Czech Foreign Minister Jan Masaryk in March 1948, the Eastern Bloc strengthened under Stalin's leadership Masaryk had sought good relations with the West and was the only bourgeois government member who did not resign following the Prague Coup. He represented Czechoslovakia in the ECE and played a leading role there. Masaryk also worked for Czechoslovakia to receive Marshall Aid. He was found dead in his pajamas in the courtyard outside his official residence at the Foreign Ministry in Prague. Officially, his death was ruled

---

[42] Sevón (1995, p. 247).
[43] Sevón (1995, p. 251).

a suicide, but this assessment has been questioned since 1989. After Masaryk's death, the coldest period of the Cold War began, and the Eastern countries reduced their participation in the ECE's technical committees.

The Soviet Union was critical of international cooperation with the West, especially in the economic area. Instead, the Soviet Union consolidated its influence by establishing communist rule in Eastern Europe. Emphasis was placed on East Germany, Poland, and Czechoslovakia for strategic and economic reasons. These countries had been staging areas during World War II and now served as vital communication links between Moscow and Soviet forces in Germany. Hungary was also considered important, while Romania, Bulgaria, Albania, and Yugoslavia played a less strategic role for both the Soviet Union and the USA.

Although the Soviet Union initially rarely participated in the ECE's technical meetings, Eastern countries were allowed to do so until the Prague Coup and Masaryk's death. The Soviet Union obstructed the ECE's annual meetings with long political declarations. Myrdal pointed out that these meetings were his annual headache. On one occasion, he was so sick and tired that he tried to sleep during the propaganda tirades from both sides, hidden under a pair of large, dark glasses, so no one would see that he was sleeping.[44]

The Soviet Union's economic strategy was to establish self-sufficiency, autarky, through rapid industrialization. Soviet hegemony over Eastern Europe disrupted historical trade relations, where Eastern countries had exchanged raw materials for industrial goods from Western countries. Now, Eastern countries' trade was redirected to the Soviet Union, with a centrally planned economy, state trade monopoly, and five-year plans for the entire economy (Fig. 8.2).

Duels Between Dag Hammarskjöld and Gunnar Myrdal

In the great game of the Cold War, Dag Hammarskjöld and Gunnar Myrdal played diametrically opposed roles. Hammarskjöld quickly became a leading actor in the OEEC in Paris, which was to coordinate Marshall Aid from the USA to Europe. Hammarskjöld participated in developing the OEEC's long-term program. He was a proponent of the British line, which meant that Marshall Aid should be limited to the reconstruction of Western Europe.[45]

At a dinner in Paris in May 1948, a major clash occurred between Myrdal, who proposed all-European cooperation, and those advocating that Marshall Aid should only be given to Western Europe. The dinner was attended by Edmund Hall-Patch, chairman of the OEEC's Executive Committee, Robert Marjolin, Secretary-General of the OEEC, Dag Hammarskjöld, Swedish representative and responsible for the OEEC's long-term program, and Gunnar Myrdal, head of the ECE. After the dinner,

---

[44] Gunnar Myrdal interviewed by Kostelecký in 1978, see Stinsky (2021, p. 97).
[45] Stinsky (2021, p. 95).

Fig. 8.2 In the drawing, Uncle Sam is seen with Western Europeans around the Marshall cake and Stalin surrounded by Eastern Europeans. The drawing was on the wall in Myrdal's office in Geneva. (Source: The UN brochure published in 2007 on the occasion of the 60th anniversary of the ECE)

Hall-Patch reported back to the Foreign Office. Hall-Patch noted that Myrdal's main theme was that the goals of the European Recovery Program couldn't be met without significantly increasing East-West trade.[46] Hall-Patch said that the Soviet government clearly intended to sabotage the ERP and did not share his optimism. Myrdal then argued that the OEEC was overly suspicious of the Russians and that cooperation was possible. The morning after this dinner, Hall-Patch received a note from Hammarskjöld, deploring Myrdal's lack of tact and naivité.

Hammarskjöld played a pivotal role in integrating Sweden into the Western bloc. His approach did not focus on rebuilding East-West trade, unlike Myrdal. Hammarskjöld believed that increased productivity was the most central issue in reconstruction. He argued that Marshall Aid should be used to boost the production of goods in Western Europe that could replace imports from the USA and also be exported there.[47] On the other hand, Myrdal aimed to restore East-West trade to pre-war levels, which also underpinned the assumptions in the Marshall Aid calculations at the State Department.

East-West trade was at the core of the problems handled by the ECE at this time. In 1947, trade volume was only just over 40% of the pre-war level. From the end of

---

[46] Stinsky (2021, p. 95).

[47] Stinsky (2021, p. 95).

1947, Western powers, led by the USA, progressively imposed a strategic export embargo against communist countries.[48] Consequently, East-West trade continued to decrease. The trade committee established at the ECE was shut down. The outbreak of the Korean War in June 1950 further intensified the tensions between the superpowers, dimming prospects for East-West trade even further. At this time, there was no multilateral trading system in place. Trade was characterized by short-term bilateral barter agreements without strong legal frameworks.

Gunnar Myrdal adamantly asserted that the ECE virtually monopolized handling trade problems between East and West. The ECE was the only organization with a mandate to conduct multilateral trade relations that included socialist countries. According to Myrdal East-West trade was the responsibility of the ECE par préférence because it cannot be taken over by the OEEC.[49] When trade issues were stagnant, the ECE had to choose between accepting defeat or taking further initiatives to progress. Myrdal chose the latter. He intensified efforts to break the deadlock between the Eastern and Western blocs. The ECE now devoted considerable energy to depoliticizing trade problems and treating them as technical issues. Moreover, Myrdal used the needs of European countries to establish or restore trade with countries in the opposing bloc. The ECE and Myrdal offered countries in both blocs the opportunity to conduct bilateral talks within a multilateral framework.[50]

However, a new duel soon emerged between Gunnar Myrdal and Dag Hammarskjöld. The context was that the USA was the world's largest economy, with an unscathed production apparatus after the war. The USA could supply goods to European countries. However, there was a shortage of dollars to pay for the needs arising from the enormous devastation. The GATT, which came into effect in 1948, contributed to reducing tariffs and increasing trade, but it did not eliminate the dollar shortage. Marshall Aid provided aid in dollars, but it did not cover the long-term dollar needs.

Two strategies were discussed to reduce the dollar shortage in Europe.[51] The first strategy, advocated by the ECE and Myrdal, was to diversify trade, increasing exports in all directions, to both Western and Eastern countries. The second strategy, favored by the OEEC and its long-term program authored by Hammarskjöld, was to increase productivity rather than diversifying exports.[52] The OEEC also advocated trade liberalizations within the Western bloc, which were implemented early on. However, East-West trade was left to the ECE, which Myrdal realized required patience until the worst period of the Cold War was over. He insisted that the ECE

---

[48] Karlsson (1992, p. 237).
[49] Stinsky (2021, p. 102).
[50] Stinsky (2021, p. 102).
[51] Stinsky (2021, p. 106).
[52] The OEEC also established a European Payments Union (EPU) in September 1950, facilitating payments in a multilateral system that benefited trade within the Western bloc.

should function as a bridge between East and West, stating that such a bridge must be built, even if no one was crossing it now.[53]

The period from 1949 to 1953 was the coldest period of the Cold War. Nevertheless, the ECE made persistent attempts to restore trade relations between East and West. The negotiation machinery was in place in Geneva and ready to be utilized. The ECE's leadership continued to be independent and focused on depoliticizing trade issues, treating them as technical matters. Gunnar Myrdal was also keen on modifying negotiation techniques when positions were deadlocked. After a long stalemate during the worst years of the Cold War, an opportunity for a breakthrough for Myrdal's bridge-building ideas also opened. But who were the people building the bridge?

A Fearless Leader Sought Competent Staff with High Integrity

As the head of the ECE, Myrdal was driven by the idea that international officials should function as a kind of international engineers—akin to the social engineers who built the welfare state.[54] They should be ideologically unbound, rational, and focused on solving problems. The officials should be able to analyze, understand, and propose improvements that supported the public interest and not special interests. Regarding staff recruitment, Myrdal believed it was important to prioritize competence and avoid appointments controlled by governments.[55] It was also crucial that the staff had sufficient integrity and could resist national pressures. At a meeting with delegation leaders, he emphasized that ECE employees worked only on behalf of the United Nations and were not allowed to receive instructions from their home countries. He was determined to ensure the organization's right to its own initiatives in its areas.

Myrdal put a lot of effort into shaping a department for research and planning. A significant economist, Nicholas Kaldor, was recruited as the department's first head. He worked on developing the theory of cumulative processes and applied it to analyses of the industrial sector. Another well-known economist was Walt Rostow, the person in the American administration who first proposed an UN-based organization for Europe's reconstruction.[56] Rostow later became known for his theory of various stages in the rise of capitalism, which will be revisited in Chap. 11. Rostow also became one of the architects of the Vietnam War in the 1960s, covered in Chap. 12. Other famous economists working for Myrdal included Ester Boserup, a population expert and anti-Malthusian who also participated in the work on Asian Drama,

---

[53] Stinsky (2021, p. 139).
[54] Stinsky (2018, p. 67).
[55] Kostelecký (1989, p. 80).
[56] Rostow's early initiatives that led to the ECE are described by Kostelecký (1989, pp. 20–22).

and her husband Mogens Boserup. Ingvar Svennilson, one of the Stockholm economists and head of the Swedish Industrial Institute for Economic and Social Research, was also recruited to the ECE, where he contributed significantly to a major study on growth and stagnation in Europe.

At its peak, over 60 people worked in the department, about half of whom were economists or statisticians. The department was tasked with providing the commission and its committees with analyses. This involved assessments of the economic situation in European countries and in-depth studies in specific areas. Great importance was placed on analyzing various obstacles to economic recovery, such as shortages of labor, industrial capacity, raw materials, and energy. The ECE early on highlighted the inflationary pressure that existed beneath the surface in many economies after the war due to the situation of scarcity.

Myrdal was careful to ensure that the analysis was policy-relevant and not primarily of academic interest. Practically usable analysis and research were sought at the ECE. He also arranged conferences with invited researchers and drove a scholarship program aimed at younger researchers, financially supported by the Rockefeller Foundation.

The content of the ECE's annual reports and special analyses should, according to Myrdal's guidelines, be guided by the criterion of truth. He did not hesitate to publish analyses that could cause dissatisfaction from individual countries' governments. France was criticized for tolerating a black currency market, and the United Kingdom for wasteful coal consumption.[57] The ECE was the only international organization during the Cold War that published regular analyses and comparisons of developments in Eastern and Western countries.[58] The reports received mixed reviews.

However, the USA's State Department praised the quality of the ECE's annual economic overview. According to the State Department the survey was a rich source book, and it would be hard put to name any UN publication in the economic field that is more valuable.[59] But at the same time, the USA felt that the ECE often presented too bleak a picture of development in the West. Soviet representatives, on the other hand, thought that the ECE painted too bleak a picture of development in the East. Myrdal thus managed to upset both sides, which is a sign of great independence for the ECE and its head.

---

[57] Barber (2008, p. 104).
[58] Stinsky (2021, p. 156).
[59] Stinsky (2021, p. 156).

The Export Embargo Against Communist Countries

A significant factor that influenced the operations of the ECE was the strategic export embargo against communist countries.[60] As early as December 1947, the USA decided to start controlling all exports to Europe.[61] The aim was to prevent the Soviet Union from accessing strategic American goods. The Marshall Aid Act was amended to subject participating countries to American control measures. The initiative was taken by the USA, which imposed it on its Western allies and, with varying effectiveness, on the entire non-communist world.

In June 1948, the Soviet Union began to block ground connections between West Berlin and West Germany, initiating the Berlin Blockade, which lasted until May 1949. The blockade was Stalin's response to the Western powers forming a German state from their own occupation zones and introducing the Deutsche Mark as the currency on June 20th, 1948, without consulting the Soviet Union. West Berlin was saved by a substantial air bridge, primarily by American aircraft. The Western powers agreed on a counter-blockade, initially disrupting trade between the different occupation zones in Germany. After the Prague Coup and in the shadow of the Berlin Blockade, the North Atlantic Treaty was formed in April 1949 by 12 countries: Belgium, Denmark, France, Iceland, Italy, Canada, Luxembourg, the Netherlands, Norway, Portugal, United Kingdom and the USA, which later gradually evolved into the NATO defense alliance.[62]

The secret export embargo contributed to further reducing East-West trade but caused tensions between the USA and its European allies. In the fall of 1949 and early 1950, the Coordinating Committee for Multilateral Export Controls (CoCom) was secretly established in Paris to streamline the export control of strategic goods from the USA, its NATO allies (except Iceland), and Japan. Sweden declined to participate, citing its policy of neutrality.[63]

Gunnar Myrdal assessed that the embargo policy intensified the Cold War. Once again, a vicious cycle described the process: an action from one side led to a counteraction from the other. The political events during the coldest days of the Cold War were a kind of "cooperation" between the leaders of the Western and Eastern blocs. From a Stalinist perspective, the embargo policy was advantageous and could be used in propaganda to blame the West—especially the USA—for the Cold War. The embargo lists also gave the Eastern states crucial information about which goods

---

[60] See Gunnar Myrdal's foreword to Adler-Karlsson (1970).

[61] Karlsson (1992, p. 237).

[62] Greece and Turkey became NATO members in 1952. West Germany was admitted as a NATO member on May 6, 1955, on the condition of never acquiring nuclear weapons. A little over a week later, on May 14, 1955, the Warsaw Pact was formed with Albania, Bulgaria, Poland, Romania, Czechoslovakia, Hungary, and East Germany under Soviet leadership The next day, on May 15, 1955, the major powers and the Austrian government signed a state treaty restoring Austria's sovereignty.

[63] Nilson (2008).

they needed to produce themselves. Thus, the export embargo served as a decisive argument for consolidating the communist bloc under Moscow's leadership.

Hard Work for Dag Hammarskjöld

In the years 1948–1949, Sweden began to receive Marshall Aid after prolonged negotiations, led by Dag Hammarskjöld on the Swedish side. A condition for receiving Marshall Aid was a commitment not to export strategic goods to the Soviet Union and Eastern Europe that were produced using American goods purchased with loans or grants from the USA.[64] Hammarskjöld also handled the issue of Swedish participation in the Western export embargo. In a letter to Karin Kock in September 1948, he outlined what the Americans were working towards. He had been informed by OEEC's Secretary-General Marjolin that the USA wanted to see increased trade between the West and East, but only under two conditions. One was that goods that could strengthen the military potential of Eastern countries should not be exported eastward. The other was that the volume of trade should not become so extensive that it created a more pronounced dependence between the West and East.[65]

However, Sweden had to take further steps towards adapting to the USA's embargo policy. In 1949, a ban on the export of strategic goods to produce nuclear energy was introduced.[66] Additionally, the definition of war material was redefined to include machines and tools for producing war material.[67]

A dilemma for Swedish neutrality policy was the need for advanced military equipment to maintain an effective defense. Sweden depended on imports of military high technology from the UK and the USA. Following the outbreak of the Korean War in June 1950, the Western powers tightened their restrictive stance on exporting war material to Sweden. The Americans obstructed the export of modern radar stations for air surveillance, command, and control. In the fall of 1950, Foreign Minister Undén traveled to the USA and met Secretary of State Acheson but could not secure a partial war trade agreement for the radar stations. In early 1951, ambassadors from the USA, the UK, and France approached the Swedish government, requesting Sweden to join the Western economic warfare against Eastern Europe.[68]

The Korean War further increased the pressure on Sweden to adapt to the embargo policy under US leadership. Sweden was the only Western democracy that abstained on February 1th, 1951, when the UN General Assembly voted on the US

---

[64] Nilson (2008, p. 69).
[65] Stinsky (2021, p. 109).
[66] Nilson (2008, p. 69).
[67] Karlsson (1992, p. 238).
[68] Nilson (2008, p. 73).

proposal to brand China as the aggressor in Korea.[69] Foreign Minister Undén asserted that the decision was a consequence of the neutrality policy, a view not shared by Dag Hammarskjöld, who unsuccessfully tried to change his chief's opinion. According to the diary of Prime Minister Tage Erlander, Sweden had become isolated through the China vote which caused offense to the Americans just when difficult negotiations with them were underway.[70] However, Erlander still believed the government had acted correctly. If it had bowed, it would have had no remnant of independence left.

Concern about the future grew at the Ministry of Foreign Affairs. According to Hammarskjöld the situation was starting to become dangerous, and the threat of war was a reality. The government might face the most difficult decisions vis-à-vis the Western powers in the coming months and it must be prepared to make very far-reaching concessions, short of joining NATO.[71] In February 1951, Hammarskjöld was promoted to cabinet minister and entered the Swedish government with the task of handling East trade issues, among others. Hammarskjöld continued a gradual adaptation to CoCom policy.

Negotiations between Hammarskjöld and the American ambassador William Walton Butterworth led to results in June 1951.[72] It was not a formal agreement between two parties. Instead, it was a clarification of how neutral Sweden intended to conduct its trade policy, aimed at avoiding issuing licenses and specifying quotas for the export of goods subject to a complete embargo. The USA accepted that existing agreements had been fulfilled.

One could say that Sweden's formal neutrality was accepted by the USA, provided that its meaning was adapted. It can also be argued that Sweden, on formalistic grounds, claimed full independence while practically accommodating the USA. During the negotiations, Sweden noted a success in access to American military high technology. The export of American radar stations to Sweden was now allowed, albeit after a long delay.[73] Both Prime Minister Erlander and Foreign Minister Undén thanked the American ambassador in Stockholm, Butterworth, for approving the export order. The contacts were kept secret. According to Sverker Åström of the Ministry of Foreign Affairs' political department, these contacts were initially strictly secret as they did not want them to be used for propaganda purposes by domestic communists or by the Soviet Union. But to themselves they said that if the Swedish people had been fully informed, the reaction would generally have been understanding.[74] It was also clear that Sweden needed to continue its security policy adaptation to the Western powers.

---

[69] Nilson (2008, p. 74).
[70] Nilson (2008, p. 75).
[71] Sven Dahlman, undated, see Nilson (2008, p. 75).
[72] Karlsson (1992, p. 238).
[73] Nilson (2008, p. 78).
[74] Åström (1992, p. 64).

Prime Minister Tage Erlander visited the USA in April 1952 under the pretext of visiting old Swedish settlements. But in practice, it was about confidential consultations and lunch with President Harry S. Truman. The central issue for Sweden at the time was what was required for continued war material purchases in the USA. The answer was that Sweden could be placed in the same category as NATO countries if it complied with the prescribed regulations.[75] When Erlander returned home to Sweden, Dag Hammarskjöld informed the Americans that Sweden fully understood that the demands of the American military assistance act had to be met.[76]

On July first, 1952, another secret agreement was reached between the USA and Sweden concerning a guarantee against the re-export of war material and secrecy protection in the exchange of secret military-technical information. On this basis, Sweden was given the right to purchase war material in the USA. This agreement has sparked much debate. Some researchers believe that it represented a decisive step towards a secret Swedish-American defense cooperation. Others argue that the agreement was kept secret for political and psychological reasons, supported by researchers who have studied the archives of the Ministry of Foreign Affairs.[77] However, there is support for the agreement presupposing a covert Swedish adaptation to the Western powers' economic warfare. A central source supporting this analysis is the Swedish Chief of the Defense Staff Richard Åkerman. He wrote in his diary on July second, 1952, about the agreement reached between Sweden and the USA.[78] Åkerman noted that agreement was made with the USA on the purchase of materials in the USA. With sophistical formulations the diplomats agreed to the conditions that placed Sweden on par with NATO countries. It was also clear the agreement could not be publicized. If it was publicized the Soviet Union would be right that prime minister Erlander visited the USA for the purchase of war material to be accepted. However, according to researchers Swedish security policy did not constitute a breach of neutrality in international law. The Western contacts established did not contain binding mutual commitments, at least no formalized ones.[79]

---

[75] Agrell (2014, Chap. 11).

[76] Agrell (2014, Chap. 11).

[77] A few weeks before the agreement, a Swedish DC-3 disappeared over the Baltic Sea, and 2 days later, a Catalina plane searching for the DC-3 was shot down by Soviet fighter jets. These events were behind the decision to keep the US-Sweden agreement confidential, according to documents in the Swedish Foreign Ministry's archives. There is also evidence that a precondition for the US agreement was Sweden's full participation in the Western powers' economic warfare against the Soviet Union, see Nilson (2008) for the discussion on the agreement. Sweden long concealed that the DC-3 was involved in signal intelligence on Soviet radar stations. It was not until 1974 that Tage Erlander revealed in his memoirs that it was a signal intelligence mission. In 2002, it was disclosed that the signal intelligence was conducted in collaboration with the United Kingdom, and the Swedish government then apologized to the relatives: 'Sweden was threatened... These eight men contributed to protecting Sweden's security and independence', Holmström (2011, p. 53).

[78] Agrell (2014, Chap. 11).

[79] However, it poses a problem on the political level due to the discrepancy between the public perception of security policy and its actual implementation, Agrell (2014, Chap. 11).

The Bridge Between East and West in Use After Gunnar Myrdal's Innovative Approach

Much of the ECE's work in several committees was centered on international trade, with the embargo policy receiving significant attention. During the escalation period, it served as a major impediment to the commission's work. Myrdal's efforts were focused on breaking the deadlock that shackled many economic relations in Europe. The scope of restrictions increased until 1953, when the Marshall Aid phased out, Stalin died, and the Korean War ended. Embargo lists for Western European allies began to be scaled down. When the trend reversed, the ECE contributed to the resumption of trade between West and East.

After Stalin's death in March 1953, a kind of thaw occurred, and the view on trade between Eastern and Western countries became more positive. This meant that the bridge Myrdal and his team had built could begin to be utilized. Between April 13th and 24th, 1953, the ECE held its second consultation on East-West trade. It started with a multilateral session with representatives from all countries, followed by bilateral meetings involving all 26 countries, with over 100 such meetings held. The consultation concluded with a multilateral session.

This international meeting marked a major breakthrough in discussions about trade between Western and Eastern countries. Myrdal had devised a clever way to avoid superpower quarrels and political battles.[80] The format was a consultation by the Executive Secretary, Myrdal, with trade experts appointed by governments, hence not an intergovernmental meeting. The entire consultation was conducted privately. Especially the bilateral negotiations were secret. No minutes were recorded, other than the notes taken by the participants themselves. No journalists or outsiders were allowed. This format also allowed Myrdal to chair the multilateral meetings himself, thus avoiding the normally tedious and politically charged process of delegates choosing a meeting chair. Without minutes, without the election of a chairperson, and without a joint report, the meeting became a miracle, especially considering the tense atmosphere, according to Myrdal.[81]

During the initial multilateral round, many Western delegates were surprised by the realistic trade proposals launched by the Russian side. By facilitating bilateral talks in a multilateral context, the ECE succeeded in arranging bilateral meetings between all countries, even those without diplomatic relations. The Eastern European countries surprised the West by requesting large quantities of consumer goods. The bilateral talks became an important starting point for future bilateral trade agreements.

In the multilateral closing phase, opportunities were provided for triangular trade agreements, such as between Finland, the Soviet Union, and Poland. The conclusion after the consultation was that the ECE seemed to have found a technique that broke the deadlock in trade negotiations between East and West. Another

---

[80] Stinsky (2021, p. 169–170).

[81] Stinsky (2021, p. 172).

conclusion was that Myrdal, with his clever setup, managed to prevent the USA from controlling the event. Reportedly, after the meeting, US Secretary of State John Foster Dulles sent panicked telegrams to his ambassadors in Western Europe, asking them to find out what information the countries had about what was being agreed upon at the meeting.[82]

Gunnar Myrdal also played a role as a bridge-builder between East and West in the international agreement that restored Austria as a sovereign nation in 1955. Like Germany, Austria had been occupied by the Soviet Union, USA, UK, and France after World War II. The agreement was the first between the USA and the Soviet Union in 10 years concerning troop withdrawals in Central Europe. It was Bruno Kreisky, Austrian Vice Minister of Foreign Affairs and Myrdal's old friend from the Little International, who actively worked to reach an agreement between East and West. The first meeting between Kreisky and Soviet representatives took place in Myrdal's private apartment in Geneva, in conjunction with an ECE meeting in 1954.[83]

Myrdal's oldest daughter, Sissela Bok, noted that Gunnar Myrdal was the only head of any of the UN's organizations who did not yield to American demands during the McCarthy era to interrogate American officials about their political views. According to Myrdal, officials working for the ECE were international officials, and neither Americans, Russians, nor others had the right to interrogate them.[84]

Myrdal himself was suspected of being pro-Soviet in an intelligence report from the American military.[85] The US Department of State stated in a confidential memo that Myrdal seemed to support the Soviet Union. The reason was believed to be Myrdal's opposition to the Marshall Plan and his effort to ensure that the ECE included all countries in Europe, aligning with the Soviet position. However, the memo was criticized by a leading American at the ECE, who argued that Myrdal, while perhaps naive, was not a communist or sympathizer, but rather a great admirer of America.

ECSC, the European Coal and Steel Community

In May 1950, the French Foreign Minister Robert Schuman presented a plan to replace the ECE's coal allocation mechanism with a coal and steel community in Europe. The Schuman Plan was based on the idea that both coal and steel are central commodities in the war industry. A supranational body was needed to control the Franco-German production of coal and steel. Schuman proposed the establishment of a high authority that would act in the common European interest, not national

---

[82] Stinsky (2021, p. 171).
[83] Stinsky (2021, p. 178).
[84] Bok (1987, p. 203).
[85] Jackson (1990, p. 324).

interests, to prevent future war between France and Germany. A treaty was signed in April 1951 in Paris, and in July 1952, the European Coal and Steel Community (ECSC) was established, with France, West Germany, Italy, Belgium, the Netherlands, and Luxembourg participating.

The ECSC benefited from the ECE's work between 1947 and 1951. The ECE had played a central role in distributing coal after the war. But now, the ECSC took over the allocation of coal from the ECE, which contributed expertise, reports, and technical assistance to the establishment of the European Coal and Steel Community. The chairman of the ECE's Coal Committee, François Vinck, became one of the general directors at the ECSC. The ECSC emerged as a new supranational organization with more independence than both the ECE and the OEEC and wielded significantly more power than previous organizations for economic cooperation in Europe. For example, it could determine production quotas when demand rose and impose fines on companies that did not follow the rules.[86]

For the ECE, the formation of the ECSC mainly affected coal analysis. The Committee for Coal Allocation was disbanded but replaced by a Coal Trade Committee. It provided an opportunity for the six countries participating in the ECSC to exchange important information with other importing countries. The ECE also expanded its analysis of other energy sources such as oil and gas.

Meanwhile, the old rivalry between the ECE in Geneva and the OEEC in Paris continued. However, Myrdal realized that the ECE could benefit from the formation of the ECSC. This was because the ECSC, as a supranational organization, posed a greater threat to the OEEC than to the ECE. The American representative in Geneva noted in a message to the State Department that the ECE could be used to strengthen NATO and the OEEC through its strong research department and lack of hierarchies.[87] He also mentioned that the British hoped to use the ECE as a counterbalance to the ECSC.

Thus, the ECE continued its operations even after Western European cooperation began to be built up in a supranational spirit. The ECE directly contributed to European cooperation and indirectly as support to other organizations. It was the ECE that introduced a system for classifying the thousands of different types of coal in Europe. The ECE's work laid the groundwork for a global coal classification system in the 1990s.[88] In the 1950s, the ECE also started several international projects in the transport sector, which still influence traffic systems in Europe and other parts of the world today. These included standardized road signs and traffic rules and the European network of motorways: the European routes. The ECE also initiated the international transport system, TIR. TIR is an international customs convention with about 70 participating countries worldwide, allowing goods to be transported without customs declaration at each border.[89] The ECE also became an

---

[86] Stinsky (2021, p. 206).
[87] Stinsky (2021, p. 212).
[88] Stinsky (2021, p. 203).
[89] Stinsky (2018, p. 59; 2021, p. 141).

important base for international cooperation on major infrastructure projects—hydropower, electrical transmission, and more.

Later, the ECE took the initiative for the first treaty that guarantees environmental protection for all: the Aarhus Convention. It is the UN Convention on Access to Information, Public Participation in Decision-making, and Access to Justice in Environmental Matters.[90]

Alva Made Herself Independent and the Family Split

As the head of the ECE, Gunnar Myrdal was, as usual, fervently active and an extremely absent parent. He was completely absorbed by the task of addressing the post-war reconstruction problems. Everything unrelated to his work was excluded. He was admired by colleagues and staff and escaped the stifling and toxic atmosphere in Sweden. However, for Alva, the situation became critical. She had long felt that her own space diminished as Gunnar's involvement increased. In a letter to Karin Kock a few years earlier, she compared her situation to Karin's. The more definitively Gunnar devoted himself to politics, the less Alva could appear in these broader contexts. Everything Alva did could easily be interpreted as the women's association variant of their firm or family.[91] Alva Myrdal believed that Karin Kock was better off since she and her husband did not have overlapping tasks. Moreover, Karin Kock had chosen a profession that could not in any way be said to have a feminine character. Now, confined in Geneva, Alva concluded, as Sissela Bok noted, that the ECE had become everything for Gunnar, and the family and herself nothing.[92]

Contributing to the crisis was the close relationship between Gunnar and his secretary, Annika de la Grandville, who was efficient, multilingual, and willingly served as his hostess at various ECE events. Alva suffered from being excluded from Gunnar's community. Sissela claimed that Alva never asked Gunnar what had actually happened in the 40 years that followed. Jan pointed out that although Alva was in the house, Annika increasingly took over the hostess role. Jan noted that Gunnar was unusually happy and relaxed when she was in the room. Jan noticed that his face became almost boyishly open when he looked at her and assumed they had an affair.[93] However, Annika had told Kaj about her family situation—born in Czechoslovakia, divorced from a French nobleman who threatened to take the children at her slightest misstep—which, according to my interview with Kaj Fölster, suggests that Gunnar and Annika "did not cross the line".

---

[90] It came into effect in 2001.
[91] Letter from Alva Myrdal to Karin Kock, April 20th 1945, see Niskanen (2007, p. 122).
[92] Bok (1987, p. 187).
[93] Myrdal (1994, p. 223).

Alva's dream of a complete marriage between spouses and work colleagues was hardly possible to realize under the existing conditions. Nor could Alva's other dream—her own significant professional career—be fulfilled in Geneva. During her time in Geneva, she devoted herself to social issues, especially child pedagogy and children's rights. In 1948, she became the first world chairperson of OMEP, an organization for preschool teachers she had helped to found, with advisory status to UNICEF, UNESCO, and the Council of Europe. It is an international voluntary organization of great significance for post-war child development, but not as well-known as the international organizations that Gunnar and Dag worked for. However, in early 1949, the path opened for a significant international career for her too. Alva Myrdal became head of the UN's social department in New York. Gunnar did not want to accompany her, and daughters Sissela and Kaj stayed in Geneva under the supervision of Karin Anger. The family split. But Gunnar supported Alva by providing extensive information through letters on how the complex UN machinery worked. Alva Myrdal led a department of more than 200 employees, managing social programs and allocating funds to the UN's projects worldwide. She thus became the highest-ranking woman in any international organization. She later wrote: "Now I see clearly that I only became a free person in 1949. And so happy, in New York, in Paris, in New Delhi."[94]

In Geneva, the daughters felt abandoned, with Sissela being 15 and Kaj 13. Sissela claimed that Gunnar was immersed in his work, deeply egocentric even then, and with an inner insecurity that drove him to try to belittle anyone who could be a competitor, he often said that children did not interest him.[95] Gunnar, however, tried to keep up appearances for a while and wrote letters to Alva about how the girls were doing in school, that Kaj had cut her hair, and that Sissela was beautiful and wearing Alva's clothes. He also wrote a letter to Alva on March 13th 1949:

> I think the girls like me—more and more as they get older, although they don't get much from me. I think they understand me on a deeper level, that I'm hardworking and doing important things, that I mean well, that I look good and am fun and youthful and generous to them... I notice nothing of father complexes in them like in Jan. They also know how proud I am of them.

Jan also visited with his wife and first grandchild, moving Gunnar to tears. The relationship with Jan was decent, Gunnar reassuringly wrote to Alva—no conflicts since, Gunnar gave up trying to make him a normal person.[96] But the atmosphere worsened as Gunnar increasingly realized that running the household was his responsibility, from the winter of 1949 to the end of 1952, when the residence in the large house at Les Feuillantines was dismantled. Gunnar buried himself in work more than ever, and Karin Anger became ill. She was overworked, isolated, and depressed and decided to leave Geneva. Alva rushed over and arranged for Karin to return to Sweden. The daughters felt that people were starting to seriously pity

---

[94] Bok (1987, p 195).
[95] Bok (1987, p. 168).
[96] Hirdman (2006, p. 309).

them.⁹⁷ The youngest daughter, Kaj, felt abandoned in the villa in Geneva and found a beloved teacher's family, with young children, sheep, chickens, apple trees, who let her move in with them for a year.⁹⁸ Gunnar visited Kaj in the German family once but fell out with the man of the house. He later reproached Alva for letting Kaj stay with "that Nazi." Kaj was struck by Gunnar's overbearing manner and, and his inability to converse, not even listen, instead harboring preconceived opinions, as the men in her family showed towards people who were important to Kaj.⁹⁹

Alva ensured she got another top job at the UN and was head of UNESCO's social science department in Paris from 1950 to 1955, closer to Gunnar and the family in Geneva. UNESCO, founded in 1945, declared in its charter that the war had been made possible through the denial of the democratic principles of the dignity, equality, and mutual respect of men, and through the substitution of ignorance and prejudice for the doctrine of the inequality of men and races.¹⁰⁰ UNESCO also produced a notable statement on the race issue, with the help of leading researchers in sociology, biology, ethnology, and anthropology; among them was the pioneering social anthropologist Claude Lévi-Strauss. The statement was sent out to more scientists for feedback, including Gunnar Myrdal, who thought the statement should more clearly oppose the biological basis for dividing humans into different races. The text was revised and published in UNESCO (1950) and stated in the first sentence that scientists had reached general agreement in recognizing that mankind is one and that all men belong to the same species, homo sapiens.

During this time, Alva wrote a book with Viola Klein titled *Women's Two Roles*, published in 1956, discussing women's status in Sweden, England, France, and the USA. Women's emancipation involves choosing both a profession and marriage. The idea is that a woman can have the best of both worlds if she just makes an effort. However, it has been pointed out that the book does not foreshadow the 1970s' parental leave and a continuous working life outside the home for women. Instead, a woman's life is divided into three phases: education and career, home with young children, and career again.¹⁰¹

Gunnar in Deep Crisis

Gunnar experienced a serious car accident in Denmark on October 30th, 1952, while on his way to Sweden with colleague Ingvar Svennilson, who was driving; the incident has been described by Stellan Andersson.¹⁰² They were hit by a drunk driver

---

⁹⁷ Bok (1987, p. 200).
⁹⁸ Fölster (1992, p. 90).
⁹⁹ Fölster (1992, p. 90).
¹⁰⁰ Berg, Lundberg, and Tydén (2021, Chap. 4).
¹⁰¹ Myrdal and Klein (1957), written between 1951 and 1956, see Hirdman (2006, p. 344).
¹⁰² Andersson (1998).

who had crossed onto the wrong side of the road near Helsingør. Gunnar hit the dashboard, fainted, lost some front teeth, and injured his hip. He was first treated in Helsingør and then at Lund Hospital. For Gunnar Myrdal, the car accident marked a turning point. From being very active, it suddenly became difficult for him at the age of 53 to move unhindered in the world. He suddenly felt old. He became depressed, more complaining than usual, and difficult to handle for those closest to him. His depression reached a low point in April 1953, when Dag Hammarskjöld was appointed the new Secretary-General of the UN. It was a job he had wanted, but instead, it went to another Swede, a younger economist, whose dissertation Gunnar had opposed and been involved in grading, and who had since developed into a powerful adversary in the Swedish finance bureaucracy.

Trygve Lie had announced in November 1952 before the UN General Assembly his wish to resign as Secretary-General. In recent years, he had been constantly attacked by both the Soviet Union and the USA. During the Korean War, when the US military action was carried out under the UN flag, the Russians boycotted the Security Council and refused to recognize Lie as Secretary-General. He had experienced the coldest period of the Cold War and faced mistrust internally. Dwight D. Eisenhower became the new US president in January 1953, and Stalin died in Moscow in March.

The Security Council deliberated on potential successors to Lie. Names from various quarters were put forward as potential successors to Trygve Lie in the Security Council. Gunnar Myrdal was one of those mentioned early in the speculations by the international press, with his name proposed in the Manchester Guardian, the Observer, and Zurich's Volksrecht newspaper.[103] However, it was a complicated process to find a candidate acceptable to both the USA and the Soviet Union. Internally at the UN, Gunnar Myrdal was apparently never a serious contender.[104] After a Canadian diplomat was voted down by the Soviets, Hammarskjöld was proposed by the British and French, familiar with him from his work in the OEEC.

The Americans were ready to approve him immediately because he was deemed competent, pro-Western, and "as good as we may get," according to Henry Cabot Lodge, the US Ambassador to the UN.[105] He was also accepted by the Russians, although it is unclear how much they knew about Hammarskjöld. It was probably a significant factor that he came from neutral Sweden and was the Deputy Foreign Minister to Östen Undén, who was considered to have an understanding of the Soviet Union. The extent of the Soviets' knowledge of Hammarskjöld's role in the embargo policy is uncertain. After the Security Council's secret meeting on March 31st, 1953, it was announced that the Council had agreed to recommend Dag Hammarskjöld as the new Secretary-General of the UN to the General Assembly.

---

[103] Andersson (1998).

[104] Sweden's ambassador to the USA, Erik Boheman, was mentioned in the internal process, see Landberg (2012, p. 561).

[105] Berggren (2016, p. 105).

Hammarskjöld's appointment as the head of the organization where Gunnar Myrdal was active was a harsh blow to Myrdal's self-esteem. Moreover, it closed the doors to a continued career in top positions in international organizations. In a letter to Alva, Gunnar had pointed out that the only two international jobs he cared about were Secretary-General of the UN and Director-General of the FAO.[106] To Alva, Gunnar wrote on April second 1953:

> Obviously, Dag's appointment means quite a lot to me, though nothing immediate. Probably it will be a bit difficult for us to work in this new relationship—but we will wait and see. It quite definitely closes my further career—FAO can hardly also be given to a Swede… I must concentrate on getting my books out.

He also told Alva that he dreamed about Dag at night. For the first three nights after the announcement, he could not sleep until around three in the morning. Gunnar noted in a letter April fourth 1953: "I am probably very sad deep down inside."

Václav Kostelecký, who worked as Myrdal's assistant at the ECE at this time, claimed that when Myrdal received the news of Hammarskjöld's appointment, he said nothing, but his face and body language expressed surprise and disappointment.[107] Kostelecký said that Myrdal had been prepared to take the entire ECE group to New York to sort out the UN after Trygve Lie's tenure. Kostelecký also claimed that Myrdal, who had been working for the UN since 1947, wanted to offer friendly advice to Hammarskjöld but received evasive and hostile responses. Hammarskjöld was always on guard and did not want to cooperate. The atmosphere between the two top Swedish officials was very cool, according to Kostelecký, until Gunnar Myrdal visited Dag Hammarskjöld in October 1956 and announced his intention to leave the ECE in 1957. In his memorial speech to the Stockholm Student Union after Hammarskjöld's death in September 1961, Gunnar Myrdal described his view of Hammarskjöld's selection as Secretary-General, quoted in Andersson (1998):

> The choice of Dag Hammarskjöld as Secretary-General was, of course, a remarkably fortunate coincidence, and I am sure as surprising to him as to the rest of the world.

Gunnar Myrdal continued his work at the ECE for a while. He began delivering renowned lectures on underdeveloped countries and wrote several books on international economics, utilizing much material from his work at the commission and testing his theses with a broader audience. He hoped that it was as the author of major scientific works that he still had a future. He also managed a couple of trips to South Asia and the Central Asian republics of the Soviet Union while remaining at the ECE (Fig. 8.3).[108]

---

[106] Hirdman (2006, p. 322).
[107] Andersson (1998).
[108] Myrdal (1968, Preface, p. vii).

Fig. 8.3 On April 12, 1957, Gunnar Myrdal's resignation from the ECE was accepted by the UN Secretary-General, Dag Hammarskjöld. (Courtesy of UN Photo)

Conclusions

Myrdal's most significant contribution during his tenure as Executive Secretary of the ECE from 1947 to 1957 was his intense work for increased cooperation within Europe and detente between the West and East. His earlier work on welfare reforms contributed to the idea of seeing international officials as independent technicians who analyze and solve problems rationally, without national biases. According to Myrdal, economic advancement—better economic conditions for the population—was the focus for all countries, and he tried to show that the means to achieve this goal could be made into technical issues. His experience from the Little International spoke for the task of creating a bridge between the West and East. His time as Minister of Trade showed the importance of striving for international cooperation, even in the face of strong headwinds from the superpowers.

In a speech that Myrdal gave when the ECE had been operational for almost 7 years, he evaluated the activities.[109] He noted that the current era was characterized by national integration and international disintegration. This meant that governments had not been prepared for a higher degree of cooperation, not even in the economic field. Despite this, the ECE had fulfilled important functions. Particularly important was the fact that many international disputes had been resolved with the support of the commission. He pointed out the responsibility to support multilateral and bilateral contacts between the West and East. He also noted the importance of the meetings that occurred "off the record" between ECE experts and government representatives of the countries, which evolved into consultations.

Historians have later pointed out that the ECE was a very important but underrated international organization.[110] The ECE combined European internationalism and American ideals without becoming a tool for the confrontational policy during the Cold War. The organization played a central role in distributing coal from Germany to other countries and supporting Europe's reconstruction between 1947 and 1950. Afterwards, the European Coal and Steel Community took over the task, with support from the ECE.

Several Eastern countries were very active when the ECE started its operations, but after the Prague Coup in 1948, Moscow's influence increased, and they began to withdraw from work in the technical committees. When the Eastern countries did not actively participate in the ECE, the problem of duplication of work in relation to the OEEC also increased; both organizations were dominated by Western countries. When the OEEC focused on Western Europe it was up to ECE in Geneva to use its bridgehead and try to save the cooperation between East and West, according to Myrdal.[111]

One can say that Gunnar Myrdal waited out the Cold War, and when the worst of the cold was over, he could move on to new tasks. He left the ECE in 1957 for his work on the *Asian Drama* in New Delhi, where Alva Myrdal served as the Swedish ambassador to India. Meanwhile, the construction of the Swedish welfare model was in full swing, largely according to the blueprints of one of its main architects.

References

Adler-Karlsson G (1970) Western economic warfare 1947–1967, with a foreword by Gunnar Myrdal. TEMA, Rabén & Sjögren, Stockholm

Agrell W (2014) Fred och fruktan Sveriges säkerhetspolitiska historia 1918–2000 (Peace and fear Sweden's security policy history 1918–2000). Historiska Media, Lund

Andersson S (1998) Skiss till en fallstudie Gunnar Myrdals beslut att skriva Asian Drama (Sketch for a case study Gunnar Myrdal's decision to write Asian Drama). Manuscript. The Labor Movement's Archive and Library, Stockholm

---

[109] The speech was given at Bedford College in London on February 25th, 1954, see Barber (2008, p. 110).

[110] Stinsky (2021, p. 241).

[111] Stinsky (2018, p. 61).

Åström S (1992), Ögonblick. Från ett halvsekel i UD-tjänst (Moments: Half a Century in Diplomatic Service), Bonnier Alba, Stockholm

Barber W (2008) Gunnar Myrdal an intellectual biography. Palgrave Macmillan, New York

Berg A, Lundberg U, Tydén M (2021) En svindlande uppgift Sverige och biståndet 1945–1975 (A dizzying task Sweden and aid 1945–1975). Ordfront, Stockholm

Berggren H (2016) Dag Hammarskjöld Att bära världen (Dag Hammarskjöld bearing the world). Max Ström, Stockholm

Bok S (1987) Alva, ett kvinnoliv. Bonniers, Avesta. English edition: Bok S (1991) Alva Myrdal. A daughter's memoir. Radcliffe biography series. Perseus Publishing, Cambridge

Dagerman S (1947) Tysk höst (German Autumn). Norstedts, Stockholm

Ekström T, Myrdal G, Pålsson R (1971) Vi och Västeuropa Andra ronden, andra upplagan av vi och Västeuropa (1962), inklusive första upplagan, ny inledning och fem nya kapitel (We and Western Europe second round, second edition of we and Western Europe (1962), including first edition, new introduction, and five new chapters). TEMA, Rabén & Sjögren, Halmstad

Fölster K (1992) De tre löven En myrdalsk efterskrift (The three leaves a Myrdalian postscript). Bonnier, Stockholm

Gaddis J (2005) Strategies of containment a critical appraisal of American National Security Policy during the cold war, revised and, Expanded edn. Oxford University Press, Oxford

Hirdman Y (2006) Det tänkande hjärtat. Boken om Alva Myrdal. Ordfront, Stockholm. English edition: Hirdman, Y (2008) Alva Myrdal: the passionate mind. Indiana University Press, Bloomington

Holmström M (2011), Den dolda alliansen. Sveriges hemliga NATO- förbindelser (The Hidden Alliance: Sweden's Secret NATO Ties), Atlantis, Stockholm

Jackson W (1990) Gunnar Myrdal and America's conscience. Social engineering and racial liberalism 1938–1987. The University of North Carolina Press, Chapel Hill & London

Karlsson B (1992) Handelspolitik eller politisk handling Sveriges handel med öststaterna 1946–1952, (Trade policy or political action Sweden's trade with the Eastern Bloc 1946–1952, dissertation. Department of Economic History, University of Gothenburg

Kostelecký V (1989) The United Nations economic commission for Europe the beginning of a history. Graphic Systems AB, Göteborg

Lagercrantz O (1966) Den pågående skapelsen: En studie i Nelly Sachs diktning (The ongoing creation: a study in the poetry of Nelly Sachs). Wahlström & Widstrand, Stockholm

Landberg H (2012) På väg … Dag Hammarskjöld som svensk ämbetsman (On the way Dag Hammarskjöld as a Swedish civil servant). Atlantis, Stockholm

Lowe K (2012) Savage continent Europe in the aftermath of world war II. Picador, St Martin's Press, New York

Menand L (2021) The free world, art and thought in the cold war. Picador, New York

Myrdal G (1968) Asian drama an inquiry into the poverty of nations. Twentieth Century Fund, New York

Myrdal J (1994) När morgondagarna sjöng (When the tomorrows sang). Norstedts, Stockholm

Myrdal A, Klein V (1956) Women's two roles, Routledge & Kegan Paul Ltd, London

Niskanen K (2007) Karriär i männens värld Nationalekonomen och feministen Karin Kock (Career in a man's world: the economist and feminist Karin Kock). SNS Publishing, Stockholm

Sevón C (1995) Visionen om Europa, svensk neutralitet och europeisk återuppbyggnad 1945–1948 (The vision of Europe, Swedish neutrality, and European reconstruction 1945–1948). Bibliotheca Historica 3, Helsinki

Stinsky D (2018) A bridge between east and west? G Myrdal and the UN economic commission for Europe 1947–1957. In: Christian M, Skott S, Ondrej M (eds) Planning in cold war Europe competition, cooperation, circulations (1950s–1970s). De Gruyter, Oldenburg

Stinsky D (2021) International cooperation in cold war Europe the United Nations economic commission 1947–64. Bloomsbury Academic, London

UNESCO (1950) Statement on race, July 1950, see four statements on the race question, UNESCO and its programme, COM.69/II.27/A, 1969

Chapter 9
The Swedish Welfare Model: Increased State and Societal Capacity

Gunnar and Alva Myrdal were instrumental in the development of the Swedish welfare state, although its foundations were laid by politicians like Per Albin Hansson, Gustav Möller, Ernst Wigforss, Tage Erlander and Gunnar Sträng. The Swedish welfare state relied on both state intervention and active civil society engagement to drive transformational pressure. Myrdals approach anticipated modern theories suggesting that a strong state and strong civil society fosters increased capacity in both sectors. The Swedish economic policy of the 1950s and 1960s, influenced by Myrdal, focused on full employment and low inflation, supported by both demand- and supply-side measures. Key reforms included universal social insurance, education policy changes, and family policies promoting gender equality. Social democracy also aimed for political hegemony through welfare policies, influencing sectors like the labor market and public education. Despite challenges, the Swedish model achieved significant economic growth, low unemployment, and equitable income distribution. However, some regulations, such as rent controls and agriculture policies, led to economic imbalances. These regulations, combined with political deviations from some of the model's main principles, meant that the economy had difficulty adapting when external pressures increased in the 1970s.

Introduction

Gunnar and Alva Myrdal significantly influenced the establishment of the modern welfare state in Sweden. However, it is also true that the Swedish welfare state began to take shape several decades before their entry into reform work. Gustav Möller played the most central role in the Social Democratic Party for the implementation of the basic security model that eradicated poverty and distress in Sweden. Ernst Wigforss was the party's most influential ideologue for a long time. Before the reforms, Myrdals encountered resistance within their own party, from the bourgeoisie, and the business community. Nonetheless, many of the welfare reforms and policies for modernization, rationalization, and high resource utilization in the economy were long influenced by the Myrdals' thinking, as well as regulations that proved unsustainable in the long run.

State and Civil Society Both Contribute to the Strong Transformational Pressure

"Planned economy" is a term that Gunnar Myrdal often revisited, in his inaugural lecture, the Social Democrats' post-war program, and the book *Beyond the Welfare State*.[1] Planned economy easily conjures images of state ownership, centrally controlled planning, absence of competition, and a lack of freedom, as underscored by economist Friedrich von Hayek, whom Myrdal's opponents cited during the 1940s planned economy debate. Myrdal's critique of the market economy largely concerned its need for efficiency. The private sector was deemed inefficient, but Myrdal believed that an element of planned economy was required to preserve Sweden's democratic and private capitalist structure, as noted in Chap. 7.

After the war, many of the most socialist proposals in the post-war program were abandoned by the Social Democrats. Opposition leader Bertil Ohlin noted in his memoirs about the period 1940–1951 that essentially were implemented the proposals common to the Liberal Party's program and the Social Democrats' post-war program.[2] Myrdal himself argued that social control could be intensified without resorting to socialization.[3]

The implemented framework somewhat resembles the development of both the state and the civil sector's capacity—a theme that has become relevant in modern research on the welfare state.[4] It is about strengthening the transformational pressure in society. The state alone cannot achieve this, as it becomes too strong, authoritarian, and even despotic. Nor can civil society develop on its own; without general laws, regulations, and institutions, societal trust risks being lost.

In a post-war lecture, Myrdal emphasized that the Swedish state is legalistic and democratic.[5] It rigorously defines and binds the legal state between people with more passion than in many other countries. Myrdal also indicated that the continuous

---

[1] The book was published in English (Myrdal 1960) and in Swedish (Myrdal 1961).
[2] Ohlin (1975).
[3] However, he believed that the threat of socialization could be an effective deterrent. Myrdal wrote: "Whether it is a family business or a more impersonal corporation, it is already substantially 'socialized'. Moreover, these activities are constantly influenced by the realization among their owners—as well as corporate leaders—that they must justify their existence as private enterprises every year or risk being more closely regulated or perhaps nationalized," see Myrdal (1961, p. 79).
[4] Acemoglu and Robinson (2019).
[5] Speech to the Stockholm Merchants' Association on January 8, 1946, reproduced in Appelqvist and Andersson (1998, p. 246).

increase in state interventions during various crises has raised the demand for more systematic coordination of efforts. Myrdal was also of the opinion that as people become more aware of protecting their interests, they form organizations that, unlike what liberal theory assumes, aim to change the conditions under which they act.[6] This means that Myrdal recognized that a strong state can promote a strong civil society, which utilizes the state for its purposes.

The state might also need to step in and replace a no longer functioning automatic market mechanism. This largely involved creating a price regulation that fulfills the market principle, especially when large-scale operations and power plays disrupt the pricing mechanism.

In his book on planned economy in the welfare state, Gunnar Myrdal discussed how the government in a Western country tries to coordinate society's actions more rationally to achieve desirable political goals. He also highlighted that under state control, organizations have gained influence and expanded their activities. State authorities usually coordinate with these organizations and often work together with them.[7] Myrdal thus anticipated modern institutional theory. Leading institutional scientists, economist Daron Acemoglu and political scientist James Robinson, co-winners of the Nobel Memorial Prize in Economic Sciences in 2024, suggest that both cooperation and competition between the state and civil society are needed to drive the transformational pressure in the welfare state.[8] Acemoglu and Robinson argue that a welfare state like Sweden resembles the dynamics in Lewis Carroll's children book *Alice Through the Looking Glass*. They particularly highlight the role of the Red Queen in maintaining the pace.[9] Alice competes against the Red Queen, and both run fast, but the trees and everything around them seem to stand still.[10] Alice later recalls that they held each other's hands and that the Queen ran so fast that Alice could barely keep up. Yet, the Queen incessantly shouted, Faster! Faster! Alice felt that she could not run any faster, but she was so out of breath that she could not say it. The strangest thing was that no matter how fast they ran, they did not seem to pass anything. Alice said that in her country, you generally get somewhere else if you run fast for a long time. The Queen considered Alice's homeland to be a sluggish country. In Looking-Glass Land, one maintained one's place only by running as fast as one could. To move forward, it was necessary to increase speed in another way.

In a similar race in modern society, both the state and civil society must move forward to maintain their position, according to Acemoglu and Robinson. If neither the state nor civil society runs as fast as possible, society risks stagnation. Modern theory claims that as the state strengthens, it also becomes harder to monitor. Therefore, civil society must also become stronger to demand accountability and maintain its relative position against the state. In a country like Sweden, it is the

---

[6] Appelqvist and Andersson (1998, p. 251).
[7] Myrdal (1960, Chap. 4, Section 3).
[8] Acemoglu and Robinson (2019).
[9] Acemoglu and Robinson (2019, p. 41).
[10] Carroll (1998, pp. 130–132).

competition between a strong state and a robust civil society that drives development, according to Acemoglu and Robinson. Gunnar Myrdal, preceding them, pointed to a similar link and feedback between the strength of the state and the strength of civil society. In addition to state interventions, local and provincial authorities, as well as other organizations outside the state, are also taking action, according to Myrdal. The increased market intervention by these organizations has led to more state interventions and a greater need for coordination. This has significantly expanded the scope of market interventions.[11]

Acemoglu and Robinson also suggest that when the state is balanced by civil society, cultural norms develop that favor an inclusive society.[12] Gunnar Myrdal, for his part, claimed that people generally liked regulations in Western countries as they are perceived as consequences of a societal process, in which the people themselves participate in steering.[13] However, it is also true that in some instances, Swedish regulatory policies were unsustainable and required modification or complete abandonment, a fact that became increasingly apparent in the 1970s.

Economic Policy

Overall, Swedish economic policy was successful during the 1950s and 1960s, featuring elements of both demand- and supply-side policy, focused on full utilization of both labor and capital. The economic policy was based on the state's active participation in the restructuring and efficiency of the private sector. Gunnar Myrdal's influence was significant in several areas, despite his leaving Sweden in 1947. Many of his colleagues in various projects stayed behind and new ones joined. Karin Kock, Richard Sterner, and Ingvar Svennilson, all participants in the Myrdal Commission, contributed to developing the Swedish model. The Economic Research Department of the Swedish Trade Union Confederation (LO), established in 1943 at the initiative of Gunnar Myrdal and LO's chairman, August Lindberg, was strongly influenced by Myrdal's ideas.[14]

Myrdal and Lindberg almost acted as a tandem, with a joint ambition to fundamentally transform Swedish society.[15] Richard Sterner became the department's first head, and Gösta Rehn, a former student of Myrdal, became a central collaborator. Sterner and Rehn had also served as secretaries in the labor movement's postwar program. Rudolf Meidner then succeeded Sterner as head of LO's research department when the latter was appointed State Secretary to Gunnar Myrdal in 1945. Meidner, a Jewish refugee fleeing Nazism, arrived in Sweden in 1933, where

---

[11] Myrdal (1960, Chap. 4, Section 3).
[12] Acemoglu and Robinson (2021, p. 10).
[13] Myrdal (1960, Chap. 4, Section 3).
[14] Meidner (1998, p. 16).
[15] Ekdahl (2005, p. 109).

Myrdal became his most important teacher at the university and also a strong support during years of great insecurity when Swedish refugee policy was very restrictive. Myrdal ensured Meidner's participation in research projects, helped him secure employment when his German passport was a barrier, and supported his application for Swedish citizenship. Several other economists who had a major influence on economic policy were inspired by Myrdal.

During the war, various regulations of economic activity were introduced, including controls on prices, rents, interest rates, and wages, as well as currency regulation. The labor movement's post-war program and the Myrdal Commission had proposed the gradual removal of many of the war's regulations, which was also carried out. However, price control and control of capital movements with currency regulation were retained, as recommended in both programs.[16]

Currency regulation isolated Sweden from the global financial world and for a long time formed the basis of the stabilization policy of the Swedish model. The Swedish krona's exchange rate against the US dollar was fixed. Cross-border capital flows were limited to what was necessary to support foreign trade. The Swedish central bank (the Riksbank) also regulated domestic lending and particularly facilitated financing of housing construction at low interest rates. Fiscal policy played a central role in achieving full resource utilization, equitable income distribution, and a growing public sector. Fiscal policy was refined by introducing new instruments to control investments, housing construction, and more.

An economic policy model for full employment and low inflation across the entire economy was introduced in the 1950s. It was developed by LO economists Gösta Rehn and Rudolf Meidner, both closely associated with Gunnar Myrdal. In the fall of 1944, Myrdal published an article in the trade union movement's magazine arguing that the most urgent task was to resist inflation with all might. The dilemma Myrdal formulated concerned maintaining full employment without leading to inflation.[17] He emphasized the need to make the economy more efficient. In a speech to LO's representative assembly in April 1945, Myrdal claimed that with the Social Democratic policy, the trade union movement was entering a new phase. Wage policy had to depend on the production capacity of the economy. The only way to counter the threat of inflation at full employment was by streamlining the economy and broadening the production base.[18] The trade union movement had to ensure that wage demands corresponded to the increase in productivity, otherwise, it would lead to inflation. Myrdal also called for centralization of wage policy.

Rehn and Meidner were inspired by Myrdal but realized that it was difficult for the trade union movement to take such a large overarching societal economic responsibility on its own. They identified excess demand in good times as an important cause of wage increases—wage drift—beyond the agreements. Rehn and Meidner therefore developed a theory for full employment based on a generally

---

[16] Lindbeck (1968, p. 28).

[17] Ekdahl (2005, p. 143).

[18] Ekdahl (2005, p. 150).

restrained fiscal policy, combined with expansive, selective measures to increase employment in the weakest sectors. According to the Rehn–Meidner model, trade unions should pursue a solidarity wage policy, meaning equal pay for equal work. Thus, wage differences between sectors would decrease, contributing to rationalizations and rapid structural transformation. The state assisted in moving and training people for employment in new, profitable industries when old, unprofitable ones were phased out. The model was presented in a report to the LO congress in 1951 and became a central part of the Swedish model from the mid-1950s.

The Swedish government effectively fostered innovation through various means, including public procurement, technical cooperation, regulation, and the establishment of standards in housing, safety, and environmental protection. Corprorate allocations for investments were tax-favorable through a system of state investment funds, inspired by Gunnar Myrdal and other economists. Allowing for the free deducation of R&D expeditures meant that 90% of the R&D spending in the Swedish manufacturing sector was financed internally by the firms themselves. Large public investment projects were financed through taxes and by channeling houshold savings into public pension funds.

Economic historians have pointed out that several development blocks were created when the state collaborated with private actors.[19] Electricity was at the center of one such development block, where the state-owned Vattenfall was the purchaser of equipment from ASEA (General Swedish Electrical Company), which became a world-leading supplier with cutting-edge expertise in high-voltage technology. The interaction between the state-owned Televerket (Telecommunications Company) and LM Ericsson was another example of how cooperation between state orders and privately owned production led to technological advancements in telephony. A third development block was the expansion of the public road network, the emergence of motoring, and the Swedish car and truck industry. Behind the protective measures of tariffs and import restrictions, and bolstered by tax subsidies, Scania and Volvo emerged as two of the world's three largest manufacturers of heavy trucks.

The policies stimulated and supported high growth and propagated the established large-scale industrial firms with concentrated private ownership but deliberately ignored the formation of new firms and the importance of small firms: a dynamic but aging social economy with a large public sector.

Social Reforms

The social reforms implemented were universal, intended to benefit everyone in the spirit of Möller, Wigforss, and Myrdal. In 1955, a general and compulsory insurance against income loss, funded about 80% by employer contributions and the rest by the state, was introduced. The labor market parties LO (The Swedish Trade Union Confederation) and SAF (The Employers´ Organization), played a

---

[19] Schön (2014, p. 335).

significant role in establishing the system. Unemployment insurance became almost universal two decades later, in 1974.[20]

The foundations of the new education policy were laid out in the labor movement's post-war program in 1944, with Alva Myrdal as a central driving force.[21] The idea was to replace the existing school forms with a unified 9-year comprehensive school, the grundskola, and to remove economic barriers to higher education. The aim of the education policy was to achieve increased social equality both in education and in society at large.

As we saw in Chap. 5, it was Gunnar Myrdal who pushed through a proposal for free school lunches in the Population Commission's work in the 1930s. This gradually began to be realized in the 1950s and 1960s. The reform has recently been evaluated by combining data from its gradual introduction with extensive registry data.[22] The conclusion is that the free school lunches had significant positive consequences. The nutritious lunch contributed to an increase in students' body length. Moreover, the duration of education increased, as did the likelihood of progressing to university studies. The free school lunches also had positive lifelong economic consequences. According to the study, the school lunches are an economic success. The children's increased lifetime incomes were almost four times greater than the cost of the free school lunches.

In the 1950s, the focus of Swedish family policy shifted from population policy to social policy, under family minister Ulla Lindström.[23] In 1946, she was recruited as an expert to the Ministry of Commerce by Gunnar Myrdal, then Minister of Trade. Myrdal thought Lindström was capable and should be appointed chair of an inquiry into the Swedish furniture industry. When he brought up the matter in the government, there was little enthusiasm for a woman leading the inquiry. In the end, it was supported by the Prime Minister Per Albin Hansson who noted that it was probably a good proposal and he was ready to invest more in such young people, especially if they were women, as too few of them had been given a chance.[24]

By the end of the 1960s and the beginning of the 1970s, a vision of an equitable gender contract emerged, with a fair distribution between men and women of wage and home work.[25] Ultimately, however, society, state, and municipality had overarching responsibility for children's conditions in line with the ideology of Myrdals. Alva Myrdal increasingly made her mark in Swedish politics in the 1960s. She was elected to parliament in 1962 and succeeded Lindström in the government in 1967. Myrdal was responsible for, among other things, disarmament and equality (Fig. 9.1).

---

[20] In 1974, a cash labor market support was introduced for those not in any voluntary unemployment insurance fund. The aim was to provide basic economic security for those entering the labor market.

[21] Rothstein (2010, p. 103).

[22] Lundborg and Rooth (2022).

[23] Sjögren (2003).

[24] Myrdal (1982, p. 201).

[25] SOU (1990, p. 44).

Fig. 9.1 Alva Myrdal and Olof Palme were both known for combining a strong interest in welfare issues with a passionate international commitment. Here they are together at the Social Democratic Party Congress in 1973. (Courtesy of the Swedish Labor Movement's Archives and Library)

Alva Myrdal also led a working group on equality issues jointly appointed by the Social Democrats and LO. A report to the party congress in 1969 stated that the two-income family should be the norm for long-term changes in social policy. An expanded maternity insurance was made gender-neutral. The work contributed to transforming maternity insurance into parental insurance, introduced in 1974, making Sweden the first country in the world to introduce insurance that enabled fathers to take parental leave.[26] The expansion of municipal childcare was accelerated through special state subsidies. More and more women began to work, and for a long time, the demand for childcare places exceeded the supply.

The description above is a sketch of some central components of the Swedish model during the first decades after World War II when physical and human capital, welfare, and the public sector increased in a way that attracted international attention. The period was successful both in terms of economic growth and reduced economic inequality. Employment increased in service production and particularly in public service production. Public sector expenditures rose from a quarter of GDP in 1950 to about two-thirds of GDP in the second half of the 1970s. The idea was to both streamline the market economy and expand the public sector. Sweden was one of the first countries to achieve "near-permanent full employment."[27]

---

[26] Wennemo (2014, p. 168).

[27] Unemployment in recessions peaked at 2–2.5% and in booms at 1–1.5%. Assar Lindbeck noted a lack of success in fighting inflation, which had been slightly higher than the OECD average.

Disruptions and Imbalances

However, some regulations within the Swedish model led to various disruptions and imbalances, sparking debate and political revisions. Gunnar Myrdal had already pointed out in two articles in Tiden in the early 1950s, which reported that direct price controls were ineffective as a means against inflation.[28] Myrdal warned of the risk that policy degenerates into a guerrilla war against price movements, caused by inflationary pressure which the planning authorities lacked the will or strength to prevent.[29] He advocated instead for general, coordinated demand-restricting measures, particularly fiscal policy, to eliminate inflationary pressure, in line with the Rehn–Meidner model.

Other regulations contributing to imbalances were established in housing policy, heavily influenced by Gunnar Myrdal. The direction of Swedish housing policy after the war was set by the *Bostadssociala utredningen* (the Housing Social Investigation), which published its main report in 1946 and 1947. Myrdal was one of the members, and Alf Johansson, one of Myrdal's oldest friends, worked as the inquiry's secretary.[30] The inquiry proposed general measures to raise housing standards, eliminate overcrowding and housing shortages. Alf Johansson became the leading ideologue of social housing policy and in 1948 became the director-general of the National Board of Housing. The state regulated financing, building norms, and large, rationally, and industrially planned building projects. Banks and insuranc companies were compelled to invest in public bonds, which funded a substantial housing program.

Rent regulation contributed to relatively low rents and high demand for housing but also to constraining building and limiting supply. This led to a housing shortage, a surplus of demand for housing. Several economists argued that the cause of the housing shortage was rent control. The housing shortage could only be eliminated with higher and more flexible rents.[31] However, the official policy was that higher rents could not eliminate the housing shortage and were also not desirable for social reasons. Therefore, a decision was made to eliminate the housing shortage by building one million apartments during 10 years. However, so many apartments were built that supply exceeded demand; instead of a shortage of apartments, there was a shortage of single-family homes. Rent regulation and several other elements in housing policy have contributed to low mobility in the Swedish housing market. This is a legacy of the Swedish model that is still intensely debated.

However, during the period 1945–1965, the average annual inflation was 3.8% in both Sweden and the European OECD countries, Lindbeck (1968, pp. 18, 19, 191).

[28] Myrdal (1951).

[29] Myrdal (1951, p. 146). See also Lewin (1967, pp. 348–349).

[30] However, Myrdal resigned from the investigation in November 1945, a few months after his appointment as minister.

[31] Sven Rydenfelt and Eli Heckscher were early critics of rent regulation. Alf Johansson was the main defender of the official housing policy, Lindbeck (1968, p. 151).

Political Ideology and Hegemony of Social Democracy

Thus, state regulations contributed to imbalances in the economy and were criticized by economists. Another type of criticism concerned the political dominance of social democracy, present on both the left and right. Anders Isaksson, author of a classic biography of Per Albin Hansson, noted that Swedish society as a whole never became permeated with socialism, but there was an aspiration of social democracy for political hegemony, based on the welfare state's policies of security, care, health, and labor market, and to some extent in education. Isaksson argued that during the heyday of the welfare state, social democratic politicians built a hegemony over the public sector based on an army of social workers, employment agents, doctors, nurses, and preschool teachers.[32] The Labour Market Board (AMS) and employment offices were staffed with union and politically active personnel, dominated by labor market organizations, especially the LO.

Political scientist Bo Rothstein, in his thesis, den *socialdemokratiska staten* (the Social Democratic State), provides evidence that a cadre of union activists was recruited to implement labor market policy according to new principles. In the recruitment to AMS, founded in 1948, and the county labor boards, no formal competence requirements were set. Promotion was free and not based on years of service, as in traditional civil service. Many individuals with LO backgrounds were promoted to managerial positions. The outward communication aimed to create public understanding of the policy and, among other things, promote mobility in the labor market.

A chief economist at SAF noted that the head of AMS had been so successful in his propaganda that it became ingrained in the public consciousness that one should move, which was not the case in other countries.[33] Using Gunnar Myrdal's terminology, one might say that AMS managed to ensure that the Swedish people adopted the opinions they should have to correspond with a "more complete and accurate perception of reality." Rothstein noted that AMS and the county labor boards achieved good results, with precise goal management, great operational freedom for staff, and support for reform policy.[34]

The ideology of the welfare state was evidently inserted into a context where both the state and civil society were strengthened. However, historian Åsa Linderborg in her thesis argued that social democracy confirmed and strengthened a social-liberal hegemony rather than challenging it.[35] Against this view, historian Sten O. Karlsson argued that social democracy is an independent ideology that seeks to reform society based on the notion of a genuinely social, societal individual and opposes both individualism and class struggle doctrines; the folkhem (the people's

---

[32] Isaksson (1996, chapter "The System Shift").
[33] Rothstein (2010, p. 173).
[34] Rothstein (2010, p. 238).
[35] Linderborg (2001).

home) can even be seen as an organism.[36] But Gunnar Myrdal and contemporary social researchers like Daron Acemoglu and James Robinson emphasize rather that the construction of the Swedish model was characterized by the dynamics and competition between a strong state and a strong civil society, contributing to increased capacity in both sectors and the emergence of an inclusive welfare society.

Conclusions

During the emergence of the Swedish welfare state, general welfare reforms were combined with an economic policy for high resource utilization of both labor and capital. The measures of society were coordinated to streamline the economy. The goal was to achieve rapid development towards higher prosperity. The state actively participated in the modernization of the business sector. Business and workers' organizations were included in the reform work. The Swedish model also contained regulations that contributed to imbalances in the economy. These regulations, combined with political deviations from some of the model's main principles, meant that the economy had difficulty adapting when external pressure increased, which became clear in the 1970s when the international currency cooperation collapsed and oil prices skyrocketed.

Until then, Sweden had for several decades succeeded in increasing citizens' living standards, combining low unemployment with low inflation, and ensuring that income distribution became relatively even, in accordance with the ideas from Myrdal's think tank. Alva Myrdal also gained increasing space in Swedish politics in the 1960s, while Gunnar Myrdal after 1947 mostly worked abroad or with international issues. Instead, many of Gunnar Myrdal's disciples or recruits participated in the construction of the Swedish welfare state. One of the most important collaborators was Ulla Lindström. Their cooperation also concerned development issues in the third world and the construction of Swedish aid to poor countries, as we will see in the next chapter.

References

Acemoglu D, Robinson J (2019) The narrow corridor, states, societies, and the fate of liberty. Penguin Press, New York
Acemoglu D, Robinson J (2021) Non-modernization power-culture trajectories and the dynamics of political institutions. Working Paper, MIT
Appelqvist Ö, Andersson S (1998) Vägvisare – Texter av Gunnar Myrdal. Norstedts, Stockholm. English edition: Appelqvist Ö, Andersson S (1998) The essential Gunnar Myrdal. The New Press, New York
Carroll L (1998) Through the looking glass, original edition 1871. Classic Publishers, Stockholm

---

[36] Karlsson (2001).

Ekdahl L (2005) Mot en tredje väg. En biografi över Rudolf Meidner. II. Facklig expert och demokratisk socialist (Towards a third way. A biography of Rudolf Meidner. II. Union Expert and Democratic Socialist). Arkiv förlag, Lund

Isaksson A (1996) Per Albin 3 Partiledaren (Per Albin 3 the party leader). Wahlström & Widstrand, Stockholm

Karlsson S (2001) Det intelligenta samhället (The intelligent society). Carlsson, Stockholm

Lewin L (1967) Planhushållningsdebatten (The debate on planned economy). Almqvist & Wiksell, Stockholm

Lindbeck A (1968) Svensk ekonomisk politik (Swedish economic policy). Bonnier, Stockholm

Linderborg Å (2001) Socialdemokraterna skriver historia (Social democrats writing history). Dissertation. Atlas, Stockholm

Lundborg P, Rooth DO (2022) Skollunchens effekt på utbildning, hälsa och livsinkomst (The effect of school lunches on education, health, and lifetime income). Ekonomisk Debatt 3(22):42–52

Meidner R (1998) Some reminiscences and lessons. In: Appelqvist Ö, Andersson S (eds) The essential Gunnar Myrdal. The New Press, New York

Myrdal, G (1951) Utvecklingen mot planhushållning I och II (The development towards planned economy I and II) Tiden, pp 71–84 and 134–150

Myrdal G (1960) Beyond the welfare state. Yale University Press, New Haven & London

Myrdal G (1961) Planhushållning i välfärdsstaten. Tiden, Stockholm

Myrdal G (1982) Hur styrs landet? (How is the country governed?). Rabén & Sjögren, Stockholm

Ohlin B (1975) Socialistisk skördetid kom bort (The lost harvest of socialism). Bonniers, Stockholm

Rothstein B (2010) Den socialdemokratiska staten (The social democratic state). Arkiv Publishing, Lund

Schön L (2014) En modern svensk ekonomisk historia (A modern Swedish economic history). Studentlitteratur, Lund

Sjögren M (2003) Familjen i servicedemokratin Ulla Lindström som familjeminister 1954–1966 (The family in service democracy Ulla Lindström as family minister 1954–1966). Socialvetenskaplig Tidskrift 1:66–90

SOU 1990:44, Demokrati och makt i Sverige: Maktutredningens huvudrapport (Democracy and power in Sweden: the main report of the power inquiry)

Wennemo I (2014) Det gemensamma Om den svenska välfärdsmodellen (The common welfare about the Swedish welfare model). Premiss Publishing, Stockholm

Chapter 10
Integration, Development, and Aid to Poor Countries

After World War II, anti-colonial struggles intensified, with many European colonies gaining independence. Ralph Bunche and Gunnar Myrdal played significant roles in advocating for decolonization and analyzing the underdevelopment of former colonies. Myrdal's work emphasized the importance of institutional analysis in understanding and addressing the causes of poverty in these countries. Myrdal's lectures and books on development highlighted the need for economic integration and equal opportunities, arguing that such integration was essential for both national and international progress. He warned of the risks posed by the growing disparity between wealthy and poor nations and advocated for comprehensive national plans for development in underdeveloped countries. Myrdal's work faced criticism from liberal economists but inspired new research on path-dependent development. Myrdal influenced Swedish aid policies, advocating for increased international aid and the establishment of new aid organizations. His interdisciplinary approach and advocacy for international solutions shaped much of the debate on development aid and policies in the mid-twentieth century.

Introduction

After the World War II, many people still lived in countries that were European colonies. The anti-colonial struggle intensified, and the colonies began demanding independence, spurred by the United Nations (UN) Charter of 1945 and the Universal Declaration of Human Rights of 1948. By the late 1940s, India, Pakistan, Ceylon (Sri Lanka), and Burma (Myanmar) had gained independence from Britain. The winds of independence grew stronger in the 1950s. However, colonial powers resisted the liberation movements in what began to be known as the Third World. Ralph Bunche, a key collaborator in Gunnar Myrdal's *An American Dilemma* played a central role in the dismantling of European colonial empires.

Bunche was a leading architect at the UN for the process of nations gaining independence. Gunnar Myrdal's work also increasingly shifted towards analyzing the poor countries of the Third World, whose weak institutions were a legacy of colonial times. Myrdal became an international pioneer in comprehensive institutional analysis of the causes of underdevelopment. He also wrote the foreword to Richard Wright's book on the 1955 Bandung Conference, which brought together 29 Asian and African countries and laid the foundation for the Non-Aligned Movement. Myrdal was also active in the Swedish debate on aid to poor countries, alongside main actors Ulla Lindström and Olof Palme.

Lectures and Books on Development and Underdevelopment

The lectures and books Gunnar Myrdal published in his last years at ECE focused on international issues, integration, development, and aid. They played a significant role in the debate on development aid from wealthy to poor countries.

Myrdal's Cairo lectures at the Central Bank of Egypt in 1955 discussed the disparity between rich and poor countries and were widely noted.[1] The underlying values in these lectures were the desirability of political democracy and equal opportunities for all. In 1956, Myrdal published the comprehensive book *An International Economy*. The book was a revision of the keynote speech he was invited to give at Columbia University's bicentennial celebration in 1954. He detailed his value premises in analyzing problems in the world economy outside the Soviet sphere. The book became a crucial component in Myrdal's long-term work on underdevelopment and poverty.

Value Premises

Myrdal based his value premises on what he believed to be the traditional ideals of freedom and equality in Western countries. He advocated economic integration as an ideal, meaning equal opportunities for all countries and peoples. Integration was viewed at the time as a desirable goal for adaptation within and between nation-states, which had quickly become more interdependent. Myrdal argued that economic integration was not just an economic issue, but also a matter of political science, sociology, and social psychology. He believed that the gradual development toward equal opportunities for all presupposes the emergence of a society with more free social mobility, founded on a more complete realization of the norms of equality and freedom.[2]

---

[1] Myrdal (1957).

[2] Myrdal (1956, p. 26).

Myrdal noted that economic integration is a complex phenomenon requiring a comprehensive analysis. He assumed that general economic advancement in a country is necessary for the ideal of equal opportunities to be realized. At the same time, he argued that increased equality is essential for rapid and sustained economic progress. Myrdal's formulated value premises include:

- economic integration—both national and international.
- equal opportunities in relations between peoples of different countries.
- a democratic form of government is desirable.

In his book, Myrdal pointed out that international trade between advanced and underdeveloped countries had not led to the equalization of prices for production factors (labor, capital) according to traditional trade theory. Instead, the development tends toward a cumulative process away from equilibrium. Myrdal warned that the growing gap between the wealth of the Western world and the poverty in countries in Africa, South America, and Asia could lead to a political disaster. He called for domestic reforms in underdeveloped countries. Western countries must also realize that only when poor countries achieved equality in terms of opportunities has the world become integrated.

Vicious and Virtuous Circles in Underdeveloped Countries and Regions

Gunnar Myrdal addressed the issue of vicious and virtuous circles in several works. He recalled the ambition from *An American Dilemma* to analyze how various external forces affect internal variables in a complete system. In his books, he also referred to contemporary development economists working with similar approaches, mainly Paul Rosenstein-Rodan and Ragnar Nurkse. Rosenstein-Rodan had developed the idea that development required resources to be invested broadly across a range of complementary industries to achieve what he called balanced growth. Nurkse had analyzed the existence of vicious circles due to both low supply (low productivity) and low demand (low incomes). He aimed to break these vicious circles with broad investments in the domestic markets of developing countries, targeting balanced growth.

Myrdal similarly argued that it was pointless to seek a single dominant root factor in analyzing the problems of underdeveloped countries. Many factors—economic and others—needed to be considered. He believed that measures targeted at important factors could improve the entire system. If well-balanced actions are taken at strategic points, they can lead to cumulatively enhanced final effects. Myrdal also warned that poor regions or countries risked a backwash effect when richer regions or countries develop The idea was that the free play of market forces tended toward increasing disparities as market expansion and liberation favored already developed centers of expansion.

Planning for Development

Myrdal believed that a country or region in the process of development could neutralize the backwash effect. This required combating poverty and fully utilizing human resources. In an underdeveloped country, a national plan for a cumulative economic development process was needed. The plan's aim was to maximize overall economic progress, considering the sacrifices the population could accept.[3] The value of larger investments, increased consumption, and improved health and education needed to be considered in the causal cycle, resulting in a final outcome, measured as increased national income, significantly higher than the initial costs that started the process.

Myrdal's books on international economics faced sharp criticism from economists in the liberal tradition. They critiqued Myrdal's pessimistic conclusions about the role of trade and market forces in stagnation and underdevelopment, citing weak analytical and empirical bases for his assessments. The most critical economist was P. T. Bauer, a market liberal opponent of state intervention in the economy. He argued that the price mechanism and individual choices play a central role in the development process. Bauer believed that Myrdal completely overlooked these core aspects of the economic system in his over-reliance on planning and government interventions.[4] However, much later, these books inspired a new research area emphasizing that development is path-dependent. For instance, Brian Arthur analyzed how a rapidly developing region benefits from a combination of good infrastructure, specialization, and economies of scale, leading to a cumulative process in the spirit of Myrdal.[5]

Development Aid and Moral Dilemmas

Myrdal called for increased international aid from advanced industrial countries to poor countries. He became one of the pioneers advocating for development aid through assistance policies.[6] He also highlighted the need for an international capital market to ensure capital imports to underdeveloped countries and increased mobility of people between countries.

Myrdal noted a moral dilemma in Western countries related to "the welfare state – which we have built up, with which we deeply identify, which we are not prepared to compromise on, and which we are determined to continually improve – being nationalistic."[7] He pointed out that solidarity developed rapidly but remained

---

[3] Myrdal (1957, p. 120).
[4] For an overview of the criticism against Myrdal's books in the 1950s, see Lundahl (2021, Chap. 5).
[5] Arthur (1994).
[6] Myrdal (1956).
[7] Myrdal (1956, p. 420).

confined within national borders, even as nations became increasingly interdependent. This moral dilemma between the national welfare state and international solidarity later became prominent in many European welfare states.

The Bandung Conference

At this time, the underdeveloped countries began to be referred to as the Third World, a term coined in 1952 by French demographer Alfred Sauvy, to indicate that the Third World, like the Third Estate during the French Revolution, wanted to become something from nothing. Several of these countries met in 1955 at a conference in Bandung, Indonesia. Organized by Indonesia's President Sukarno with support from India's Prime Minister Jawaharlal Nehru, the Bandung Conference brought together 29 countries from Asia and Africa. The Soviet Union was not invited, while China was represented by Premier Zhou Enlai. The conference agreed on ten principles, later playing a significant role in the founding of the Non-Aligned Movement in Belgrade in 1961. These principles included equality between all races and between small and large countries and not participating in collective defense alliances favoring any superpower's interests.

Gunnar Myrdal wrote the foreword to Richard Wright's book on the conference, *The Color Curtain. A Report on the Bandung Conference*. Wright, born in 1908 in a poor family in Mississippi, became the most famous black author in the world with his breakthrough novel *Native Son*, the first book by a black author to be chosen as a Book of the Month in the USA, and *Black Boy*, describing his upbringing in Mississippi. When the Myrdals lived in New York, Wright was one of their friends who often visited. He was part of a circle of cultural workers whom Alva believed were important to understand African-American culture.[8] In 1946, Wright moved to Paris with the help of Gertrude Stein and Claude Lévi-Strauss, where he met authors Jean-Paul Sartre, Simone de Beauvoir, and Albert Camus. When Wright arrived in Paris, a journalist from the resistance newspaper Combat asked him if the problem of blacks in the USA was close to being solved. Wright's response, "There is no black problem in the USA, there is a white problem," has been interpreted as echoing the main thesis of *An American Dilemma*, published 2 years earlier.[9] Wright also influenced Simone de Beauvoir about Myrdal's major work on race, contributing to her decision to write a similarly impactful book on women's status, resulting in her groundbreaking work *The Second Sex*.[10]

Wright, a former communist who left the party during the war, attended the Bandung Conference as a representative for the Congress for Cultural Freedom,

---

[8] Bok (1991, p. 135).
[9] Menand (2021, p. 390).
[10] Kirkpatrick (2019, Chap. 11).

unknowingly sponsored by the Central Intelligence Agency (CIA).[11] Key themes at the conference included colonialism, racism, and Western powers' attempts to sideline Asian countries' interests during the Cold War. Additionally, the conference discussed the significant tension between the USA and China and the hope of establishing cooperation between poor countries—the Third World now becoming a central concept.

Richard Wright was one of those who ensured that Bandung, in retrospect, became associated with solidarity among the people of the Third World against the white Western world. It has been claimed that the book's title, *The Color Curtain*, is a metaphor clearly alluding to the Cold War and suggesting a global confrontation based on race rather than ideology.[12] Wright warned in his book that it represented the last call of Western-aligned Asians to the moral conscience of the Western world. If the West did not change its stance, there was a risk that China would exploit the situation. China could step into an anti-Western house built on the reaction against colonialism and racism, according to Wright.[13] However, other observers, like New York Times Asia correspondent Tillman Durdin, believed Wright exaggerated the risk of a race-based confrontation.[14] Durdin argued that Bandung was not about a manifestation of colored people against white people. A later analyst, Louis Menand, suggested that the conference was largely pro-Western, and solidarity among oppressed races was not particularly prominent at that time.[15]

Gunnar Myrdal praised Richard Wright in his foreword to Wright's book.[16] He noted that Wright did not intend to write a documented analysis of the Bandung Conference. He only recounted what he, as a visiting reporter from a foreign land, heard, saw, felt, and thought. Wright focused on two forces beyond Left and Right: Religion and Race. These forces united and separated people from the West. They also caused internal divisions and conflicts. Religion, shaped by thousands of years of history, influenced their culture and values. Race represented their reaction to Western prejudice and colonialism. Consequently, Asia and Africa carried irrational elements from both East and West, according to Myrdal's interpretation of Wright's book.

Swedish Development Assistance

In the first decades following the war, Swedish aid to developing countries was guided by the United Nations' visions. In 1949, the UN Economic and Social Council (ECOSOC) established a framework for bilateral aid programs based on

---

[11] Menand (2021, p. 410).
[12] Menand (2021, p. 411).
[13] Wright (1956, p. 202), also cited in Menand (2021, p. 412).
[14] Menand (2021, p. 412).
[15] Menand (2021, p. 410).
[16] Gunnar Myrdal's preface to Wright (1956).

cooperation, coordination, and mutual respect.[17] The UN's Expanded Programme for Technical Assistance (EPTA) encouraged wealthy countries to offer their experts for development in poor countries and to accept scholars from these countries. In 1951, Sweden's representative in ECOSOC was Richard Sterner, a collaborator of Gunnar Myrdal from the Population Commission, the book on the American dilemma, and a secretary during his tenure as Minister of Trade. Working for the Foreign Office under Dag Hammarskjöld, Sterner reported international pressure from underdeveloped countries for resources for an international Marshall Plan. Sweden's contributions to EPTA were lower than many other wealthy countries, even considering its population. This was coupled with criticism of Sweden's neutrality during the war and its refusal to join NATO, formed in April 1949 by 12 Western countries led by the USA. A generous Swedish aid policy would better emphasize a desire to remain apart from military and political engagements.

Cabinet Secretary Arne S. Lundberg at the Foreign Office thus drafted a proposal for a national committee with representatives from civil society movements and labor market parties, to help coordinate, prioritize, and distribute aid efforts. A unified national effort was needed for the underdeveloped countries, whose problems were long-term, and Swedish activities should be sustainable. Public education about the need for aid to poor countries became a central part of the operation. Aid was not a limited campaign but a permanent demand on people's conscience.

The Central Committee for Technical Assistance to Less Developed Areas (CK)

The established organization was named the Central Committee for Technical Assistance to Less Developed Areas (CK) and functioned as an umbrella organization active from 1952 to 1961. Its operation rested on three pillars: organization, education, and a small number of bilateral projects. It was funded both by government funds and voluntary contributions. The committee was largely led by an inner circle of directors, diplomats, academics, politicians, and trade unionists from the upper echelons of public Sweden. The chair was Axel Gjöres, a former cooperative leader and Minister of National Economy.

Ulla Lindström became Sweden's first Minister for Development Cooperation in 1954. She was a Swedish delegate to the UN from 1947 to 1966 and one of the few women participating in the UN General Assembly during its early years. A proponent of multilateral aid like Gunnar Myrdal, Lindström sometimes clashed with those in CK who emphasized Swedish bilateral efforts. She believed overpopulation was a primary cause of hunger and poverty, a view shared by Gunnar and Alva Myrdal.

---

[17] Berg, Lundberg, and Tydén (2021, Chap. 4).

Lindström focused on the need for family planning aid in developing countries. CK organized pioneering projects on family planning in Ceylon (Sri Lanka) in 1958 and Pakistan in 1961. However, family planning was a sensitive topic at the time. In 1960, Lindström candidly spoke at the UN about the need for birth control and contraceptives to curb the dramatic population increase. After her speech, UN Secretary-General Hammarskjöld jokingly noted that the whole UN blushed.[18]

In 1960, the UN adopted a variant of the 1% target for aid from rich to poor countries.[19] A decade of development was proclaimed by the UN General Assembly the following year. At that time, Sweden was at the bottom internationally, providing aid equivalent to 0.05% of its Gross National Product, while the average in other developed countries was around half a percent. This meant a significant need for Sweden to increase aid funding, strengthen diplomatic relations with recipient countries, and enact new legislation.

Committee for International Aid

Consequently, the Swedish state stepped in and gradually took control of foreign aid. NIB (The Committee for International Aid) was established as a traditional government agency, following a proposal by Minister Ulla Lindström, and was active from 1962 to 1965, when it was replaced by Sida (Swedish International Development Cooperation Agency). The government gained significant influence over aid. Multilateral aid, channeled through international organizations, was placed under the Foreign Office. Olof Palme, then Agency Manager of the Prime Minister's Office, outlined in Parliament what the new agency would not do: financial aid, trade policy, and multilateral efforts. NIB focused on specific bilateral aid projects. The fundamental principles of foreign aid were developed in a separate process and presented in bill 1962:100, with Olof Palme as a leading actor.

Alva and Gunnar Myrdal were active as inspirers and administrators in shaping Swedish state aid policy. As Sweden's envoy and ambassador to India—also responsible for Ceylon (Sri Lanka), Burma (Myanmar), and Nepal—Alva was involved in negotiations on various aid efforts in South Asia, including the family planning pilot project in Ceylon, discussed more in the next chapter.

Upon her return to Sweden, Alva Myrdal became a board member of NIB, alongside Olof Palme. Aid became a new political area involving many different actors and interests. Several organizational problems arose when it was launched.

---

[18] Bjereld et al. (2008, p. 211).

[19] The aid target initially encompassed flows from both private and public sectors in developed countries but was later modified to 0.7% of Gross National Product, applying to public aid. Since 1974, the target has been expressed as a percentage of the Gross National Income of developed countries.

Preparation for International Aid Issues

The Preparation for International Aid Issues—the U-Committee—was appointed by Prime Minister Tage Erlander to discuss the challenges of aid policy in broad consensus. Representatives from the state, business, and civil society were included. The goal was to unite forces and demonstrate Sweden's international solidarity and responsibility. It operated for a year from spring 1961 to early 1962. About 50 people were engaged, including several ministers and Erlander as chairman.

Gunnar Myrdal participated in the U-Committee's first meeting in early 1961 and gave a speech. He argued that when it came to helping underdeveloped countries, it was crucial to highlight the huge, unstable social, economic, and political reality with a complex and hard-to-understand movement system, which was only partially understood.[20]

Regarding the organization of aid, Myrdal believed there were strong reasons for it to be primarily provided through intergovernmental bodies. This approach would increase total resources. Intergovernmental bodies were also more independent than national ones, had greater acceptance in recipient countries, and could draw experts from around the world.

However, there were also reasons for Swedish efforts in areas where intergovernmental organizations were not effective. Myrdal promoted, for example, spreading knowledge about birth control—family planning—in poor countries, as there was a shameful alliance between Catholics and Communists in intergovernmental bodies that prevented effective work in this area.[21]

He wanted to prioritize three areas of assistance: providing food to starving people, supporting agricultural production, and focusing on health, medical care, and birth control. He was also positive about supporting Non-Governmental Organization (NGOs) with special expertise in operating in poor countries.

Myrdal also pointed out that in facing development problems, everyone was a newcomer. He compared the challenges of aid to those faced by a marching army in volcanic terrain. The way back was forever closed, even though aid workers were equipped with good maps and even though the ground was shaking beneath them, it was necessary to march on and find the way.[22]

U-Group and Bill 1962:100

Within the U-Committee, there was a working group known as the U-group, led by Olof Palme. This group, comprising officials from various departments, was where most of Bill 1962:100 was formulated. The bill was approved in Parliament in May

---

[20] Myrdal (1964, p. 129).

[21] Myrdal (1964, p. 143).

[22] Myrdal (1964, p. 128).

1962. The process leading to this renowned aid bill was subject to intense criticism. The Minister for Development Cooperation, Ulla Lindström, felt overlooked. She was not even allowed to sign the bill, which was done by the Prime Minister, Tage Erlander.

A historian has claimed that allowing an independent working group to shape aid policy breaks with practice; issues of this magnitude should be prepared by state investigations.[23] Gunnar Myrdal shared this view. He participated in meetings with the U-Committee and was not afraid to spark debate on the issue. Myrdal criticized in an article in the daily newspaper Stockholmstidningen, that it was an expression of inner circles and the establishment's alleged secrecy.[24] Olof Palme responded to Gunnar Myrdal in Stockholmstidningen, October 7th, 1962, defending the handling. He argued that it saved time, as a normal investigation would have taken at least another year. Palme also noted that the U-Committee itself, with participants from political parties and civil movements, emphasized that it was about a mobilization for international solidarity. According to Palme, more material had been published than in many other issues, thanks to the work in the U-group. Olof Palme concluded by stating:

"The handling of development aid does not seem to be a particularly fine example of 'secrecy.' It is further an area where Gunnar Myrdal, through his own involvement, should have particularly good knowledge of the actual circumstances. This gives rise to the suspicion that he also lacks a basis for his very sweeping accusations in other areas".

According to Olof Palme's biographer, Kjell Östberg, the U-group's work was an early example of Palme's ability to improvise and find solutions that did not always follow the rule book, perhaps not even the constitution, but achieved the desired results.[25]

With Bill 1962:100, the principles for Swedish aid policy were established for a long time. The goals were now formulated and would endure for several decades. The aim of aid giving was to raise the living standards of the poor people. Concretely, this meant eliminating hunger and mass poverty, eradicating epidemic diseases, reducing child mortality, and overall creating bearable living conditions.[26] Aid became an expression of international solidarity, a moral duty, and part of foreign policy, characterized by mutual cooperation rather than unilateral help. During 1963–1966, aid increased by about 30% per year, and the number of partner countries grew. The aid was to gradually increase to match 1% of the Gross National Product. During this process, the term underdeveloped countries was also replaced with developing countries. Gunnar Myrdal primarily advocated international solutions. In his view, the Swedish aid effort, even if it were ten times larger than now,

---

[23] Östberg (2010, p. 225).
[24] Östberg (2010, p. 225).
[25] Östberg (2010, p. 225).
[26] Berg, Lundberg and Tydén (2021, Chap. 7).

was still vanishingly small compared to the need for help—like "spitting in the sea," as his grandmother in Dalarna used to express it dramatically.[27]

From the mid-1960s, the foreign policy dimension of aid policy was strengthened when Sweden began supporting liberation movements, mainly in South Africa, Namibia, Southern Rhodesia (Zimbabwe), and the Portuguese colonies of Angola, Guinea-Bissau, Cape Verde, and Mozambique. When the government in 1966 did not fulfill the promise to increase aid to 1% of GDP, Ulla Lindström resigned from the government in protest.

Conclusions

The books Gunnar Myrdal published on the world economy introduced theories on trade and integration, development, and underdevelopment, which in several respects shaped the debate in the 1950s and 1960s. They dealt both with the need for international cooperation and the difference between rich and poor countries as colonial empires were dismantled and the Third World rose. Myrdal, however, received criticism from liberal economists for underestimating the role of market forces and foreign trade in economic development. Alva and Gunnar Myrdal both actively participated in shaping state aid policy, but it was Ulla Lindström and Olof Palme who were the central figures in deciding the principles and direction of Swedish state aid.

The books Gunnar Myrdal published in the 1950s were preparations for his work on *Asian Drama*. Gunnar Myrdal had become one of the world's most distinguished institutional economists, fully equipped to implement his interdisciplinary approach in a novel context. Angresano (1997, p. 1) has pointed out that Myrdal combined the same conception with an interdisciplinary method of analysis in *An American Dilemma*, implementation of economic recovery measures in Europe after World War II, and investigation of the causes of poverty in underdeveloped nations. Myrdal viewed the economy not as a static entity, but as an ongoing process comprised of the aggregate of institutions which perform economic functions and determine economic conditions. These institutions behave according to working rules, many of which are established by authorities who allocate scarce resources while answering questions pertaining to production and distribution of goods and services. Working rules are both formal and informal, and exist at different levels (for example, household, firm, nationwide) either with or without sovereign power exercised by the state.

Alva's service as Swedish ambassador to India made it possible for them to live together again. This contributed to Gunnar embarking on an all-consuming task where, according to a letter from Alva to Gunnar on July 15th 1956, he could shape a "new message of equality, in a scientifically intelligent form. Darling, there is so much worth living for".

---

[27] Myrdal (1964, p. 142).

References

Angresano J (1997) The political economy of Gunnar Myrdal – an institutional basis for the transformation problem. Edward Elgar, Cheltenham

Arthur W (1994) Increasing returns and path dependence in the economy. The University of Michigan Press, Ann Arbor

Berg A, Lundberg U, Tydén M (2021) En svindlande uppgift Sverige och biståndet 1945–1975 (A dizzying task Sweden and aid 1945–1975). Ordfront, Stockholm

Bjereld U, Johansson A, Molin K (eds) (2008) Sveriges säkerhet och världens fred (Sweden's security and world peace). Santérus, Stockholm

Bok S (1987) Alva, ett kvinnoliv. Bonniers, Avesta. English edition: Bok S (1991). Alva Myrdal. A daughter's memoir. Radcliffe biography series. Perseus Publishing, Cambridge

Kirkpatrick K (2019) Becoming Beauvoir: a life. Bloomsbury Academic, London

Lundahl M (2021) The dynamics of poverty circular, cumulative causation, value judgements, institutions, and social engineering in the world of Gunnar Myrdal. In: Cohen A, Harcourt G, Kriesler P (eds) Palgrave studies in the history of economic thought. Palgrave Macmillan, Cham

Menand L (2021) The free world, art and thought in the cold war. Picador, New York

Myrdal G (1956) An international economy, problems and prospects. Harper and Brothers Publishers, New York

Myrdal G (1957) Economic theory and underdeveloped regions. Gerald Duckworth, London

Myrdal G (1964) Vår onda värld (Our evil world). Rabén & Sjögren, Stockholm

Östberg K (2010) I takt med tiden. Olof Palme 1927–1969 (In step with the times. Olof Palme 1927–1969). Leopard, Stockholm

Wright R (1956) The color curtain a report on the Bandung conference with a foreword by Gunnar Myrdal and an afterword by Amritjit Singh. New edition 1994 banner books University Press of Mississippi, Jackson

Chapter 11
Asian Drama

Gunnar Myrdal's ambitious project *Asian Drama* tackled development issues in South Asia. Myrdal's work aimed to understand the complexities of underdevelopment from an institutional perspective. Myrdal highlighted the challenges of selecting value premises for Asian nations due to their heterogeneity and the low political participation outside the elite. He emphasized modernization ideals like rationality, productivity, and social discipline while critiquing the "soft state" for its weak implementation of policies. Myrdal addressed the significant role of non-economic factors like attitudes and institutions, arguing that these must change to break the cycle of poverty. He underscored the importance of family planning in tackling rapid population growth in order to increase living standards. But he criticized the practical implementation of planning in South Asia, noting that it often favored the upper social strata. *Asian Drama* published in 1968 received mixed reviews, praised for its comprehensive analysis but critiqued for not emphasizing that development requires more market mechanisms and foreign trade. Despite criticism, Myrdal's institutional approach and focus on both economic and non-economic factors when implementing policy to reduce poverty remain influential.

Introduction

The work of Gunnar and Alva increasingly focused their attention on international development issues. Alva's work at UNESCO led to an invitation to visit India in late 1952. The visit was overwhelming, almost like a conversion, she wrote to Gunnar.[1] She was deeply moved by the country's culture and met Jawaharlal Nehru, India's first Prime Minister, becoming personal friends with him, whom she

---

[1] Hirdman (2006, p. 322).

described as the white man in her life.² Their first encounter was at a seminar on Gandhi. During a photo session, Alva was placed next to Nehru on a lawn when Ralph Bunche walked in, and she noted, in a draft written on October 7th 1982, that:

> he was sparkling as usual with interest in everything and everyone. I rushed to him, forgetting convention, we embraced, hugged, and kissed. A bit embarrassed, I returned to my place beside Nehru and muttered apologetically, 'We're such old, good friends.' And Nehru, with a laugh in his voice, said, 'Don't explain. Don't make it worse.'³

In the fall of 1953, Gunnar Myrdal also visited India. He traveled around South Asia with the head of the UN Economic Commission for Asia and the Far East, Professor PS. Lokanathan, meeting government representatives, experts, academics, and visiting industries and villages.⁴ The idea of a new major book on the development problems in Asia began to take shape. Myrdal thought New Delhi would be a suitable city to write such a book. He described this journey in *Asian Drama* (Preface, p. vii.):

> I made a six-weeks' tour of South Asia in the autumn of 1953, visiting Pakistan, India, Burma (Myanmar), Thailand, and Indonesia. [...] Since the visit, I have never been free of an intense awareness of the monumentous human drama of the desparate strivings for national consolidation and economic development in South Asian countries. I decided then that as soon as I could free myself with good conscience from my duties at ECE, I would return for a couple of years to these countries and devote myself to studying economic underdevelopment, development, and planning for development.

At this time, Alva Myrdal was beginning to engage in dialogue with the Swedish government about an ambassadorial post abroad. When the Foreign Office asked in the summer of 1955 if she wanted to become Sweden's first female envoy to India, she gladly accepted. She served as Sweden's ambassador to India, Ceylon (Sri Lanka), Burma (Myanmar), and Nepal from 1955 to 1961.⁵ On a flight from Zurich to Karachi, on her way to take up the post in New Delhi, Alva wrote in a letter to Gunnar on November 30th 1955:

> This is to be the last great ambitious foray into the world that lasts and works far beyond our personal fates, we have agreed on that... Gunnar – here I am traveling to India – to what was a land of youthful dreams of pearls and turbans, of rajas, of Mughal history, and Gandhi and Tagore and Buddha. I'm traveling there, paid by our own Swedish state with sleeper and all conveniences over the Alps and everything. Gunnar, just put it back into our study-hungry, upstart-unsure childhood. We who met on a fence and found that we wanted so much, can now come together in houses prepared for us in this land of wonders, with human contacts that exclude us from no one.

As ambassador, Alva Myrdal made significant contributions to strengthening relations between Sweden and India. She looked after Swedish interests and wrote reports back to the Foreign Office. Beyond traditional diplomatic tasks, she spent

---

² Bok (1987, p. 210).
³ Myrdal (1982).
⁴ Andersson (1998).
⁵ Lindskog (1981, p. 177).

much time traveling around India and talking about Sweden, often with educational elements and said in an interview that she believed that her many lectures were useful propaganda and the Indians got her message when she talked about Swedish popular education, local self-government, etc.[6] She tried to get them to understand that even with quite simple means, valuable practical things could be learned. She wanted them to start by learning to count. As there are only ten digits they could learn them, according to Alva. Then, it would be possible to check how many sacks of rice they had delivered and how many the merchants ticked off.

During Alva Myrdal's ambassadorship, a new Swedish mission was established in the diplomatic quarter of Chanakyapuri in New Delhi. The Indian state sold the 40,000 square meter plot to the Royal Building Board. The Swedish embassy, with a residence, representation hall, staff housing, and recreational spaces, was designed by Jöran Curman and Sune Lindström, believed to be inspired by the Indian village and making it an architectural and social landmark.[7] The outer walls were painted pink, balustrades and sunshades white. Doors, windows, and built-in cabinets were made of Indian teak and manufactured on-site. Floors were made of concrete mosaic and in some places marble. Electrical installations and office furniture were imported from Sweden, giving the interior a Swedish touch. The contrast between the Swedish residence and the Indian village was, however, striking.

No other member of the diplomatic corps in New Delhi had as good a relationship with Prime Minister Nehru as Alva Myrdal. During her tenure as ambassador in India, Nehru visited Sweden in 1957, with Alva participating in the visit. Prime Minister Tage Erlander noted in his diary that Nehru's visit was a great success for Nehru, and no setback for himself.[8] When Nehru had retired for the night at Harpsund, Tage offered the lingering guests a late-night snack with schnapps, beer, and sandwiches. Alva could not help but regret that the distinguished guest missed out on this Swedish social specialty. The good relations between the countries led to Tage Erlander making a successful reciprocal visit to India at the end of 1959.

Gunnar Myrdal was positive about moving to India and sought financial support for a study of development problems in South and Southeast Asia. He was turned down by the two foundations that had previously supported him generously, the Rockefeller Foundation and the Carnegie Corporation. However, the Twentieth Century Fund agreed to finance for two and a half years.[9] It turned out that the study took 10 years and faced several difficulties before being published in 1968 in three volumes totaling 2284 pages.

Among the staff involved in the early stages were Ester Boserup, a population expert, and her husband Mogens Boserup, both from the research department at Economic Commission for Europe (ECE). Ester Boserup was a Danish development economist who turned Malthus's population theory upside down, arguing that

---

[6] Lindskog (1981, p. 98).
[7] Berggren (2008, p. 91).
[8] Harrison (2017, p. 550).
[9] Barber (2008, p. 121).

greater population density created conditions for the introduction of better agricultural tools and irrigation facilities. Therefore, higher population pressure could contribute to increased agricultural production. She also contributed pioneering work on women's roles in the economy and linked population and gender issues.[10]

However, Ester and Mogens Boserup left the Asian Drama project after a few years, as Ester and Gunnar did not agree on the analysis. In the project's early stages, Gunnar was also assisted by young economists from Oxford, Kamal Azfar and Michael Lipton. Myrdal himself traveled to Oxford in the summers to work on the book. In the early 1960s, however, the entire project was moved to the newly established Institute for International Economics at Stockholm University, where Gunnar Myrdal became professor and its first head in 1962. The project also involved other professors, such as George Wilson and William Barber, and Paul Streeten, who had translated Gunnar Myrdal's earlier methodological books.

Alva Myrdal played an important role, especially in the chapters on health and education, and utilized the five lectures on health and education for economic development she held in 1955 at the tropical medical training at the University of London.

Value Premises

The title *Asian Drama: An Inquiry into the Poverty of Nations* consciously echoes Adam Smith's classic book *An Inquiry into the Nature and Causes of the Wealth of Nations* from 1776. Myrdal's book, focusing on development problems in South Asian countries, is written from a broad, institutional, and social science perspective. The countries covered include India, Pakistan, Ceylon (Sri Lanka), Burma (Myanmar), Malaysia, Thailand, Indonesia, the Philippines, and to some extent Cambodia, Laos, and South Vietnam. Central to the drama are the peoples and the educated elite of South Asian countries, focusing on the internal conflict experienced between high hopes and the harsh realities of life, between the desire for change and the obstacles that can be raised against these changes.

Myrdal pointed out that selecting value premises for analyzing South Asian countries is more difficult than for similar studies in Western countries. This is due to a lack of knowledge about how people in different social groups and locations truly experience their living conditions and to what extent they would be influenced by political actions. Contributing to this are the uncertain and, from a viewpoint of equality, skewed political processes in South Asia, with low participation from people outside the elite. Moreover, Myrdal considers these countries to be significantly more heterogeneous than Western nations, which have been consolidated as nations over a long time, and where the emergence of the welfare state has contributed to increased social harmony.

---

[10] Berg (2012, p. 458).

He also noted that after gaining independence, most countries in South Asia have adopted some form of modernization ideal, more explicitly in India, Pakistan, Ceylon (Sri Lanka), and the Philippines, than in Burma (Myanmar) and Indonesia.

Modernization Ideals

The modernization ideals identified by Myrdal are as follows: rationality, development and planning for development, increased productivity, improved living standards, social and economic equalization, improved institutions and attitudes, national consolidation, national independence, political democracy, grassroots democracy, and social discipline.

According to Myrdal, policy proposals should be based on rational considerations. In line with such an ideal, it is about countering superstitious thought patterns and accepting modern technology in a broad sense to increase productivity. Social and economic institutions need to change to lay the groundwork for higher work productivity, efficient competition, greater mobility, more efficient business, more equal opportunities, increased well-being—in short, to contribute to development.

People's attitudes need to undergo major changes. Myrdal calls for increased efficiency, more diligence, accuracy, and punctuality. Additionally, frugality, honesty, and rationality (freedom from superstition and groupthink) are essential. He advocates a readiness to change and seize opportunities, a stronger entrepreneurial spirit, and highlights the importance of integrity and self-confidence, willingness to cooperate and trust in others, and the ability to take a long-term perspective.

Myrdal was deliberately vague about the importance of political democracy. He points out democratic deficiencies in several South Asian countries. He also believes that the democracy premise, unlike other value premises, is not critical to introducing the other modernization ideals. These ideals can also be embraced by an authoritarian regime, although such a regime naturally does not guarantee that the ideals will be realized.

Regarding the need for social discipline, Myrdal stated that all the countries studied are *soft* states. This means that many decided political measures are never implemented, and the state does not make sufficient demands on people. It is clear that Myrdal wants to strengthen the state's ability for welfare policy by meeting modernization requirements both by the intellectual elite and the general population.

Overall, Myrdal called for measures to increase living standards and equality by proposing value premises that entail extensive reforms of institutions and attitudes. He aims to replace *soft* states with strong societal institutions and promote new attitudes in the population that strengthen work ethics.

The Gender Issue

Myrdal did not include the gender issue in the selection of value premises.[11] This is somewhat surprising, considering that it is a topic addressed in several parts of the book, including the workplace. According to Myrdal, education is clearly poorer for girls than boys in South Asia at the time described. Fewer girls than boys attend school. Girls often leave school early. The literacy rate is lower among women than men.[12] A clear discrimination exists, rooted in pre-colonial attitudes and religious beliefs. Health conditions are also worse, and mortality is higher for women than for men.[13] Women's health risks are largely associated with pregnancy and childbirth. The number of births per woman is large, hygiene is lacking, and midwives often lack training, especially in rural areas. Young women are discouraged by their parents from seeking vocational training in healthcare, as they are expected to marry young.

High birth rates also mean that women's participation in the workforce outside the home is held back. However, there are differences in women's employment rates. It is also influenced by social and religious background. Employment rates may be higher for women belonging to a low caste and for women in whose lives Islam does not play a significant role. There are also indications that when a family's income rises, social pressure increases for the women in the family to withdraw from the labor market, regardless of religious affiliation.[14]

Migrant labor contributes to the disintegration of family life. Men largely leave the villages to work alone in the cities. In Calcutta, there are twice as many men as women, leading to a high degree of prostitution, broken relationships, and lost security.[15] Generally, women's employment rates are lower in the countries of South Asia than in Southeast Asia. In Southeast Asia, prejudices against women's professional lives are less. Women are more active outside the home and work independently, not under a man, which is common in India and Pakistan.[16] In India, women often take simple, manual jobs that men reject, such as in the construction industry.[17] But when legislation strengthens women's conditions in the workplace—equal pay for equal work—employers tend to replace them with men.

Myrdal noted that in Delhi women are generally offered all kinds of unskilled jobs and have to work as hard as men. It has been found that more than 60% of the unskilled tasks in construction activities are performed by women. The explanation given by those responsible for recruitment is that women are preferred over men for

---

[11] Yvonne Hirdman argues that the choice of value premises excludes gender issues from the analysis, see Hirdman (2006, p. 346).

[12] Myrdal (1968, p. 1672).

[13] Myrdal (1968, p. 1409).

[14] Myrdal (1968, p. 1073).

[15] Myrdal (1968, p. 1107).

[16] Myrdal (1968, p. 1132).

[17] Myrdal (1968, p. 1135).

several reasons: not only are women's wages lower, but female workers are also more often subjected to unauthorized deductions, incorrect account statements, and delayed payments. Since female workers are more compliant, keep time better, and work hard, much more work can be extracted from them.[18]

Useful Concepts

In the book, Myrdal continued his crusade against traditional economists' lack of interest in the central role of non-economic factors in a country's development. He argues that attitudes, institutions, and productivity consequences of very low living standards are of such crucial importance in underdeveloped countries that they cannot be ignored in economic theory and planning.

This means Myrdal put a lot of effort into clarifying which concepts can be used in analyzing underdevelopment in South Asian countries. A central issue is the situation in rural areas, where land ownership is organized like a pyramid with the landowner at the top and landless laborers at the bottom. To the extent that there are self-owning farmers, they are somewhere in the middle of the pyramid. The attitudes mean that it is high status not to work. Only those who are forced choose to work. The large landowners do not work at all and are also not present. They are in another place, living on rent. The rent system also hinders the renter's efficiency. The yield of increased labor effort falls to the landowner. The conclusion is that traditional concepts of work, employment, and unemployment do not suffice in analyzing underdevelopment in South Asia. These concepts presuppose a functioning labor market with established norms and definitions that do not exist. Instead, Myrdal chose to base his analysis of labor utilization on simpler concepts concerning observable facts: who is working at all, during what times of the day, week, and year do they work, and with what intensity and efficiency?[19] Subsequently, it became possible to begin the analysis by considering in an institutional context how labor utilization is influenced by measures to increase labor demand, as well as attitudes and other institutional conditions in society.

---

[18] Myrdal (1968, p. 1135).
[19] Myrdal (1970, p. 29).

Cumulative Processes or Stage Theories?

A central issue in this work too was the value premise of the cumulative process, which is considered in several contexts in the main text and described more extensively in the second methodological appendix.[20] The appendix analyzes the mechanism that keeps a country in poverty. Myrdal examines which value premises should underlie a plan to lift stagnation and start a virtuous cycle in line with the cumulative development process.

Myrdal noted that the idea of a positive cumulative process for a country's development shares similarities with the theory of various stages of development that all countries undergo. This notion is found in the radical social critic and historical materialist Karl Marx, author of *The Communist Manifesto* (with Engels) in 1848 and *Capital* in 1867. It is also present in Walt Rostow, Myrdal's colleague at ECE, who in 1960 published the much-discussed and influential book, *The Stages of Economic Growth: A Non-Communist Manifesto*, about how various stages of economic growth lead capitalism to an ever-improving society.

Marx emphasized how internal contradictions in a particular stage of development lead to crises that establish new modes of production, with history following a predetermined path: feudalism, capitalism, socialism, and communism. Rostow's stage theory includes five stages: traditional society, preconditions for take-off, take-off, drive to maturity, and age of high mass consumption.

Myrdal was critical of both these stage theories. He was particularly critical of the idea of identical development in different countries and at different historical times.[21] He distrusted the idea of history's development as purpose-driven and inevitable. He argued that there are no people or organizations that can choose different development paths at various historical moments. He also had noted, in an earlier book, that Marx lacked a system for economic policy in his analysis.[22]

Nevertheless, Myrdal acknowledged that Marx was a skilled social scientist who, within the framework of his stage theory, had made important and lasting contributions to almost all social and economic fields.[23] He was more critical of Rostow, who had not delved as deeply into empiricism and conceptual analysis as Marx.[24]

Myrdal's conclusion, as usual, was that social researchers should state their value premises early in their work, in a clear and open manner, before starting empirical research.

---

[20] Appendix 2 The Mechanism of Underdevelopment and Development and a Sketch of an Elementary Theory of Planning for Development.
[21] Myrdal (1968, p. 1847).
[22] Myrdal (1957, p. 186).
[23] Myrdal (1968, p. 1849).
[24] Myrdal (1968, p. 1855).

The System's Main Variables

Regarding the development process in South Asian countries, Myrdal began by identifying six main variables in the social system.

1. Production and Income. The most important economic factor is low labor productivity, meaning low production per worker or per capita, a central part of underdevelopment.
2. Production Conditions. A low proportion of industrial production, low savings, and low investments contribute to the low production per capita.
3. Living Standards. The low standard of living for the vast masses in South Asia means inadequate food supply, low housing standards, lack of hygiene and healthcare, and inadequate education. It is primarily caused by low production per capita. In turn, low living standards cause low workplace efficiency.
4. Attitudes to Life and Work. Low work discipline, punctuality, and orderliness; superstition and irrationality; lack of ambition and adaptability; contempt for physical labor; authoritarianism; lack of cooperation; all these together form conditions for underdevelopment.
5. Institutions. The *soft state* means weakly developed institutions for enterprise; lack of national consolidation; weak authority in national authorities' actions; low efficiency in both national and local public authorities.
6. Politics. Politics refers to decided changes that affect one or more of variables (2)–(5) above.

The main variables (1)–(3) are economic factors while (4) and (5) are non-economic factors. The institutional weaknesses reinforce each other mutually. Additionally, there is a mutual relationship between institutions and attitudes to life and work. Institutions and attitudes significantly affect production, production conditions, and living standards negatively. The sixth factor, politics, can affect both economic and non-economic variables.

If there is an improvement in one of the variables, it is in itself a desirable improvement, such as a higher standard of living in different respects. The main theory is the same as encountered in earlier works by Myrdal. An improvement in one component can lead to improvements in other variables. Thus, the spread of modernization ideals contributes to breaking stagnation and leading the country onto a positive development path according to a cumulative process. However, several negative factors can slow down the virtuous circle or even prevent it from starting. Extensive primary changes are needed for development to take off, but secondary social counterforces that hinder it cannot be ruled out. Myrdal noted that it is somewhat of a mystery what causes countries to develop and not get stuck at a low societal level.[25] However, when it came to identifying the biggest obstacle that needed to be overcome, he had no doubt: population growth was the overarching problem in South Asia.

---

[25] Myrdal (1968, p. 1871).

Family Planning

Gunnar Myrdal followed Malthus's footsteps closely in *Asian Drama*. The rapid and accelerating population growth at the time was, according to Myrdal, a primary reason for poverty. Attitudes opposing family planning must be changed. Family planning was the only means to tackle this issue. In all concerned countries, high and rising population growth held back living standards. If birth rates did not decrease with family planning and other measures, the countries risked falling into the poverty trap.

A Swedish government bilateral aid project on family planning started in Ceylon (Sri Lanka) in the late 1950s, when Alva Myrdal was ambassador in India and also responsible for Ceylon.[26] An agreement was signed between the governments of Sweden and Ceylon. Gunnar Myrdal was also engaged as an advisor to the Ceylonese government on population issues, which he utilized in his work on *Asian Drama*.

Alva Myrdal's interest in the global overpopulation problem dated back to her time at the UN, where she published a pamphlet in 1949 with French demographer Paul Vincent titled *Are We Too Many?* It called for a population policy that took local conditions into account and was based on sociological knowledge. When she became head of UNESCO's social science department, her interest in the issue increased. She became more convinced of global overpopulation as a problem that needed to be prevented with social measures. The population explosion became a topic in the general debate in the 1950s and 1960s. A Swedish food scientist, Georg Borgström, had a significant influence with several books, which related the global population explosion to the earth's limited resources and advocated radical measures.

Alva Myrdal was very active in planning the family planning project in Ceylon, which started in June 1958 and continued until the mid-1960s. The project became one of Sweden's first own aid projects. It served as a flagship for Swedish aid policy and was described in *Asian Drama*, which contains chapters on population policy and an appendix on family planning.

Ceylon's Prime Minister Solomon Bandaranaike was convinced of the dangers of overpopulation. He was eager to prioritize the population issue in the upcoming 10-year plan. Therefore, he organized a special group of advisors with Gunnar Myrdal at the helm, including Ester and Mogens Boserup. They met in Ceylon several times between March 1958 and May 1959 and contributed several pages on the population issue to the 10-year plan that was later published. However, political turmoil in the country led to the assassination of the Prime Minister. He was succeeded by his widow, Sirimavo Bandaranaike, who had a documented interest in family planning.

The Swedish family planning project continued after Alva Myrdal had confirmed that the overall impression of the operation was very positive and appreciated. The project expanded in various ways, including the training of state-employed doctors

---

[26] Berg et al. (2021, Chap. 11).

in family planning, education of the population in the villages, and among plantation workers. When the project concluded in the mid-1960s, the birth rates in the affected area had decreased from around 30 to 20 per thousand people between 1958 and 1964.[27] According to the project leader, the experiences showed that family planning could be integrated into maternal and child health care across the country without significant extra costs. The Ceylon government decided on a large nationwide family planning program starting in 1966.

The Swedish aid project received significant international attention as it was considered the world's first government aid project focused on family planning.[28] The project was subject to both praise and criticism. Praise came from aid veterans for combating poverty and supporting women's rights. Criticism arose as it was seen as part of the Western world's attempt to control and dictate life in the Third World. Researchers who have studied the project retrospectively found that it was somewhat successful, especially considering the goal of learning about the possibilities for family planning in new environments for the Swedes. However, women's health and human rights were less in focus during the first decades than the primary goal of curbing population growth and preventing famine.[29]

Gunnar Myrdal noted in *Asian Drama* that the Swedish project had successes. Attitude surveys showed that 65–70% of married women of childbearing age and 85% of those with two children or more were positive about learning methods of birth control.[30] However, he pointed out that the Swedes had overlooked the ethnic division in Ceylon between Sinhalese and Tamils. The Swedish project started in villages with a Sinhalese population. The Sinhalese, therefore, suspected that birth rates would decrease in their group but not among the Tamils.[31]

Another issue discussed is whether Gunnar and Alva Myrdal advocated sterilization as a method of contraception in poor countries at the time. Elise Ottesen-Jensen, founder of the Swedish Association for Sexuality Education (RFSU,) claimed in her memoirs that she changed her stance on the issue when she was elected as the chair of the International Planned Parenthood Federation (IPPF) congress in New Delhi in 1959.[32] She believed that Gunnar Myrdal had convinced her that her opposition to sterilizations would lead to children dying of hunger. However, there is no empirical evidence that Myrdal was a strong advocate of sterilizations. In *Asian Drama*, he suggested that condoms and coitus interruptus were the best methods for birth control in India. He noted that sterilization could be effective for couples with many children but a lack of surgeons and equipment argued against the method for

---

[27] Berg et al. (2021, Chap. 11).

[28] Population aid was a controversial issue in the UN system at this time due to resistance from several Catholic and communist countries.

[29] Berg et al. (2021, Chap. 11).

[30] Myrdal (1968, p. 1519).

[31] Myrdal (1968, p. 1508).

[32] IPPF is a global organization for family planning and reproductive health formed in 1952.

reducing birth rates.³³ Neither did Alva Myrdal advocate sterilizations when she spoke about the population threat in the early 1960s.³⁴

Gunnar Myrdal devoted important sections in *Asian Drama* to the population issue. He argued that when the countries in South Asia began a population policy in the neo-Malthusian spirit, there was no other way than to focus on voluntary solutions. It was crucial to run awareness campaigns about the use of contraceptives and a rational approach to family size. Myrdal opposed the idea that those who had many children should suffer economically. At the same time, he believed there were reasons to be cautious with economic support to parents with many children. There was a dilemma between achieving both increased living standards and lower birth rates.

After considering the issue, Myrdal realized that the conflict only arose if benefits were paid in cash to the parents and if these resources were used for purposes other than their children. His conclusion was to link support for families to welfare initiatives that reached the children directly, bypassing the parents. This involved healthcare, education, and school meals. Welfare services for children should, in Asian countries, be managed more by society than in Western countries and be organized at the local level.³⁵

Planning for Development

In the book, Myrdal deepened his analysis of what economic planning means in an underdeveloped country. He was keen to emphasize that it was not about the type of state command planning over nationalized companies introduced in socialist countries in the East. Nor was it about the type of pragmatic and coordinating measures that gradually emerged in Western countries as a consequence of industrialization. In underdeveloped countries, particularly in South Asia, conditions are different. In these countries, the idea of planning takes shape before it begins to be realized.³⁶

The Ideal Plan Demands Much

Myrdal returned to value premises when discussing the role of planning. He described the prerequisites for the ideal plan. Fundamentally, it is about influencing the main category 4, *attitudes to work*, reinforced by main category 5, the *institutions* and the *soft state*. Modernization ideals thus encounter serious resistance in

---

[33] Myrdal (1968, p. 2160).
[34] Berg et al. (2021, Chap. 11).
[35] Myrdal (1968, p. 1503).
[36] Myrdal (1968, p. 739).

the planning process. The ideal plan should increase people's choices and show that modernization ideals are an alternative to people's actual attitudes.[37] Myrdal noted that planning can constitute the intellectual matrix for the whole idea of modernizing an underdeveloped country. At the same time, he was aware of the many difficulties with such an all-encompassing vision.[38] Myrdal emphasized that many conditions must be met for economic planning to work. It requires a stable, effective, and united government, law and order, social discipline, and national consolidation.[39]

Economic Planning Does Not Work Well in Practice

Myrdal was highly critical of how planning worked in practice. Planning in reality was not about developing an ideal plan and then trying to implement it. He argued that in South Asia, planning is a process, a constant negotiation between the national government, state governments, and companies. He pointed out that planners themselves are part of the social game and have their own economic and political interests to protect. This often results in compromises where the upper social strata in trade and industry gain significant influence. The poor people do not feel the effects of economic planning to any noticeable extent. Nor does any equalization of living conditions occur. Economic power continued to be concentrated among the upper strata.[40]

Furthermore, Myrdal pointed out that the government used bureaucratic control measures to influence the economy. Companies could hardly take any important actions without first seeking permission from state and state authorities.[41] Overall, the system meant that competition within the business sector was restrained and planning in practice favored the large and established monopolies and oligopolies.[42] He also warned that a legacy of authoritarian rule and the common interest of high-level administrators, politicians, and business leaders could strengthen the "illiberal" state.[43] Myrdal's own value premise was that bureaucratic control measures are the wrong way to go. He advocated that the state should stimulate and facilitate production and consumption with more general measures.

---

[37] Myrdal (1968, p. 1883).
[38] Myrdal (1968, p. 711).
[39] Myrdal (1968, p. 719).
[40] Myrdal (1968, p. 737).
[41] Myrdal (1968, p. 921).
[42] Myrdal (1968, p. 929).
[43] Myrdal (1968, p. 933).

Industrialization and Rural Development

Gunnar Myrdal was not particularly optimistic about the possibility of a rapid industrialization process that would absorb the large underemployed masses in the countryside, at least in the short term.

In the long term, however, population growth may be tempered by family planning, and employment in the industry could increase. Myrdal was not overly optimistic about the export sector's ability to compete in the global market. He viewed positively the idea of supporting domestic companies that replace the need to import goods from the outside world. A strategy for import substitution would, however, require national protective measures against competition from foreign companies, which he supported. But he was cautious. There were hopes that the import substitution strategy could trigger a positive cycle, but there were opposing factors that could slow the process: a lack of trained personnel, a lack of technical knowledge, a shortage of raw materials and semi-finished goods, and a lack of infrastructure.

Regarding rural development, he saw both difficulties and opportunities. The underutilization of labor was a very difficult issue to solve, especially if one does not believe in rapid industrialization. However, he saw positive elements in the new agricultural methods—*the Green Revolution*—which began to gain attention at that time. These included improved and more resilient seeds, irrigation, and education in the new methods. He supported the emergence of capitalist agriculture, which he argued is something entirely different from laissez-faire. He wanted those who own the land to also cultivate it. Myrdal suggested that landownership without cultivation should be penalized with taxes by the authorities, and he wanted to prohibit the possibility of selling land to those who do not cultivate it. There was also a need for new credit systems to free agricultural workers from landowners at the top of the pyramid and village moneylenders who charged high interest rates. Self-owning farmers with strong motives to improve agricultural methods and yield could play a central role in the development of countries. He also advocated for the redistribution of land to the landless, to give them increased dignity.

Reception

Asian Drama was not received as an instant classic in the same way as *An American Dilemma*.[44] Indeed, it was reviewed by Western academics who were impressed by Myrdal's deep attempt to understand the conditions of underdevelopment and his critical methodological analysis. His examination of traditional concepts, such as unemployment, and focusing on other methods to measure underemployment to find out who is working and how intensively the work is being performed, were noted.

---

[44] Barber (2008, pp. 143–144) and Lundahl (2021, Chaps. 7–8) provide overviews of the book's reception.

However, he also received criticism for being overly pessimistic and for not clarifying the differences between countries. There is a significant difference between a large and densely populated country like India and smaller countries in Southeast Asia, which are more sparsely populated. Additionally, liberal economists criticized him, emphasizing that development requires more market mechanisms and deregulations.[45] Left-wing critics highlighted China with its revolution and strong state as a model for India, arguing that China had made more progress in health and education for the masses than India, which had lagged due to the lack of a radical upheaval and the soft state.[46]

In Asia, Myrdal's book also had a mixed reception. Some acknowledged the breadth of the analysis and considered the book a significant advance in institutional analysis. Others criticized Myrdal for downplaying the possibility of industrialization and having an overly pessimistic view of foreign trade's role in development.

The choice of modernization ideals as value premises was criticized. These ideals might seem obvious to many social scientists and people in Asia striving for a living standard on par with the Western world. But there was criticism of the modernization ideals from those defending traditional cultures, religious values, or the environment's fundamental role in sustainable development.

Some researchers argued that Myrdal's choice of value premises was influenced by Western ethnocentric values. The explanation could be that Myrdal largely identified with the Indian elite, which received British education during colonial times. This criticism implied that the book's stereotypical depiction of India revealed his own hidden prejudices about rationality being a European trait.[47] However, it could be argued that this criticism was possible precisely because Myrdal clearly motivated his choice of modernization ideals as the value premises for the Asian drama. He is entirely open with his premises, which counters the notion of hidden prejudices. In the book, he also discusses why different groups oppose the idea that attitudes, living conditions, and institutions can be obstacles to development.[48] According to Myrdal, for Western academics, it could be a matter of diplomatic reasons not wanting to discuss these issues, while for local academics in the countries, influenced by Western ideals, it could be more about national pride or an assessment that only a radical and authoritarian social transformation is possible in these countries.

---

[45] P T Bauer, Myrdal's conservative and market-liberal counterpoint, launched a broadside against the book, criticizing its equality goals and the concept of cumulative processes as misguided.

[46] Criticism from the left included Joan Robinson, a leading British economist who, alongside research on monopolistic competition and capital accumulation, wrote several books on China, positively highlighting the cultural revolution. Robinson was a leading figure in post-Keynesianism, a school also influenced by Gunnar Myrdal.

[47] Cherrier (2009, p. 51).

[48] Myrdal (1968, p. 117).

The Challange of World Poverty: A World Anti-Poverty Program in Outline

The book *The Challange of World Poverty: A World Anti-Poverty Program in Outline* was a continuation of *Asian Drama*. It was based on a lecture series that Gunnar Myrdal gave in the USA in 1969 at Johns Hopkins University. After the criticism of *Asian Drama*, Myrdal realized that he needed to make a general summary of the political conclusions of the book. He writes in the preface to the American edition that it can be seen as the missing eighth link to the previous book.[49] However, much of the content was taken from *Asian Drama*. The political conclusions still applied to South Asia, especially India and Pakistan, but there is also an appendix on the Latin American powder keg. Myrdal claimed that his analysis is so general that it often applies to the entire so-called underdeveloped world. The value premises were again the modernization ideals, but now he seemed to sharpen his stance. He emphasized that the traditional values in the underdeveloped countries are not aimed at promoting change but are too static. Therefore, they cannot be used to set goals for planning. Myrdal used a paternalistic tone when he noted that the superiority of the modernization ideals are organized under the principle of rationality and must be accepted, as soon as development is set as a goal.[50]

Myrdal returned to several of the themes he had dealt with in Asian Drama. It was about the need for countries themselves to introduce institutional reforms to increase equality. Agriculture needed to be reformed so that the masses in the countryside gained access to better social and technical conditions—*the Green Revolution*—and thereby increased motivation to exert themselves. The population explosion was still an acute dilemma that needed to be handled with a robust state policy for birth control.

Myrdal also returned to the soft state and tried to deepen the analysis. He stated that social control was insufficient and now called for more bureaucratic control mechanisms, within the framework of village development and cooperation. He believed that the primary explanation for the soft state was that all power lay in the hands of the upper class at the top of the pyramid, and he argued that rapid development required a fight against corruption and greater social discipline and such cannot be achieved without laws and regulations based on compulsion.[51]

---

[49] Myrdal (1970, p. 16).
[50] Myrdal (1970, p. 39).
[51] Myrdal (1970, p. 161).

Conclusions

In several countries in Asia, better social and economic development occurred than Gunnar Myrdal and many others anticipated in the 1960s, especially in countries that balanced between state and market and opened up to trade with the outside world. It is also possible that population development was better than expected due to the investments in family planning made with support from Myrdal and others. However, development in Asia has been very uneven. There are still significant differences in living standards between different countries and groups.

Three central lessons can be drawn from Myrdal's books for the analysis of development issues. The first lesson is that development is a value in itself. All modernization ideals may not be universally accepted, but goals that involve reduced poverty, lower child mortality, increased life expectancy, and reduced inequality are shared by most.

The second lesson is that foreign trade plays a more significant role in development than Myrdal counted on. Increased trade with the outside world strengthens the positive cumulative process in many countries and has meant a lot for reducing poverty in India.

The third lesson is that Myrdal's institutional holistic perspective is worth striving for. Development encompasses many aspects that are not economic factors. In modern institutional economics, the balance between state and civil society plays a decisive role in whether countries develop according to the good circle or are pushed into a vicious circle by power-hungry autocrats. We will return to these issues in Chap. 16.

References

Andersson S (1998) Skiss till en fallstudie Gunnar Myrdals beslut att skriva Asian Drama (Sketch for a case study Gunnar Myrdal's decision to write Asian Drama), manuscript. The Labor Movement's Archive and Library, Stockholm
Barber W (2008) Gunnar Myrdal an intellectual biography. Palgrave Macmillan, New York
Berg C (2012) Global ekonomi – en introduktion till samhällsekonomi och politisk ekonomi (Global economy an introduction to economics and political economy). SNS Förlag, Stockholm
Berg A, Lundberg U, Tydén M (2021) En svindlande uppgift Sverige och biståndet 1945–1975 (A Dizzying Task Sweden and Aid 1945–1975). Ordfront, Stockholm
Berggren H (2008) Första försvar Diplomati från ursprung till UD (First defense diplomacy from origin to the Ministry of Foreign Affairs). Atlantis, Stockholm
Bok S (1987) Alva, ett kvinnoliv. Bonniers, Avesta. English edition: Bok S (1991). Alva Myrdal. A daughter's memoir. Radcliffe biography series. Perseus Publishing, Cambridge
Cherrier B (2009) Gunnar Myrdal and the scientific way to social democracy, 1914–1968. J Hist Econ Thought 31(1):33–55
Harrison D (2017) Jag har ingen vilja till makt, Biografi över Tage Erlander (I have no will to power, biography of Tage Erlander). Ordfront, Stockholm

Hirdman Y (2006) Det tänkande hjärtat. Boken om Alva Myrdal. Ordfront, Stockholm. English edition: Hirdman Y (2008) Alva Myrdal: the passionate mind. Indiana University Press, Bloomington

Lindskog L (1981) Alva Myrdal Förnuftet måste segra(Alva Myrdal reason must prevail). Sveriges Radios Förlag, Kristianstad

Lundahl M (2021) The dynamics of poverty circular, cumulative causation, value judgements, institutions, and social engineering in the world of Gunnar Myrdal. In: Cohen A, Harcourt G, Kriesler P (eds) Palgrave studies in the history of economic thought. Palgrave Macmillan, Cham

Myrdal G (1957) Economic theory and underdeveloped regions. Gerald Duckworth, London

Myrdal G (1968) Asian Drama an inquiry into the poverty of nations. Twentieth Century Fund, New York

Myrdal G (1970) Politiskt manifest om världsfattigdomen. Rabén & Sjögren, Stockholm. English edition: Myrdal G (1970) The challenge of world poverty: a world anti-poverty program in outline. Pantheon Books, New York

Myrdal A (1982) Draft by Alva Myrdal: Nehru, a romantic relationship that never became a relationship. The Swedish Labour Movement's Archives and Library

Chapter 12
Stances in the 1960s

In the early 1960s, Gunnar and Alva Myrdal returned to Stockholm. Gunnar Myrdal was active internationally, particularly in the US, where he was a popular speaker and wrote extensively on economic and international issues. The civil rights movement in the US gained momentum in the 1950s and 1960s and led to significant legislative changes, supported by the Supreme Court's reinforcement of constitutional amendments ensuring equal rights. Gunnar Myrdal addressed structural unemployment and the emergence of a new underclass in the US. His term "underclass" gained traction in sociological discourse. Myrdal's emphasis on public measures for education and retraining highlighted his commitment to eradicating poverty and promoting equality. Gunnar Myrdal participated in a heated public panel debate in New York with the black author James Baldwin. Gunnar's relationship with his son Jan Myrdal was strained, particularly over differing views on the Vietnam War, and led to a rift between them.

Back in Stockholm: Alva Myrdal's Career Takes off

In the early 1960s, Gunnar and Alva Myrdal moved back to Stockholm. They had bought a property on Västerlånggatan in the Old Town, a three-story maisonette with its own elevator and a view of Riddarfjärden. Gunnar thought they would spend a lot of time together. However, Alva Myrdal was appointed as the Swedish representative in the nuclear disarmament negotiations in Geneva, starting in 1962. Alva was often traveling, and Gunnar sometimes felt despondent and abandoned.

The disarmament work aimed to establish agreements between nuclear powers to refrain from further testing and ensure that other countries did not acquire nuclear weapons by signing non-proliferation treaties. This work occupied Alva for many years. She was also elected to the Swedish Parliament in 1962, became a board member of the Committee for International Aid (NIB), and in 1964 chaired the UN

Security Council's expert group on South African issues. She investigated Prime Minister Erlander's plans—possibly her own idea—for an international peace research institute in Stockholm, SIPRI (Stockholm International Peace Research Institute), and became its first chairperson. She became the Minister for Disarmament in the Swedish government in 1967, worked on gender equality issues, and was responsible for a study on separating the church from the state and another on future issues.

Gunnar Works on Many International Issues

Gunnar Myrdal often visited the USA and gave lectures. He was a popular speaker at universities and in political contexts, one of the most sought-after European intellectuals in the USA at that time. His lectures were mainly based on his own work and focused on American and international issues. He chose not to engage in the debate about his own book on the American dilemma, responding to critics by saying that he was primarily working on other issues. However, the civil rights movement gained momentum and new legislation was introduced to prohibit segregation. A new edition of *An American Dilemma* was published. On a few occasions, Gunnar Myrdal joined the debate on the American racial issue and also became a sharp critic of the Vietnam War. He succeeded Alva as the chairperson of SIPRI in 1967, when she joined the government.

In addition to his major work on the *Asian drama*, which was now based at the Institute for International Economics in Stockholm—founded by Gunnar Myrdal in 1962—he wrote several books on economic and international issues. He published books on planned economies in the West, challenges of the welfare state in the USA, and a critical analysis of the West European cooperation organization that had started operating in Brussels.

As an author of books in many different areas, Gunnar Myrdal read an enormous amount. The National Librarian, Uno Willers, pointed out that Myrdal usually acquired the books himself. When a material was thoroughly examined and the work completed, Myrdal would always send a message to the Royal Library that he had a cubic meter of books that he no longer needed and asked if they could come and pick them up the next day.[1]

---

[1] Willers (1971).

The Civil Rights Movement and Civil Rights Laws

From the 1950s onwards, the US Supreme Court played an increasingly significant role as an independent political actor in ensuring that the American Constitution's amendments on equal rights for all Americans were upheld. These amendments included the 13th Amendment of 1865, which prohibits slavery; the 14th Amendment of 1868, which prescribes equal rights for all Americans; and the 15th Amendment of 1870, which states that no citizen should be denied the right to vote based on race or color.

In May 1954, the Supreme Court's decision to prohibit racial discrimination in schools referred to *An American Dilemma*, as noted earlier. Another significant event occurred in December 1955, when the black bus passenger Rosa Parks refused to give up her seat to a white passenger in Montgomery, Alabama, and was arrested, sparking strong reactions. Rosa Parks' courageous act led to an extensive bus boycott in Montgomery, where black people collaborated and nearly bankrupted the bus company. The boycott was led by a young pastor at the Dexter Avenue Baptist Church, named Martin Luther King, only 26 years old. Rosa Parks' protest became a starting point for the fight against racial segregation in the Southern States. On December 21, 1956, the US Supreme Court declared it illegal to segregate users of buses and other public transportation.

Revisiting the American Dilemma

About 20 years after the first edition of *An American Dilemma*, a new edition was released in 1962. The book was supplemented with a lengthy section by Arnold Rose, who had followed the dilemma's development on the ground in the USA, while Myrdal worked on other issues in other parts of the world. Rose observed that the developments between 1942 and 1962 brought about significant changes for the black population. Technological and industrial development, increased collective awareness among African Americans, greater sensitivity in the country to international opinion, and the civil rights movement's fight at the federal, state, and local levels for equal rights were important components of the change that had begun.

Housing segregation was a significant dilemma, especially in the Northern states, according to Rose. The influx of African Americans into the major cities in the North and West was followed by an exodus of white people to the suburbs. Housing prices in black areas decreased, and many areas became slums. Meanwhile, segregation in the Northern states began to decrease in many public environments, restaurants, hotels, and stores. In the Southern states, the situation was more tense, and civil rights activists resorted to civil disobedience (sit-ins) to protest discrimination.

Rose argued that, overall, the comprehensive system of racial discrimination had been dismantled; many prejudices remained, but racism as an ideology did not have the same influence as when Myrdal's book was written. The civil rights movement, however, became increasingly active during the 1960s but also faced opposition. White racists attacked demonstrations and meetings. James Meredith, the first African American to enroll at the University of Mississippi, was protected by federal troops sent by President Kennedy to Oxford, Mississippi. Martin Luther King led civil rights marches in Birmingham, which became known worldwide. When non-violent activists there were bitten by police dogs, the USA lost esteem both domestically and internationally.

The March on Washington for Jobs and Freedom gathered more than 250,000 participants in August 1963. Martin Luther King delivered his famous "I Have a Dream" speech in front of the Lincoln Memorial. He himself quoted *An American Dilemma* in 1967, the year before he was assassinated (Fig. 12.1).[2]

Fig. 12.1 Martin Luther King, Coretta Scott King, and Ralph Bunche at the UN headquarters on December 4, 1964. Bunche was the first African American to win the Nobel Peace Prize in 1950 and he is here congratulating Martin Luther King for being awarded the same prize in 1964. Ralph Bunche participated in Gunnar Myrdal's *An American Dilemma*, a book Martin Luther King referred to in a speech in 1967, the year before he was murdered. (Courtesy of UN Photo, UN7767857)

---

[2] Morey (2021, p. 242).

Following the assassination of President Kennedy in November 1963, civil rights legislation was expedited. Civil rights laws, complementing the Constitution's 13th, 14th, and 15th Amendments, were enacted between 1957 and 1968.[3] These laws established a Civil Rights Commission to gather information on how citizens were being denied voting rights due to color, race, religion, or national origin. Additionally, a federal inspection was set up to investigate voter registration at the local level. They ensured equal access to public facilities, equal employment rights irrespective of race. It became illegal to require literacy tests for voter registration. Harsh penalties were introduced for those obstructing free voting participation. Finally, discrimination was prohibited in relation to selling, renting, and financing in the housing market.

More Books and Debates with Kenneth Clark and James Baldwin

The civil rights movement and strengthened civil rights legislation were largely in line with Myrdal's message. However, in the 1960s, a more clearly formulated critique began to emerge, defending black culture against white dominance. The black author Ralph Ellison published his review of *An American Dilemma* in 1964, which had been unpublished for 20 years. Ellison appreciated much of the book but critiqued it on several points. He was skeptical of the idea that blacks should wait for whites to realize that their behavior needed to change. Ellison also noted that black culture itself was worth preserving and fighting for. He loved Harlem, its black churches, and dance halls, he pointed out to a journalist.[4]

Gunnar Myrdal's book *Challenge to Affluence* was published in 1963. The book provided a sharp analysis of how technological development contributed to stagnating demand for low-skilled labor. Those affected by structural unemployment in the USA were often black people, creating a new underclass for whom equality became increasingly absent.

In the book, the Swedish term "underklass" was introduced, becoming *underclass* in English and thereafter a widely used term in sociological analysis. The concept of the underclass had been used by the author and playwright August Strindberg, who defined it as the nourishing, governed, in contrast to the consuming, governing upper class.[5] In Myrdal's definition, the underclass included the unemployed and persistently underemployed and their families, forming a strata at the bottom of society, not integrated into society, a useless and miserable bottom

---

[3] Kubiak (2013, pp. 223–224).

[4] Morey (2021, p. 237).

[5] August Strindberg's A Little Catechism for the Underclass was likely written in 1884, but first published in 1913 in his Collected Works.

layer.[6] Myrdal's concept was later used by sociologists like William Julius Wilson in influential books about American urban ghettos.

Myrdal again pointed out the role of vicious cycles when work performed by people in slums was no longer needed, leading to more unemployment, underemployment, and outright exploitation. He called for comprehensive public measures for education and retraining and a number of reforms to eradicate poverty.[7] He also revisited a commencement lecture he delivered in 1962 to students at Howard University. Howard was established post-Civil War as a university for African Americans. It was from this university that several of the most influential and radical contributors to *An American Dilemma* were recruited, such as Ralph Bunche and Doxey Wilkerson.

In the lecture, Myrdal provided an overarching history of the black group's status in the USA. He noted progress in the past 20 years in several areas. He highlighted the right to equal conditions in several respects, where segregation and discrimination were gradually being broken down. In Myrdal (1963, p. 205) he praised the ongoing fight for black causes, which he believed had now entered the phase of victory. He claimed that when whites and blacks come together in work and leisure, they discover they are the same kind of people with participation in the same culture.

Myrdal also believed that a black intellectual, alongside their profession, must be active as a spokesperson for their race. He looked forward to the day when all educational institutions in America are open to all, regardless of race and skin color, and when the composition of the faculty and student body at Howard University does not differ from other universities.

However, Myrdal could not refrain from paternalistically pointing out to the students that those practicing black professionals in the middle and upper classes must give up the economic monopoly they still held among black customers. He believed they should prepare for their competence to be measured by the norms of the rest of American society and that a society of equality offered much greater opportunities, but it also made much harder demands on them than the society made on earlier generations of black people.[8]

In the 1960s, Myrdal reconnected with Kenneth B. Clark. He had participated as a young, black psychology student in the work on *An American Dilemma* and was struck by Myrdal's treatment of him as an equal. He recalled that Myrdal had not been socialized into racism, often the case with white Americans at that time.

Clark emphasized that Myrdal insisted that social scientists should be thoughtful, rational, moral, and uphold central human values. According to Clark, it was an important weapon in the fight against injustices.[9] Clark was the first African American to earn a doctorate in psychology at Columbia University and became a professor in 1942. Together with his wife, psychologist Mamie Pipps Clark, he

---

[6] Myrdal (1963, p. 52).
[7] Myrdal (1963, p. 87).
[8] Myrdal (1963, p. 207).
[9] Jackson (1990, p. 290).

developed famous color tests, where African-American children coloring pictures of themselves often chose a lighter skin color than their real one.

Kenneth B. Clark also published a notable book, *Dark Ghetto*, in 1965 with a foreword by Gunnar Myrdal. The book provided a shocking description of life in the black urban population's ghettos. Clark had conducted pioneering systematic fieldwork to map the inhabitants' lives. Life in the ghetto was affected by cumulative effects of racial oppression and economic discrimination. Formal and informal institutions for social control had weakened. Street violence and crime had increased. Fear of violence contributed to rising hostility towards the white society and its institutions. Dark Ghetto showed how the inhabitants adapted to various ways against the backdrop of structural oppression. Women's roles in households increased while men partied more extensively. Conflicts between men and women were subdued in various ways. Household compositions became more flexible, and informal life outside the household increased.[10]

In March 1964, a public panel debate was held in New York between the black author James Baldwin and three white liberals, one of them Gunnar Myrdal, one of his appearances in the USA on the racial issue. Kenneth B. Clark was in the audience. James Baldwin had become known for his strong criticism of white American culture, which he perceived as racist. Baldwin had been obsessed with identity throughout his life and became a role model for those who did not want to be defined by others. He was born in 1924 in Harlem, the eldest of nine children, and grew up under difficult conditions. As a teenager, he attended a high school in the Bronx with mostly white students and an English teacher, Abel Meeropol, who wrote the lyrics to the anti-lynching song Strange Fruit, recorded by Billie Holiday in 1939.[11]

After the war, Baldwin moved to Paris, met black author Richard Wright, and got to know French intellectuals who wrote about race, prejudices, colonialism. Baldwin returned to the USA in 1957 following the successful bus boycott in Montgomery and became a spokesperson for the civil rights movement. In 1963, Baldwin's essay collection *The Fire Next Time*, Baldwin (1963), exploded into the American political race debate. He stated that Americans not yet fully recognized as citizens had to learn to despise themselves from the moment their eyes open to the world. The world had countless ways to make the difference between black and white perceived, known, and feared. The theme for the New York panel debate in 1964 between James Baldwin and Gunnar Myrdal was Liberalism and the Black Man. In the debate, Baldwin argued that he and everyone he knew did not believe in the American creed. He criticized the white liberals' missionary attitude and their conviction that they should show the way for the black man. Black people realized that they must live outside the system, real education happened outside the world of books.[12]

---

[10] Clark (1965).
[11] Menand (2021, p. 386).
[12] Jackson (1990, p. 299).

Gunnar Myrdal, on the other hand, still believed in integration and assimilation, and looked forward to a color-blind society. He also asserted that white liberals often need a push. He pointed out to Baldwin that he must rely on liberals as it was not the conservative politicians who would implement major reforms, eradicate poverty, and create a free society where everyone has the opportunity to advance through education and hard work to liberate the entire oppressed social group.[13]

It was then that Kenneth B. Clark stood up in the audience and supported Baldwin because he helped him and others with the difficult problem of handling white liberals, who in fact, in relation to black people, had not been as liberal as they pretend.[14] Clark noted that he himself identified with American liberalism for most of his adult life but added that he now had to admit that he primarily saw the adjective "white" in white American liberalism. He warned black people that they needed to learn to handle these strange and insidious opponents. Clark turned directly to Gunnar Myrdal, and said that as so far as the black man was concerned, the ethical aspect of the American liberalism was primarily verbal. According to Clark there was a peculiar kind of ambivalence in American liberalism, a persistent verbal liberalism that was not capable of overcoming an equally persistent illiberalism of action.[15]

Myrdal continued to assert that the fight against poverty is an overarching goal. He emphasized the need for civil rights, integration, assimilation, and equal opportunities, while Baldwin and Clark presage and inspire the black consciousness movement that emerged in the 1960s.[16]

In the mid-1960s, extensive riots with many deaths began to occur in black areas in several American cities, including Detroit, Los Angeles (Watts), Chicago, and Newark. Many Americans blamed the riots on foreign agitators and young, angry black men. A federal commission, appointed by President Johnson and led by Otto Kerner, countered this assumption.[17] The Kerner Commission concluded in 1968 that white racism, rather than black anger, had been the triggering factor. It was also about deficiencies in police actions, poor housing, weak education, high unemployment, and poor social security. The commission also suggested that the media bore some blame in the development by presenting the white man's view of the events, and claimed that the American nation was moving towards two societies, one black and one white—separate and unequal.

However, the Kerner Commission was criticized in some key areas.[18] It did not deepen the analysis of the causes of white racism, did not analyze differences in power and money, did not specify whose interests were favored by the system. It also missed considering the significance of the new black consciousness movement that began to grow in the 1960s. The fight to preserve black culture, foreshadowed

---

[13] Jackson (1990, p. 300).
[14] Jackson (1990, p. 300).
[15] Jackson (1990, p. 300).
[16] Jackson (1990, p. 300).
[17] Gooden and Myers (2018).
[18] Gooden and Myers (2018).

by authors such as James Baldwin, Ralph Ellison, and Richard Wright, now began to appear more tangibly with movements like *Black Power* and *Black is Beautiful*.

Much later, Baldwin's stance and storytelling ability were highlighted by the author and philosopher Aleksander Motturi (2019). In his view, James Baldwin is not content with analyzing the racial power structure black people are already familiar with. Baldwin belongs, along with Frantz Fanon, to the few who manage to depict the depth of this experience and at the same time make it perceptible even to people—whites, innocents, liberals, and others—who do not themselves have to endure its violent, harsh, and inhumane side. According to Motturi, this also becomes a struggle with language, with what is depicted, and with how the depiction will be made possible.

Sweden and Western Europe, the First Attempt

In the 1960s, Gunnar Myrdal also entered the debate about a possible Swedish membership in the European Economic Community (EEC), which had been created by the Treaty of Rome in 1957 and preceded by the European Coal and Steel Community (ECSC) in 1951, which was linked to the EEC. In the EEC were Belgium, France, Italy, the Netherlands, Luxembourg, and West Germany. Myrdal had worked with issues of European cooperation as the executive secretary of the UN agency ECE for 10 years when the EEC was formed. Before the ECSC was established, it was Myrdal and the ECE that ensured the distribution of coal from Germany to other countries and supported Europe's reconstruction. Myrdal and ECE had also supported the coal and steel community with resources when it was formed. Coal and steel were the main ingredients in the war material industry, and the vision was, among other things, to prevent a future war between France and West Germany.

Sweden chose not to participate in the EEC. Instead, Sweden decided to enter a free trade area, European Free Trade Association (EFTA), with Norway, Denmark, the United Kingdom, Switzerland, and Austria, which began operating in 1960. However, Swedish business organizations and some conservative parties were positive about participating in the common market.

In August 1961, Prime Minister Tage Erlander held the so-called Metal Speech, an important policy speech on Swedish European policy.[19] According to Erlander, Swedish membership in the EEC could not be considered. The EEC's supranational tendencies posed a threat to neutrality and welfare policies. However, Erlander's conclusion was that an association agreement with the EEC could be acceptable for Sweden without questioning the neutrality policy.[20]

---

[19] The speech was delivered at the Metalworkers' Union Congress on August 22, 1961, developed with the assistance of Sverker Åström and Olof Palme.

[20] Ekengren (2005, pp. 70–71).

In August 1961, the British government decided to apply for membership in the EEC, as did Denmark. The pressure increased on the other members of EFTA to act. Together with Austria and Switzerland, Sweden submitted an application for association with the EEC on December 15, 1961.

Myrdal argued that after the Metal Speech, the Social Democrats and the government began to downplay the risks of Swedish participation in the EEC. Together with two other Social Democrats, he wrote a debate book—*We and Western Europe. A call for reflection and debate*—published in early autumn 1962.[21]

Myrdal and his co-authors argued that membership in the EEC meant that Sweden had to give up its position as a neutral state. Myrdal warned against subordinating Sweden to a supranational order for entire fields of economic policy. Myrdal warned that in Europe, the trade union movement had not achieved collective bargaining as an equal party.[22]

When the book came out, it was seen as heretical. According to Prime Minister Erlander, quoted in the second edition by Ekström et al. (1971, p. 19), it was a political "huge miss." However, the Swedish association agreement with the EEC did not materialize. French President Charles de Gaulle stopped Britain's application to the EEC in January 1963, and with it fell Sweden's and the other EFTA countries' applications.[23]

Criticism of US Foreign Policy

In the 1960s, Gunnar Myrdal was also active in the debate on the major international issues of the time. It was largely about the foreign policy of the United States. It was about China, the Soviet Union, the Vietnam War, and the developing countries, which were now often called the third world.

Regarding China, Myrdal criticized the American foreign policy for excluding the country from normal political relations with the outside world. He reminded of the great powers' century-long incursions into China to obtain various privileges. He argued that China's exclusion from the UN since 1949 meant that the country had been thrown into the arms of the Soviet Union.[24]

Myrdal also returned to the issue of the export ban on strategic goods to the Soviet Union, which he opposed already as the head of ECE. He believed that American foreign policy in this respect had failed. The blockade gave the

---

[21] Ekström, Myrdal, and Pålsson (1962). The book was republished in a second edition in 1971 with a new introduction and five new chapters, while the original chapters remained unchanged. The page reference below refer to the new edition.

[22] Ekström, Myrdal and Pålsson (1971, p. 136).

[23] Charles de Gaulle's reluctance was due to viewing Britain as a rival that could gain too much influence, for example, over support for French agricultural policy. Britain's close ties to the USA could also make Europe dependent on the Western superpower, Ekengren (2005, pp. 79–80).

[24] Myrdal (1963, p. 140).

communists a propaganda argument and helped them consolidate their rule. The focus on self-sufficiency was strengthened in the communist bloc, while the main purpose of the blockade, to prevent the development of highly efficient military weapons, had not been successful, according to Myrdal.[25]

The Vietnam War

Gunnar Myrdal became a sharp critic of the Vietnam War—or what was referred to in Vietnam as the American War. He viewed the war as stemming from the Cold War, which he analyzed as a cumulative process or a vicious cycle, where both blocs knew that an escalation by one side would lead to a hostile response from the other, necessitating a countermove.[26]

In America, the Cold War developed into a nightmare about a Communist conspiracy against the United States and the entire "free world." The Domino Theory became an extension of the containment policy, suggesting that Third World countries must be kept free from Communist influence. Preventing the spread of Communism worldwide became the driving force behind U.S. foreign policy. Walt Rostow, a former colleague from ECE, became one of the key architects of the Vietnam War.[27] Military spending increased, military bases were established worldwide, especially around Communist countries, and political and military alliances were formed with various governments in the encirclement policy. In developing countries, support was given to undemocratic regimes, creating an image of the U.S. as supporting oppression on a global scale. The U.S. government continuously escalated the war in Vietnam.

In the Western world, a strong opinion and protest movement against the U.S. involvement in Vietnam emerged in the 1960s. Gunnar Myrdal became one of the most influential European critics of the American government's foreign policy. At a mass meeting in Madison Square Garden in New York in December 1966, he was one of the speakers.[28]

Myrdal reviewed the development in Vietnam, from French colonial oppression in Indochina to the French defeat at Dien Bien Phu in 1954. He noted that the provisional division of Vietnam into north and south had not been followed by the promised referendum. He vehemently opposed the American escalation of support for the South Vietnamese regime and the escalating war efforts. He also argued that the unjust war in Vietnam threatened to morally and politically isolate the U.S. from other countries. He described the U.S.'s allies in Asia—the Philippines, South

---

[25] Myrdal (1963, p. 146).
[26] Myrdal (1973, p. 272).
[27] Rostow held high positions at the State Department. He was Deputy National Security Advisor to President Kennedy in 1961 and became National Security Advisor to President Johnson from April 1, 1966 to January 20, 1969. He was succeeded in this position by Henry Kissinger.
[28] Vinterhed (2003, p. 270).

Korea, and Thailand—as client states lacking popular support. He also stated that the relations between the rich, white minority in the world and the poor, colored majority risked being poisoned as the immense American war power poured death and misery over Vietnam.

Conflict with Jan Myrdal

In Sweden, the Vietnam War led to the creation of a new popular movement, the united FNL groups, supporting the national liberation of South Vietnam and fighting U.S. imperialism. The FNL groups were largely a youth movement. They organized meetings, study circles, and demonstrations and had a significant influence on public debate. One of the most sought-after speakers was Jan Myrdal, the son of Gunnar and Alva. At that time, Jan Myrdal was an established author and strongly pushing the leftist winds. He left home and school without a diploma at the age of 17 and became a volunteer at Värmlands Folkblad, thanks to Gunnar Myrdal's contacts. Early on, Jan was active in young communist movements and participated in several World Youth Festivals in Eastern Europe in the 1950s. However, it was the Cold War, and in the U.S., authorities systematically tracked down Communists, suspected Communists, and sympathizers. Gunnar and Alva Myrdal were among those the FBI collected information on.[29]

Before Alva Myrdal took over as head of UNESCO's department in Paris, there was hesitation from the American side about possible Communist sympathies. The U.S. embassy in Stockholm, however, declared that she was not a Communist but noted that her son, Jan Myrdal, was a sympathizer. He had attended a youth festival in East Berlin. When Alva Myrdal landed at the airport in New York in March 1953, she was denied entry. She was to attend meetings at the UN as a UNESCO representative. Alva Myrdal was forced to sign a conditional agreement. She was allowed to visit New York on the condition that she will not leave the city without first obtaining permission from the State Department. The U.S. immigration authorities did not give a reason for treating her this way.

Alva Myrdal did not publicize the incident, but it led to one of the first crises that Dag Hammarskjöld had to manage as the new Secretary-General at the UN. Likely, zealous passport controllers had acted based on information from the FBI. The story leaked to the press. The New York Times published an article based on statements from an anonymous government official.[30] It was claimed that the case involved applying a law intended to prevent the entry of foreigners who had engaged in subversive activities. In France, a newspaper thought that Alva Myrdal was a victim of McCarthy hysteria. In Sweden, the newspaper *Dagens Nyheter* published an article stating that Alva Myrdal was suspected of subversive activities due to Jan Myrdal's

---

[29] Jackson (1990, pp. 327–328).
[30] Jackson (1990, pp. 327–328).

Communist activities. Another newspaper, *Aftonbladet*, interviewed Jan Myrdal by phone, who was in Bucharest organizing a Communist youth festival. He regretted if it was true that his mother was persecuted because of him and explained that his parents were honorable people whom he highly regarded and respected. Jan Myrdal also knew that they respected his opinions, despite the differences.

After Hammarskjöld's intervention, the U.S. declared that Alva Myrdal should have unhindered access to the United States. However, no apology or explanation was given. Only in 2008 was the reason published by Hans Hederberg, who had access to archives at the State Department and the FBI. The background was that a source at the American embassy in Stockholm, according to Hederberg (2008), had reported that Alva Myrdal was affiliated with the Communist Party as a propagandist or secret agent. However, the person had not checked the claim with Ambassador Butterworth. When he confronted the source, it turned out that there was no evidence for the allegations. Butterworth was upset that the information had not been checked against facts and not submitted to the embassy.

Jan Myrdal's breakthrough as an author had come in the 1960s with the books *Report from a Chinese Village* and *Confessions of a Disloyal European*. In the latter book, he examines his own lack of action in the face of a friend's impending suicide. He equates it with how European intellectuals are aware of Western massacres in the Third World but refrain from acting. He highlights how the peoples of the Third World have been oppressed under colonialism; they have their own valuable culture, rise against oppression, and create their future. He wrote regularly in the newspapers and became highly influential. It was largely Alva Myrdal who supported Jan's writing with money, feedback, and suggestions for direction, according to her grandson Janken Myrdal, a professor of history, who reviewed previously unpublished letters within the family.[31] It was Alva who initially suggested that Jan should write about the peoples of the Third World. As early as 1948, she had suggested in a letter that he should give voice to the colored peoples and their concerns. Only then would what he wrote be of general significance.

Jan's relationship with his parents was sometimes conflict-ridden, but he often lived with them when they were abroad. He lived for a year in Geneva with his first wife, Nadja, and a year in Paris with his second wife, Maj. Jan also lived with his third wife, the artist and photographer Gun Kessle, in periods between trips to Asian countries at the residence in New Delhi with Gunnar and Alva. They shared a common interest in Asia. However, the Vietnam War contributed to a break in contacts between Jan and his parents. Jan was beaten by the police during a notorious Vietnam demonstration in Stockholm on December 20, 1967, but did not feel support from his parents, leading to a significant rift. It is important to note that Alva Myrdal was a member of the government and defended its domestic and foreign policies. Jan accused Alva of being complicit in police violence as a government member. Gunnar suggested that Jan should go to Vietnam and fight against the Americans himself, instead of demonstrating on the streets of Stockholm, which

---

[31] The letters have been published in Myrdal et al. (2023).

can be seen against the backdrop that Jan Myrdal was a militant communist at the time and advocated for a socialist world revolution.[32]

Gunnar Myrdal Chairman of the Swedish Committee for Vietnam

In January 1968, Gunnar Myrdal became the chairman of the Swedish Committee for Vietnam, an umbrella organization that brought together churches, trade unions, women's associations, and other civil organizations in support of Vietnam under slogans less militant than those of the FNL groups.[33] From the FNL groups' perspective, this was seen as the Social Democrats attempting to take control of the Vietnam movement.[34]

With Gunnar Myrdal as its first chairman, the start of the Swedish Committee for Vietnam was tumultuous. Myrdal, known for his authoritarian leadership style and politically insensitive statements, nearly dismantled the organization.[35] He used his position to attack his son Jan, labeling Vietnam activists as "confused minds" and "America-haters."[36]

Jan Myrdal responded by comparing his father to a Belgian socialist who had collaborated with the Nazis during the war. Gunnar Myrdal's fundamental criticism of the war in Vietnam was overshadowed as those on the left of the Social Democrats attacked him, and he himself was provoked into more outbursts, following the logic of the vicious cycle.

Olof Palme Secured the Social Democrats' Position on the Vietnam Issue

However, in February 1968, the committee organized a torchlight procession through Stockholm, led by Education Minister Olof Palme and North Vietnam's ambassador to Moscow, Nguyên Tho Chan, along with Gunnar Myrdal. A photo of Palme and Chan in fur hats, each holding a torch, circulated globally, particularly in

---

[32] Speech by Jan Myrdal on Walpurgis Night 1967 in Uppsala (Verdandi), see Myrdal (1968, pp. 139–140).

[33] Berggren (2010, p. 386).

[34] Olle Svenning, who worked for Prime Minister Erlander at the time, noted that the Swedish Foreign Minister Torsten Nilsson was active in the preparations for the committee and the selection of Gunnar Myrdal as chairman, see Svenning (2018, Chap. 7).

[35] Svenning (2018, Chap. 7).

[36] Berggren (2010, p. 386).

the U.S.[37] The demonstration led to a diplomatic crisis between Sweden and the U.S., with the American ambassador in Sweden, William Heath, being recalled.[38] This event, much larger than the Myrdal family feud, significantly impacted public opinion in Sweden and other countries, cementing the Social Democrats' stance on the Vietnam issue.

In 1971, Gunnar Myrdal was succeeded as chairman of the Swedish Committee for Vietnam by Birgitta Dahl, a Social Democratic Member of the Parliament.

Interactions with Leading Opinion-Makers

When in Sweden, Alva and Gunnar Myrdal enjoyed socializing with politicians and cultural figures in the Swedish elite. At a dinner at the Myrdals' on Västerlånggatan, the author and member of the Swedish Academy Per Wästberg, noted Gunnar Myrdal's exhaustion after finally completing *Asian Drama*, yet he was still writing articles and lectures at a remarkable pace. Wästberg also noticed that Alva, with her Indian experience, was an unrecognized co-author of the major work.[39] When Wästberg hosted a dinner for them, he observed that Gunnar was alert as long as he spoke himself but fell asleep during coffee. Those who listened to him received the label of being particularly gifted. In between, he displayed seemingly modest self-criticism.

Per Wästberg (2010, p. 333) also believed that Alva Myrdal was driven by a duty to a society and a vision greater than the self. Not a dinner went by without a discussion with leading opinion-makers. Alva did not try to shine but absorbed knowledge. Gunnar withdrew to the punch where he could dazzle a few loyal friends. Their gatherings seemed meticulously orchestrated, according to Wästberg.[40]

References

Baldwin J (1963) The fire next time. Dial Press, New York
Berggren H (2010) Underbara dagar framför Oss En biografi över Olof Palme (Wonderful days ahead a biography of Olof Palme). Norstedts, Stockholm
Clark K (1965) Dark ghetto dilemmas of social power. Wesleyan University Press, Middletown
Ekengren AM (2005) Olof Palme och utrikespolitiken (Olof Palme and foreign policy). Boréa, Umeå
Ekström T, Myrdal G, Pålsson R (1971) Vi och Västeuropa Andra ronden, andra upplagan av. Vi och Västeuropa (1962), inklusive första upplagan, ny inledning och fem nya kapitel (We and

---

[37] Berggren (2010, p. 388).

[38] After Olof Palme's speech on Christmas 1972, which sharply condemned the U.S. bombings of Hanoi, diplomatic relations between the USA and Sweden were frozen for a year.

[39] Wästberg (2010, pp. 332–333).

[40] Wästberg (2010, p. 333).

western Europe second round, second edition of we and western Europe (1962), including first edition, new introduction, and five new chapters). TEMA, Rabén & Sjögren, Halmstad

Gooden S, Myers S (2018) The Kerner commission report fifty years later revisiting the American dream. Russel Sage Foundation. J Soc Sci 4(6):1–17

Hederberg H (2008) Så kartlade FBI makarna Myrdal (how the FBI mapped the Myrdals). Axess 1:16–19

Jackson W (1990) Gunnar Myrdal and America's conscience. Social engineering and racial liberalism 1938–1987. The University of North Carolina Press, Chapel Hill & London

Kubiak H (2013) The American dilemma 70 years later. Krakowskie Studia Miedzynarodowe 1:199–229

Menand L (2021) The free world. Art and Thought in the Cold War, Picador, New York

Morey M (2021) White philanthropy, Carnegie Corporation's an American dilemma and the making of a white world order. The University of North Carolina Press, Chapel Hill

Motturi, Aleksander (2019). "Förord", i ny upplaga av. Baldwin (1964), Nästa gång elden. James Baldwin (Foreword to the new edition of Baldwin (1964), Next Time the Fire. James Baldwin.). Norstedts, Stockholm

Myrdal G (1963) Amerikas väg. En uppfordran till överflödssamhället. Rabén & Sjögren, Stockholm. English edition: Myrdal, G (1963) Challenge to affluence. Vintage Books, New York

Myrdal J (1968) Skriftställning (Writings). PAN/Norstedts, Stockholm

Myrdal G (1973) Istället för memoarer. Prisma, Stockholm. English edition: Myrdal G (1975) Against the stream. Vintage Books, New York

Myrdal A, Myrdal G, Myrdal J (2023) De hemliga breven (The secret letters with contributions by Kaj Fölster, Janken Myrdal and Bosse Lindquist). Albert Bonniers, Stockholm

Svenning O (2018) År med Erlander (Years with Erlander). Albert Bonniers förlag, Stockholm

Vinterhed K (2003) Kärlek i tjugonde seklet En biografi över Alva och Gunnar Myrdal (Love in the twentieth century a biography of Alva and Gunnar Myrdal). Atlas, Stockholm

Wästberg P (2010) Hemma i världen En memoar (At home in the world a memoir). Wahlström & Widstrand, Stockholm

Willers, U (1971), Fredspristagarna, i Alva och Gunnar Myrdal i fredens tjänst, sammanställd av Ulrich Hertz (The Peace Prize Laureates, Alva and Gunnar Myrdal in the Service of Peace), compiled by Ulrich Hertz, Rabén & Sjögren, Stockholm

Chapter 13
The Pinnacle of the Swedish Model and the Nobel Prize

During the 1970s crisis, Myrdal criticized the direction of Sweden's economy, highlighting issues like high taxes and excessive state dependency that stifled innovation and productivity. His environmental advocacy was significant, as seen in his keynote speech at the UN's 1972 environmental conference, where he emphasized the need for governmental action to address environmental issues. Myrdal's influence extended to the establishment of the Sveriges Riksbank Prize in Economic Sciences in Memory of Alfred Nobel, which he won in 1974. However, he was dissatisfied with sharing the prize with Friedrich Hayek, reflecting his contentious relationship with free-market economists. Myrdal's legacy includes the founding of the Institute for International Economics at Stockholm University, fostering a hub for world-class economic research and policy debate. His work influenced many prominent economists and contributed significantly to economic policy discussions in Sweden and beyond.

Introduction

At the beginning of the 1970s, Sweden had reached a peak compared to many other industrialized countries. However, an international crisis began with the collapse of the Bretton Woods system of fixed exchange rates.[1] The crisis continued with sharply rising oil prices throughout the 1970s. The adaptability of the Swedish model proved weaker than expected. Discussions about Swedish membership in the Western European Economic Community resurfaced for the second time. Gunnar

---

[1] The Bretton Woods system meant that participating countries' currencies had a fixed exchange rate against the dollar, which in turn was linked to gold. The fixed exchange rate in Sweden was abandoned in November 1992, and the inflation target was announced in January 1993. Sweden chose not to adopt the euro.

Myrdal re-entered the debate, publishing a new edition of his book criticizing Swedish membership. Around the same time that the Swedish model peaked, he was awarded the Sveriges Riksbank Prize in Economic Sciences in Memory of Alfred Nobel. He also delivered lectures, and wrote articles and reviews on the issues he had worked on throughout his life.

The economic crisis influenced many of Gunnar Myrdal's lectures and papers, which were largely retrospective in his later years. He also drew attention to emerging problems and devoted a forward-looking central lecture on environmental issues at the United Nations' first environmental conference in Stockholm.

Stagflation, Stimulus Policy, and Persistent Inflation

The international crisis of the 1970s placed a significant strain on the Swedish model. The crisis led to high inflation and weak resource utilization, known as stagflation. In the following decades, Sweden experienced slower productivity growth and worse income development compared to many other industrialized countries.[2]

Several economists argued that the Swedish crisis stemmed from the Swedish model evolving in the wrong direction.[3] Many organizations in the civil society gradually became financially dependent of the state: labor unions, tenants' organizations, cultural and educational organizations, political parties, and the mass media. Strong trade unions, regulations—currency, credit market, rents, agriculture—and a vast public sector financed by rising tax pressure characterized the economy, according to this view. This created tensions that hindered renewal. In particular, the marginal tax rate, the tax on income increase, was considered too high. Gunnar Myrdal agreed with the assessment when looking back at the Swedish model. Legislation had also begun to replace the traditional negotiation model in the labor market. The Employment Protection Law (LAS) and The Co-determination Law (MBL) were introduced. A proposal for wage-earner funds, launched by Rudolf Meidner and intended to give trade unions power over large companies, led to an intense debate with the business community and the center-right parties, becoming a millstone around the neck of Social Democracy.[4]

Economists claimed that domestic imbalances were exacerbated when the economy was hit by international disturbances. High wage increases contributed to a cost crisis in the Swedish industry. As long as the public sector expanded,

---

[2] Schön (2014, p. 401).

[3] Lundberg (1983, p. 150 and Lindbeck (1997, p. 16).

[4] The proposal for wage-earner funds was developed by Rudolf Meidner and the Swedish Trade Union Confederation (LO) and entailed that a portion of companies' profits would be paid into the funds, which could eventually own more than half of the shares in large companies. When wage-earner funds were introduced in 1983, the funds' maximum ownership in a company was limited to 8%. The wage-earner funds were abolished following the center-right victory in the 1991 general election.

employment could be maintained despite the industry's weakness. However, this expansion could not continue indefinitely. Several economists argued that the public sector's *production monopoly* in healthcare, eldercare, education, and childcare was associated with inefficiency and welfare losses and, therefore, should be abolished.[5] Politically inclined attitudes toward spending had developed during the years of rapid growth when there were abundant resources to distribute. However, increasing public expenditures and higher taxes led to a vicious cycle of rising public spending as share of GDP and falling productivity growth.[6] The competitive sector's share of the economy decreased. Sweden recorded large deficits both internally (state budget) and externally (balance of payments).

But it could also be argued that certain aspects of the Swedish model did not hinder development. According to the traditional Swedish model, the government should refrain from supporting stagnating companies and industries through subsidies or devaluations.[7] Despite this, the economic policy was oriented towards trying to bridge the international crisis with a highly expansionary fiscal policy. The bridging policy was supported by several influential economists, while Finance Minister Gunnar Sträng tried to resist but was overridden by Prime Minister Olof Palme and some younger ministers. The Swedish state then, under center-right governments from 1976 to 1982, intervened with substantial support for the crisis-stricken shipbuilding, mining, and steel industry, contrary to the traditional model. The companies did not survive in the global competition. The state then tried to increase competitiveness post facto by devaluing the krona, leading to rising inflation and more devaluations, in a vicious *devaluation cycle*, also contrary to the traditional model. The rapidly growing budget deficits were covered by domestic and foreign borrowing, with the government debt as a share of GDP beginning to rise. This was accompanied by low efficiency in production and a lack of consumer choice. An indicator of the lack of competition was that the prices of a large number of goods in Sweden were significantly higher than in other countries, as were the costs of public service production.[8] Particularly high price differences prevailed in the food and construction sectors, due to a lack of competition following state regulations (agriculture, housing construction).[9] It became evident that the Swedish model exhibited a dual shortcoming: on one hand, there was a noticeable fragility within the large, established, and specialized corporations; on the other, there was a marked absence of emerging companies in progressive sectors. Capital remained entrenched in existing enterprises. Moreover, financial regulations constrained the expansion of new businesses that relied on equity market financing for growth.

---

[5] SNS (1986, p. 45).
[6] SOU 1993:16, p. 9.
[7] Erixon (2020, p. 177).
[8] According to the OECD, the price level in Sweden was 20–40% higher than the average price level in OECD countries for nearly the entire period from 1970 to 1990, see SOU 1993:16, p. 70.
[9] SOU 1993:16, p. 73.

Sweden and Western Europe, the Second Attempt

After de Gaulle's resignation as President of France in April 1969, a new start for cooperation in the European Economic Community (EEC) occurred. An investigation was initiated, focusing on foreign policy, the Davignon Plan, and another report on monetary cooperation, the Werner Plan, both of which were approved. The Davignon Plan meant that the EEC member states would formalize cooperation in foreign policy matters. The Werner Plan proposed creating an economic and monetary union with a common currency among the member states.

In the spring of 1970, Prime Minister Olof Palme toured Europe, maintaining that Swedish membership in the EEC was entirely conceivable. Palme focused on strengthening ties with Europe. Palme also believed that Sweden was well-prepared to reap economic benefits from joining the EEC.[10] By early 1971, however, Palme became more doubtful about the feasibility of membership, considering the Davignon Plan and neutrality.[11]

Gunnar Myrdal and his co-authors were now fully engaged in a second edition of their 1962 book. The new edition contained five new chapters and criticized how the EEC had evolved, as well as the Swedish government's handling of the EEC issue.[12] In several areas, the criticism from 1962 was repeated, while in others, it was deepened. Myrdal argued that the equality policy goals clearly marked in Sweden were missing from the European Economic Community. Myrdal and his co-authors, having reviewed the Werner Plan, noted that budget, tax, and monetary policies were to be coordinated in preparation for a common currency. Gunnar Myrdal opposed these far-reaching restrictions on domestic economic policy.[13] Myrdal and his co-authors also reviewed the Davignon Plan. Myrdal concluded that full membership in the EEC was incompatible with Swedish neutrality.[14]

In November 1970, negotiations between Sweden and the EEC began. However, in March 1971, Prime Minister Olof Palme declared that EEC membership was not an option for Sweden. According to Palme, Swedish participation in the foreign policy cooperation, as outlined in the so-called Davignon Report, was not compatible with a firm Swedish neutrality policy.[15] Prolonged negotiations for a free trade agreement between Sweden and the EEC ensued, ultimately resulting in an agreement signed in Brussels in July 1972.

---

[10] Ekengren (2005, p. 107).
[11] Ekengren (2005, p. 128).
[12] Ekström et al. (1971).
[13] Ekström et al. (1971, p. 83).
[14] Ekström et al. (1971, p. 94).
[15] Ekengren (2005, p. 128).

The Environmental Issue

The UN's first environmental conference was held in June 1972 in Stockholm, hosted by the Swedish government. At the conference, the Stockholm Declaration was adopted, and the United Nations Environment Programme (UNEP) was established, later leading to the formation of the UN's Intergovernmental Panel on Climate Change (IPCC).

Gunnar Myrdal was invited as a keynote speaker. In his lecture, titled "The Economics of Environmental Improvement," Myrdal began by emphasizing the grave seriousness of the environmental issue.[16] He foresaw that unguided development would not save humanity. According to Myrdal it was necessary to undertake large-scale governmental actions to defend the environment. Even if economists managed to develop a theory for such planning, he doubted both the willingness and the ability of governments to decide and implement such systematic actions to the necessary extent. He highlighted the rapid growth of the world's population, which was likely to continue for several decades, potentially leading to a catastrophic development unless societies were prepared to introduce and enforce various restrictions and changes in the direction of production and consumption, indeed their entire way of life. Myrdal criticized economists for rationalizing the general public's preferences and supporting the psychology and ideology of constant and unlimited growth. He specifically targeted the concept of Gross National Product (GNP), which did not account for resource consumption and environmental destruction in a useful way. He dismissed all attempts to find objective measures of "social utility."

Myrdal pointed out two different ways to introduce and enforce measures against resource consumption and pollution. One was direct state regulation of people's behavior, prohibiting them from doing certain things and obliging them to do others. The other was to use pricing policy, i.e., to use taxes and/or subsidies to make price formation send different signals to producers and consumers.[17]

Myrdal called for a large-scale correction to get the entire population to behave differently. He discussed the difficulties of introducing centrally mandated and enforced planning of almost all economic and human activity. However, he hesitated over the risk that the control apparatus would become too costly and not accepted by the people. He then suggested that it was better to work with pricing policy and other steering means that place far more manageable demands on the administrative apparatus than direct, discretionary state prohibitions and regulations.[18]

Myrdal discussed the political prospects of implementing measures that improve the environment. He believed that awareness of environmental problems had increased. He especially highlighted the UN's role in preparing for the Stockholm

---

[16] Myrdal (1973, p. 205).

[17] Myrdal (1973, p. 211).

[18] Myrdal (1973, p. 213).

Conference and its plans for a permanent body for continued environmental work. He noted the creation of new national government agencies for environmental control and popular demands to protect nature, flora, and fauna, and also stated that industry will participate, partly under the compulsion of state regulations, sometimes softened by subsidies in various forms, but undoubtedly partly due to social responsibility.[19]

He concluded by calling for a new lifestyle. At the same time, he acknowledged that it was easy to make general declarations in favor of a new lifestyle, but warned that the habitual lifestyle had a great capacity to persist, especially in a market-driven economy, where each group was eager to defend and raise their incomes and living standards.

The Economics Prize in Memory of Alfred Nobel

The Sveriges Riksbank Prize in Economic Sciences in Memory of Alfred Nobel was initiated by the Governor of the Riksbank, Per Åsbrink, and announced in 1968, as the Swedish central bank celebrated its 300th anniversary, as the world's oldest central bank. Åsbrink had asked Professor Assar Lindbeck, an advisor to the Governor of the Riksbank, if he thought Swedish economists could agree on awardees without divisive conflicts.[20] Lindbeck replied that he believed so, but Åsbrink Should contact four economists at KVA (Kungliga Vetenskapsakademien), the Royal Swedish Academy of Sciences: Gunnar Myrdal, Bertil Ohlin, Erik Lundberg, and Ingvar Svennilson. The KVA was expected to be the awarding authority, as it was for the original Nobel Prizes.

However, there was existing opposition within the Academy of Sciences to establishing new Nobel Prizes. Resistance now primarily came from a number of physicists, according to what Lindbeck heard from Lundberg and Svennilson. On the other hand, the economists vigorously argued for a prize—notably Gunnar Myrdal and Bertil Ohlin, who both later became laureates. Assar Lindbeck played a role in the creation of the prize through contacts with both the Riksbank and the Wallenberg financial family, represented on the board of the Nobel Foundation.[21] The Nobel Foundation sent a person to discuss the matter with the oldest living representative of the Nobel family, a clear-minded 87-year-old woman, who realized that the prize could not be stopped, but sressed that it must be clear that the prize was not an original Nobel Prize.

Eventually, the proposal was approved by both the Nobel Foundation and the KVA, with the addition that it should not be an actual or original Nobel Prize. The prize was named the Sveriges Riksbank Prize in Economic Sciences in Memory of

---

[19] Myrdal (1973, p. 226).
[20] Lindbeck (2012, Chap. 5).
[21] Offer and Söderberg (2016, pp. 98–102).

Alfred Nobel. The Riksbank Board of Directors made the decision about the prize on May 14, 1968, the day before the 300th-anniversary celebration began.

The prize amount was the same as that of the original Nobel Prizes. The Riksbank committed to paying the prize money and the annual administration costs. The first prize committee consisted of Bertil Ohlin (chairman), Erik Lundberg, Ingvar Svennilson, Herman Wold, and Assar Lindbeck, with Ragnar Bentzel as secretary. The process of selecting a laureate works as follows: The prize committee in the KVA submits a proposal for the winner to the social sciences class in the KVA. The social sciences class, in turn, submits its own proposal to the full assembly meeting of the academy, where the formal decision is made.[22] The first Sveriges Riksbank Prize in Economic Sciences in Memory of Alfred Nobel was awarded in 1969. In the media, there had already been speculations about a possible Swedish recipient. Aftonbladet even asked, "Gunnar Myrdal, Will He Be the First to Receive the Nobel Prize in Economics?"[23] However, the prize went to the Norwegian economist Ragnar Frisch and the Dutch economist Jan Tinbergen, for having developed and applied dynamic models for the analysis of economic processes, two skilled empirically-oriented economists. The following year, the prize was awarded to the American economist Paul Samuelson, who had developed economic theory and contributed actively to raising the level of analysis in economic science, a skilled and influential theorist who had reformulated much of the central theory.

Gunnar Myrdal had to wait until 1974, when he was awarded the economics prize but had to share it with a political adversary, the Austrian economist Friedrich von Hayek, for their pioneering work in the theory of money and economic fluctuations and for their penetrating analysis of the interdependence of economic, social, and institutional phenomena. Myrdal was more cited than Hayek at the time, whose star had waned in the decades leading up to the economics prize. In the 1930s, Friedrich Hayek was an opponent of Keynesian analysis, which focuses on total demand in the economy. In Hayek's works, economic upswings halt and reverse due to a lack of savings—not a lack of demand—as Keynes and Myrdal often emphasized. Hayek challenged Keynes's analytical methods and opposed government interventions in the economy. Hayek emphasized the overriding role of the price system as an information carrier in a modern, decentralized market economy. His most famous work, *The Road to Serfdom*, sharply criticizes governmental planning measures in the economy, which he believed could lead to totalitarian development. The book fueled the campaign against Myrdal when he was Minister of Trade from 1945 to 1947, as described in Chap. 7.

Myrdal did not appreciate sharing the prize with Hayek, a sentiment he demonstrated during the Nobel festivities in Stockholm. At a meeting of the Economic

---

[22] According to Assar Lindbeck's memoirs, it was, in reality, the original proposal of the price committee that was announced as the winner, see Lindbeck (2012, Chap. 5).

[23] Aftonbladet, August 6th, 1969, see Offer and Söderberg (2016, p. 101).

Club with both laureates, Myrdal demonstratively turned his back on Hayek, stating that he did not wish to speak with "such a person."[24]

Gunnar Myrdal also reacted strongly when Milton Friedman was awarded the Economics Prize in 1976. Like Hayek, Friedman was a staunch advocate of a free-market economy and a critic of Keynesianism. Friedman's influence became significant for economic policy in the Western world. He visited several countries, advising governments, including those in Eastern Europe. His visit to Chile in 1975, under the dictatorship of Augusto Pinochet, was particularly notable. Friedman lectured and met with Pinochet. The announcement that Milton Friedman had won the Economics Prize in 1976 was met with protests due to his connection with the Chilean regime, including from four former Nobel laureates who wrote a letter published by The New York Times.[25] In Sweden, the Chile Committee, a solidarity movement against the dictatorship, organized protests against Friedman's prize. During the award ceremony at the Concert Hall, a protester rose after Erik Lundberg's speech and shouted down with capitalism, freedom for Chile. After the protester was escorted out, Erik Lundberg reassured the audience by saying, it could have been worse.[26]

On the same day as the award ceremony, Gunnar Myrdal published a lengthy article in *Dagens Nyheter*, criticizing the secret procedure used by the Royal Swedish Academy of Sciences' prize committee in deciding the laureates. He argued that awarding the prize to Friedman tarnished the reputation of the Economics Prize and regretted accepting the prize 2 years earlier.[27] The Academy published a kind of white paper defending the decision to award Friedman, but it continued to face opposition when the book was reviewed, including by two radical economists from the Stockholm School of Economics, one of whom became a future professor of economics and advisor to the Riksbank, and the other a future governor of the Riksbank and CEO of the Nobel Foundation.[28]

Recipients of the prize are often highly regarded by other economists before being honored. When a laureate is criticized, it often relates more to their political views than their scientific achievements. Economists awarded the Sveriges Riksbank Prize in Economic Sciences typically receive significant and positive attention. However, some economists who had begun to fade into obscurity receive a significant boost in popularity from being awarded the prize. A good example is Hayek, as mentioned above. When he received the prize, the curve of how often his works were cited shifted upward significantly.[29] Other economists have a more typical, bell-shaped curve, where the citations increase until the prize is announced and then

---

[24] Lindbeck (2012, Chap. 5).

[25] New York Times, October 24th, 1976, see Offer and Söderberg (2016, p. 193).

[26] Lindbeck (2012, Chap. 5).

[27] Dagens Nyheter, December 14th, 1976, see Offer and Söderberg (2016, p. 194).

[28] The white paper is Axell and Swedenborg (1977), while the debate article is a review of the book, written by Englund and Heikensten (1977), see Offer and Söderberg (2016, p. 194).

[29] Offer and Söderberg (2016, p. 130).

gradually decline, as was the case with Paul Samuelson. There are also economists whose influence is on the rise when they are awarded the prize and continues to increase significantly, such as development economist Amartya Sen, who received the Economics Prize in 1998.

Gunnar Myrdal was among those economists who were well-known and widely cited both before and after receiving the Economics Prize. The prize, however, helped him maintain and, to some extent, strengthen his prominent position. This was not the case for his old friend and colleague in the Stockholm School, Bertil Ohlin, who received the prize in 1977 for his contributions to international trade theory in the 1920s and early 1930s.[30] Ohlin was cited less frequently than Myrdal during the post-war period, and the prize hardly affected the number of citations. He had long since left the research field for a political career as the leader of the Liberal Party.[31]

Regarding the focus and broader significance of the Economics Prize, debate is sometimes intense, as it should be in a pluralistic society. However, the prize has undoubtedly contributed to stimulating contacts between Swedish and international research institutions and scholars.

Reflections

After receiving the Economics Prize, Gunnar Myrdal continued to write overviews and articles on issues that had engaged him throughout his long career. At the centenary of the Swedish Economic Association in 1977, he contributed an article titled "A Good Country That Could Have Been Much Better."[32] The premise was that Sweden had been unusually fortunate with its natural resource endowment, the development of sound institutions, years of peace, and a homogeneous population.

However, inflation had become a major problem in the economy lately. He also warned of newly discovered environmental risks, the depletion of non-renewable resources, consumerism, and the deterioration of inherited work ethics.[33]

The following year, he published an article titled "Time for a Better Tax System!" which garnered significant attention. He proclaimed that Swedish honesty had been a source of pride for him and his generation. Now, he had a feeling that Sweden, through bad laws, was becoming a nation of dodgers.[34] The background issue was the need to finance the extensive welfare state. The socialization of consumption, primarily in education and healthcare, advocated by Alva and Gunnar in the 1930s,

---

[30] Bertil Ohlin shared the prize with the British economist James Meade.
[31] Ohlin was elected to the parliament in 1937 and was party chairman of the Liberal Party from 1944 to 1967. After retirement, he returned to academic questions about the Stockholm School and Keynes, see Larsson (1998).
[32] Myrdal (1977).
[33] Myrdal (1977, p. 247).
[34] Myrdal (1978, p. 500).

had been realized to an extent they hardly could have anticipated.[35] However, the expansion of the public sector meant that taxes had risen almost continuously throughout the century, according to Myrdal. He criticized taxes with harmful side effects, particularly the income taxes that had reached the ceiling, and citizens did what they could to evade them. High marginal taxes led people to reduce their declared income in various ways, including tax evasion.

Myrdal concluded by highlighting the value-added tax as a good tax. In the area of taxation, Myrdal's assessments influenced policy and some of his forecasts came true: the marginal tax rates have been lowered and the role of the value-added tax in the economy has increased.[36]

Institute for International Economic Studies

The Institute for International Economic Studies was founded by Gunnar Myrdal in 1962 at Stockholm University and has developed into a world-class institution in economic research. The Institute and its economists play a vital role in advancing research, developing contacts between Swedish and international scholars, participating in economic and political debate, and advising Swedish authorities.

During Myrdal's tenure as head, the Institute mainly served as a base for the large study on development in Asia, *Asian Drama*. The researchers were temporarily employed foreign collaborators in Myrdal's own projects. Myrdal lacked interest and patience to supervise more than a few doctoral students; the most notable was Gunnar Adler-Karlsson, who wrote a thesis on the West's economic warfare against communist countries in the East.

The Institute Myrdal founded was not large. However, he was foresighted and ensured that the Institute had its own charter, board, and budget title.[37] This contributed to the Institute's ability to develop an independent position and eventually grow. Myrdal's aim was to avoid the "meddlesome, power-hungry, and constantly striving for uniformity on a common low level, oversized and ever-growing meeting bureaucracy."[38]

During Assar Lindbeck's tenure as head of the Institute from 1971 to 1995, its current direction was established. The operation focused on research that could compete with the best research internationally.

Assar Lindbeck was one of the most influential Swedish economists of the postwar era. He was appointed to the Economics Prize committee in 1969 and served as its chairman from 1980 to 1994. Lindbeck was very active in public debate,

---

[35] Myrdal (1978, p. 493).

[36] Myrdal (1978, p. 505). The Value-Added Tax (VAT) is a state tax on consumption that replaced the turnover tax in 1969.

[37] Myrdal (1982, p. 59).

[38] Myrdal (1982, p. 59).

engaging in opposition to various governmental regulations, such as in agricultural policy and the rental market. Internationally, he gained recognition for his analysis of the new left's economy in the 1960s, *The Political Economy of the New Left*, published in book form in 1971, with an enthusiastic foreword by Paul Samuelson.

Lindbeck believed that the left-wing movement of the 1960s raised important questions about unequal distribution of income and wealth, causes of environmental problems, and racial and gender discrimination. However, he was critical of the left's proposed solutions to these issues. According to Lindbeck, the fundamental weakness in the new left's view of economic matters was that they generally opposed both markets and central economic planning, unlike the old left's enthusiasm for central planning. Analysis of the labor market became one of Assar Lindbeck's most important contributions as a researcher. He developed the theory of how already employed individuals (insiders) are favored while the unemployed (outsiders) are disadvantaged, which gained international attention and was published in the book *The Insider–Outsider Theory of Employment and Unemployment*, co-written with Dennis Snower.

Assar Lindbeck collaborated with Olof Palme for several decades but left the Social Democrats in 1982 due to a conflict over wage-earner funds. He headed the so-called Lindbeck Commission, appointed by the conservative government after the Swedish krona's fixed exchange rate collapsed in November 1992, to propose reforms in the light of the economic crisis, as discussed in Chap. 15.

When Assar Lindbeck took over as head of the Institute for International Economic Studies in 1971, a solid regulatory framework was in place. The Institute had a high degree of autonomy from Stockholm University and its own budget, as ensured by Gunnar Myrdal. Assar Lindbeck had known Gunnar Myrdal since the 1950s and held him in high regard as a researcher. According to Lindbeck, Myrdal was a pronounced empiricist, critical of narrow model work, and obsessed with research and social debate.

Many have testified that Gunnar Myrdal was not a man of dialogue. A Danish economist and finance minister who sat next to Myrdal on a plane from Rome to Copenhagen was asked what they had talked about, and the reply was: Talked? Gunnar spoke about Asia.[39]

Lindbeck once pointed out to Myrdal that he had less ability to listen than to speak. Myrdal then replied that he could listen and talk simultaneously.[40] Assar Lindbeck also noted that Myrdal never renounced earlier opinions when adopting new ones. Gunnar Myrdal's views thus resembled a rich tapestry of archaeological layers that he had adopted over the years. During the day, he wrote about the need for central planning, but in the evenings he talked about the shortcomings and mistakes of politicians. According to Lindbeck, Gunnar was a central planner by day and a liberal, sometimes almost an anarchist, by night. He was not only highly

---

[39] Hertz (1971).
[40] Lindbeck (2012, Chap. 9).

intelligent but also a hardworking person and in private conversations, Gunnar almost always discussed significant social issues.

Assar Lindbeck built up the Institute for International Economic Studies by enthusing young and talented doctoral students, giving them time to research, and thus shaping a modern, creative research environment according to international models.[41] Securing funding required significant effort. The state grant was quite small when Lindbeck took over. The foundation created by Myrdal was based on his book royalties and some donations but was insufficient to expand the Institute's operations as Lindbeck planned. He intensively cultivated contacts with private research foundations, which contributed scholarships to individual researchers. Later, it became possible to seek funds from state foundations as well, including the Riksbank's Jubilee Fund, established in conjunction with the Riksbank's 300th anniversary in 1968. Gunnar Myrdal jokingly told Assar Lindbeck that he had chosen what Myrdal called 1920s-style builder financing, financing more than three-quarters of operations via a motley collection of external funds.[42]

Assar Lindbeck's ability to combine successful research with active participation in the economic-political debate played an important role for many Swedish economists, such as Lars Calmfors, who succeeded Lindbeck as the head of the Institute and was prominent as a researcher, investigator, and debater on many issues.[43] Lars Calmfors led the EMU Inquiry, recommending that Sweden should not join the European Union's monetary union when the euro area was established in 1999. His deputy, Hans Tson Söderström, became the CEO of SNS (Studieförbundet näringsliv och samhälle), (Center for Busines and Policy Studies) and was a leading advocate for deregulation and the introduction of norms for fiscal and monetary policy in the 1980s; more on that later. Nils Lundgren was influential as both an economist and politician. He was the leader of the eurosceptial June List and was elected to the European Parliament in 2004. Torsten Persson, who followed Calmfors as the head of the Institute for International Economic Studies, became a world-leading researcher in macroeconomics, international economics, and political economics, incorporating elements from other social sciences like political science. Lars E.O. Svensson became the most cited Swedish economist in the generation after Assar Lindbeck. He introduced rational expectations and credibility analysis in models for fiscal and monetary policy as well as for financial stability policy. Particularly significant was his contribution to the analysis of how central banks' monetary policy can be based on forecasts and targets for inflation and unemployment. He served as deputy governor of Sveriges Riksbank from 2007 to 2013. Other prominent economists at the institut include Harry Flam, Nils Gottfries, John Hassler, Per Krusell, Mats Persson, and Jakob Svensson. Harry Flam, who specializes in research on international trade and economic integration in Europe became

---

[41] Calmfors (2021, Chap. 3).
[42] Lindbeck (2012, Chap. 9).
[43] Lars Calmfors was the head from 1995 to 1998, Torsten Persson from 1998 to 2009, Harry Flam from 2010 to 2014, and Jakob Svensson from 2015 onwards.

the head of the institute after Torsten Persson, participated in the EMU inquiry, and chaired the Inquiry into the Financial Independence and Balance Sheet of the Riksbank (SOU 2013:9). John Hassler has conducted research on the development of the welfare state and the connection between climate and the environment, and he is actively involved in the debate, particularly on climate issues. Jakob Svensson became the head of the institute in 2015 and has published research on topics such as development aid, economic growth, democracy, and corruption in developing countries, often utilizing new survey-based methods to gather data directly from those affected by a study.

Lars Calmfors, Torsten Persson, Lars E.O. Svensson, John Hassler, Per Krusell, and Jakob Svensson all became members of the Royal Swedish Academy of Sciences and have participated in the work with the Sveriges Riksbank Prize in Economic Sciences in Memory of Alfred Nobel.

References

Axell B, Swedenborg B (1977) Milton Friedman and the Nobel prize in economics. Akademilitteratur, Lund
Calmfors L (2021) Mellan forskning och politik 50 år av samhällsdebatt (Between research and politics 50 years of public debate). Ekerlids förlag, Stockholm
Ekengren AM (2005) Olof Palme och utrikespolitiken (Olof Palme and foreign policy). Boréa, Umeå
Ekström T, Myrdal G, Pålsson R (1971) Vi och Västeuropa Andra ronden, andra upplagan av Vi och Västeuropa (1962), inklusive första upplagan, ny inledning och fem nya kapitel (We and Western Europe Second Round, second edition of We and Western Europe(1962), including first edition, new introduction, and five new chapters). TEMA, Rabén & Sjögren, Halmstad
Englund P, Heikensten L (1977) Böcker: Bo Axell-Birgitta Swedenborg, Milton Friedman och Ekonomipriset, Ekonomisk debatt 1977 (5):318–320
Erixon, Lennart (2020), Att legitimera en ny ekonomisk politik (To Legitimize a New Economic Policy), i red. Ekdahl, Lars m.fl., Politik och marknad. Kritiska studier av kapitalismens utveckling (Politics and Markets: Critical Studies on the Development of Capitalism), Dialogos, Stockholm
Hertz U (1971) Två livsöden i vår tid Alva och Gunnar Myrdal i fredens tjänst (Two destinies in our time Alva and Gunnar Myrdal in the Service of Peace). Rabén & Sjögren, Stockholm
Larsson SE (1998) Bertil Ohlin Ekonom och politiker (Bertil Ohlin economist and politician). Atlantis, Stockholm
Lindbeck A (1997) The Swedish experiment. SNS Publishing, Stockholm
Lindbeck A (2012) Ekonomi är att välja Memoarer (Economics is about choices memoirs). Bonnier, Stockholm
Lundberg E (1983) Ekonomiska kriser förr och nu (Economic crises then and now). SNS Publishing, Stockholm
Myrdal G (1973) Istället för memoarer. Prisma, Stockholm. English edition: Myrdal G (1975 Against the stream. Vintage Books, New York
Myrdal G (1977) Ett bra land som borde kunnat vara mycket bättre (A good country that could have been much better). In: Herin J, Werin L (eds) Ekonomisk debatt och ekonomisk politik, Nationalekonomiska föreningen 100 år. Norstedts, Stockholm
Myrdal G (1978) Dags för ett bättre skattesystem! (It is time for a better tax system!). Ekonomisk Debatt 7:493–506

Myrdal G (1982), Hur styrs landet? (How is the Country Governed?), Rabén & Sjögren, Stockholm

Offer A, Söderberg G (2016) The Nobel factor: the prize in economics, social democracy, and the market turn. Princeton University Press, Princeton & Oxford

Schön L (2014) En modern svensk ekonomisk historia (A modern Swedish economic history). Studentlitteratur, Lund

SNS (1986) Tson Söderström H (ed) Nya spelregler för tillväxt (New rules for growth). SNS Publishing, Stockholm

SOU (1993) 16 Nya villkor för ekonomi och politik, Assar Lindbeck m.fl., Lindbeckkommissionen, Stockholm. English edition: Lindbeck A, Molander P, Persson T, Petersson O, Sandmo A, Swedenborg B, Thygesen N (1994) Turning Sweden Around, MIT Press, Cambridge

Chapter 14
Revisiting the American Dilemma and the Final Years

In the 1970s, Gunnar Myrdal again tried to revisit the themes of *An American Dilemma*. Despite legislative advances since his original publication, racial inequalities in education, labor markets, and housing remained significant. Myrdal criticized both the conservative retreat from equal rights policies and the left's focus on identity politics, which he felt neglected the broader issues of poverty and power. Recent criticism of *An American Dilemma* has been deepened by Maribel Morey. She has pointed out that in Myrdal's book, one value premise involves assimilation into American culture and traits appreciated by the white group. How did this questionable value premise enter the book? Myrdal's later years were marked by continued engagement in public discourse, including criticism of the new Swedish constitution. In 1982, Jan Myrdal published *Childhood*, with an unflinching portrayal of Alva and Gunnar, which darkened their final years. Janken Myrdal analyzed his father's book and found that he obscured much of the help Jan had received from his parents. Gunnar Myrdal passed away in 1987, leaving a legacy of profound contributions to social science and public policy.

Introduction

We have seen that Gunnar Myrdal was heavily engaged with international issues after leaving Sweden in 1947. Upon his return to Sweden in 1961, research and social debate still played the most significant roles in his life. His interest in his children and grandchildren was limited, according to his daughter Kaj Fölster.[1] Gunnar radiated strength and charm, and his encouraging contrarian thinking opened new realms of thought. He quickly exposed intellectual dishonesty and had

---

[1] Fölster (1992, p. 54).

no respect for social privileges. He never dryly spoke about economic problems; it was always about people. Gunnar only expressed warmth for Alva and, as Kaj later realized from the letters, for Jan.

Gunnar Myrdal continued to divide his time between Sweden and visits to other countries, primarily the USA, where he revisited the *American Dilemma*. He also participated in the Swedish debate, albeit sporadically, as we have seen. His work after *Asian Drama* largely involved summarizing and popularizing his central ideas. He increasingly began to cite himself. Sissela Bok asserts that after the car accident in 1952, the sparkling originality and genius of Gunnar became rarer, self-citations then became a passion.[2]

The physical inactivity after the accident may have contributed to a decline in his memory. He often returned to his own books and contributions. Eventually, he wrote a book about the genesis of *An American dilemma* and a memoir providing an overview of Swedish development from a longer perspective. Both books were published in Swedish only.

Alva Myrdal and the Arms Reduction Game

As the 1970s began, Alva Myrdal was still in the Swedish government. Gunnar had finished his major work on the *Asian Drama* but remained a sought-after lecturer and contributor to various works on his key issues. They were jointly awarded the German Book Publishers' Peace Prize in 1970. Alva's health began to deteriorate, and doctors recommended that she resign, but she resisted for a couple of years.

In 1973, however, she left the government to write *The Game of Disarmament*, a comprehensive analysis of the negotiations in Geneva, in which she had participated as the Swedish representative since 1962. The negotiations were about an agreement between nuclear powers to refrain from further nuclear tests. They also aimed to persuade non-nuclear countries to sign a non-proliferation treaty. The successes were limited in both cases. Although an agreement to limit nuclear testing was indeed concluded, it was done directly between the USA and the Soviet Union, bypassing the negotiators in Geneva, and contributed to continued arms escalation. Nuclear weapons also spread to more countries, contrary to the negotiators' intentions.

Alva Myrdal worked hard on the book about the disarmament negotiations. In the fall of 1973, Alva and Gunnar had the opportunity to spend a year at a research center for democratic studies in Santa Barbara, California. Alva worked on her disarmament book, and Gunnar began planning a revisit to the *American Dilemma*, a book project that would prove difficult to realize.

Alva's book required much more work than planned. By the summer of 1976, *The Game of Disarmament* was nearing completion. Gunnar set aside his work and

---

[2] Bok (1987, p. 212).

thoroughly reviewed her manuscript. He called for clearer formulations, as if it were his own book. After tremendous efforts, they worked on the Swedish and English versions simultaneously until both were satisfied. After posting the final version, Alva and Gunnar went on vacation to Mariefred. The next day, Alva suffered a combined stroke and heart attack and lost her ability to speak for a few days. However, she recovered and was able, against doctors' recommendations, to travel to the USA in the fall to launch the book and participate in a Senate hearing. From there, she wrote some letters to Gunnar, cited in Hederberg (2004, p. 219):

> You might even see from my handwriting that I am shaky. Heartbeats, I suppose. But these are the first days I can remember when I have no duties over me… Traveling with you, I will surely manage. And I long to return to caring, dear you.

A few days later:

> You should know how much I long for you—and how deeply grateful I am to you for sacrificing so much… I believe my health is improving. But apparently, any extreme exertion is a setback, especially the Boston trip to and from New Hampshire. This is evidenced by greater difficulties in writing and speaking quickly and fluently. So weaknesses have something to do with the brain's supply, which is a horrendous price. Therefore, I have now decided to avoid all appearances… I think so much of you and how dull you have it… Then I long to cook something good for you—to feel at home, with us, to be together. The Senate's questions were tough, but I answered openly and hard. I thought that my three sections of the statement could make a fine article series. No, now the pen just won't anymore.

The Second Revisit to the American Dilemma

Gunnar continued his work on the new book project about a revisit to the American dilemma in the 1970s. After the publication of *An American Dilemma* legislation for civil rights had been strengthened. However, the differences in living conditions between black and white people—such as education, labor market, and housing—were affected by how well the legislation on civil rights was implemented in practice.[3]

In connection with the Supreme Court's decision in 1954 in the case of "Brown vs the Board of Education of Topeka," school segregation was prohibited. This led in the following years to a large number of lower court decisions opposing school segregation. What impact did these decisions have? Scientific analysis of all 868 court decisions between 1954 and 1970 has assessed the impact on school resources, educational level, and incomes after education.[4] The results suggest a clear increase in school integration. Four years after a court decision, school spending per student had also increased significantly, especially in areas with many black American students.

---

[3] Hahn et al. (2018).
[4] Johnson (2011).

The court decisions contributed to an average increase in each student's schooling of about one and a half years. Moreover, the average wage for black students after completing their education increased by more than half. Adult black poverty decreased by a third. Thus, a virtuous circle seems to have been set in motion following the Supreme Court's historic decision. However, by Myrdal's revisit in the 1970s, the proportion of black students advancing to higher education was still lower than that of white students.[5]

Nevertheless, a clear equalization of income disparities between black and white people occurred in the labor market between 1940 and 1975. The legislation on Equal Employment Rights, established in 1964 and strengthened in 1972, significantly contributed to higher employment and incomes for both black men and women. A study focusing on black women's employment and wages revealed a distinct trend shift before and after 1964. In the southern states, the proportion of black women in domestic work significantly decreased, while employment in service occupations increased, even surpassing that of white women. Additionally, wages for black women began to rise, narrowing the gap with white women's wages.[6] However, the equalization in wage differences between white and black Americans slowed in the latter half of the 1970s, possibly due to new technology, higher educational requirements, and decreased federal pressure for equal treatment.[7]

One of the most significant differences between white and black Americans concerns wealth, largely due to disparities in home ownership between the groups.[8] White Americans more commonly own their homes, their properties appreciate more in value than those of black Americans, and they receive better terms for housing loans. An estimated two million instances of discrimination against African Americans occur annually on the housing market.[9]

However, the racial wealth gap is not only driven by the racial homeownership gap. The racial wealth gap contributes to the continued existence of a black American urban underclass, despite advancements in the struggle for equal rights.[10]

Thus, substantial disparities between black and white Americans persisted in the USA when Myrdal revisited the dilemma in the 1970s. Myrdal's concept of the underclass was adopted by William Julius Wilson in his notable books about black urban ghettos in the 1970s and 1980s. The low-educated group, the underclass, was particularly affected when the USA's import of labor-intensive goods from low-wage countries increased. The black underclass often lived in areas with higher unemployment rates. They were disadvantaged when businesses moved workplaces to suburbs farther from black neighborhoods. According to Wilson, attitudes and values hindered integration. William Darity Jr. and co-authors later posed the

---

[5] Allen and Jewel (1995).
[6] Hahn et al. (2018).
[7] Ferguson (1995).
[8] Hahn et al. (2018).
[9] Thomas et al. (2018).
[10] Darity (1995).

question of whether the presence of a black underclass is a permanent phenomenon.[11] There is a fundamental rigidity of social stratification in American society, according to them. Social mobility has slowed down. The inequalities are determined by the advantages the better educated, wealthier parents can bestow upon their children. It is much easier to maintain a downward spiral than to initiate an upward one.

During Gunnar Myrdal's revisit, the American dilemma was still prevalent and he began to realize that a major project on the development of the dilemma would be challenging to execute. He recognized that the social and political landscape had changed since he published his book. He was troubled by conservative forces on the right, distancing themselves from policies for equal treatment, and dogmatic academics on the left, who criticized capitalism. Moreover, a general trend emerged focusing on multiculturalism rather than integration and assimilation, which Myrdal believed should be the focus in the fight for equal rights.

Criticism Against the Idea of Assimilation

Many sociologists started to believe that ethnic background played a more significant role in the lives of Americans than Gunnar Myrdal had understood when he wrote *An American Dilemma* 30 years earlier.[12] Myrdal himself was careful not to criticize the black consciousness movement, whose influence had grown. Instead, he criticized the ethnic discourse among white upper-class intellectuals, which, in his opinion, missed the fact that the social problem was about poverty, not ethnic background. The focus on ethnicity and identity politics served, according to Myrdal, to preserve injustices because it avoided questions of power, money, and class.[13]

Recent criticism of Myrdal's book has been deepened by Maribel Morey.[14] Morey pointed out that in *An American Dilemma* Myrdal had assumed the white person's need for black people to assimilate. It is also clear, as we have seen earlier, that Myrdal advocated for assimilation in the book. Morey argued that it was about assimilating into "white Anglo-American whiteness."[15] The value premise in Myrdal's book involves assimilation into American culture and traits appreciated by the dominant white group; here Morey is correct. It is peculiar that this questionable value premise is found in Chap. 43 of *An American Dilemma*, which Myrdal himself did not write. Chapters 43 and 44 of the book were written by Arnold Rose. Gunnar Myrdal seemed to sense that he could not fully stand by the content when

---

[11] Darity (1995) and Darity et al. (2018).
[12] Jackson (1990, p. 353).
[13] Jackson (1990, p. 354).
[14] Morey (2021).
[15] Morey (2021, p. 207).

he wrote in the book's foreword that, in its present form, Rose was responsible for these two chapters.[16]

Chapter 43 of *An American Dilemma* states that it is not about the white culture being superior to other cultures.[17] The Black culture differs somewhat from the general American culture, but the difference has American causes. Broken family relationships originate from the devastating impact of slavery, migrant labor, and racial discrimination.[18]

Morey noted that in the book's final Chap. 45, it is said that the USA might remain the "strongest white nation for several decades." She then added that Myrdal believed that such a "white nation" needed to demonstrate its moral superiority to maintain its global dominance.

In the final chapter of *An American Dilemma,* the American ideals of equal rights were a central message. However, Myrdal also wrote, as quoted in Myrdal (1944, p. 1019):

> America then will have the major responsibility for the manner in which how humanity approaches the long era during which white peoples will have to adjust to shrinkage while the colored are bound to expand in numbers, in level of industrial civilzation and in political power.

Myrdal then stated in the book that few white people in the USA realize what needs to be done, while the insight was greater among black organizations. He concluded *An American Dilemma* by, quoted in Myrdal (1944, p. 1021), saying that:

> The Negro problem is America's greatest failure but also America's incomparably great opportunity for the future…America can demonstrate that justice, equality, and cooperation are possible between white and colored people.

There are questionable formulations in the last chapter of *An American Dilemma,* as pointed out by Morey. Myrdal realized this when he revisited the topic in the 1970s and 1980s and wrote a short book, Myrdal (1987). He regretted some of the content in the final chapter, which he deemed was a description of a dream world, acknowledging that it was very unfortunate that this dream concluded a serious scientific work. He also tried to disavow responsibility for this chapter.[19] However, Gunnar Myrdal is solely responsible for the content of the book, as he pointed out in the book's foreword in 1944.[20]

---

[16] Myrdal wrote in the foreword: "When I delivered the manuscript and departed from America, there was still a great deal of checking to be done and gaps to be filled in for which he (Rose) was responsible, as well as for the proofreading. He also had to write Chaps. 43 and 44, on the Negro community and culture, and sections 1 and 4 of Appendix 10. For the present form of these two chapters and the appendix, Rose is himself responsible." See Myrdal (1944, p lxvi).

[17] Myrdal (1944, p. 929).

[18] Myrdal (1944, p. 931).

[19] He also claimed that the person responsible for printing the chapter was not himself but Arnold Rose, see Myrdal (1987, p. 120).

[20] Myrdal (1944, p. lxviii).

Myrdal Needs Assistance

Gunnar Myrdal understood that he could not undertake a large project on the current state of the American dilemma by himself. He renewed his contact with psychologist Kenneth B. Clark, with whom he had previously collaborated. Clark had continued his research, after the publication of the book *Dark Ghetto*. He also published a collection of essays titled *The Negro American* with sociologist Talcott Parsons, where he developed his critique of the white power structure in the USA.

Clark shared Gunnar Myrdal's visions of integration, assimilation, and reforms within the economic system's framework. When Myrdal reached out to Clark in the 1970s with a proposal for them to jointly revisit the American dilemma, Clark agreed. With the support of the Carnegie Corporation and a team of collaborators, they planned to produce a comprehensive review of the literature and assess how well America was living up to its ideals of equal opportunities for black and white people. Gunnar Myrdal continued the project with Clark during the 1974–1975 academic year as a visiting professor at New York City University.[21] However, it soon became apparent that the two could not collaborate on this project. Myrdal's health was faltering. He was also not easy to work with. Clark was accustomed to leading research projects himself. Tensions arose between Myrdal and Clark, leading Clark to leave the project.

Gunnar Myrdal took over the chairmanship of SIPRI (Stockholm International Peace Research Institute) after Alva joined the government in 1967. He participated, among other things, in a presentation of a book on South Africa's escalating warfare in southern Africa in 1976.[22] The book described the Western world's support for the apartheid regime's warfare against surrounding countries and the similarities with the USA's warfare in Vietnam. He also continued with the project on the American dilemma independently and spent the 1977–1978 academic year as a visiting professor at the University of Texas in Austin.

Author Per Wästberg believes that Gunnar and Alva Myrdal were heavily dependent on each other. Behind his confident appearance, Alva admired Gunnar's energy and ideas but also sensed his doubt and anxiety. He saw himself as part of the intellectual elite and worried that others did not see it. Despite his honorary doctorates, he feared being forgotten.[23]

Per Wästberg recounted how he was invited to a formal meeting with Gunnar Myrdal, who tried to secure Wästberg's commitment to complete the project "An American Dilemma Revisited."[24] However, Wästberg believed he could not match Myrdal's comprehensive ambitions and, he did not want to inherit the local and international prestige Myrdal promised. With a mix of sadness and irritation Myrdal continued to press Wästberg, and Wästberg responded by saying he knew as little

---

[21] Appelqvist and Andersson (1998, p. 183).
[22] Landgren-Bäckström (1976).
[23] Wästberg (2010, p. 333).
[24] Wästberg (2010, pp. 333–334).

about Myrdal's core subjects as about the ancient relics in his ancestral valley, and no princely fee would make it easier to live up to his expectations.

Wästberg also recalled an episode involving the author Sven Lindqvist and Gunnar Myrdal. In 1979, Lindqvist was to be appointed an honorary doctor at Uppsala University but refused to wear a tailcoat and attend the ceremony. Instead, Per Wästberg and Margareta Ekström, along with Gunnar and Alva Myrdal, were invited to dinner at Lindqvist's villa in Älvsjö. After dinner, Lindqvist asked Gunnar to put the doctoral ring on him and declared his disdain for all rituals. Gunnar became furious, as he was an honorary doctor at countless universities and refused to put the ring on Sven. Not wanting to wear a tailcoat in the noble traditions was ridiculously rebellious, according to Gunnar. "Alva, call a taxi."[25]

Gunnar Myrdal could not complete the project on revisiting the American dilemma as intended. It only resulted in a small memoir published in 1987. Towards the end of the 1970s, both Alva and Gunnar's health deteriorated, and their energy for travel waned. Alva suffered another stroke in the fall of 1979 and broke her femoral neck in the winter of 1980.[26] However, when she was awarded the newly established Albert Einstein Peace Prize in 1980, she managed to accept it.

How Is the Country Governed?

Gunnar also increasingly struggled with mobility; the old hip injury plagued him, and it was discovered he had Parkinson's disease, diagnosed in 1979.[27] However, he needed to continue writing and ensured that the doctors prescribed both calming and stimulating pills. The most important book he wrote during this period, titled *Hur Styrs landet?* (How is the Country Governed?), was published in 1982. It was a peculiar book that did not attract the same attention as several of his earlier works. It begins with a self-declaration where Myrdal emphasizes that he continuously worked on problems not directly related to Sweden after 1947. His analysis can be seen as if he, like in science fiction literature, "had been frozen this long time and now wakes up and looks around with curious and surprised eyes."[28]

The book includes retrospectives on intellectual predecessors, often several generations back, the Stockholm School economists, collaboration with leading Social Democrats, political adversaries, and his time as Minister of Trade. The book also provides a description of certain aspects of the Swedish model's development after the war. Myrdal directs sharp criticism in some areas. He points out that he is thereby continuing a radical line. He believes it is both a right and a duty for a Social

---

[25] Email from Per Wästberg dated October 3, 2022.
[26] Hederberg (2004, p. 220).
[27] Hederberg (2004, p. 220).
[28] Myrdal (1982a, p. 8).

Democrat to "constantly question and seek to change established positions to the best of one's ability."[29]

He criticizes the municipal reform that led to merging municipalities and the building of extensive bureaucratic systems that prevent citizens' traditional self-governance. He disliked the strong centralization of the judicial and police systems and criticizes the large, monotonous, and poorly constructed residential complexes around Stockholm and the unnecessary demolition in the old city centers. He was also critical of the large-scale Swedish university education—both the "excessive" expansion of administration and the quality of teaching and research, which cannot compare with that at elite academic institutions in the USA and England.[30]

Myrdal devoted a long and thorough chapter to the new Swedish constitution. He believed that the constitution, which, among other things, replaces the two-chamber parliament with a single chamber, came into being in an oblivious climate when the economy was developing well. The spirit of the times meant that politicians become more interventionist. This led them to draft a new and extensive constitution instead of settling for minor adjustments needed to introduce a one-chamber parliament. Myrdal argued that the constitution does not lead to efficiency and stability in governance, which is needed in times of turmoil and great danger. Myrdal directs sharp criticism at the Speaker's role in approving a new prime minister. Myrdal dislikes that a person can be appointed prime minister without needing to present a government program or a government. Furthermore, it was sufficient if half of the parliament did not vote against the appointment. If the Speaker's proposal was voted down four times, they could call a new election. A fundamental flaw was that the electoral period was fixed. A new election only applied until the next regular election. Myrdal argued that there would have been greater stability in government if a new election granted a mandate for a new full period. This issue was highlighted in 2021, when several votes of no confidence against the sitting prime minister were held in the parliament, but no extra election was held. However, it was considered understandable that the parties were reluctant to restart the parliament given Sweden's peculiar constitutional arrangement under the conditions.[31] As almost the only country in history, an extra election does not become the starting point for a new mandate period.

Myrdal also foresaw the risk that the budget for the following year could be prepared by a government without the parliament's confidence. He believed that the Swedish rule system for government formation after elections or government resignation would likely cause great concern within the now uncertain future.[32] He also directed sharp criticism at embedding detailed rules in the constitution to limit constitutional emergency rights if the country was at war and wholly or partially occupied. He lacked provisions for a government-in-exile, formed by Swedish patriots who had fled abroad.

---

[29] Myrdal (1982a, p. 12).
[30] Myrdal (1982a, p. 110).
[31] Dagens Nyheter December 28, 2021.
[32] Myrdal (1982a, p. 121).

The Final Years

Alva Myrdal was awarded the Nobel Peace Prize in 1982 for her work with disarmament negotiations and the book *The Game of Disarmament*, which maps the superpowers' actions. She shared the prize with Mexican diplomat Alfonso Garcia Robles, who received the award for his work on an agreement aimed at making Latin America and the Caribbean nuclear-free zones.

When Alva Myrdal received the Nobel Prize news in October 1982, her life was overshadowed by the book *Childhood*, which her son, Jan Myrdal, had started publishing excerpts from the newspaper *Expressen* during the summer and which was published in October. *Childhood* garnered significant attention for its unflinching portrayal of Alva and Gunnar. The book was written from a child's perspective and presents a picture of the parents filled with hatred. Alva is depicted as an icy, fluting woman, only interested in her son as a psychological subject of study. Gunnar is portrayed as a teasing and malicious man with no interest in children whatsoever. The parents' careers depended on other people taking care of the children and household. Thus, the Myrdal family was a social façade. The conflict between Jan and his parents became a topic of conversation among the Swedish cultural elite at the time. It escalated to the point that when Alva received the Nobel Peace Prize in Oslo in December 1982, some claimed that Jan had stolen the entire show.[33]

Janken Myrdal had analyzed his father's book against the background of previously unknown letters between Alva, Gunnar, and Jan Myrdal.[34] According to Janken, the letters contradict Jan's claim in *Childhood* and subsequent books that the parents did not like him, and he obscures much of the help he received from Alva and Gunnar over the years. Jan also claims that Alva did not understand him, despite using her notes from his childhood that she had sent him. Janken also contends that Jan was untruthful about spending most of his childhood with relatives. In reality, he lived most of the time with his parents.

Janken has confirmed the story Jan tells in his childhood suite about Gunnar forgetting to meet him at Central Station in New York when he returned from a stay with acquaintances. However, Gunnar, having received vague information about the train name, met several trains until Jan arrived, and then treated him to ice cream and took him home.

It is evident that *Childhood* darkened Alva's and Gunnar's final years. This is apparent from the letters Alva wrote to Sissela and Kaj, according to my interview with Kaj Fölster in May 2023. It is also reflected in Gunnar's reactions. He regarded Jan's book as deceitful. When Jan got the opportunity to read his book as a serial in Swedish Radio, Gunnar was so enraged that he called friends and asked them to

---

[33] Hirdman (2006, p. 385).
[34] A book, De hemliga breven (the Secret Letters), with letters between Alva, Gunnar and Jan Myrdal and comments by Kaj Fölster and Janken Myrdal was published in 2023, see Myrdal et al. (2023).

exert pressure to stop the radio broadcasts.[35] He went through the book with a pen in hand, noting all the lies he could find. One might say that Jan set a literary trap. Jan had written an autobiographical novel from a child's perspective, without claiming all details were accurate. When Kaj Fölster asked Jan why he lied about events that she and other relatives knew were untrue, she received the reply, "you see, I am primarily a novel writer."[36] However, Gunnar approached the book as a scientific text, which may not have been a great idea but is understandable considering the attacks. During the Nobel festivities in Oslo, Gunnar took the opportunity to publicly criticize Jan. The Norwegian newspapers then wrote about Gunnar's statement that Alva had considered taking her own life after Jan's book.[37] This could perhaps be interpreted as both Jan and Gunnar contributing to stealing the show from Alva when she received the Nobel Prize.

With Sissela's book published after the parents' death, much of the picture of the difficult upbringing of the Myrdal children was confirmed. Especially Gunnar's egocentricity, aggressive teasing, and detachment from the children are evident in her portrayal. Alva had realized early on that behind Gunnar's heroic masculine mask was a depressive and scared boy. Sissela also describes how Gunnar could unexpectedly behave like an incomprehensible, unpredictable little boy. She disowned him as a father by drawing him as a child at the age of ten, lined up with Jan, Kaj, and Sissela, next to Alva as the mother to them all.[38]

Kaj Fölster also published a book a few years later about her upbringing, remembering Gunnar in all the workrooms he had.[39] In these rooms, there were always large tables with heaps of drafts, his ashtray overflowing with cigarette butts, burn marks on the tabletop and the paper in front of him. He looked up a bit distracted, and lamented—"poor Uvve who has to work so hard"—which touched Kaj in a distant way, as he obviously wanted to return to his thought constructions. Kaj never voluntarily stepped into these workrooms, to avoid feeling the inner tightness.

After Alva was awarded the peace prize, the couple continued to live for some time in their apartment in Old Town. As their health worsened, they moved to Blomsterfondens' elderly care home Svalnäs in Danderyd, north of Stockholm City, with support from Tore Browaldh. However, Alva suffered from speech difficulties and headaches, which turned out to be due to a brain tumor. She underwent unsuccessful surgery and lay in the care clinic Stortorp in Huddinge, South of Stockholm City. Alva endured 3 years of terrible suffering and longing for death, according to Kaj Fölster.[40] Alva consciously felt her cognitive powers diminishing, not as dementia but as puzzle pieces falling out of an active brain that continued to think, perceive, feel, and understand. She rejoiced in the visits of her family and Gunnar's

---

[35] Hederberg (2004, p. 224) and Lindbeck (2012, Chap. 9).
[36] Email from Kaj Fölster dated May 13th, 2023.
[37] Vinterhed (2003, p. 298).
[38] Bok (1987, p. 170).
[39] Fölster (1992, p. 50).
[40] Fölster (2021).

weekly visits despite his advancing Parkinson's and blindness. They tried to understand, until the end, why they weren't allowed to end their lives together. She avoided other visitors as they reminded her too much of the active life she once led. Alva passed away on February 1, 1986. A photograph of the bright man in her life, Jawaharlal Nehru, was found next to her hospital bed. A memorial service took place in Storkyrkan (the Stockholm Cathedral) on February 16, attended by official Sweden and Prime Minister Olof Palme, who delivered one of his last and most powerful speeches, before he was murdered 12 days later.

Gunnar Myrdal's last efforts were dedicated to a short memoir about the American dilemma. His deteriorating health contributed to the book never being published in English. Instead, it was posthumously published by SNS under the title *Historien om An American Dilemma* (The Tale of An American Dilemma), the same year Gunnar Myrdal passed away. The book provides a picture of the genesis behind *An American Dilemma*, the choice of value premises, how Myrdal organized the work, and ends with a sketch of how the dilemma evolved.

Gunnar Myrdal passed away on May 17th, 1987, exactly 33 years after the Supreme Court's decision in the case "Brown vs. Board of Education of Topeka." After a memorial service in the SIPRI banquet hall, the burial took place in a chapel at the Northern Cemetery in Stockholm.[41] One of his last remarks on his deathbed was that "he was glad he didn't have to be ashamed of anything he had written."[42]

The ashes of Alva and Gunnar Myrdal are scattered at the Northern Cemetery, with no stones erected.

References

Allen W, Jewel J (1995) African-American education since an American dilemma. Daedalus 124(1):77–100

Appelqvist Ö, Andersson S (1998) Vägvisare – Texter av Gunnar Myrdal. Norstedts, Stockholm. English edition: Appelqvist Ö, Andersson S (1998) The essential Gunnar Myrdal. The New Press, New York

Bok S (1987) Alva, ett kvinnoliv. Bonniers, Avesta. English edition: Bok S (1991). Alva Myrdal. A daughter's memoir. Radcliffe biography series. Perseus Publishing, Cambridge

Darity W (1995) The undesirables, America's underclass in the managerial age beyond the Myrdal theory of racial inequality. Daedalus 124(1):145–165

---

[41] Jan Myrdal never reconciled with his parents and did not attend their funerals. However, he defended their intellectual legacy after their passing, highlighting their political writings that helped shape Swedish society from the 1930s to the 1970s. Jan Myrdal also revised some aspects of his own upbringing. He pointed out that it was Gunnar Myrdal who, by speaking with his first chamber colleague John Sandén, the editor-in-chief of Värmlands Folkblad, made it possible for Jan to join the newspaper as a volunteer in the autumn of 1944, which opened life and freedom for him. See Myrdal (2019, pp. 263–264).

[42] Fölster (1992, p. 22).

References

Darity W, Hamilton D, Paul M, Aja A, Price A, Moore A, Chiopris C (2018) What we get wrong about closing the racial wealth gap. Samuel DuBois Cook Center on Social Equity, Duke University

Ferguson R (1995) Shifting challenges fifty years of economic change towards black-white earnings equality. Daedalus 124(1):37–76

Fölster K (1992) De tre löven En myrdalsk efterskrift (The three leaves a Myrdalian postscript). Bonnier, Stockholm

Fölster K (2021) Bedjande ögon, Tal om Alva Myrdals sista tre år (Pleading eyes, speech on Alva Myrdal's last three years). In: RTVD (Rätten till en värdig död) – bulletinen 1:6–7 (Reprinted in RTVD (The Right to a Dignified Death) Bulletin 1:6–7)

Hahn R, Truman B, Williams D (2018) Civil rights as determinants of public health and racial and ethnic health equity health care. Education, employment, and housing in the United States. SSM Popul Health 4:17–24

Hederberg H (2004) Sanningen, inget annat än sanningen sex decennier ur Alva & Gunnar Myrdals liv (The truth, and nothing but the truth six decades from Alva & Gunnar Myrdal's life). Atlantis, Stockholm

Hirdman Y (2006) Det tänkande hjärtat. Boken om Alva Myrdal. Ordfront, Stockholm. English edition: Hirdman, Y (2008), Alva Myrdal: the passionate mind. Indiana University Press, Bloomington

Jackson W (1990) Gunnar Myrdal and America's conscience. Social engineering and racial liberalism 1938–1987. The University of North Carolina Press, Chapel Hill/London

Johnson R (2011) Long-run impact of school desegregation & school quality on adult attainments. National Bureau of Economic Research, Cambridge

Landgren-Bäckström S (1976) Southern Africa, the escalation of a conflict. A politico-military study. SIPRI, Almqvist & Wiksell, Stockholm

Lindbeck A (2012) Ekonomi är att välja Memoarer (Economics is about choices memoirs). Bonnier, Stockholm

Morey M (2021) White philanthropy, Carnegie Corporation's an American dilemma and the making of a white world order. The University of North Carolina Press, Chapel Hill

Myrdal G (1944) An American dilemma the negro problem and modern democracy, 1st edn. Harper & Row Publishers, New York. Cited edition: Transaction fiftieth anniversary edition 1996, Transaction Publishers, New Jersey

Myrdal G (1982a) Hur styrs landet? (How is the country run?). Rabén & Sjögren, Stockholm

Myrdal J (1982b) Barndom (childhood). Norstedts, Stockholm

Myrdal G (1987) Historien om an American dilemma (The tale of an American dilemma revisited). SNS Publishing, Stockholm

Myrdal J (2019) Ett andra anstånd (A second respite). Norstedts, Stockholm

Myrdal A, Myrdal G, Myrdal J (2023) De hemliga breven (The secret letters with contributions by Kaj Fölster, Janken Myrdal and Bosse Lindquist). Albert Bonniers, Stockholm

Thomas M, Moye R, Henderson L, Hayward H (2018) Separate and Unequal. The Impact of Socioeconomic Status, Segregation, and the Great Recession on Racial Disparities in Housing Value. Sociology of Race and Ethnicity, 4(2), pp 229–244

Vinterhed K (2003) Kärlek i tjugonde seklet En biografi över Alva och Gunnar Myrdal (Love in the twentieth century a biography of Alva and Gunnar Myrdal). Atlas, Stockholm

Wästberg P (2010) Hemma i världen En memoar (At home in the world a memoir). Wahlström & Widstrand, Stockholm

Chapter 15
The Legacy of Myrdal: Is the Swedish Welfare State Dead?

The Swedish model, originally insulated from international financial influences, became obsolete with the rise of global financial markets in the 1970s–80s. Financial deregulation in the 1980s led to rapid credit expansion, asset price inflation, and increased indebtedness, culminating in a severe banking crisis by the early 1990s. The government's response included abandoning the fixed exchange rate and introducing economic reforms. Confidence in the financial system was restored by comprehensive and transparent action. Despite the crisis, the welfare state persisted, although modified. The 1990s saw privatization and deregulation in various sectors. Sweden became the home of several of Europe's largest tech companies. New challenges like wealth inequality and immigrant integration emerged. Following Russia's invasion of Ukraine in 2022, the dilemma for Swedish security policy from the coldest period of the Cold War returned. Sweden became a member of NATO in March 2024, which completed the Western-friendly line of Dag Hammarskjöld. The dream of a Myrdalian bridge between East and West now seemed dead, even though Myrdal's contributions during the Cold War still are worth recognizing.

Introduction

The emergence of the Swedish model post-war provides evidence for the notion that both competition and cooperation between the state and civil society are necessary to create a strong transformative pressure and develop the welfare state. Gunnar Myrdal frequently emphasized the need for more rational coordination of societal actions to accelerate the development towards higher prosperity. The state played an active role in modernizing the industry and ensured the inclusion of both business and employee organizations in this process. The state was instrumental in allowing the economy to operate "at full capacity," fully utilizing both labor and capital. Important development blocks such as electricity, telephony, road construction, and housing were areas where the state collaborated with private companies. The social reforms were universal, providing insurance against loss of income, funded by mandatory fees, and established in consensus with labor market parties. Increasing numbers of women began to work, maternity benefits were transformed into parental insurance, and childcare services were expanded. Employment, living standards, and equitable public welfare services improved impressively, garnering international admiration.

However, the Swedish model also consisted of regulations that contributed to low efficiency and lack of competition in several areas. The public sector, monopolizing welfare service production, was expected to grow and employ more people. This necessitated progressively higher taxes and employer contributions, which became increasingly challenging during the international crises that severely impacted the Swedish economy in the 1970s. Domestic regulations and imbalances were exacerbated by these international disturbances, as seen earlier, leading to the deregulation of the financial system in the 1980s. In the early 1990s, the Swedish model faced a profound economic and political crisis.

Did the Swedish Model Also Die?

The crisis unfolded against a backdrop where Sweden's traditional regulatory instruments were no longer effective within the country's new global contact, by more liberal financial regulations. Economic policy had predominantly favored the largest publicly traded companies, promoting financing through retained earnings. Simultanously, it had offered less support for equity markets and the financing of startups in emerging sectors.

Historically, the Swedish model relied on an economy that was financially insulated from international influences. However, the growth of a larger international financial market during the 1970s and 1980s made these regulations obsolete. Companies, having become more international, required financial support for their overseas endeavors. In response, Swedish banks advocated for a level playing field with their international counterparts, seeking equal opportunities in the global market.

In the mid-1980s, the Riksbank decided to eliminate the cap on bank's lending, which led to a rapid expansion of credit, increasing asset prices, and growing levels of indebtedness. This deregulation allowed banks to extend their lending without constraints of regulatory limits. The boom in asset prices was further amplified by the fact that nominal interest rates were fully deductible against high income taxes. This deduction policy contributed to rising asset prices, which, in turn, increased the value of collateral, further fueling the expansion of credit. The abolition of currency regulations in 1989, which had been in place since World War II, resulted in capital outflows from Sweden. Despite these developments, monetary policy remained anchored to the fixed exchange rate, preventing the use of interest rate adjustments to temper the overheated economy. Fiscal policy also failed to counteract the boom.

The situation escalated into a crisis when real interest rates surged rapidly, driven by an increase in real interest rates in Germany following reunification, a tax reform in Sweden that diminished the deductability of mortgage interest, and lower inflation rates. In an attempt to defend the krona's exchange rate, the Riksbank raised interest rates dramatically, at points reaching up to 500%, but ultimately capitulated in November 1992.

After the asset price boom, asset prices collapsed, plunging the Swedish economy into a period of debt deflation. The balance sheets of households, firms, and banks became fragile as asset values, particularly property prices, fell below the values of their collateral. This precipitated a severe banking and financial crisis that depressed the economy, leading to three consecutive years of falling GDP, very high unemployment, and increasing government debt. Consequently, the government was compelled to significantly revise its economic policies. Operating under a fixed exchange rate, Sweden encountered a Catch-22 scenario: capital outflows required higher interest rates, whereas the banking crisis required lower rates. The resolution was to abandon the fixed exchange rate, allow the krona's rate to fluctuate, and lower interest rates to manage the financial crisis effectively.

The Swedish model, after receiving intensive care in the banking emergency room—officially known as the Bank Support Auhority, an agency under the Ministry of Finance tasked with managing the politically decided bank support measures—managed to survive.

Almost all Swedish banks were affected, with a substantial amount of bad debt stemming from the collapse of the property market. Broad political consensus was essential for the early, comprehensive, and transparent action needed to restore confidence in the financial system. The Bank Support Authority, led by Stefan Ingves, adhered to four principles: (1) minimizing the use of government funds, (2) ensuring equal treatment of banks, (3) recapitalizing the "good" part of the bank, and (4) transferring the banks' bad assets to a separate asset management company. The handling of the Swedish banking crisis garnered significant international interest, especially during the global financial crisis of 2008–2009.

Before the Swedish economy could recover, several comprehensive reforms were implemented. The crisis unfoldened a few years after the deaths of Alva Myrdal, Olof Palme, and Gunnar Myrdal, leading to claims that the Swedish model also was in severe trouble. However, the notion that the welfare state has passed away is greatly exaggerated. It is evident that extensive modifications to the welfare model were necessary, yet many elements from Myrdal's and other leading ideologists' agendas have persisted. This is particularly true for publicy subidized welfare services aimed at providing universal access to quality care and eduction and mitigating unequal living conditions among different groups. Nonetheless, old dilemmas persist, and new challenges have emerged, including the increased production of private or civil tax-financed welfare services, choice reforms, rising income and wealth disparities, and the inadequate integration of foreign-born individuals,

The Swedish Welfare Model Has Transformed But Is Staying Alive

The Swedish welfare model has undergone significant transformations since the crisis years of the 1990s. After the collapse of the fixed exchange rate, a new anchor was needed for economic policy. Price stability became the primary goal for the economy in the 1991 financial plan. In January 1993, the Riksbank introduced a price stability goal in the spirit of Knut Wicksell and Gunnar Myrdal, becoming a new anchor for economic policy.[1] Gunnar Myrdal's monetary policy book, scarcely mentioned, foresaw much of the setup six decades ago: a numerical target for inflation measured by consumer prices, a tolerance interval around the target, and a focus on establishing credible future expectations for monetary policy against the backdrop of a "free currency policy," as seen in Chap. 4. The inflation target laid the foundation for recovery, along with robust public finance sanitation and a new framework for public finances.[2]

The new public finance framework aligned with Gunnar Myrdal's thoughts on financial policy soundness. It included, among other things, a numerical target for the public sector's financial savings over an economic cycle, allowing for annual deviations. Additionally, the Riksbank became independent, a long-term wage agreement was reached between labor market parties, and a state mediation institute was established.

In the early 1990s, under the center-right government, numerous significant reforms were introduced in the public welfare services sector. Subsequently, the production of welfare services in private or civil hands within healthcare, education, and childcare increased from a very small share to nearly one-fifth of all tax-financed welfare services.[3] The generosity of various benefit systems were reduced. The Swedish welfare state, however, remained extensive by international standards. The welfare system was also largely tax-financed compared to other countries.[4] During

---

[1] The inspiration was largely drawn from other countries like Canada and New Zealand. Knut Wicksell's norm and the price stability target in the 1930s were also known. For an overview of the experiences guiding the Riksbank's work after the transition to a floating exchange rate, see Sveriges Riksbank (1992).

[2] The marginal tax rate was also reduced in conjunction with a major tax reform in 1990–1991. Some corporatist elements were abandoned when interest organizations were no longer represented on the boards of public administration, see Rothstein (1998).

[3] In 2017, production in the private or civil welfare sector accounted for an average of 17% of the entire welfare sector. That year, independent schools educated 26% of high school students. In primary care, private actors accounted for 37% of net costs, while only 7% of specialist healthcare was provided in civil terms. Personal assistance at home for the disabled was performed by private providers to 74%, see Blix and Jordahl (2021, Chap. 1). There are also significant regional differences. The share of privately run healthcare centers was 68% in Stockholm and 13% in the Västerbotten region, see Lindgren (2022, p. 15).

[4] In Sweden, private health insurance accounted for 1% of total health costs in 2015, while the corresponding share in the United Kingdom was 3%, France 14%, and the USA 35%, see Blix and Jordahl (2021, Chap. 4).

the 1990s many public monopolies were also deregulated, including, taxis, electricity, telecommunications, railways, and domestic air travel services. Sweden has become the home of Europe's largest tech companies, benefiting from both the series of market reforms and the robust social and physical infrastructure provided by the welfare state.

After the fall of the Berlin Wall in 1989 and the dissolution of the Soviet Union in 1991, the Cold War ended, and Sweden's membership in the European Community became a topic for the third time. Economic considerations largely motivated the membership, with traditional security policy being a secondary factor. Sweden's entry into the European Union (EU) in 1995 intensified competitive pressure and stiffer anti-cartel rules were introduced. It affected the Swedish economy in several ways. EU membership led to an alignment of Swedish food prices with EU's lower price levels, but also increased agricultural expenditures in the state budget.[5] The civilian or private competitive sector grew, while the public sector shrank.[6] The tax burden decreased and marginal taxes have been lowered since the 1970s' record levels.

Overall, the economic and political reforms meant that the long-term inflation expectations remained stable even during the global financial crisis of 2008–2009 and the COVID-19 pandemic of 2020–2021. Adjusted for inflation, the average wage increases for Swedish workers were significantly better during the period from the reform of the Swedish model up to Russia's invasion of Ukraine in early 2022, than during the 1970s and the 1980s.[7] Labor force participation and employment rose to levels that, in 2020, were among the highest in the EU.[8] However, unemployment remained higher than in the 1970s and 1980s, particularly high among the less educated and non-European immigrants.

Rent control, a long-standing legacy of the Swedish model, along with the conversion of rental apartments into condominiums, protracted planning processes, and weak competition in the Swedish construction sector, contributed to low mobility in the Swedish housing market.[9]

---

[5] There are a number of negative socio-economic consequences of Sweden adopting the EU's common agricultural policy, as pointed out by Rabinowicz (2020).

[6] According to the Swedish Central Bureau of Statistics (SCB)'s socio-economic classification, employment in the private sector increased from 51% in 1984–1985 to 61% in 2014–2015, while it decreased in the public sector from 39% to 28% during the same period, see Ahrne, Stöber and Thaning (2021, pp. 31–32).

[7] Between 1995 and 2021, real wages increased by an average of 2.1% per year, which cumulatively became about 70%. Real wages increased more in the mining and manufacturing industries than in the state and municipal sectors and more for women than for men, according to SCB's monthly wage statistics.

[8] In the EU, only the Netherlands and Germany had a higher employment rate than Sweden in 2020 according to the OECD.

[9] See Bergman and Nyberg (2021).

Women's status improved, and the wage gap between men and women narrowed. Sweden achieved the EU's highest employment rate among women.[10] However, women still had a lower employment rate, shorter working hours, higher absence from work, and lower wages than men. Attitudes and prejudices still affected women's situations in the labor market, as Karin Kock had noted in the 1930s.

Some New Dilemmas

Following the major overhaul of the Swedish model, new dilemmas have emerged. Incomes increased for all income deciles during the decades after 1995, but the incomes of the richest income decile rose the most. Primarily, increased capital incomes related to real estate and closely held corporations contributed to a more uneven income distribution.[11] Wealth distribution in Sweden became one of the most unequal internationally, due to rising housing prices, the abolition of the wealth tax, and significantly reduced property taxes on expensive homes.

However, the welfare system in Sweden helped counteract increasing income disparities. Publicly subsidized welfare services such as childcare, education, healthcare, and elderly care reduced income differences by over a fifth.[12] Consequently, the distribution of disposable annual incomes remained lower than in many other countries.[13]

Another dilemma was the sharp contrast between the Swedish creed's ideal of equality and the actual reality in many segregated areas following a period of increased immigration and weak integration.[14] Immigrants have played a crucial role in Sweden's labor market, filling shortages in both high-skill and low-skill occupations, particularly important in sectors such as healtcare and services. However, foreign-born individuals are overrepresented in the Swedish working class, and many are poorly integrated into the Swedish labor market.[15] People with foreign backgrounds faced the risk of discrimination at work, though the degree of

---

[10] In Sweden, the employment rate for women was 78.3% in 2020, while the average in the EU was 66.7% the same year, according to Eurostat.

[11] Swedish Government Budget Proposal 2020/21:1 Appendix 3.

[12] The Gini coefficient is a measure of income distribution inequality. When the value of individual public services is included, the Gini coefficient was 0.24 in 2018. Without them, it was 0.31. Welfare services thus contributed to reducing inequality by 23%. See Swedish Government Budget Proposal 2020/21:1 Appendix 3.

[13] Waldenström (2020) and Björklund and Waldenström (2022).

[14] The share of foreign-born individuals increased from 11.3% of the population in 2000 to 19.7% at the end of 2020, ESO (2022, p. 40).

[15] According to the SCB's Labor Force Survey (AKU), the share of workers among foreign-born individuals was 50% in 2016, while the corresponding share for Swedish-born was 36%, Neergaard (2021, pp. 502–503).

vulnerability varied.[16] In recent years, however, employment among foreign-born individuals has risen significantly.[17] The increased employment among foreign-born individals appears to be due to changes in the functioning of the economy. For foreign-born individuals, employment has increased in all wage categories of jobs, but most notably in the lowest-paid jobs. This differs from the employment rate for native-born individuals, where the increase is entirely due to relatively high-wage jobs, while employment has decreased in low- and mid-wage jobs. Thus, both native and foreign-born have contributed to the job polarization that has occurred in Sweden.

Education holds a special place in the Swedish model. It is constitutionally guaranteed; the right to free education applies to everyone subject to compulsory education.[18] The difference in reading comprehension between the best and weakest students in Sweden was smaller than the EU average in 2018.[19] Sweden was also among the EU countries that spent the most resources per student in primary school.[20]

However, the Swedish primary school had become more segregated, both socially and ethnically. The difference in reading ability between Swedish pupils with and without an immigrant background was among the highest in the EU in 2018.[21] A significant part of the increased school segregation since the early 1990s was due to residential segregation.[22] The Swedish charter school system with equal school funding and free establishment also contributed to profitable students being attractive to independent schools, while unprofitable students were referred to municipal schools.[23] Municipal schools have a responsibility to accept all students, incurring costs that independent schools do not have.

There were signs of cumulative processes of a Myrdalian type. Socioeconomically strong families, for example, had greater preferences for schools with socioeconomically strong students and good results. These schools, in turn, also had an

---

[16] Neergaard (2021, p. 501).

[17] Konjunkturinstitutet (2023).

[18] Pålsson and Samuelsson (2022, p. 37).

[19] According to the OECD, the difference in reading comprehension between the top and bottom quartiles of students was 23% in Sweden in 2018, while the corresponding figure in the EU was 28% on average and 30% in the OECD, see OECD (2021).

[20] The cumulative cost per student for the entire primary school period of 6–15 years was SEK 1,151,807 in Sweden in 2018, while the EU average was SEK 900,519. Within the EU, only Luxembourg and Austria spent more resources per student than Sweden. Source: OECD (2021) Indicator C1, converted from purchasing power parity-adjusted USD to Swedish kronor at the Swedish Riksbank's exchange rate of 8.69 SEK/USD for 2018.

[21] In Sweden, 70% of students with immigrant backgrounds in 2018 achieved the same level in reading comprehension as other students. In EU countries and the OECD area, the corresponding figure on average was about 80% the same year, see OECD (2021) Indicator 4.1.1.

[22] SOU (2020, p. 28).

[23] The share of students in charter schools amounted to 15% in primary school and 30% in high school in 2020. Seventy percent of charter schools were operated as joint-stock companies, Pålsson and Samuelsson (2022, p. 45).

easier time retaining teachers for longer periods. A virtuous circle was established for the well-off, as schools with a strong student body attracted more strong students and teachers who stayed, while a vicious circle was established for the underclass. With residential segregation came a return of Swedish overcrowding. The living space per person in Sweden was among the highest in the EU, but at the same time, Sweden had a higher proportion of overcrowded people in the population than most Western EU countries, only Greece and Italy had a greater proportion of overcrowded people.[24] School results were negatively affected for children growing up in overcrowded families, according to the logic of the vicious circle. A vicious circle was the escalation of shootings between criminal gangs, which occurred in both major and medium-sized cities.

To reverse these vicious circles, interventions were needed on several fronts, including labor market, housing, education, social, and criminal policy. A social scientist, Carl-Ulric Schierup, who analyzed issues of discrimination and exclusion in Europe—a European dilemma—was inspired by the method in *An American Dilemma* and participated in Swedish public inquiries on migration, labor market, and welfare state.[25]

Myrdal's Approach to Bridging East and West Expires

Sweden's policy of neutrality granted it a status as an independent actor in global politics, taking on the role of a bridge-builder between East and West in the spirit of Östen Undén and Gunnar Myrdal. Sweden's entry into the EU in 1995 meant abandoning its policy of neutrality. The commitments undertaken implied that neutrality towards another EU state became legally and politically unsustainable. Since 2003, the government's foreign declaration merely stated that Sweden is non-aligned. Additionally, the defense clause enacted in 2009 obliges EU member states to support and assist any member state subjected to armed attack on its territory with all available means.

A significant dilemma arose for Swedish security policy following Russia's invasion of Ukraine in 2022. From a security policy perspective, Sweden was no longer a regional powerhouse as it had been during the heydays of the welfare state and neutrality policy. Post-1980s, Sweden lost much of its status as an independent actor in world politics, a role previously played by figures like Östen Undén, Gunnar and Alva Myrdal, and Olof Palme. The robust Swedish defense that underpinned

---

[24] Bergman and Nyberg (2021).
[25] Schierup (1996, 2006, 2010).

neutrality policy was reduced following the end of the Cold War, shifting the focus of Swedish defense efforts largely to international peacekeeping missions.[26,27]

However, the post-Cold War calm proved short-lived. The disintegration of Yugoslavia in the 1990s and ethnic, violent conflicts initiated a Myrdalian vicious cycle of international interventions, growing fissures in the UN's peacekeeping efforts, and increasing mistrust between superpowers. The Balkan Wars were increasingly referred to as genocides.[28]

East-West tensions gradually escalated. More Eastern European countries chose to join NATO and the EU.[29] Russian President Putin claimed at a security conference in Munich in 2007 that the Western world had overstepped its authority.[30]

With escalating conflict between Russia and NATO/EU, the dilemma for Swedish security policy from the coldest period of the Cold War returned. During that period Prime Minister Tage Erlander and Dag Hammarskjöld had been instrumental in deepening the Swedish, often secret, security cooperation with Western countries. Once again, it was about managing the small state's interests near an aggressive superpower. Finland and Sweden applied for NATO membership in May 2022. This completed the Western-friendly line from the days of Marshall Aid and embargo policy all the way from short of joining NATO to applying for full membership.[31]

Ukraine's extraordinary resistance at all levels and support from the democratic Western world positioned it at the forefront of defending the European security order. However, the risks of a prolonged war of attrition or an escalation of the conflict were significant. The dream of a Myrdalian bridge between East and West now was dead or very distant. But Myrdal's contributions during the coldest period of the

---

[26] The Swedish defense budget as a percentage of GDP declined from around 4% in the early 1950s to 3.1% in 1975, and was 1.2% in 2020. In March 2022, the government announced an increase to 2% of GDP, in response to Russia's invasion of Ukraine.

[27] Initially, Swedish efforts mainly involved United Nations-led missions in places like Bosnia, Liberia, and Mali. However, after joining the EU, Sweden prioritized NATO-led operations, such as those in Afghanistan, Kosovo, and Libya, and EU-led missions in Mali and Somalia.

[28] The Srebrenica massacre of approximately 8000 Bosnian Muslim men and boys in the summer of 1995 was carried out by Bosnian-Serb forces. UN Protection Force soldiers attempting to halt the killings were prevented from intervening by the UN, according to Dahl (2022, p. 88).

[29] NATO expanded to include Poland, the Czech Republic, and Hungary in 1999; Bulgaria, Estonia, Latvia, Lithuania, Romania, Slovakia, and Slovenia in 2004; Albania in 2009; Montenegro in 2017; and North Macedonia in 2020. The EU's expansion included Cyprus, Estonia, Latvia, Lithuania, Malta, Poland, Slovakia, Slovenia, the Czech Republic, and Hungary in 2004; Bulgaria and Romania in 2007; and Croatia in 2013.

[30] He also pointed to planned American missile defenses in Central Europe and the US-led invasion of Iraq in 2003 as collective threats to Russian security interests. He argued that the global security architecture needed revision and that countries like Russia and China should be given a more significant role. Putin interpreted the Rose Revolution in Georgia in 2003 and the Orange Revolution in Ukraine in 2004–2005 as part of a Western strategy to weaken Russia, see Kragh (2022, p. 13).

[31] Finland became a NATO member in April 2023, while Sweden's membership application was ratified by Turkey in January 2024 and Hungary in March 2024 and Sweden became a NATO member in March 2024.

Cold War are worth recognizing, as is his analysis of how international conflicts can escalate in the fight against authoritarian despots.

Conclusions

It is clear that the Swedish welfare model has been subjected to many strains due to domestic and global crises in the decades following Gunnar Myrdal's death. However, an assessment of how well the Swedish model has fared depends largely on the value premises one starts from. It is also evident that new dilemmas continue to emerge, contributing to tensions affecting everyone in Sweden, Europe, and our entire world.

How Gunnar Myrdal would view this development is hard to say. We only know that he never renounced previous opinions when adopting new ones, and thus his views formed a "rich tapestry with archaeological layers accumulated over the years." Perhaps the Swedish model can be similarly perceived. It appears as a rich tapestry with archaeological layers, many of which undoubtedly stem from the reform agenda contributed by Gunnar and Alva Myrdal since the early 1930s.

References

Ahrne G, Stöber N, Thaning M (2021) Klasstrukturen i Sverige (Class structure in Sweden). In: Suhonen D, Therborn G, Weithz J (eds) Klass i Sverige (Class in Sweden). Arkiv förlag, Lund

Bergman M, Nyberg S (2021) Konkurrens och prisbildning på den svenska bostadsmarknaden (Competition and pricing in the Swedish housing market). November 2021, SNS Analys 81, Stockholm

Björklund A, Waldenström D (2022) Fördelningsdebatten inför valet 2022. Centrala frågor och försök till svar (The distribution debate before the 2022 election. Key questions and attempts at answers). Ekonomisk Debatt 3(22):5–18

Blix M, Jordahl H (2021) Privatizing welfare services lessons from the Swedish experiment. Oxford University Press, Oxford

Dahl AS (2022) NATO Historien om en försvarsallians i förändring (NATO the story of a defense alliance in change). Historiska Media, Lund

ESO (2022) Tryggare kan ingen vara? En ESO-rapport om socialförsäkringar och välfärdssystem (Can anyone be more secure? An ESO report on social insurance and welfare systems), vol 2. Bergh A, Kruse A, Expertgruppen för studier i offentlig ekonomi 2022:2, Elanders Sverige AB, Stockholm

Konjunkturinstitutet (2023) Utrikes föddas uppåtgående sysselsättning: Hur mycket förklaras av demografi? (The upward employment trend among foreign-born individuals: how much is explained by demographics?). Specialstudie, Stockholm

Kragh M (2022) Det fallna imperiet Ryssland och väst under Vladimir Putin (The fallen empire Russia and the west under Vladimir Putin). Fri Tanke, Stockholm

Lindgren AM (2022) Varje förslösad skattekrona Bokslut över privatiseringar och marknadsexperiment i svensk välfärd (Every wasted tax Krona a review of privatizations and market experiments in swedish welfare). Tankesmedjan Tiden, Stockholm

Neergaard A (2021) Klassamhällets rasifiering i arbetslivet (Racialization of the class society in the workplace). In: Suhonen D, Therborn G, Weithz J (eds) Klass i Sverige (Class in Sweden). Arkiv Publishing, Lund

OECD (2021) Education at a glance 2021

Pålsson AM, Samuelsson P (2022) Marknadsskolan En rapport till Lärarnas Riksförbund (The market school: a report to the national teachers' union). Lärarnas Riksförbund, Stockholm

Rabinowicz E (2020) Sverige i EU efter 25 år Jordbruket och livsmedelsindustrin (Sweden in the EU after 25 years: agriculture and the food industry) 2020, vol 7. SIEPS, Stockholm

Rothstein B (1998) Den svenska modellens uppgång och fall. En essä (The rise and fall of the Swedish model: an essay). Statsvetenskaplig Tidskrift 1:41–49

Schierup CU (1996) Ett europeiskt dilemma: Aktualiteten i Gunnar Myrdals amerikaanalys (An European dilemma: the relevance of G Myrdal's American analysis today). Tvärsnitt 1:52–69

Schierup CU (2006) Kapitel 2. In: Den sociala exkluderingen i Sverige Migration, arbetsmarknad och välfärdsstat i förändring (Social exclusion in Sweden: migration, labor market, and welfare state in transition). SOU 2006:59

Schierup, CU (2010) Diversity and social exclusion in the third way Sweden the Swedish model in transition, 1975–2005 REMESO, TheMES, Themes on Migration and Ethnic Studies, Occasional papers and reprints, p 35

SOU 2020:28 En mer likvärdig skola – minskad skolsegregation och förbättrad resurstilldelning (A more equitable school system – reduced school segregation and improved resource allocation)

Sveriges Riksbank (1992) Monetary policy under a floating exchange rate (Special issue of Sveriges Riksbank Economic Review, December 1992)

Waldenström D (2020) Perspektiv på den ekonomiska ojämlikheten i Sverige (Perspectives on economic inequality in Sweden). Ekonomisk Debatt 4(20):13–25

Chapter 16
The Legacy of Myrdal: The Role of Institutions in Social Theory

Gunnar Myrdal's principal works on development issues focused on South Asia. His analysis emphasized the role of institutions and the cumulative process in development. However, criticisms include his failure to recognize the development potential in an open economy. Myrdal's concept of the "soft state" was relevant to India's 1960s economic policies, but broader economic openness and market reforms in Asia led to unexpected rapid growth, especially in Southeast Asian "tiger" economies and China and later also in India. Modern institutional theory, that reminds of Myrdals analysis, highlights the interplay between state capacity and civil society, necessary for developing inclusive welfare states. Countries with strong state and civil society capacities tend to form virtuous circles of development, while those with weak institutions often face stagnation. Myrdal's holistic perspective on development anticipates modern social research, underscoring the dynamic interplay between a strong state and a strong civil society.

Analysis of Colonialism and Underdevelopment

It has been over half a century since Gunnar Myrdal published his significant works on the conditions of people in developing countries emerging from colonialism. He worked with value premises on economic integration, equal opportunities in the relationship between peoples, and a democratic form of government. Poverty was to be combated with extensive social and economic reforms. Modernization became the catchword and underlying value premise. Superstition was to be counteracted, and modern technology accepted. Social institutions needed fundamental transformation, and people's attitudes had to change and become more rational. The accelerating population growth was a primary cause of poverty. Opposition to family planning had to be overcome to prevent countries from being trapped in poverty and stagnation.

Myrdal introduced the concept of the soft state, implying that politically decided actions were rarely implemented, and few demands were placed on the people. Therefore, the state needed strengthening to ensure the acceptance of the modernization ideals. Development required fighting corruption and greater social discipline; law and order needed consolidation. With the help of the modernization ideals, stagnation could be broken, and a virtuous cycle could begin. His principal works on development issues were *Asian Drama* and *The Challange of World Poverty: A World Anti-Poverty Program in Outline*. The books primarily focus on countries that were part of British India during colonial times: India, Pakistan, and Ceylon (Sri Lanka).

Development in Asia After Myrdal's Books

It has been a long time since the books were published, facilitating an evaluation of their analysis and message. They provide valuable analytical insights upon reflection, especially regarding the role of institutions and the cumulative process, a relevant tool for analyzing development.[1] Myrdal's introduction of value premises in the analysis is a step forward.[2]

However, there is relevant criticism of Myrdal's use of value judgments. He bases much of his selection on official figures and political documents, often landing on value premises that are his own. Today, researchers have better and more sophisticated methods for determining people's values, including all those affected by development.

There's also criticism of the concept of soft states, not considered universally applicable. Myrdal can be criticized for not recognizing the development potential in the open economy. But these issues are interconnected. The soft state was highly relevant in India in the 1960s when the government based economic policy on state planning and regulation, hindering competition in business and favoring the upper echelons of society. When Myrdal wrote his books, India's birth rates were considerably higher than Sweden's in the mid-nineteenth century, when the Swedish population boom began. India's population explosion was a fact when Myrdal wrote *Asian Drama*. Only after 1980 did the significant decline in birth rates in India occur, contributing to poverty reduction, partly due to increased focus on family planning that Myrdal had advocated.[3]

A key factor in the development process was increased openness to trade and investment. Foreign trade played a much larger role than Myrdal had anticipated. The development was driven by rapid economic growth, led by exports and high

---

[1] Nayyar (2018, Chap. 1).
[2] The use of value premises, however, has not gained widespread acceptance in development research or social science, as pointed out by Lundahl (2021, Chap. 9).
[3] The number of children born per woman decreased from 5 to 2.7 between 1980 and 2009.

investments, which changed the composition of production and employment, thereby reinforcing the cumulative process.

The development in several Asian countries turned out much better than expected after Myrdal's books were published. The development was particularly successful in the Southeast Asian tigers: South Korea, Taiwan, Singapore, and Hong Kong. Even socialist planned economies that introduced clear elements of market economy—China in 1978 and Vietnam in 1986—achieved rapid economic development. India opened up to the world only in 1991, 13 years after China.[4] Asia's economic growth rate was more than double that of the traditional industrialized countries. This led to Asia's share of the world's total GDP increasing from one-tenth to around 45%. Birth rates have decreased, child mortality fallen, and life expectancy increased. However, the difference in development and welfare is still significant between various countries in Asia.

Myrdal's Influence on Modern Theory

It is sometimes said that Gunnar Myrdal and other Stockholm economists did not form a school. That is true. However, Myrdal became a significant inspiration for many economists in his international work.[5] Like several of his contemporaries in development economics, he chose not to create consistent, testable models. He was skeptical of the value of models as reality is multifaceted. The theoretical development in economics had not advanced enough to include everything needed to analyze institutional factors consistently. For a period, a kind of bifurcation occurred between development economics and the main current in economics.[6] The main current in economics focused on answering relatively precise questions, with economists developing testable models using statistics from developed countries. In development economics, Myrdal and other researchers often had to settle for more general reasoning. It was challenging to establish consistent models, especially with a lack of reliable statistics from developing countries. Myrdal demonstrated that development has value in itself and is influenced by society's institutions. Myrdal's institutional holistic perspective is worth striving for and has been accepted in modern social research, which naturally has more roots than Myrdal alone.

Pioneers in institutional economics include Thorstein Veblen, while Myrdal's contemporary economist Ronald Coase paved the way for later institutionalists like Oliver Williamson, Douglass North, and Ellinor Ostrom, all four, like Myrdal, recipients of the Nobel Memorial Prize in Economic Sciences. North, for example,

---

[4] For a comparison of developments in India and China, see Berg (2012, p. 511).

[5] One of the leading economists following in Myrdal's footsteps was Nicholas Kaldor, a Hungarian-born economist in England. Appointed by Myrdal as the research director at ECE, Kaldor later became a professor in Cambridge and an advisor to the Labor Party. Influenced by both Keynes and Myrdal, Kaldor developed Myrdal's theory of cumulative processes with empirical support.

[6] Lundahl (1981) provides an overview of the state of development economics in the early 1980s.

analyzed the crucial role of institutions in economic history and which frameworks contribute to development. Ostrom showed how common natural resources are at risk of exploitation—pastures, forests, lakes—can be collectively managed with good decision-making frameworks.

New Institutional Economics

Today, analyzing the role of society's institutions is crucial for understanding what is necessary for countries to develop into democratic welfare societies and the risks of authoritarian development. Modern theory focuses on both the state's role in establishing stable frameworks and civil society's importance in keeping the state in check. Fundamentally, a functioning legal system is required, contributing to a strong degree of trust and confidence between people and society.[7]

In recent decades, the concept of good and evil circles has reemerged in institutional social analysis. Political scientist Bo Rothstein has highlighted the need to move beyond the level of one-directional causal explanations in social science.[8] Instead of looking only at how certain interests/norms give rise to certain institutions, or vice versa, Rothstein calls for explainations how the causal logic between these relationships occurs over time. According to him institutions give rise to certain interests and norms, which in turn either strengthen or undermine the original institutions. In other words, he points to a double-acting causal logic between institutions and interests/norms. In everyday language, this is often referred to as the existence of good versus evil circles, according to Rothstein.

The gap between mainstream economics and development economics has also narrowed. Social scientists, especially economists and political scientists, emphasize how a virtuous circle can be established in countries with inclusive political and economic systems. This is shown by Daron Acemoglu, Simon Johnson and James Robinson, awarded the Nobel Memorial Prize in Economic Sciences in 2024 for their studies of how institutions are formed and affect prosperity.[9] It means that the opportunity for all to participate in political activities is balanced by everyone's opportunity to be active in business. Inclusive political systems contribute to a virtuous circle by allowing free media and open debate, preventing threats against the inclusive system. With pluralistic political systems, it is more challenging for a dictator or a narrow power group to seize power and monopolize resources for their benefit. Pluralism and democracy play a significant role in fair and equal treatment of all citizens, fostering trust and cooperation.

Inclusive economic systems mean that economic freedom prevails; all people are allowed to engage in business activities if they follow laws and regulations. Many

---

[7] North (1991).
[8] Rothstein (2010, p. 172).
[9] See the influential book Acemoglu and Robinson (2012).

countries that are wealthy today achieved their status by introducing inclusive institutions at some point in history, which were strengthened and preserved following the logic of the virtuous circle. Other countries became European colonies, exploited as suppliers of raw materials and slaves. The indigenous population was excluded from political rights, leading to exclusive economic institutions intended to enrich a few. Countries imposed with weak institutions by colonial powers often have weak institutions long after gaining independence.[10]

State and Civil Society Capacity

In modern institutional theory, several aspects reminiscent of Myrdal's thought exist.[11] Two leading researchers in political economy, Timothy Besley and Torsten Persson, have noted that the feedback between various forms of state capacity and people's incomes and welfare largely aligns with Gunnar Myrdal's view of development.[12]

There are two important dimensions that affect societal structure, according to this modern theory. The first dimension is *state capacity*, concerning the state's ability to efficiently collect taxes and legislate, leading to legal protection for citizens and the business community.[13] State capacity also considers the ability to transform resources into collective services that benefit all: the common welfare. This includes the population's education, health, and expected life standard throughout the life cycle, from childhood to pension.

There is a clear positive relationship between state capacity, incomes, and welfare in a country. Increasing state capacity contributes to greater trust in the common good, strengthening public interest. In weak states, however, public interest is weak, tax systems are deficient, legal protection is low, and public welfare systems are insufficient.

The second dimension concerns the *capacity of civil society*. Civil society's capacity involves the ability of all people to engage in business activities, organize, be included in politics, and hold the state accountable. A strong civil society requires peaceful conditions, free from violent conflicts or political repression.

Civil society's capacity is influenced by a country's political governance and the extent of democracy.[14] After the end of the Cold War, a wave of democratization

---

[10] Berg (2012, Chap. 1).

[11] The inspiration comes from, among others, Acemoglu and Robinson (2012), Besley and Persson (2011), Acemoglu and Robinson (2019) and Besley, Persson, and Dann (2021).

[12] Besley and Persson (2013, p. 20).

[13] Besley and Persson (2011) analyze the relationship between state capacity and other variables in a profound and innovative way, see also Berg (2012, Chap. 6).

[14] A robust civil society presupposes a *full democracy*, designated as a liberal democracy: a multiparty system, free and fair elections, and several requirements for democratic institutions. Civil society is weaker in an *electoral democracy*, with a multiparty system and free elections but certain

began, and some expected democracy to triumph worldwide. However, over the past decade, the liberalization wave has slowed and been replaced by a wave of autocratization: countries moving towards undemocratic and authoritarian directions. The degree of democracy in 2023 had regressed to levels seen in 1985; more than three decades of democratic progress had been erased. The share of the world's population living in autocratizing countries has overshadowed the share living in democratizing countries.[15] The democratic decline is stark in Eastern Europe and South and Central Asia. A few years after the turn of the millennium, the positive trend concerning the number of civil wars and the use of violence also broke. Both civil wars and political repression became more common again after a certain decrease following the end of the Cold War.[16]

The modern theory of the role of institutions in economic development can be illustrated by categorizing countries into different groups. The classification focuses on three combinations of the two dimensions. In summary, the following three types of systems describe the theory.[17]

The first group is *welfare states*, combining strong state capacity with policies aimed at high common social welfare while civil society has significant capacity.[18] The political system is democratically organized with clear accountability of those in power. This favors long-term investments in common welfare because the rulers realize that even the opposition will benefit the common interest after a power shift. These countries have effective tax systems and general welfare programs. The average income of residents in welfare states, measured as GDP per capita, is high.[19] The group includes many developed Western countries in North America and Western Europe, such as the Nordic welfare countries, which also top the list of the index ranking the strength of liberal democracy in the world's countries.[20]

---

legal restrictions. It is even weaker in *electoral autocracies*, countries with a mix of democratic and authoritarian features: multiparty elections and suffrage combined with manipulation, threats, and repression against the opposition in civil society. Finally, *closed autocracies* are countries without democracy, where opposition and free media are absent, and civil society is extremely weak. The categorization of countries' governance types is sourced from the V-Dem Institute at the Department of Political Science, University of Gothenburg, see Democracy Report (2022).

[15] 71% of the world's population—5.7 billion people—live in autocracises—an increase from 48% 10 years ago, see Democracy Report (2024).

[16] Democracy Report (2022) and Besley, Persson, and Dann (2021).

[17] The statistics are from Besley, Persson, and Dann (2021).

[18] Welfare states include: Australia, Austria, Belgium, Canada, Czech Republic, Denmark, Finland, France, Germany, Iceland, Ireland, Italy, Japan, Luxembourg, Malta, Netherlands, Norway, New Zealand, Portugal, Spain, Sweden, Switzerland, United Kingdom, and USA.

[19] In welfare states, GDP per capita increased by 50% between 1990 and 2016. During the same period, these countries' share of the total global production (GDP) decreased from two-thirds to about 45%, while their population share decreased from 19% to 16%. See Besley, Persson, and Dann (2021).

[20] The index measures the strength of democracy in 179 countries. Top ten in 2023: 1. Denmark, 2. Sweden, 3. Norway, 4. Switzerland, 5. Estonia, 6. New Zealand, 7. Belgium, 8. Ireland 9, Costa Rica, and 10. Finland. Democracy Report (2024, p. 444).

The second group, called *redistributive states* or states governed by special interests, comprises countries with medium state capacity and social welfare.[21] In these countries, the political system often favors a leading elite, not under the same accountability as in welfare countries. Political stability can be quite high. However, investments in state capacity are often used for repressive measures against the civilian population, holding back investments in common welfare. Civil capacity can vary significantly between different countries in the group. The average income measured as GDP per capita is lower than the level in welfare countries.[22] The group includes several Asian countries, such as Malaysia, South Korea, and Thailand. In some countries, development has advanced significantly. For example, South Korea has caught up and surpassed several Western countries in terms of average income and expected lifespan.[23] However, political repression is more common than in welfare states, and a growing number of countries in this group have become electoral autocracies, with a mix of democratic and authoritarian features, including Thailand.

The third group is characterized as *weak states*, countries where the capacity of the state and civil society, and social welfare, are generally much lower than in welfare states.[24] Like in redistributive states, the accountability of the rulers is weak. In addition, political instability prevails, meaning the interest of the rulers in investing in common welfare is low. Tax systems are underdeveloped, and property rights are limited. The average income is significantly lower than in welfare states.[25] The group includes India, Pakistan, and Sri Lanka, which were the focus of *Asian Drama*. Development has been uneven. In India, GDP growth has been high, birth rates have fallen, life expectancy has increased, the middle class has grown, and the IT sector has expanded. India is the world's fifth-largest economy, but poverty is still widespread. Additionally, India and Pakistan are electoral autocracies, political government has weakened democratic institutions, media freedom, and the capacity of civil society. In many other countries in this group, stagnation persists due to weak institutions and low trust. An example is Sri Lanka, where the state collapsed

---

[21] Redistributive states include: Albania, Argentina, Barbados, Brazil, Bulgaria, China, Chile, Costa Rica, Cyprus, Dominican Republic, Egypt, Greece, Hungary, Iran, Jamaica, Jordan, Malaysia, Mauritius, Poland, Romania, South Korea, Thailand, Trinidad & Tobago, and Uruguay.

[22] In redistributive states, GDP per capita doubled between 1990 and 2016, reaching about 40% of the level in welfare states. The share of global production (GDP) in redistributive states also increased from 22% to 37% during the same period, while their population share slightly decreased from 44% to 42%. See Besley, Persson, and Dann (2021).

[23] South Korea has slightly higher values than Sweden regarding life expectancy, 83.5 years compared to 83.3 years (2020, according to UN statistics).

[24] Weak states include: Algeria, Benin, Bolivia, Democratic Republic of Congo, El Salvador, Guatemala, Haiti, India, Ivory Coast, Malawi, Morocco, Myanmar, Niger, Pakistan, Paraguay, Peru, Philippines, Senegal, Sri Lanka, Togo, Turkey, and Zimbabwe.

[25] In weak states, GDP per capita doubled between 1990 and 2016, reaching just under one-sixth of the level in welfare states. The share of global production (GDP) in weak states increased from 11% to 17% during the same period, while their population share rose from 37% to 42%. See Besley, Persson, and Dann (2021).

in 2022 due to corruption and prolonged mismanagement. Political violence and civil wars also occur more frequently in weak states than in welfare states.

Before the pandemic and the Russian invasion of Ukraine in 2022, incomes had risen on average in all three country groups. However, the difference in living standards between individual countries was vast. In the group of welfare states, several countries were in a virtuous circle. In the group of redistributive states, some countries were in a virtuous circle, while development had regressed in others. In the group of weak states, several countries were stuck in a vicious circle, where weak institutions contributed to a lack of trust and stagnation. Few individual countries changed groups over a quarter-century, reinforcing the thesis that the development process does not follow a given path.[26] It is the dynamics and competition between a strong state and a strong civil society that creates conditions for increased capacity in both sectors and the emergence of an inclusive welfare state, stronger, more equitable, and more viable than the authoritarian, despotic state.[27]

Modern research shows that development is a cumulative process influenced by many components. Norms and attitudes also play a role in development, as emphasized in *Asian Drama*. Trust between citizens is important as a complement to state institutions in strengthening society's capacity, according to new research. For example, there is a correlation between the state's legal capacity and civil society's norms of right and wrong regarding various types of crime (thefts, bribes).[28] The broad, institutional perspective from Myrdal recurs when researchers today approach development issues with new data and models.

Conclusions

We have seen that the analysis of the role of institutions in the economy has evolved after Gunnar Myrdal. A virtuous circle is established in countries with inclusive political and economic systems, while a vicious circle can arise in countries with exclusive institutions where autocratic forces threaten democracy. War and political repression pose obstacles to development that began to increase again after the turn of the millennium. The state has a central role in strengthening the transformation pressure, but it should not be allowed to do so on its own, as it then becomes too strong and authoritarian. A strong and stable civil society with democracy, economic freedom, and organizational life plays a central role by balancing state influence, demanding accountability, contributing to solutions to collective problems, and strengthening trust between people.

---

[26] Over a 25-year period, relatively few countries changed categories. Between 1990 and 2016, three countries moved from redistributive states to weak states: Algeria, Paraguay, and Turkey. Two countries moved from welfare states to redistributive states: Cyprus and Greece. One country moved from redistributive states to welfare states: Malta. See Besley, Persson, and Dann (2021).
[27] See Acemoglu and Robinson (2023).
[28] Besley, Persson, and Dann (2021).

References

Acemoglu D, Robinson J (2012) Why nations fail the origins of power, prosperity and poverty, vol 29. Crown Publishers, New York, p 168

Acemoglu D, Robinson J (2019) The narrow corridor, states, societies, and the fate of liberty. Penguin Press, New York

Acemoglu D, Robinson J (2023) Weak, despotic or inclusive, how state type emerge from state versus civil society competition. Am Polit Sci Rev 117/2:407–420

Berg C (2012) Global ekonomi – en introduktion till samhällsekonomi och politisk ekonomi (Global economy an introduction to economics and political economy). SNS Publishing, Stockholm

Besley T, Persson T (2011) Pillars of prosperity. Princeton University Press, Princeton

Besley T, Persson T (2013) The Causes and Consequences of Development Clusters; State Capacity, Peace and Income, Working Paper, IIES, Stockholm University

Besley T, Persson T, Dann C (2021) Pillars of prosperity a ten-year update, CEPR, discussion paper series, DP16256

Democracy Report (2022) Autocratization changing nature? V-Dem Institute University of Gothenburg

Democracy Report (2024) Democracy winning and losing at the ballot. V-Dem Institute, University of Gothenburg

Lundahl M (1981) Teorins plats inom utvecklingsekonomin (The place of theory in development economics). Ekonomisk Debatt 8(81):603–614

Lundahl M (2021) The dynamics of poverty circular, cumulative causation, value judgements, institutions, and social engineering in the world of Gunnar Myrdal. In: Cohen A, Harcourt G, Kriesler P (eds) Palgrave studies in the history of economic thought. Palgrave Macmillan, Cham

Nayyar D (2018) Rethinking Asian drama. In: Nayyar D (ed) An inquiry into the development of nations a study prepared for the United Nations. World University for Development Economics Research, Oxford University Press, Oxford

North D (1991) Institutions. J Econ Perspect 5(1):97–112

Rothstein B (2010) Vad bör staten göra? (What should the state do?). SNS Publishing, Stockholm

Index

A
Acemoglu, D., 168–170, 177, 268, 269, 272
Acheson, D., 153
Adler-Karlsson, G., 152, 234
Åhrén, U., 66, 67
Andersson, S., 8–11, 20, 23, 38, 49, 50, 54, 57, 65, 77, 79, 81, 114, 161–163, 168, 169, 192, 245
Anger, K., 110, 140, 160
Appelqvist, Ö., 11, 38, 49, 50, 54, 57, 65, 77, 79, 111, 113, 114, 118–120, 122, 125–129, 168, 169, 245
Arthur, B., 182
Åsbrink, P., 230
Åström, S., 154, 217
Azfar, K., 194

B
Bagge, G., 22, 24, 49, 55, 111
Baldwin, J., 209, 213–217
Bandaranaike, Sirimavo, 200
Bandaranaike, Solomon, 200
Barber, W., 82, 144, 151, 165, 193, 194, 204
de Beauvoir, S., 65, 183
Bentzel, R., 231
Berggren, H., 18, 162, 193, 222, 223
Besley, T., 269–272
Bevin, E., 142
Bidault, G., 142
Bok, S. (born Myrdal), 4, 8, 18, 73, 74, 88, 110, 139, 157, 159, 183, 192, 240, 249
Borgström, G., 200
Boserup, E., 150, 193

Boserup, M., 151, 193, 194, 200
Brandt, W., 109, 110
Branting, H., 29, 66, 95
Branting-Westerståhl, S., 95
Broberg, G., 78, 79, 81–83
Browaldh, T., 114, 249
Brown, L., 2
Bryce, J., 107
Bugge Wicksell, A., 29, 38
Bühler, C., 23
Bunche, R., 87, 92–94, 179, 180, 192, 212, 214
Butterworth, W.W., 154, 221

C
Calmfors, L., 236, 237
Camus, A., 183
Carlson, A., 21, 24, 70, 71, 74–76, 79, 81, 82
Carnegie, A., 88, 89
Carroll, L., 169
Cassel, G., 7, 21–22, 24, 28–30, 45, 54–56, 73, 89, 111, 118
Churchill, W., 137
Clark, K.B., 213–217, 245
Clark, M.P., 214
Clayton, W., 140–142
Coase, R., 267
Curman, J., 193

D
Dagerman, S., 136
Dahl, B., 223
Dahlberg, G., 77, 78

Darity, W., 242, 243
Davidson, D., 29, 56
Davis, J., 90, 91
Du Bois, W.E.B., 91, 92, 106
Durdin, T., 184

E
Edin, K.A., 76
Eisenhower, D.D., 162
Ekerwald, H., 37
Ekman, C.G., 41, 63, 64
Ekström, M., 246
Ekström, T., 144, 218, 228
Eliaeson, S., 36, 37
Ellison, R., 213, 217
Embree, E., 102
Engströmer, D., 116
Erlander, T., 73, 83, 121, 126, 129, 130, 154, 155, 167, 187, 193, 210, 217, 218, 222, 261
Ersson, M.E., 16
Ersson, P.P., 16
Ezra, D., 144

F
Fisher, I., 33–34, 45
Flam, H., 236
Fölster, K. (born Myrdal), 88, 140, 159, 161, 239, 248–250
Fredrikson, M., 21
Friedman, M., 232

G
de Gaulle, C., 218, 228
Gjöres, A., 128, 130, 185
Gottfries, N., 236
Grafström, S., 130
de la Grandville, A., 159

H
Hall-Patch, E., 147, 148
Hammarskjöld, B., 57
Hammarskjöld, D., 2, 3, 29, 30, 49, 50, 56, 57, 112, 119, 120, 126–128, 135, 143, 147–150, 153–155, 162–164, 185, 186, 220, 221, 253, 261
Hansson, P.A., 49, 51, 65, 66, 80, 94, 110, 116, 119, 121, 167, 173, 176
Hassler, J., 236, 237
von Hayek, F., 118, 119, 168, 225, 231, 232
Heath, W., 223

Heckscher, Ebba, 73
Heckscher, Eli, 11, 29, 30, 45, 49, 53–56, 73, 111, 118, 119, 123, 128, 175
Hederberg, H., 123, 221, 241, 246, 249
Hirdman, Y., 12, 22, 49, 66, 67, 70–73, 75, 78, 81–83, 89, 96, 98, 116, 160, 161, 163, 191, 196, 248
von Hofsten, E., 79
Högfeldt, P., 52

I
Ingves, S., 255
Isaksson, A., 176

J
Jansdotter, S.G., 16
Johansson, A., 20, 21, 29, 30, 66, 76, 94, 95, 123, 124, 130, 175
Johansson, A.W., 94
Johnson, G., 92
Jonsson, S.-G., 67

K
Kahle, S., 4
Kaldor, N., 150, 267
Karlsson, B., 122, 124, 125, 143, 149, 152, 154
Karlsson, S.O., 51, 64, 111, 176
Kennan, G., 137, 138, 140, 141
Keppel, F., 88–91, 94, 98
Kessle, G., 221
Keynes, J.M., 21, 27, 30, 38, 43–45, 47–52, 56, 58, 59, 120, 231, 233, 267
King, C.S., 212
King, M.L., 94, 211, 212
Kjellén, R., 11, 65
Klein, V., 161
Knight, F., 23, 44, 45
Kock, K., 29, 30, 55–57, 68, 69, 76, 77, 117, 140, 145, 146, 153, 159, 170, 258
Kostelecký, V., 136, 147, 150, 163
Kreisky, B., 109, 110, 157
Krusell, P., 236, 237

L
Lévi-Strauss, C., 161, 183
Lewin, L., 111, 118, 119, 175
Lie, T., 139, 141, 142, 162, 163
Lindahl, E., 7, 21, 22, 29, 43, 46, 47, 50, 55, 56

Lindbeck, A., 171, 174, 175, 226, 230–232, 234–236, 249
Linderborg, Å., 176
Lindqvist, J., 10, 11
Lindqvist, S., 83, 246
Lindström, S., 193
Lindström, U., 173, 177, 180, 185, 186, 188, 189
von Linné, C., 7, 8, 15
Lipton, M., 194
Lokanathan, P.S., 192
Lundberg, A.S., 185
Lundberg, E., 29, 30, 44, 45, 53, 55, 57, 59, 68, 114, 118–120, 127–129, 230–232
Lundborg, H., 77, 78, 81
Lundgren, N., 236
Lundkvist, A., 63
Lynd, H., 23
Lynd, R., 23

M
Malinowski, W., 110
Malthus, T.R., 67–70, 193, 200
Marjolin, R., 147, 153
Markelius, S., 66, 67, 87, 88
Marshall, G., 140
Marx, K., 198
Masaryk, J., 146, 147
Meeropol, A., 215
Meidner, R., 170, 171, 226
Menand, L., 137, 138, 183, 184, 215
Meredith, J., 212
Mesterton, E., 63
Mitchell, W., 23
Möller, G., 2, 49, 51, 63, 64, 67, 74, 76, 79–83, 110, 121, 129, 167, 172
Molotov, V., 141, 142
Morey, M., 89, 91, 212, 213, 239, 243, 244
Motturi, A., 217
Myrdal, A., 2, 7, 35, 48, 63, 87, 109, 135, 167, 183, 191, 209, 233, 239, 255
Myrdal, J., 11, 22, 23, 87, 88, 90, 96, 110, 140, 159, 160, 209, 220–222, 239, 240, 248–250

N
Nehru, J., 183, 191–193, 250
Nguyên, Tho Chan, 222
Norgren, P., 92
North, D., 267, 268
Nurkse, R., 181

O
Odum, H., 91
Ogburn, W.F., 23, 91
Ohlin, B., 7, 22, 29, 30, 43, 45–46, 48–51, 55, 57, 111, 121, 122, 127, 130, 168, 230, 231, 233
Östberg, K., 188
Ostrom, E., 267, 268
Ottesen-Jensen, E., 67, 201
Owen, D., 110, 139

P
Palme, O., 3, 174, 180, 186–189, 217, 222–223, 227, 228, 235, 250, 255, 260
Pålsson, R., 218
Park, R., 91, 105
Parks, R., 211
Persson, A.L., 81
Persson, M., 236
Persson, T., 236, 237, 269
Pettersson, A.S., 8
Pettersson, C.A., 8, 20
Pinochet, A., 232
Putin, V., 261

R
Rehn, G., 170, 171
Reimer, A., 12, 16–18
Reimer, F., 13, 14
Reimer, L., 13, 17, 18
Reimer, R., 12–14
Robinson, J., 168–170, 177, 205, 268, 269, 272
Robles, A.G., 248
Roosevelt, F.D., 58, 95, 106, 131
Rooth, I., 56, 127
Rose, A., 98, 211, 243, 244
Rosenberg, G., 115, 117
Rosenstein-Rodan, P., 181
Rostow, W., 150, 198, 219
Rothstein, B., 17, 18, 52, 80, 83, 173, 176, 256, 268

S
Sachs, N., 135
Sartre, J.-P., 183
Sauvy, A., 183
Schierup, C.-E., 260
Siven, C.-H., 44, 48–50
Sjögren, T., 77
Smith, A., 32, 34, 194

Snower, D., 235
Söderlund, G., 120
Söderström, H.T., 236
Sorokin, P.T., 23
Staaff, K., 29
Stalin, J., 137, 140, 142–144, 146, 148, 152, 156, 162
Sterner, M., 89, 94
Sterner, R., 74, 75, 89–92, 94, 96, 98, 111, 170, 185
Sträng, G., 121, 167, 227
Streeten, P., 194
Sukarno (President), 183
Svennilson, I., 30, 151, 161, 170, 230, 231
Svensson, J., 236, 237
Svensson, L.E.O., 236, 237
Swedberg, R., 5, 37

T
Tegen, E., 116
Tegen, G., 116
Thomas, D., 23, 92
Thomas, W.I., 23, 105
Thorén, F., 21
Tingsten, H., 2, 72, 77, 95, 122–125, 130
Tito, J.B., 144
de Tocqueville, A., 107
Trägårdh, L., 18
Truman, H.S., 107, 137, 155
Tydén, M., 78, 79, 81–83, 161, 185, 188

U
Undén, Ö., 49, 78, 121, 130, 140, 153, 154, 162, 260

V
Vachon, J., 136
Västberg, D., 81
Vincent, P., 200

W
Wärenstam, E., 11
Wästberg, P., 223, 245, 246
Weber, M., 27, 30, 31, 36, 37
Wennemo, I., 70, 80, 174
Wicksell, K., 29–31, 33, 38, 43–44, 46, 47, 56, 67–70, 76, 101, 256
Wicksell, S., 76
Wigforss, E., 24, 30, 38, 41, 48–52, 56–59, 64, 67, 73, 79–81, 110, 111, 113, 118–121, 127–130, 167, 172
Wilkerson, D., 87, 92, 214
Willers, U., 115, 210
Williamson, O., 267
Wilson, G., 194
Wilson, W.J., 214, 242
Wisselgren, P., 37
Wohlin, N., 22, 74, 75, 81
Wold, H., 231
Wright, R., 180, 183, 184, 215, 217

Y
Young, D., 92

Z
Zhou Enlai, 183

www.ingramcontent.com/pod-product-compliance
Lightning Source LLC
Chambersburg PA
CBHW050556100325
23228CB00005B/248